BEHIND ENEMY LINES

These were the Army's most professional soldiers, and their most flexible. They weren't green recruits still growing up. They were mature warriors, many of them family men—who had volunteered for Special Forces and this type of hazardous duty. . . .

The team began picking off soldiers. Balwanz directed the fire like a surveyor marking spots on land. Five of the eight men on the team were expert snipers. With the telescopic sights atop their M-16s, they could kill a man 500 yards away. The Iraqis didn't have that range or accuracy with their AK-47s. The snipers began to drop them before they could get close enough to make their shots count.

The soldiers nearer to the team fared even worse. Balwanz and Hopkins carried the Heckler and Koch MP-5 machine guns, perfect for close-quarter battle with infrared laser sights fitted on them. In just the first ten minutes of fighting, the eight Green Berets had managed to coldly and methodically kill about forty soldiers. That halted the enemy advance and forced the Iraqis to hug the ground. . . .

THE
COMMANDOS

THE INSIDE STORY OF
AMERICA'S SECRET SOLDIERS

DOUGLAS C. WALLER

A DELL BOOK

TO JUDY, DREW, COLBY, AND DAVID

Published by
Dell Publishing
a division of
Bantam Doubleday Dell Publishing Group, Inc.
1540 Broadway
New York, New York 10036

Photo credits:
1, 2, 4–10, 12, 13 by Douglas C. Waller; 3 by John Marlin; 11 by Air Force Special Operations Command; 14, 16 by Bill Gentile, *Newsweek*; 15 by Chris Kleponis, *Newsweek*; 17 courtesy of Rich Comer; 22 courtesy of Skip Davenport; 24, 25, 27–30 by Special Forces Association, chapter 38; 26 courtesy of Jim Kraus; 31 courtesy of Tom Deitz; 32 courtesy of Ray Smith.

ISBN: 0-440-22046-7

Reprinted by arrangement with Simon & Schuster

Printed in the United States of America

Published simultaneously in Canada

August 1995

OPM   13   12

ACKNOWLEDGMENTS

A number of people made this book possible. *Newsweek* editor Maynard Parker spearheaded the original cover story I wrote on American special operations forces and their secret war in the Persian Gulf. He and the other senior editors at the magazine then graciously allowed me to neglect my reporting duties at times as I labored to produce a book from that project.

My literary agent, Kristine Dahl, a military brat like myself, helped me turn the inchoate ideas I had at the beginning into a book outline that would tell a story we both found so intriguing. Evan Thomas, *Newsweek*'s Washington bureau chief and one of the best editors in the business, cheerfully reviewed early drafts of the manuscript and provided invaluable suggestions to improve the narrative. Ann McDaniel and Thomas DeFrank, who were *Newsweek*'s White House correspondents during my research for the book, and national security correspondent John Barry came to the rescue a number of times with advice and facts from their beats. Dominick Anfuso, my editor at Simon & Schuster, applied a skillful hand to shaping the final product.

There were others who read parts of the manuscript and offered their wise counsel: Orr Kelly, who has written an excellent history of the Navy SEALs; Bill Arkin at Greenpeace, who shared with me a number of the military after-action reports he has collected on the Desert Storm war; Benjamin Schwarz, a RAND expert on low-intensity conflicts; Lieutenant Bruce Thomas with the Naval Special Warfare medical staff, who corrected the sections on SEAL medicine; Air Force captains Joe Becker and Ben Pulsifer, who patiently reviewed the sections on helicopter technology and operations. There were also former and current special operations officers who read particularly sensitive parts of the manuscript for accuracy, but asked not to be publicly acknowledged. They know I will be forever in their debt.

A number of experts gave many hours of their time to educate me on special operations and low-intensity conflicts. They included Ted Lunger, Chris Mellon, John M. Collins, Noel Koch, James R. Locher III, Colonel Gary Weikel, Neil Livingstone, Major General Richard Scholtes (Ret.), Lieutenant General William Yarborough (Ret.), Erik Kjonnerod, Robert Kurz, Colonel Frank Toney, and Seth Cropsy. I want to thank Chief Warrant Officer Rick Detrick, Master Sergeant Dan Kaiser, Don Murphy of the Special Forces Association (Chapter 38), Colonel Jim Kraus, now Rear Admiral Ray Smith, and Lieutenant Tom Deitz for photos they provided on commandos in the Persian Gulf. I also want to thank Hughie and Jenny Freel, who gave me refuge in Coronado, California, as I pursued my research on the Navy SEALs.

Writing about military special operations is like walking into a dark room and searching desperately for candles and matches. The military by nature maintains a distance from the news media. Special operations soldiers avoid journalists even more and their missions are usually hidden behind layers of security classifications. I am indebted to General James Lindsay (Ret.), the first commander of the U.S. Special Operations Command, who spent many hours with me sharing his insights on the history and character of this force. I also would like to thank General Carl Stiner, the second chief of special operations, for the cooperation the command provided as I pursued my research. Both generals are warriors in the finest sense of the word.

Being a public affairs officer for a special ops outfit is perhaps the most thankless job in the military. Commandos think all the PAOs do is leak secrets to the press, which I certainly never found to be the case. A number of public affairs officers bravely broached their units with my requests for information and interviews. I am particularly grateful to Colonel Jake Dye, who as head of public affairs for the Special Operations Command displayed unusual grace under fire. Major John Marlin, an Army Ranger who by now is an English professor, cheerfully spent the two weeks with me camped out among the Green Berets. Lieutenant Colonel Frank Urben patiently suffered days with me in Air Force helicopters. I am also grateful to Commander Bob Pritchard, Major Craig Barta, Steve Moore, and Lieutenant Colonel Terence Meehan.

I interviewed more than 200 commandos for this book. I want to thank the Army, Navy, and Air Force special operations students and instructors who allowed me to follow their training for weeks and interrupt it with countless questions. Scores of other special operations officers and enlisted men who fought in the Desert Storm war gave me many hours of their time for on-the-record interviews. But other officers, senior Pentagon officials, White House aides, and congressional staffers could only talk on the condition that their names not be used. I want to thank them all for helping tell this important story.

Finally, I want to thank my wife, Judy, who not only took care of our family during the time I spent writing and researching, but also labored through the manuscript correcting errors. It is to her and our three children—who put up with dad being away all the time playing commando— that this book is dedicated.

CONTENTS

THE SHARKMEN

Chad Balwanz climbed off the MH-60 Black Hawk helicopter. He turned his head slowly, looking from one end of the dark horizon to the other. He wanted to commit the scene to memory. A flat barley field laced with irrigation ditches for as far as the eye could see. It looked like Kansas in the winter. A clear, cool, strangely quiet night.

Balwanz and the seven other U.S. Army Green Berets were on a top secret mission, code-named "Giant." They were deep inside Iraq.

One hundred and fifty miles south of Balwanz's Special Forces team, the Army's 18th Airborne Corps stood poised in Saudi Arabia just south of the Iraqi border. In a little more than five hours, at exactly 4 A.M. on February 24, 1991, the 18th Corps would cross the border. Its soldiers would begin what was to go down in military history as the "Hail Mary" flanking maneuver that General H. Norman Schwarzkopf's United States Central Command had devised to encircle and destroy the Iraqi army occupying Kuwait.

It was a bold maneuver. To begin the ground war for Desert Storm, United States Marines and Arab divisions would breach the formidable defenses Saddam Hussein's army had erected along the Kuwaiti border. Meanwhile, hundreds of miles to the west the 18th and 7th Corps—made up of American, French, and British forces—would sweep through southern Iraq to bottle up the enemy in the south, cut off its lines of supply from the north.

It was a clever and bold maneuver as long as Iraqi reserve forces further north near Baghdad did not counterattack. That would trap the western flanking armies as they raced to encircle the enemy occupation forces to the south.

Chad Balwanz's Green Beret team was one of ten positioned ahead of the flankers to warn the 18th Corps if the Iraqis closed in from the north.

They were human trip wires. Balwanz and the members of his A-team, officially designated Operational Detachment Alpha-525, were assigned to keep watch on Highway 7. It was a lonely stretch of road from Baghdad that fed south into the Iraqi city of An Nasiryah along the Euphrates River—just above the point where the 18th Corps would make its right turn to envelop the enemy forces in Kuwait.

Satellites and spy planes could provide overhead photos on the disposition of Iraqi forces, but those pictures might take as long as several days to arrive at corps headquarters. Eighteenth Airborne Corps commanders, facing hundreds of miles of barren Iraqi plains where their tanks would be sitting ducks in a counterattack, wanted "eyes on the ground" and "real-time intelligence"—Army jargon for human beings lying in a foxhole ahead of the main force who would radio back to headquarters the instant they saw enemy activity ahead.

Green Berets, the elite from the U.S. Army's special operations forces, called it special reconnaissance. Saner soldiers might think it a suicide mission.

The ride in had been unnerving enough. The two Black Hawks carrying Balwanz's team had just crossed the Iraqi border when the not so subtle code words, "bag it," came over the lead chopper's radio: abort the mission, return to the refueling base at Rafha just inside Saudi Arabia. Another delay in launching the ground war.

When the choppers touched down back at Rafha, a second message came over the radio: "execute the mission." That's just like the Army, Balwanz thought. Can't make up its mind.

But now the planes were behind schedule, and would get further behind. The Black Hawk pilots, the Army's best from its secret 160th Special Operations Aviation Regiment, had calculated that they would have exactly ten minutes' worth of fuel left after they had made the round trip into Iraq. The two birds now had to sit on the runway and waste precious minutes while their tanks were topped off.

The choppers took off again at 8:45 P.M.—forty-five minutes late. The delay was critical. The flight took two hours. The Black Hawks were supposed to have landed on the west side of Highway 7 at exactly 10 P.M. That would give Balwanz's men just enough time to walk to the highway, dig two chest-deep hide sites, camouflage them, then climb into the holes to begin observing the convoy traffic before six o'clock the next morning when the sun rose.

For weeks back at their Saudi base camp at King Fahd International Airport, the team had practiced marching with the back-breaking loads they would need to build the hide sites. They had timed themselves to see how long it took to dig the holes and reinforce the walls with sandbags (four hours), then to camouflage ceilings reinforced with steel pipes (another hour). Terry Harris, the team's demolitions sergeant and a world-class scrounger, had appropriated the pipes from a construction project at the airport.

A forty-five-minute delay meant they could be finishing up those damn hide sites in broad daylight, Balwanz worried.

The two Black Hawks, each carrying four members of Balwanz's team, roared across the border at over 100 miles per hour, staying no more than twenty feet off the ground to avoid Iraqi radar. Decoy helicopters had been sent out earlier to conduct false insertions to confuse Iraqi border patrols. Balwanz felt like he was on a roller coaster that could crash at any minute as the Black Hawk plunged and zigzagged to avoid radar tracks and enemy outposts. Looking out a side window through his night vision goggles, Balwanz could see only endless sand dunes that blended into the sky.

Suddenly the plane lurched up, knocking him back. He heard a crashing sound in the rear of the chopper. The craft shook like a car that had jumped a curb.

"What's happening?" Balwanz screamed into the microphone of the helmet the crew had provided him.

"Aw, nothing," the pilot radioed back matter-of-factly. "We just struck a sand dune."

Helicopter pilots, Balwanz thought to himself. Nothing gets them excited. Only later would he learn that when the pilot jerked the cyclic stick to avoid hitting a dune, the Black Hawk's tail had dipped and hit the ground, shearing off the rear wheel. Before the chopper could land back at Rafha the ground crew had to slip a crate underneath the tail.

As the Black Hawk passed An Nasiryah, the pilot turned around in his seat with more bad news. "We've lost the satellite coverage," he shouted to Balwanz through his intercom mike.

In the modern age of instant communications and microchip computers, military helicopters, trucks, even soldiers on foot can pinpoint their exact location anywhere in the world using a small box called GPS, which stands for global positioning system. But GPS depends on an overhead satellite, which feeds the position coordinates to the person on the ground. The GPS satellite would have been over the Black Hawks' position feeding them exact coordinates if they had been at the drop-off point on time. But forty-five minutes later, the satellite had already passed.

The MH-60 had backup navigation systems. "But we're probably not going to land exactly where you wanted to be," the pilot warned.

"Just get as close as you can to that original spot," Balwanz said. He tried not to sound like he was pleading. Special Forces soldiers are trained to adjust quickly to the friction and fog of war. To be innovative, unlike the hidebound regular military, is a matter of pride for these men —the reason they are called "special."

"As close as you can" turned out to be about a mile and a half further north.

It would feel like a hundred miles. Each man was loaded down with up to 175 pounds of gear. The team had to carry enough to live on its own in the hide sites for up to six days, just in case the 18th Corps' attack was delayed or became bogged down during the western sweep. The hide site kits alone added thirty pounds to each pack. Then there were survival rations, bayonets, knives, shovels, signal mirrors, ammunition, machine guns, rifles, grenade launchers, plus five redundant radio systems to talk among themselves and with Air Force planes.

A Green Beret doctor had prescribed a weight-lifting regimen and a high-carbohydrate diet to help their bodies retain water. Still, an extra mile and a half of walking was a grueling addition to the mission.

But Balwanz wasn't the kind to be discouraged as the Black Hawks lifted off. His men called him "Bulldog" because he was muscular, stocky, had short brown hair and dark brown eyes—and because he could be tenacious on a mission. The son of a factory worker, Balwanz had spent enough time slaving in the coal mines of the Ohio Valley as a young man to know that somewhere else there was a better life. That was the Army, where he rose through the enlisted ranks to eventually become a warrant officer in the Green Berets.

Balwanz was also the kind of leader who gave his men plenty of latitude in carrying out orders. Maybe it was because he had served in the enlisted ranks and knew that sergeants detested officers who told them how to do their jobs. But it was also because Green Berets were trained to operate independently, more so than regular soldiers. People who couldn't think on their feet usually washed out of Special Forces training. As long as they produced, Balwanz was content to leave his men alone. But he expected results.

Soft-spoken, Balwanz was intensely committed to his job. It was that quality that his wife, Rhonda, had held in awe when they first met. She had been in the Army herself. Both had been stationed at an Army post in Texas. She was an impressionable young private. He was a young Green Beret sergeant.

Balwanz didn't want to fall in love. Life would be hard married to a Green Beret, he warned his wife-to-be. The work was dangerous. There would be long separations while he was on overseas training missions or secret operations. Balwanz was proud of what he did. On his income tax return, he liked writing "professional soldier" in the block where it asked for his occupation.

Balwanz was right. The job did put tremendous strain on the marriage and family life. They would never forget their daughter's first birthday. Both had to be away for military deployments, so they dropped Maggie off at a relative's house. As they drove away, they cried because they would miss that important day with her.

Balwanz had only taken command of this Special Forces A-team two months earlier. They were a cocky bunch, he thought. Scuba teams were like that. Detachment-525 was one of a handful of Special Forces units that were cross-trained to be underwater divers in addition to their commando skills. They had nicknamed themselves "the Sharkmen." You could always pick out the scuba teams with their barrel chests from the heavy regimen of swimming and their arrogant manner. On some teams the divers pierced their nipples and strung a gold chain across their chests as a sign of rebellion.

Balwanz's confidence wasn't false bravado. For all but one, this was the first time in combat. Yet each of his men were seasoned sergeants who had spent years training in special warfare tactics. Charlie Hopkins, the team's senior noncommissioned officer, was a combination dive supervisor, free-fall parachutist, sniper, Ranger-trained commando, and escape and evasion expert. The team had sequestered itself for three weeks in isolation planning for everything that might go wrong in this mission. Jim-Bo Hovermale, the team's weapons sergeant and the only one who had seen combat (in Grenada), had "what-iffed" the mission to death, spending sleepless nights planning for contingencies like the one they now faced—being in the wrong spot.

The team members hoisted their backpacks—one man had to pull up another with the groaning 175-pound weight lashed to him—and began trudging across the barley fields. They ducked into the irrigation canals whenever they could to reduce their silhouettes. They walked through the canal's ankle-deep water so they wouldn't leave tracks.

About a mile south and two miles west of Highway 7, they halted. Hopkins and Dan Kostrzebski, the team's medic and a former high school basketball star, began digging a cache to hide supplies and a PRC-104 radio. If the mission was compromised and the team had to flee, the secret cache might come in handy later.

Balwanz and Hovermale went ahead to check an area about 300 yards east of Highway 7 where the hide sites would be built. On the west side of the road ran the Shatt al Gharraf, a tributary that fed into the Euphrates further south. They had to position themselves dangerously close to the highway so that at night when they peeped through their porthole with night vision goggles they could clearly identify vehicles on the road. The 18th Corps wanted details. The men had to be close enough to the road to tell a T-72 tank from a T-54.

Shortly after midnight, the team began furiously digging the holes: one north of a canal that jutted perpendicular from the road, the other on the south side. By six the next morning, the hide sites were finished. The exhausted Green Berets climbed in and began observing the road.

At 6:30 A.M. they radioed their first report code-named "Angus." The team had spent weeks poring over intelligence folders of Iraq's mostly Soviet-supplied equipment so they could identify anything traveling on the road. Travel patterns were important. Were enemy vehicles withdrawing to the north or moving south as reinforcements?

But as dawn broke, the team began seeing more than just trucks. "Man, there are people out there," whispered James Weatherford, a communications specialist who was in one of the hide sites with Balwanz and taking his turn at peering out the square porthole.

Children were playing along the road. Women with veils across their faces gathered wood. Bedouins herded sheep, goats, and cattle. Weatherford squinted and looked from one side of the porthole to the other. Six-thirty in the morning and it seemed like Grand Central Station out there. Balwanz, who crouched behind him along with two other team members, could now hear voices. And for the next three hours, the voices sounded as if they were inching closer.

Rob Gardner, one of the most intense intelligence sergeants Balwanz had ever met, had spent hours reading every scrap of intelligence on Iraq from the cables fed to the Green Berets. The team knew that the area where the hide sites would be dug was populated. Nearby was a tiny farm village called Suwayj Ghazi, just off the Shatt al Gharraf. Intelligence analysts from headquarters had even calculated the number of people per square mile.

But they had made one incorrect assumption. In the winter American farmers almost never set foot on their fields. The intelligence section assumed that Iraqi farmers didn't either. This wasn't a harvest season. Overhead photos showed no signs of life at least when the satellites passed. But in the off-season, Iraqi farmers in fact roamed their fields gathering wood and herding animals on foot.

This isn't how it's supposed to work, Balwanz thought to himself. Weatherford became even more nervous. Children were playing and giggling around the hide site, some no more than twenty feet away.

"Just watch the road," Balwanz whispered soothingly. "Don't worry about them." The hide sites were well camouflaged. During rehearsals at King Fahd, Balwanz had other teams come out to look for them when they were dug in. They were never spotted. In fact when the allies began the air war a search party frantically hunted for their practice hide sites in the Saudi desert, fearing they might be hit by a stray Iraqi Scud missile. No, the only way someone could spot this site was if he walked on top of it, Balwanz thought.

Which is exactly what happened. The laughing outside abruptly stopped. Weatherford looked out the peep hole. An Iraqi girl no more than eight years old stared back. She screamed. He jumped back. With the green and tan camouflage paint covering his face, Weatherford must have appeared to her like a man from Mars.

"We're seen," he said excitedly, turning to Balwanz. "They've caught us."

The little girl and her two playmates took off. Kostrzebski and Robert DeGroff, another weapons expert on the team, bolted out of the hole. Silencers were attached to their Heckler and Koch submachine guns. They looked at Balwanz, who could read the question on their faces.

He shook his head. "No children are going to be shot," he said firmly. He thought Kostrzebski and DeGroff would have fired at the youngsters, but only if he had ordered it. And Bulldog Balwanz wasn't about to begin his first day in combat gunning down little kids.

Besides, it wouldn't have served any purpose, he reasoned. No one would have heard the muffled shots and the bodies could have been dragged into the holes to continue the mission. But surely someone would have come looking for the missing children. Half the men on the team were married with children. But cold calculations were made on operations like this. Lives were not senselessly taken.

Balwanz grabbed one of the radios and called Hopkins, who was in charge of the other hide site seventy-five yards away. It hadn't been spotted.

"We've been compromised," he said curtly. "Pack up your equipment. We'll meet out in the canal in a few minutes." If one site was discovered, it wouldn't be long before the second was found as well. Both groups had to get away from those holes. There was no time to dismantle the sites. They had to move fast. They left water behind that would weigh them down.

Out in the canal, Weatherford unfolded the spider-webbed antenna to his SATCOM radio and keyed the microphone. Balwanz grabbed it.

"Look, we've been compromised," he shouted into the mike. "We need emergency exfil. We need to be moved out of here!"

On the other end of the line was the special operations liaison officer at 18th Corps headquarters. "Exfil," which stood for exfiltration, which meant sending in a rescue chopper to a hot zone where the enemy would be lying in wait, was not a word the liaison officer particularly enjoyed hearing. He began grilling Balwanz, as if the questions might change the Green Beret's mind about being pulled out. What happened? What's the extent of your compromise? Are you sure you need us to come get you?

Balwanz could not have been more sure. "These children have compromised us," he repeated with an edge to his voice that he hoped the liaison officer would pick up.

"Okay, we'll work on getting you out," came the reply finally.

Weatherford folded up the SATCOM antenna. Balwanz ordered the team to move east 300 more yards away from the road where they could be hidden in a deeper part of the canal.

At the new position, Balwanz peered over the canal with his binoculars. "Something's funny here," he told Hopkins. "Nobody's come looking for us. Nobody's excited. Nobody's running to see what was in our holes." The women were still gathering wood in the fields. The farmers were still herding sheep, all as if nothing had happened.

Maybe the children didn't know what they saw, Balwanz thought. If they did, maybe they didn't tell anyone. Or maybe they told someone and he didn't believe them. Maybe their hide site had been compromised but not their mission.

Balwanz radioed back to 18th Corps and canceled the exfiltration. They would continue the surveillance and report back what they saw. At nightfall they would move further south and establish another temporary hide site. For the next two hours the team watched the road and radioed back the vehicle movement it saw.

At noontime, Balwanz took a shift at the watch and crawled up to the ridge of the canal. "Damn, this place is crowded," he muttered to himself. He could count at least thirty people around him. Some strolled along Highway 7. Others wandered to his rear. At least they were several hundred yards away, he sighed.

But not for long. Balwanz turned around and could see a group of women and children at his northeast flank walking closer. Within minutes, he looked east down the canal. Was that children peeking their heads out from a bend in the canal?

It was. The children's faces froze. This time there were no screams. For an instant, Balwanz thought he was staring them right in the eyes.

He slid down the ditch and collared DeGroff. "I think the kids might have seen me," he whispered.

DeGroff decided to take a look for himself. Short and muscular, he clambered up to the edge of the canal and poked his head out. In an instant he scrambled back down.

DeGroff didn't even have time to tell what he saw. The team looked up. Standing directly over them at the top of the ditch were two more children. Several adults walked up behind them.

A middle-aged man wearing a white robe with his head swathed in a red and white checkered khafia parted the children and peered down into the canal where the Green Berets looked up squinting into the sunlight.

"*Salam alaikum*," Balwanz said with the best smile he could muster. It was Arabic for "peace be upon you." Before the mission, Balwanz had laughed over an intelligence report he had reviewed. When he had asked the G-2 about what the reaction of Iraqi civilians might be if they happened upon Americans, the intelligence section had responded: They might be friendly. They might ignore you and be neutral. Or, they might be hostile. Boy, that was a big help, Balwanz remembered thinking.

The Iraqi who stared blankly at him now gave no hint of which category he fell into. The man turned around and walked at a fast clip toward the village of Suwayj Ghazi. Again, it was no use shooting him. There would only be more.

And there were. The Iraqi who had confronted them before came back with what seemed to Balwanz like the entire town of Suwayj Ghazi. This time some were carrying World War II–vintage bolt-action rifles.

Up the canal behind the team what appeared to be the local gang of teenagers came sauntering up. Balwanz ordered them to halt. They stepped forward defiantly. He brandished his machine gun and snarled. They backed off.

Bedouins tried to sneak about, comically almost, with their long rifles hidden underneath their robes. Others were more bold, walking straight to the team's position, their weapons hoisted onto their shoulders.

Minutes later, four large convoy trucks came to a screeching halt along the road and deposited a company of Iraqi soldiers. Balwanz counted more than a hundred. He got on the radio to 18th Corps.

"We have been compromised again," he spoke into the mike quickly, not giving the liaison officer time to ask questions. "We're about to be in a firefight. We need help. We need emergency exfiltration and we need close air support!" Balwanz described the force slowly surrounding him. The liaison officer realized it was a firefight the team could quickly lose.

"We're going to get you close air support first," the officer promised. "And we're going to work on the exfil." But it would take a half hour for the Air Force's F-16 Falcon jets to reach the highway.

"We're going to be in trouble," Balwanz said, clicking off the mike and turning to his team. "Let's destroy this stuff." The team had a prearranged emergency destruction plan for its radios and classified equipment, such as secret cryptographic gear that scrambled radio messages back to headquarters. They had rehearsed the plan back at King Fahd, hoping that they would never have to implement it. Harris pulled the plastic explosive charge out of his rucksack and plugged in a one-minute time fuse. The team stacked the rucksacks and radios on top of the charge. Only a LST-5, a high-tech transmitter for satellite communications back to 18th Corps, and two small PRC-90 survival radios were left out.

Meanwhile, the enemy 400 yards away maneuvered around the team. The Iraqi soldiers, armed with AK-47 assault rifles, split into flanking platoons to the right and left. The armed Bedouins ran east to come up on the team from its rear. The soldiers, who obviously had not had much military training, stood upright and bunched together as they marched across the open field. But Balwanz ordered the team not to shoot until it was fired upon.

The field was cluttered with unarmed civilians. Old men of the town, women, and children had gathered near the soldiers to gawk. Balwanz found it surreal, like something out of the Civil War when ladies twirling parasols would ride up in coaches to enjoy the spectacle of battle. In this case, to watch the Americans be captured or killed.

Practically surrounded, Harris set the explosive charge's timer and the team ran east, snaking through the canals, searching for a decent defensive position to hold off an attack or perhaps even an avenue of escape. Balwanz was still hoping he could avoid a fight. His was such a tiny force, certainly no match for an infantry company.

Iraqi soldiers crept up to the pile of rucksacks and radios. The fuse detonated the plastic explosive. Dirt, canvas, and radio parts flew into the air. The soldiers were knocked back. A loud boom echoed across the field.

All hell broke loose. The Iraqi soldiers began firing wildly at the Green Berets' position. The Bedouins with their antique rifles turned out to be better shots. Hunters no doubt, Balwanz thought. Dirt kicked up around his head from the rounds of their more accurate fire.

The team crouched down in the canal as volley after volley of fire came overhead. "God, this isn't good," Balwanz mumbled to himself. The F-16s were still twenty minutes away. As the Iraqis charged, they let out a blood-curdling war cry. DeGroff and Kostrzebski, who had become close friends on the team, looked at each other from opposite ends of the defensive perimeter they had established in the canal. They waved as if saying goodbye for the last time.

Should they surrender, someone asked? If tanks and armored personnel carriers next pulled up on the road, should they hoist a white flag?

Fuck that, they decided. Green Beret teams were high-priced commodities in battle. Their heads were filled with all kinds of secrets and plans for covert operations.

The commandos had stripped all the ranks and Special Forces insignia from their uniforms before beginning the mission so if they were captured the enemy might not know the prize they had.

But fat chance of that fooling them for long, Balwanz thought. If they surrendered, they wouldn't be just roughed up a little and paraded before television cameras in Baghdad. They'd be tortured for every last bit of information they had, then killed.

The decision not to surrender wasn't taken in panic. That's what separated Green Beret teams from conventional units. Cold calculations were being made. These were the Army's most professional soldiers, and their most flexible. They weren't green recruits still growing up. They were mature warriors, many of them family men—who had volunteered for Special Forces and this type of hazardous duty. Enlisted soldiers could not even apply to become Green Berets until they had some seasoning in conventional units as sergeants.

For days they had rehearsed this kind of contingency. What would they do if compromised and overwhelmed by an enemy force? A regular infantry squad would have lashed out to break the cordon. The Green Berets would pick it apart. Balwanz's team had the advantage of being what the Army liked to call a "force multiplier"—an antiseptic term that meant they had the commando skills to even up the odds in a case like this.

Balwanz knew the team didn't have enough ammunition for a long firefight. They couldn't set their weapons on automatic and spray the battlefield with bullets like conventional forces love to do. Each shot had to be carefully aimed. Each had to count. One bullet one body.

Hovermale and DeGroff, who had the M-16 rifles with the M-203 grenade launchers fitted underneath, began firing 40-millimeter grenades into the clusters of soldiers approaching on the left and right flanks. That broke the immediate advance.

Then the team began picking off soldiers. Balwanz directed the fire like a surveyor marking spots on land. Five of the eight men on the team were expert snipers. With the telescopic sights atop their M-16s, they could kill a man 500 yards away. The Iraqis didn't have that range or accuracy with their AK-47s. The snipers began to drop them before they could get close enough to make their shots count.

The soldiers nearer to the team fared even worse. Balwanz and Hopkins carried the Heckler and Koch MP-5 machine guns, perfect for close-quarter battle with infrared laser sights fitted on them. In just the first ten minutes of fighting, the eight Green Berets had managed to coldly and methodically kill about forty soldiers. That halted the enemy advance and forced the Iraqis to hug the ground.

A woman from the village walked onto the field of battle. The team at first thought she had been sent to recover the dead and wounded. Instead she scooped up weapons soldiers had dropped. The team shot her. When the woman picked up the weapons she had become a combatant. It posed no moral dilemma for the men. Another cold calculation at the time. Only later would they privately agonize over the killing they had been forced to make.

Next, children were sent out. The team held its fire. Thankfully, the children just dragged away bodies.

Finally, the F-16s came roaring over from the south, their pilots wondering what the hell American soldiers were doing this deep in Iraq. The team cheered. Weatherford, one of the communications sergeants, grabbed the LST-5 radio he had kept out of the destruction pile. The LST-5 provided the long-range communication they would need to direct the Air Force planes on where to drop their bombs.

But the whip antenna that the radio needed to transmit to the planes was missing. Weatherford searched frantically. No luck. The antenna must have been lost in the confusion of running from the hide site.

It was maddening. Balwanz could hear over the LST-5 the voices of the frustrated pilots 20,000 feet above pleading with him to direct their strikes. But with no antenna Balwanz couldn't use the radio to transmit. And without knowing exactly where the team was, the pilots couldn't attack the enemy around it for fear of killing the Americans.

Gardner grabbed a dish antenna and plugged its connecting cable into the LST-5. The dish provided only one-direction transmission so he held it up and pointed it to an F-16 swooping by.

"Guard, this is Cowboy," a voice crackled on the LST-5. Guard was the team's call sign. Cowboy was the F-16's. "We heard you for a minute. But you're breaking up." Gardner tried to keep the dish pointed steady at the plane, but it was no use.

"Guard, if we don't hear something in a minute, we're going to take out a target to the south," the F-16 pilot radioed back. Still no luck. So the F-16s began bombing a communications site they had spotted three miles south of the Green Beret position.

That raid helped in one respect. The women and children still on the battlefield scattered when the distant bombs fell. No more civilians to worry about hitting. But the soldiers and armed Bedouins remained—and though crawling, they kept advancing toward the Green Berets. Unless some form of communications could be established, the F-16 pilots would have to watch helplessly as the American position was overrun.

DeGroff spied one of the tiny PRC-90 radios the Green Berets had saved. Nicknamed "Buzzsaw," DeGroff was so competitive he'd sulk for hours if he lost at the putt-putt golf game the team played in the sand back at King Fahd airport. "Can we contact them on this?" he asked.

It's just a survival radio to talk to rescue helicopters, the communications sergeants said. These planes weren't tuned to that frequency and it probably didn't have the range to reach anyone else.

What the hell, DeGroff thought. What have we got to lose? He picked up the PRC-90, keyed its mike and began saying over and over again: "This is Guard. Anybody on this station? Anybody on this station? This is Guard."

DeGroff was about to give up when a tinny voice came

back over the radio. It was from an E-3 AWACS Sentry plane, one of several Boeing 707s jammed with electronics that the Air Force kept flying to monitor the air war and spy on enemy planes. The AWACS always had a radio tuned to the emergency frequency the PRC-90 used.

DeGroff explained their predicament. "Just a second," the AWACS radio man said and flipped a switch to call the F-16s. Tune your radios to the emergency frequency, the AWACS directed the fighter pilots. Cowboy could now talk to Guard.

The team directed the F-16s to attack Iraqi reinforcements climbing off trucks on Highway 7. A plane dropped a cluster bomb that broke up in the air and showered the road with deadly little bomblets. From afar they sounded like popcorn popping. Next came 2,000-pound bombs that shook the earth as they hit the enemy around the team. To halt Iraqi soldiers edging nearer, Balwanz began directing the air strikes to "danger close"—the Air Force euphemism for having bombs dumped practically on your own position.

The team had no choice. It was afternoon and Balwanz had just received a grim radio message the F-16s had relayed from the 18th Corps headquarters. The special operations helicopters from the 160th would not fly in until dark. A daylight rescue was simply too risky. The F-16s would be all headquarters could offer until then.

The Desert Storm war, that glorious conflict that brought videos into every American home of smart bombs devastating buildings from afar, was becoming more deadly and personal for eight Green Berets. Two enemy platoons began creeping through the canal to the west for a frontal attack. Hopkins radioed for more bombs danger close to blunt the attack. Balwanz grabbed Gardner, and the two men, shoulder to shoulder, maneuvered up the canal to intercept the western flankers who had escaped the bombing.

About 100 yards up they stumbled into a showdown. The lead element of the enemy flanking platoon was just twenty feet away. Balwanz and Gardner jerked up their machine guns, cutting down the soldiers before they could get off a shot. As he walked past the bodies, Balwanz heard a strange noise—what sounded like deep, throaty breathing.

It was an Iraqi soldier lying face-up in a pool of his own blood. His leg had been shattered by a cluster bomb and his stomach was bleeding, probably from one of the rounds Balwanz or Gardner had just fired.

The soldier's rifle rested by his side. Gardner covered the man with his machine gun while Balwanz crept up to him to drag the weapon away. The soldier stared vacantly. His face was as white as a sheet, which made his thick mustache look all the more black. The soldier turned his head ever so slightly to Balwanz, but his expression did not change. Suddenly from deep in the soldier's throat came a loud screech as he sucked in air. It was his last breath.

Balwanz would later have dreams of that haunting white face and that screeching sound. Dreams of the man who was a soldier just like him, who was fighting for his country in his own backyard. Who Balwanz had watched die.

But there was no time now to dwell on death. Balwanz and Gardner could only think of survival. They scooped up the enemy rifles and raced further west down the canal to where they had blown up their rucksacks. They grabbed the equipment that had not been destroyed. On Highway 7, more trucks arrived and more soldiers fell out. Hopkins directed the F-16s to drop more 2,000-pound bombs.

The sun was about to set. But it was still an hour before the choppers would arrive. That presented another problem for the team. As it got dark it would be almost impossible for the Green Berets to direct the F-16s to the right targets. Highway 7 was now littered with the charred hulks of bombed-out trucks, but enemy soldiers still surrounded the team. The F-16s patrolled overhead, but there was little more they could attack as it became nighttime.

But for the first time all day luck turned the team's way. The Iraqi soldiers who were dug in around the Green Berets advanced no further. The bombing, the sniper fire, it had all taken the fight out of them. For an awkward hour, as the 18th Corps gobbled up real estate in its dash to the Euphrates, the eight Green Berets and what was left of a reinforced Iraqi infantry company peered above their trenches at each other and observed an uneasy truce.

Shortly before 8 P.M., Balwanz heard the patter of helicopter blades striking the air. The 160th pilots were early. Balwanz learned later that the pilots, who chafed at being prohibited by headquarters from trying a daylight rescue, had cheated on their takeoff and left Saudi Arabia before dark. The Green Berets withdrew to safer ground east and formed a defensive perimeter to beacon in the two Black Hawks.

The choppers landed practically on top of them. The team scrambled aboard. Within seconds the helicopters took off and, hugging the ground as they flew, darted south to Saudi Arabia. There was always the chance the Black Hawks could be shot down on the ride back. But as far as Balwanz and his team were concerned they were safe.

They laughed and screamed and hooted and slapped their hands. They breathed in deeply the smell of jet fuel and oil and metal and canvas of the chopper's belly that had rescued them and now protected them from their nightmare in Iraq. Later they would dissect the mission in intricate detail as Special Forces soldiers do with every operation. Would there be recriminations because the team had to be rescued, Balwanz wondered briefly on the ride back? Would the mission be considered a failure?

But answers to those questions would have to wait. For now Balwanz and the other Green Berets slumped back on the deck of the helicopter, exhausted from having no sleep the past forty-eight hours. All they wanted to do now was savor the fact that they were still alive.

There were no recriminations. Just the opposite. Balwanz and his team were treated as heroes, and deservedly so. They were among the relatively few soldiers who saw any close-quarter combat in Desert Storm, a conflict fought mostly by planes, tanks, and precision-guided munitions fired from far away.

The Green Berets did manage to radio back intelligence about the convoy traffic on Highway 7 for the day they were there. Their reports and others from Green Beret teams that were not compromised gave the allies' western flankers up-to-the-minute intelligence on Iraqi troop activity in the north, which fortunately never materialized into a counterattack. The enveloping movement caught the Iraqi occupiers in the south completely by surprise.

Commando forces had many successful operations during the Desert Storm war. Air Force special operations helicopters raided enemy early-warning radars. Psychological operations teams that fight with words not bullets dropped tons of propaganda leaflets that prompted thousands of Iraqi soldiers to surrender. Navy SEALs faked an amphibious Marine landing along the coast of Kuwait that pinned down two Iraqi divisions. Delta Force commandos hunted Scud missiles Iraq had aimed at Israel. A Green Beret doctor even treated a wounded elephant at the Kuwait City zoo.

But the true character and nature of special operations and the men who wage it can be found in an obscure mission that went bad. Because of some curious children, Balwanz and seven comrades found themselves surrounded behind enemy lines. But because of their special training and their fighting skills, they managed to escape death. By the Army's rough count, of the some 150 Iraqi soldiers and Bedouins who surrounded Balwanz's team at the beginning of the firefight, only twenty were observed leaving the battlefield as the Black Hawks flew away. The others had been killed or wounded by Balwanz's sharpshooters or the F-16s. For keeping his team alive in the face of almost twenty-to-one odds, Balwanz was awarded the Silver Star medal. The other seven Green Berets received Bronze Stars.

But for more than three months, their mission and the valor they had displayed were kept secret. Not until after the air war had started would the Green Berets even acknowledge that they had men in Saudi Arabia. And not until I interviewed Balwanz at Fort Campbell, Kentucky, on a sunny spring day in May 1991 had he ever talked about the battle of Suwayj Ghazi to anyone who did not have a security clearance.

After our interview Balwanz went home to Rhonda and told her the details of the mission. It scared her. For a time she cried when she saw news reports on the war and realized that her husband could have been one of the casualties. Special operations work can be tough on families. Divorce rates among the all-male units tend to be high. Operators may be away from home as many as ten months out of the year on secret missions or training assignments, about which they can share little with loved ones. Some commandos have secret codes they exchange over the phone with their wives to let them know where they are. Most wives know not to ask. Marriages that survive tend to be strong; the wives often end up raising children as single parents because the men are away for such long stretches. And always there is the fear of a military staff car pulling into the driveway in the middle of the night and an officer knocking on the door with bad news.

It took me almost a month of negotiations with the United States Special Operations Command before I was allowed to interview Balwanz and more than three dozen other special operations commandos for a *Newsweek* cover story on their Desert Storm missions. Special operations units distrust the media and keep them at a safe distance. But the command knew full well it had to compete with other military outfits for fewer defense dollars in a post–Cold War world. No doubt it saw some value to ʼopening the window ever so slightly.

After *Newsweek* published its cover story based on my interviews, some senior Pentagon officials grumbled privately that the command had dumped the stories in my lap as a publicity stunt to protect its budget. I had to laugh. My negotiations to gain access had been tedious, and at times tense. The command declassified missions often only grudgingly. To this day, they refuse to talk publicly about many Desert Storm operations.

But the hostile reaction to the piece from some defense quarters was telling. The Defense Department has never been comfortable with its special operations forces. The American military was born from the early guerrilla fighters of the Revolutionary War—angry farmers who fired their muskets from behind trees at British redcoats marching in rigid formation at Lexington and Concord. But the American military establishment that evolved never had much use for unconventional warriors. The United States Army became a rigidly bureaucratized, conventional force. For the next two centuries it wedded itself to an attrition form of warfare that valued defeating an enemy simply with more men and hardware rather than with innovative tactics on the battlefield.

Guerrilla warfare had no place in American military tradition as it evolved. Not until after World War II was it given any official sanction in American military doctrine. And even then guerrilla warfare was viewed with disdain. Its tactics were hit-and-run. Its targets were sometimes even civilians. Europeans had a long affinity for this secretive form of fighting. But it was not the way Americans do battle, not by stealth or subversion or by firing from shadows, then running away.

The special operations soldiers who conducted this type of warfare were shunned even more. The very fact that they were elite, that they were carefully selected and specially trained fighters, was held against them. The special units in which they served possessed unique skills for difficult missions that conventional armies could not conduct—missions like sabotage or surgical attacks or sitting in a hole 150 miles inside Iraq watching a highway like Balwanz had done. Movies and novels glorify these elite forces, but American generals have long detested the notion of having them in their armies. The American military has prided itself on being an egalitarian force. Elite units were the stuff of European armies, of French legionnaires or German storm troopers, not American divisions whose citizen soldiers were trained and treated equally.

The generals have never trusted special operations soldiers. Commanders understandably don't appreciate what they can't control and there has always been an uncontrollable quality to special operations forces because the warfare they wage is so unconventional. General Douglas MacArthur wouldn't allow them in his theater during World War II. In Vietnam, special operations soldiers were regarded by the military brass as little more than trained assassins and mercenaries, an army within the Army.

It was not far from the truth. Green Berets and Navy SEALs tortured prisoners and assassinated Vietcong leaders for the CIA. Covert operators at times ran amuck, breaking laws and embarrassing the government. In the 1980s the Pentagon was beset by the Iran-contra scandal and investigations of fraud and abuse in secret military operations. Elite counterterrorist outfits like Delta Force and SEAL Team-6 were probed for financial irregularities. Investigators found clandestine Pentagon units using tax dollars to buy expensive hotel rooms, first-class airline tickets, and in one instance a hot-air balloon and Rolls-Royce. The secret warriors continued to be glorified in movies as hellraisers, loose cannons, and Rambos. In military circles they were considered more trouble than they were worth—weirdos and misfits who had to be reigned in, or rescued when their operations went awry.

But they all weren't cowboys. Far from it. During their ten years in Vietnam, the Green Berets also dug 6,436 wells, repaired 1,210 miles of road, and built 508 hospitals and dispensaries. Special operations officers are quick to point out that most of those implicated in the scandals of the 1980s were not of their ranks. Oliver North, after all, was a lieutenant colonel in the Marine Corps.

In many respects the commandos are trained to be less violent. Unlike conventional soldiers, who are instructed to bring massive firepower onto the enemy (often indiscriminately), commandos kill few people. A successful mission is usually one where they slip in, run their operations, then slip out undetected. Unnecessary killing risks compromise.

If American generals found little use for special operations forces, politicians have. Covert action is an age-old instrument of state. The atomic era rendered the superpowers' conventional armies good for not much more than deterrence. Secret unconventional armies, with their cover of deniability, became weapons of choice for the Cold War competition in the Third World. Despite any noble ideals they might profess, American presidents have always found it useful to have a force handy to fight dirty little wars that violate normal rules of conduct. Wars that circumvent the military chain of command. Sometimes even wars that the politicians themselves do not want to know about.

There are types of warfare that conventional armies cannot fight. The military has defined them as low-intensity conflicts: hostilities waged with political, economic, and psychological weapons, conflicts that involve the struggle of competing principles or ideologies and produce relatively few casualties. The infantry divisions, tanks, and warplanes of large combat armies are unsuited for resolving these conflicts. They are the insurgencies, the counterinsurgencies, coup d'etats, terrorism, short conflicts, economic and psychological warfare. Since World War II, there have been some 120 such conflicts worldwide. By contrast, a nuclear war was always a remote possibility, even more so now. The United States has only fought two conventional wars since World War II—in Korea in the 1950s and the Persian Gulf in 1991. Vietnam was a low-intensity conflict the U.S. Army mistook for a conventional war.

The Pentagon has come to accept the need for special operations forces, but not without a fight. The Army, Navy, and Air Force practically disbanded their special operations units after World War II, the Korean War, and Vietnam. In the annual budget wars, the disparate and demoralized special operations units that remained scattered among the services were routinely shortchanged on funding. The Trident badge of a Navy SEAL or the red ascot of an Air Force special operations squadron became a sure ticket to a dead-end career in the military. For years the Army even tried to ban the wearing of a green beret. "No more Vietnams"—the favorite refrain of generals after that war—meant no more attention paid to low-intensity warfare. The Pentagon became preoccupied with matching the Soviets ICBM for ICBM or repelling a Warsaw Pact invasion in central Europe.

But the real conflicts took other forms and the military was not prepared to deal with them. A raid to rescue the American freighter *Mayaguez* in 1975 was botched because of sloppy Defense Department planning. A 1980 operation to free fifty-three Americans held hostage in the U.S. embassy in Tehran ended in disaster when a Navy helicopter collided with an Air Force transport plane in a remote desert of Iran, killing eight airmen and commandos. When Italian Red Brigade terrorists kidnapped Army Brigadier General James Dozier two years later, Pentagon, State Department, and CIA officials spent as much time arguing over who would be in charge of the rescue as they did looking for the unfortunate officer. In 1983, a Shiite fanatic driving a truck packed with explosives rammed an unprotected Beirut airport barracks where Marine peacekeepers slept, killing 241 in the blast. In the Grenada invasion that same year, more than a dozen special operations commandos were killed or wounded in ill-conceived missions.

Fed up, Congress in 1987 passed a law ordering the Defense Department to establish a new U.S. Special Operations Command. As long as the commandos were treated as second-class citizens in the Pentagon bureaucracy, there would be more debacles like the Teheran rescue and Grenada invasion. Incensed over congressional meddling in military matters, the generals and admirals fought the legislation. But Capitol Hill demanded that special operations be organized under one command with more bureaucratic clout.

General Jim Lindsay, a cigar-chomping paratrooper who had been decorated for valor in Vietnam, became its first commander. Fellow generals thought Lindsay was insane to take over an organization the Pentagon had so bitterly opposed. But Lindsay proved as skilled a diplomat as he had been a warrior. After about a year of haggling with the military services, he managed to gain control of most special operations units.

Today the Special Operations Command, which is headquartered at MacDill Air Force base in Tampa, Florida, oversees more than 46,000 soldiers. The Army portion of the command is the largest, with about 30,000 members, and is made up of the famed Green Berets Special Forces teams, the Army Rangers, who are crack assault troops, the 160th Special Operations Aviation Regiment, psychological warfare groups, and civil affairs battalions that repair villages or restore order after a war. The Navy's contribution to the command are some 5,500 SEALs and their support forces, which specialize in amphibious commando raids and waterborne operations. The Air Force allocates 9,500 air commandos, who provide special infiltration helicopters, transport planes, aerial refueling tankers, and gunships. Then there are the 1,300 members of the most secretive part of the command—the Joint Special Operations Command. The Pentagon refuses to acknowledge that most of its forces even exist: the Army's Delta Force and the Navy's SEAL Team-6, which specialize in counterterrorism and special commando missions, a Ranger unit for surgical combat assaults, plus a secret Army and Air Force helicopter force and intelligence unit.

The command does not control all the special operations forces in the American arsenal. The FBI has a hostage rescue team modeled after Delta Force, which responds to terrorist threats in the United States. The turf-conscious Marines have refused to turn over the few special operations units they have.

The Central Intelligence Agency also has its own Special Operations Group, a paramilitary force of about 200 men and women. The CIA's SOG, as it's called in spy jargon, is made up of ex-military special operators who mainly infiltrate into foreign countries in civilian clothes to train foreign armies that don't want to be openly associated with American soldiers in uniform. The SOG, for example, trained contra rebels in Nicaragua and Honduras, and has worked discrete operations in the Latin American drug war.

When its force has been too small for an assignment, or on the rare occasions when it must undertake clandestine combat missions, the SOG will borrow men from the Pentagon's special operations units. The military calls it "sheep-dipping." During their tour with the agency, the military operators go off the Pentagon's books and become CIA case officers. Navy SEALs were sheep-dipped for the CIA's secret mining of Nicaraguan harbors in 1984. During the Soviet occupation of Afghanistan, Army Green Berets were sheep-dipped to train mujahedeen rebels.

To protect it from bureaucratic long knives, Congress carved out for the Special Operations Command an unusual amount of autonomy that still rankles the Pentagon brass. Unlike other combat outfits, the Special Operations Command manages its own budget, which has been steadily increasing despite the reductions in defense spending elsewhere. It even has a research-and-development shop to develop high-tech gizmos for clandestine warfare of the future. Some have likened the command to almost a fourth branch of the military, a characterization that makes conventional generals' skin crawl.

Special operations forces achieved some measure of recognition during the Bush administration. For the invasion of Panama in 1989, 4,000 special operations soldiers just coming together under the wing of the new command provided most of the surgical firepower and conducted practically all of the daring missions. Delta Force commandos rescued a jailed American and chased dictator Manuel Noriega. Navy SEALs blew up his planes and boats. Green Beret teams held off enemy convoys. Psychological operations teams talked Panamanian soldiers into surrendering. A year later, 8,754 commandos deployed in the Desert Storm war to eject Saddam Hussein's army from Kuwait.

But for all the media romanticizing of their missions—

and I've been just as guilty of it as other reporters—the commandos have always had to fight just to get into the war. At the end of Desert Storm, General Schwarzkopf singled out special operations forces as critical to the allied victory. Yet many of those forces were lucky to have even set foot in the general's theater. Schwarzkopf distrusted special operators. He considered them troublemakers. Only after intense lobbying by the Special Operations Command and under pressure from the Pentagon did he allow some special ops units to join his Persian Gulf army. And throughout the war he kept the commandos on a short leash.

Schwarzkopf's attitude toward special operations was hardly aberrant. The distrust remains among the senior military leadership. Few generals and admirals know or appreciate the capability of this growing force. Special operations will likely have to fight its way into the next war. As with the rest of the military, the commandos will have to take a hard look at where they fit in the post–Cold War world.

To this day, special operations forces remain mysterious and misunderstood—not only to outsiders but also within the Defense Department. Pentagon public relations officers paint them as "quiet professionals." Liberals portray them as bloodthirsty mercenaries for right-wing agendas. Leery generals still regard them as hell-raising mavericks and cutthroats.

None of the caricatures is really correct. On secret missions special operators can be as calm and meticulous as surgeons, as picky about details as accountants, as brainy as scientists. But they are hardly automatons programmed to fight one day and be sent to cold storage the next. For all their professions to outsiders that war is hell, commandos love to fight. They can be earthy and profane. They thrive on the thrill of combat, the excitement of clandestine operations like Balwanz's. They are a different, yet complicated, breed.

At the Hooch Bar near the regular officers club at Hurlburt Field, Florida, where Air Force commandos are headquartered, wives don't dare walk in wearing red, a helicopter unit's color, for fear it'll be stripped off and used for an ascot. But many air commandos are tee-totalers. One drunk driving charge and a pilot may be bounced from the unit.

Delta Force psychiatrists have marveled at the controlled violence their commandos can exhibit. Yet half of Delta's operatives are family men in their thirties who ride home in Toyotas and pickups to wives and children after work. Many are deeply religious.

Some Green Berets at Fort Bragg still sport flattop haircuts, Rolex watches, and divorce papers as their Vietnam-era signatures. But others wear earrings and sip Heinekens at yuppie hangouts like Bennigan's in nearby Fayetteville.

Some Navy SEALs still splash rum over the top of a bar and light it to commemorate the death of a comrade. (Many SEALs have party funds written into their wills to pay for the ritual.) But at the SEALs' main headquarters in Coronado, California, you can find a salad bar spread out in the compound's plaza for health-conscious commandos watching their cholesterol.

Soldiers join special operations units because they don't feel they fit into the conventional military. But the hot dogs and daredevils rarely make it past the special ops screening boards. Today's secret warriors are obsessive about being team players. Freelancers get their mates killed.

A small number of commandos become mercenaries after they retire. Others have organized freelance missions to recover American POWs from Vietnam—and failed. Still others have hired out to Third World tyrants. They keep alive the soldier of fortune myth. But the majority do what other military retirees do after they leave the service: enter the business world, join a defense contractor, become consultants, teach school, or just go fishing. Some try to parlay their special ops skills by setting up security consulting and personal protection firms, although a surprising number of these fail. Ex-commandos have the fighting skills, but often not the business sense.

They are a force of contradictions. Green Berets consider John Wayne and Ronald Reagan their heroes even though the former never served a day in his life in the military and the latter paid less attention to the force than liberal Democrats like John Kennedy. I found special operations officers savvy about life in the jungle but naive about politics in Washington. They serve mainly in the Third World, but few blacks are in their units. I could find no evidence that racism kept blacks out of the force. Commandos are hardly WASPs. Green Berets have a heavy concentration of men of Latin, Asian, and East European heritage. A surprising number of native American Indians are in Delta Force.

Special operations soldiers defy stereotyping. Among the Vietnam-era commandos you still find the hell-raising throat-cutters. But a new yuppie generation is infiltrating the force, officers more concerned about human rights who think the knife-between-the-teeth image is a bit outdated. Practically all call themselves conservative Republicans. Most are male chauvinists, according to their wives and girlfriends. But they are hardly dolts. Muscle-bound Conans tend to be the first to drop out of the training, which is more mentally than physically stressing. Enlisted men must have the aptitude test scores of officers just to join many special operations units and a majority of them have college degrees. Most of the officers have advanced degrees. Many are committed environmentalists and liberal on social issues like abortion. And their training is the most innovative and unorthodox in the military.

Piercing the veil of secrecy to find out what life is really like in this private world can be difficult. "All of us are behavioral chameleons," a combat-hardened Navy SEAL once told me. "Just as you compartmentalize intelligence programs, we learn to do that with our personalities. When you're on an operation, that's the violent mission side of you. It's totally different from the loving father side of you, who takes his kids to church and says hi to his neighbors."

I had no trouble meeting scores of impostors who posed as special operators. They're called "wannabes"— from the so-called unconventional warfare experts in Washington whose expertise comes mostly from reading books to the beer-bellied motorcycle drivers who turn up at Soldier of Fortune conventions bragging about commando exploits they never had. The real operators never talk about their missions in public. They avoid journalists and ridicule their peers whose names end up in newspapers. The reticence is understandable. Loose lips in their profession mean people die.

They are a clannish force even within their own services. Every Thursday night, the West Coast Navy SEALs gather for beer and private conversations at McP's, an Irish pub along Orange Drive in Coronado. Members of Green Beret teams and their wives tend to socialize among themselves instead of with the families of conventional Army soldiers. Delta Force squadrons have private bars in their secret headquarters at Fort Bragg where the young commandos can unwind. At the post's regular service clubs they have to be constantly on guard for eavesdroppers. In front of outsiders commandos behave formally with plenty of salutes and yes-sirs for officers. Behind the barbed wire fences of their compounds life is more informal. Military protocol disappears. Ability matters more than rank.

I interviewed more than 200 members of the special operations community for this book, from their senior officers to the recruits just joining the force to the wives of these secret warriors. I was the first journalist ever permitted to view some of their heretofore classified training. I spent long hours with them, hunched over campfires in the chilly night, weaving through dark mountains in helicopters, bobbing in the ocean in rubber rafts. I came away with a totally different impression of this force than the one painted by the movies—or by my colleagues in the media.

I found a force made up not of Arnold Schwarzeneggers or Sylvester Stallones, although it certainly has some of the most physically fit fighters in the world. I found a group much more complex and human in its character. It is a group that would fit into any hometown America—men from the coal mines of Ohio like Chad Balwanz, from the eastern shore of Maryland, from the farms of Kansas, the suburbs of Los Angeles, the streets of New York City. But it is a group that is really only comfortable with itself, separate and apart from the regular military.

If there is a common denominator among them perhaps it was this. I found that men joined special operations units because of a profound hunger for adventure, for something different in their lives. They are all type-A personalities, supremely self-confident of their abilities. They are intensely focused perfectionists. They are driven to succeed sometimes to the point that they wall out families and friends. They have a reputation for being mavericks, but in fact they are more physically and mentally disciplined than conventional soldiers. They are both flexible and rigid, highly individualistic yet extremely group-oriented. They are America's secret soldiers. This is their story.

Part I

THE
MAKING
OF A
COMMANDO

ROBIN SAGE

The helicopter ride was surprisingly boring. Ken Swanson had heard stories about the daring of the 160th Aviation Regiment, the U.S. Army's secret helicopter unit. The all-black MH-47 Chinook, souped up with fancy avionics and electronic countermeasures equipment could juke and dive so fast that its passengers would be flattened on the ceiling. Swanson expected the pilot to put the chopper through its paces for him and the rest of his student detachment. The fifteen Green Beret students squatted on their rucksacks, crammed together like sardines on the helicopter's deck. Four dim blue lights overhead cast an eerie pall inside the chopper's belly.

But except for flying blacked out with their night vision goggles, the Chinook's pilots kept a steady course above the pine forests and tobacco farms of North Carolina's southern Piedmont. The ride would be the only calm moment for Swanson for the next two weeks.

Kenneth Swanson. Infantry captain. The insignia on his uniform revealed he was one of the Army's rising young officers: an airborne patch showing he could parachute from planes, a pathfinder insignia designating him qualified to guide aircraft into remote jungle landing zones, an expert infantryman's badge, a Ranger tab on his shoulder.

Winning that Ranger tab had been hard. Sixty-five days of constant marches, two hours sleep a night, half starving in the field sometimes with just one meal a day. On lonely listening posts soldiers would become so hungry they'd start hallucinating about food. Army manuals called

Ranger school the ultimate in leadership training and physical stress. Swanson felt like a physical wreck afterward. Never again, he vowed.

But now Ken Swanson was on the verge of completing the most unusual training the Army had to offer. In two weeks—if he didn't screw up—Swanson would be able to add another patch to his uniform. This one would say "Special Forces." And on his head he would wear the Green Beret—that is, if he got through these next two weeks.

Over the deafening whine of the chopper's engines a helicopter crew member shouted into Swanson's ear, offering a headset to monitor the radio traffic of the pilots.

Swanson waved it off. The chopper would be landing soon enough, he thought.

That was his first mistake. If Swanson had listened to the radio chatter, he would have heard the pilots tick off their checkpoints along the way to the aircraft's final destination. He could have confirmed for himself that the pilot had landed at the right spot. Helicopters get lost when their high-tech direction-finding equipment malfunctions. The first rule of clandestine operations: never trust anyone or any machine to do what you've been told they'll do.

Swanson was forgiven this mistake. The MH-47 was not lost. A chopper crew member in the rear of the plane held up a finger. Each team member did the same down the line. One minute to touchdown.

The helicopter landed with a bump. The rear ramp door flopped down. The team members struggled to shoulder their rucksacks in the cramped quarters, shouting "Go, go!" as they piled out.

The helicopter had landed on a farmer's dirt airstrip, about three miles southwest of the village of Coleridge in Randolph County, North Carolina. As the team clambered out the rear ramp, they took up positions in a half-moon perimeter. The chopper stayed on the ground less than a minute, then lifted off.

The team crouched in the tall grass and waited several

minutes more to let their ears adjust to the silence of the
night. No one spoke. Only hand signals were exchanged.

A farmer wearing a tan jacket and baseball cap leaned
against a white two-and-a-half-ton truck with a tan canvas
top, which was parked at the other side of the runway. The
farmer waved them over.

Swanson and half his team quickly crept up to the
vehicle and circled it with a security perimeter.

The other half of the team raced up. Never taking his
eye off the open field behind the truck, Swanson motioned
his team to pile in the back. They were sitting ducks if
counterinsurgents attacked.

"Hurry," he whispered a bit out of breath, as he
climbed up himself after the last man had boarded.

The truck sped south on a dark two-lane road. Swanson and several team members hunched over tactical maps
with pen lights, desperately trying to keep up with the
twists and turns the driver made, the bridges he crossed,
the miles he had driven, so they would have some inkling
where they would be when the truck stopped.

Swanson craned his neck out the back of the truck
looking for landmarks in the darkness that he could match
on his map. He had wiped clean the acetate-covered map
the night before so that if it ever ended up in enemy hands
it would reveal none of the coordinates for his dropoff and
linkup points with the guerrillas. Those he had committed
to memory.

The driver was supposed to take Swanson's team as
far as he could to Pleasant Hill Church, where they were to
meet a guerrilla contact. But Swanson's intelligence file
had warned that these drivers, part of the guerrilla auxiliary, were not particularly reliable. The first rule of clandestine infiltration: don't begin a nighttime walk in the
woods to meet a distant contact unless you knew exactly
where you were starting from. You would only end up
hopelessly lost. If the driver decided to dump the team
along the road somewhere short of the church, Swanson
knew he had better have pinpointed where the truck
stopped on his map or he would never be able to match the

map's legends and contour lines with whatever terrain features he could make out around him at night.

Ken Swanson was not about to get lost at the start of this mission. He was a conscientious officer. Twenty-seven years old and strikingly handsome, he had bright blue eyes, wavy brown hair brushed back, a deep voice, and a gentle manner. An avid outdoorsman, he was a marathoner when Army field exercises didn't disrupt his training schedule. Ever since he was a child in Moline, Illinois, Swanson could remember wanting to camp out in the wilderness. He packed off to the University of Idaho in 1983 to major in wildlife recreation management. He wore flannel shirts and blue jeans and became a committed environmentalist.

But Swanson did not mix well with the other environmental activists on campus. They were too liberal politically. He may have been an environmentalist, but he was also deeply conservative. It was a conservatism nurtured among the small towns and farms of the Midwest, where people rose with the rooster crow and worked until dark and had little time for big government or taxes or welfare programs.

The Army seemed a natural place for Swanson. He won an ROTC scholarship after his freshman year and applied for the infantry after he graduated in 1986. It was a branch the recruiters were only too happy to give him. The infantry meant he would be outside, not in some stuffy office.

As Swanson expected, the truck stopped about two miles short of his linkup point with the guerrillas. If he had calculated it correctly, he was just north of Benchmark 121.9 on his map, on a road two miles east of Antioch Church. The driver walked to the back, unhooked the latch and dropped the cargo door. It clanged noisily.

"This is as far as I'm takin' y'all," the driver said firmly with a Southern twang. "They've had roadblocks all up and down this road and I ain't gettin' stopped by one."

Swanson's team piled out of the back of the truck. The driver stared at the captain for a minute, grumbled, then climbed into his truck cab and sped off. Swanson had forgotten to pay him for the ride. The driver might be even less reliable the next time.

Swanson had made his second mistake. There would be many more during the next two weeks of Robin Sage.

From the minute he joined the Army, Swanson had had his eye on Special Forces. There was a romantic quality to the Green Berets, or so he thought. They served in faraway lands on their own with no chain of command breathing down their necks. There was a laid-back sense of confidence in Special Forces. Swanson liked that. Ranger combat battalions were so regimented, he had found, so tightly wound like a coiled spring, you could quickly burn out. In Special Forces, everyone had a specialized skill. An officer didn't have to micromanage sergeants and sergeants weren't afraid to tell officers a better way to run a mission.

They were a cocky group. Green Berets hated to admit that anything was new to them. If a Green Beret was heard beginning a sentence with "The first time I . . ." he could end up owing his team a case of beer. The joke in student training: Green Berets lived by three rules. One, always look cool. Two, always know where you are. And three, if you can't remember where you are, at least try to look cool.

With luck, Swanson would study German or Russian and serve in Europe with the 10th Special Forces Group. The Green Berets were divided into five groups, which specialized in different parts of the world. The desert commandos of the 5th Group were responsible for the Middle East and Southwest Asia. The 3rd Group's territory was Africa and the Caribbean. Seventh Group's was Latin America, a popular assignment in Swanson's detachment. Everybody wanted to fight drug traffickers.

That didn't interest Swanson. During the Cold War the 10th Group's mission had been to be ready to infiltrate behind enemy lines in Eastern Europe with exotic weapons to disrupt a potential Warsaw Pact invasion. Now Green Berets were preparing for military training missions in the new democracies of Eastern Europe. Who knew, he might be in the old Soviet Union one day training Russian soldiers, Swanson thought.

His fellow Ranger officers considered him a traitor for wanting to join Special Forces. Green Berets were nothing but a bunch of fast-talking unconventionals, as far as they were concerned. Though the Green Berets have been mythologized in ballads and adventure movies, their history has often been sad and disappointing.

Born out of the World War II Office of Strategic Services (OSS)—which had parachuted "Jedburgh teams" into occupied France to link up with partisans—the Green Berets were organized by the Army in 1952 to harass Russians behind their lines if World War III broke out. The fighters were divided into eight-man units called Operational Detachments-Alpha, or A-teams. Each team, commanded by a captain, had experienced sergeants specializing in communications, demolitions, weapons, intelligence, or medicine. (Today's A-teams have been expanded to twelve.) Cross-trained in each other's skills, team members became experts in clandestine warfare: raids, reconnaissance, ambushes, sabotage, underground resistance networks. But the Pentagon questioned whether the force would be of much use in the instant wars of the new atomic age. Europe would be in rubble before A-teams could organize guerrillas. The Green Berets languished in search of a mission.

John Kennedy found it. Obsessed with communist insurgencies, the new president had a romantic view of unconventional warfare and quickly became infatuated with the jaunty Green Berets. Counterinsurgency became the trendy military doctrine in the Pentagon. Special Forces grew fourfold. Hundreds of A-teams were dispatched throughout the Third World to train foreign militaries battling communists. In Vietnam, however, the Green Berets and their counterinsurgency tactics were largely ignored by an Army bent on free-fire zones and body counts. Yet even if the Green Berets had been allowed to fight their kind of war, they would not have won. No Western counterinsurgency strategy would have succeeded.

After the war, the Green Beret ranks were decimated. It was just as well. During the expansion of Special Forces for Vietnam, standards had been lowered to attract recruits. The force was full of screwballs, alcoholics, and cowboys with their Montagnard tribal bracelets from Vietnam and sapphire rings from Bangkok. Ronald Reagan, who shared Kennedy's obsession with guerrilla insurgencies, rebuilt the force in the 1980s. Green Berets became the military ambassadors of the Reagan Doctrine to roll back communism in the Third World. Mobile training teams fanned out to more than thirty countries, instructing militaries in counterguerrilla tactics, building bridges and clinics, paving roads, and preaching human rights. Progress was made in some countries. But for unsavory regimes, the military training simply increased their proficiency in killing political opponents. El Salvador became the new testing ground for the Green Berets' counterinsurgency strategy. But it ended up being an impossible assignment. America could no more build a democratic nation in El Salvador than in Vietnam.

The quality of the Green Beret force nevertheless improved during the Reagan years, as did the training. The Vietnam generation of lone wolves and killers faded from the force. Before beginning formal instruction, which for some A-team specialties lasts a year or more, Green Beret applicants now must pass a grueling three-week selection course at Fort Bragg, North Carolina, the headquarters for Special Forces. Half drop out. Students march day and night with forty-five-pound packs to test physical endurance. They spend five days in a sleep-deprivation course to stress mental stamina. In one exercise to test how well they improvise, students are presented a jeep with its wheels off and an engine that won't start and told to move it from one point to another. If there is a flaw in a student's personality the testers believe it will surface from the mental and physical grind.

The vetting is important. A Green Beret must be both a maverick and a team player—two contradictory traits for a soldier. A good sergeant in the regular Army follows orders with layers of officers watching over him. A Green Beret sergeant can find himself plunked in a foreign country thousands of miles away from home advising foreign soldiers on his own. He must operate on his initiative, by his wits—yet not embarrass his own government.

After enduring the grind of selection, students begin the Special Forces Qualification Course, or "Q Course." First they spend three months to a year in classrooms studying an expertise such as demolitions, weapons, or communications. Then they are packed off to a Spartan camp fifty miles west of Fort Bragg, the Nicholas Rowe Special Forces Training Center. It was named after Colonel Nick Rowe, a Green Beret who escaped from a Vietcong prison camp after five years of captivity only to be gunned down twenty-five years later by communist terrorists in the Philippines.

For about two months at "Rowe U," students learn unconventional warfare tactics, many of which were borrowed from the CIA. During this field phase of the training, teams of seasoned Special Forces officers and noncommissioned officers (NCOs) teach courses in small-unit assaults, marksmanship, survival skills, escape and evasion. The final thirteen days are spent in Robin Sage, the code name for one of the most unusual exercises the U.S. Army has ever devised. Robin Sage covers the guerrilla warfare scenarios a team might face in the field during one year. By learning how to conduct insurgent operations, the students also learn how to combat them as counterinsurgents. Robin Sage takes students back to the original guerrilla warfare of World War II. Only this time they are jumping not into the countryside of France with the Jedburgh teams, but into the hamlets and farms of North Carolina's southern Piedmont.

Guerrilla and counterinsurgency tactics cannot be learned on an Army post with its fenced-off firing ranges and whitewashed barracks lined neatly in rows. The tactics must be learned where such a war would be fought, among people and villages, dogs and cats, churches and schoolhouses.

To an outsider driving on North Carolina's back roads, the villages of Troy and Biscoe and Siler City along the way seem no different from other Southern towns. But for the past thirty years, these towns and the farms that surround them have been the training ground for the unconventional warfare of the Green Berets.

Practically everyone gets in on the act. The townsfolk and farmers not only allow the Green Berets to use their pastures and forests, they also join in the exercises. Some villagers play the part of guerrillas driving Green Beret students around the countryside in their trucks for their clandestine missions. Others act as area commanders for fictional resistance forces the Green Beret students must train. On weekends, local police armed with paint guns square off with students in mock battles. Others lend land for drop zones that the Green Berets use to resupply student teams in the field.*

The civilians who play guerrillas take their parts seriously. In some families, the roles have been passed from one generation to the next. Patriotism runs deep in these towns of the Piedmont plateau with their quiet wide streets, general stores, and 4-H Clubs. Folks hang their flags out on holidays, attend church every Sunday, and host pig pickin's afterward to devour mounds of barbecue and hush puppies. On weekends, farm families in pickups watch student teams assault bridges.

The civilians and the soldiers look out for one another. Farmers offer up chickens, goats, and deer that the students learn to skin and cook for survival training. In return, Green Beret trainers have their students repair barns or chop firewood as part of their civic action training. The local townsfolk warn of rednecks looking for trouble— the Green Berets call them "Billy Bobs"—or strangers nosing around asking too many questions. When they spot a student lost or trying to sneak into one of the gas stations

---

*Sometimes the help is unsolicited. Occasionally a biker or Klansman or weekend wannabe in fatigues walks into a base camp wanting to join the exercise. The Green Berets politely shoo them off.

to buy a soda, the townsfolk will telephone the trainers. Students quickly learn that they can't get away with anything.

8:45 P.M., THURSDAY, FEBRUARY 20

Dan Moran was not happy. A sergeant first class, he was the trainer for Swanson's team, which was officially designated Operational Detachment-Alpha 941. Each team was assigned a seasoned Green Beret adviser who monitored their every move during Robin Sage. In this case, the exercise was barely an hour old and Swanson's team already was fouling it up. First Swanson didn't wear the headset in the chopper. Then he forgot to pay the guerrilla driver. (The Green Beret training cadre had printed up play money for the exercise. It was called "don," and Swanson's team had 20,000 don to grease palms and pay the guerrilla force it would train.) Now the team had climbed out of the truck, and, as far as Moran could see, was just milling around the open road with no perimeter security and no idea which side of the road it would cross to march into the woods.

The team half suspected that the driver wouldn't take it to the church. But the students never thought the guerrilla driver would stop the truck right in the middle of the road and order them off. (Moran had instructed the driver to do just that, to see how the students would react.) Swanson never bothered to even ask the driver where he had stopped. It would have been a good cross-check for where he thought he was on the map.

The unexpected always happened on these kinds of missions, Moran knew. Before the students ever left their staging area, they should have planned for this type of glitch. The team should have rehearsed exactly how it would climb out of the truck, how it would set up security while exposed on an open road, which side of the road it would race down. Contingencies, contingencies, contingencies. Moran had been drilling that into their heads since the beginning of the Q course. But the students were only paying it lip service when they put their plans on paper.

Ground rehearsals were critical for any small-unit operation, but even more so for special operations. Because their missions were so difficult to execute, special ops units normally had days, even weeks, to plan and rehearse. It was not enough just to point on a map where everyone should be positioned in a critical maneuver. You had to go out in an open field, have everyone physically walk through where they would be positioned so it would sink in and the team would react automatically during the mission. ODA-941 obviously hadn't done that, Moran realized. It was a sloppy start.

"Well don't just stand there like a gaggle of geese," he growled. "Do something!"

The team scampered down the twenty-foot embankment off the right side of the road. Moran would have gone to the left side. He unfolded his map to check the course the students were plotting. They may be lost, he thought. Christ, I don't want to wander through these goddamn woods until they find their way.

An Irishman from the suburbs of Chicago, Moran was a fifteen-year veteran of the Army. His Chicago roots and his last name had quickly earned him the nickname "Bugsy" in the service, after the famous gangster.

This was Moran's first student team as a trainer for the Special Warfare Center, or "swick" as the cadre called it from the acronym. He had just been transferred to Fort Bragg after serving seven years as an A-team communications and assistant operations sergeant with the 5th Special Forces Group at Fort Campbell, Kentucky. Moran had spent four months in the Persian Gulf advising Saudi and United Arab Emirate soldiers who breached the Iraqi defenses along the Kuwaiti border.

Living with Arab soldiers had been a hoot, Moran found. "Boogsie, Boogsie!" they would yell at him and laugh. "Boogsie, the Chicago gangster." Four months of eating rice and roasted goat with your right hand.

Duty in the small towns of eastern North Carolina was almost like being stationed overseas. Moran found himself having to practice the same diplomacy he employed with foreigners. The weekend before, he had hopped in his truck and driven from farm to farm along the paths his student detachment would take, to socialize and warn the locals that there might be a ruckus at night. More than 200 students in thirteen detachments would be roaming the forests and pastures during the two weeks of Robin Sage.

As student teams go, Moran thought his was a good one. Most were seasoned Rangers, already skilled in small-unit tactics when they showed up for the Q course. After years of drills and regulations and barracks bullshit, they had a healthy disrespect for the Mickey Mouse aspects of the Army.

But they were a bit too smug to suit Moran. He'd heard them talking about how the selection course was really the toughest part of Green Beret training, how the fifty days of the field phase training hadn't been that bad so far. Now they were just thirteen days away from putting on a Green Beret and they thought that all they had to do was coast through Robin Sage. Bugsy Moran would make sure that what his students remembered most from the Q course were these next thirteen days.

Swanson wasn't lost. He had managed to keep his course plotted during the twisting and turning truck ride. He knew he was about two miles short of Pleasant Hill Church, the primary linkup point with the guerrillas. Traveling off the right side of the road seemed the more logical route to him. But he had to get away from this damn road and fast. The team plunged into the forest.

Swanson was confident. He felt as if he had rehearsed every minuscule detail. If there was anything he had learned about the Green Berets the past year, it was that they were maniacs when it came to preparing for an operation. His team had spent the past five days in isolation planning for this training mission.

Every A-team went into isolation to prepare for an operation. Contact with outsiders was forbidden to ensure that no details of usually secret operations leaked. It also ensured total concentration to the task. Isolation could last as long as a month depending on the complexity of the mission. Swanson's team had been quarantined in a tin hut ringed by a barbed wire fence. At the mess hall they sat as a group by themselves. They traded colds or stomach viruses from being in such close quarters. They felt like dogs in a pound.

But every waking moment of isolation had to be spent planning the operation. Just the "Detachment Mission Planning Guide," the bare outline every Green Beret used to organize a mission, was nineteen pages long. A team had to consider 381 separate requirements and contingencies: infiltration plans, micro-terrain analysis, meteorological surveys, rules of engagement, demographics, local politics, terrorism threats, drop zones, passwords, weapons loads, training plans for guerrillas, the list ran on in eye-watering detail.

When the team first walked into its isolation compound, the trainers had dumped into Swanson's arms a three-inch-thick binder marked "Mission Analysis." It was crammed with intelligence on the battlefield, memos from his higher headquarters, plus a sixty-eight-page "Pineland Area Study."

The area study, a standard Green Beret briefing document, gives an A-team as complete a picture as it can of the foreign country it will enter. In this case, Swanson's team faced a classic guerrilla warfare scenario. Pineland was a fictitious country, what was once North and South Carolina. It had seceded from Opforland in 1915 ("opfor" in Army jargon is the abbreviation for opposition forces). Opforland consisted of the states east of the Appalachian Mountains, which had themselves seceded from the United States in 1880.

In November 1978, Opforland reinvaded Pineland, installing a puppet regime. Pineland's legal president fled to Columbia, South Carolina, where he set up a provisional government. Meanwhile, Opforland installed a repressive regime in the occupied northern territory. In the Robin Sage exercise, Opforland's conventional forces that ruled Pineland were played by 82nd Airborne paratroopers from

Fort Bragg, who lusted after the chance to spend two weeks away from the nearby post pestering Green Berets, even if they were students.

Small guerrilla bands, made up of former soldiers who hid from the Opforland invaders, roamed occupied Pineland. But untrained and poorly armed, their resistance was fragmented. The exiled government of Pineland had asked for Washington's help in training and organizing the guerrillas—although neither the exiled government nor Washington knew just how receptive the resistance fighters would be to American advisers.

Swanson's mission was to infiltrate his detachment into Pineland, link up with one of the guerrilla bands, and try to whip it into shape. Army intelligence had supplied him with a biography of the guerrilla chief he would soon meet. A CIA asset had sneaked out of Pineland and briefed him on the guerrilla band's battle record so far. It was clear Swanson had his work cut out for him.

For five days and nights, Swanson and his team wrote on notebook paper their plans for slipping into Pineland, linking up with the guerrillas, and molding them as a fighting force. Never before had the men considered so many details. In a conventional unit, a headquarters staff attended to most of them. But a tiny Green Beret team had to think like a self-contained division and plan for the entire campaign. In the field, it would be cut off from its higher headquarters perhaps for months. There would be no medical evacuation helicopters, no artillery, no tanks to come to the rescue if things went wrong. A Green Beret's combat support force had to be carried on his back.

9:30 P.M., THURSDAY, FEBRUARY 20

John Klapperich flipped open the lid to his pocket compass and cupped his hand around the instrument to see the glow of the bobbing needle, which pointed north. It took years of experience for a soldier to become expert in navigating through a dark forest at night with only a compass and a map. The skill had to be learned: matching the brown contour lines of a tactical map to the peaks and valleys the eyes tried to make out in the dark.

Night navigation could be tricky. Distances appeared shorter than they really were. Zigzagging around obstacles could throw off a compass reading. In a dense forest, disorientation could come quickly if a soldier missed a benchmark, a tree line, a bend in a creek bed.

A soldier also had to know when not to trust the map. Defense Department maps of foreign countries could be notoriously inaccurate. Army Rangers, who were among the best in the world when it came to long-range land navigation, could feel it in their bones when a map was fooling them.

Klapperich was a Ranger. After five years of leading infantry squads he wasn't about to get this team lost. He had been a fast riser in the Army, making staff sergeant in just four years. With blond hair and a mustache, he acted older than his twenty-two years. He was usually one of the first in the team to see a solution to a problem that others didn't. He wasn't afraid to tell others on the team how to solve it. Anyone else this young would be resented by older teammates. But Klapperich had an air of quiet authority to him that compelled others to listen.

But he detested the idea of being an officer. He didn't even like being around officers. With few exceptions, they were nothing but politicians, self-centered ticket punchers, he thought. Klapperich once had an appointment to the U.S. Naval Academy, but lost it when he fell in with the wrong group of kids and got into trouble in high school. He joined the Army at seventeen, his parents signing a consent form allowing him to enlist early. He grew up quickly.

Behind Klapperich no more than ten yards away, Drue Loiselle counted his paces. A twenty-two-year-old Army Ranger, Loiselle had seen combat in Panama. He considered himself lucky just to see the combat. He had parachuted with the Rangers into Río Hato Airport, jumping just 400 feet with a 100-pound rucksack onto the concrete airport tarmac. Loiselle survived the jump only to have his uniform torn to shreds as his parachute, caught by a burst of wind, dragged him along the runway as if it had been hooked to a speeding car.

Loiselle would be happy now if he could just make it through these woods. To navigate on foreign land with a map, a unit always had to know two important things: its direction of travel and how far it had walked. Otherwise it could never match the surrounding landmarks with the symbols on its map. Klapperich walked point with the compass to navigate direction. Loiselle was the pace man. Every infantryman had his own stride, his own number of paces for every 100 meters, which he had precounted hundreds of times in different terrain. Loiselle counted every time his left foot hit the ground. In an open field, his pace was 60 left-foot strikes per 100 meters. In thick brush it was 68 to 70, or even higher if he was climbing a steep ridge.

Loiselle would call out his pace every 100 meters. Klapperich would stop, check his compass heading, then shoot an azimuth to a point ahead to which the team should travel. At intervals, he would stop to compare the pace and compass reading with where he thought he was on the map. The other team members also were counting paces and checking their compasses. Every A-team member had to navigate and know where he was at all times. If the team was attacked and took losses, any team member could end up being left on his own or in command. It was a tedious process, but necessary if the team was not going to become lost and have to backtrack to get back on course— which every compass and pace duo dreaded making its detachment do.

Loiselle's pace by now was a full 70 per 100 meters. The team didn't dare take any open trails or walk across bare fields this close to its dropoff point. That meant plowing through the forests, which in Randolph County could be near impenetrable. The woods were hilly and rolling with sharp drop-offs and swift streams that sneaked up on a walker at night. An ankle could be broken in the countless potholes left from rotted pines. Walking through the scrub oak was like climbing through jungle bars in a playground. Low limbs poked eyes and whacked chests. The team wore thick gloves to keep the briars from shredding their hands. Vines wrapped around them like octopuses. Canteens and entrenching tools sticking out from their rucksacks became snarled, throwing the heavy loads on their backs off balance and tipping them over. Soldiers called them "wait-a-minute vines." They had to whisper "wait a minute" until they had untangled themselves.

Being the lead man, Klapperich was the first to face the wall of vines and briars. At some points it seemed to him that the only way the team would get through would be for him to simply flop down on the vines and have them walk over his back. The team's plan had been to fight its way through the forest some 300 yards west of the road, to be sure that it wouldn't be heard or accidentally bump into anyone wandering around at night. But now it faced another barrier it would never confront in the training areas of military reservations: barbed wire fences.

Klapperich met his first one just fifty yards off the road. He reached up to push the top wire down to climb over. Sparks flew. It felt like someone had taken a thick board and slapped the palm of his hand. The pain shot up to his elbow and knocked him off balance.

"Shit!" he said under his breath. The fence was electrified.

The bad news was passed back to Swanson. The captain quickly draped a poncho over his head, flipped on his pen light underneath, and scanned his map. It showed no houses along the road south for the next 800 yards. Swanson ordered the team to follow the fence line. Maybe there would be a break in the fence further south where they could cross.

If it had caught his eye, a notation in small print on the left-hand corner of his map might have alerted Swanson that this decision would be another mistake: "map information as of 1983."

Less than forty meters along the fence line, it happened. Dogs began barking. Not just a few. It seemed to the team like a thousand of them were yapping and howling. It was as if they had walked into a kennel. Every mutt in Randolph County must be awake and along that road, they thought. Swanson ordered the pace picked up, which was almost impossible to do because the vines and scrub oak and briars were still thick.

"What a fucking mess," Moran muttered to himself. They couldn't have attracted more attention if they had been a brass band marching down Main Street.

Moran had a more practical concern. If the dogs didn't stop barking the lights in the homes they belonged to would soon start blinking on. During the last field exercise, a team walking past a barking dog near a trailer had awakened its owner who stormed out in his undershorts with a shotgun. The training sergeant had to quickly intervene to assure the owner that the intruders were Green Berets.

Moran let the team hack its way through another 100 yards, then called a halt.

"Gather around here, I want to talk to you," he said, irritated. "You're supposed to be infiltrating. But you've got every fucking dog around here barking. You look like you're out trick-or-treating going from house to house waking up everybody.

"Sure the houses weren't on the map," he continued. "But this map is old. You should have realized that new houses would have been built since it was printed. You have to assume that wherever there's a paved road, there may be houses with barking dogs that can end up compromising your mission.

"An electrified fence shouldn't have stopped you. You could have taken off your packs, dug a trench under the bottom wire, crawled underneath it, then lifted the packs over the fence. Now if you don't want the whole world to know that you've arrived, you better move west and away from all these goddamn homes!"

12:30 A.M., FRIDAY, FEBRUARY 21
Swanson and a two-man reconnaissance party squatted in the tall brush at the base of a hill, on which Pleasant Hill Church sat. A lone street lamp illuminated the church

parking lot and the cemetery to its rear. Swanson, who had left the rest of his team on the other side of the road 500 yards north, could see anyone walking into the graveyard. But no one had come. The linkup with the guerrilla contact was supposed to have occurred at midnight. Swanson's orders were to wait until 12:30 A.M. If the contact hadn't shown by then, it meant something had gone wrong and he was to meet the guerrillas at the alternate linkup point.

Moran was the reason something had gone wrong. He had ordered the guerrilla contact not to meet Swanson at the primary linkup site. This would be one of a number of glitches Moran would introduce into the exercise.

Swanson wasn't surprised. It was probably too much to expect that the students would be allowed to meet the guerrillas on the first try and get a decent night's sleep before they began training them. But he still groaned. The team had fought its way through three miles of lousy terrain. The alternate linkup site, Riverside Church, was about four miles south by road. But they would have to travel west first to avoid the houses, then wind their way through the forest, which would make the total trip about seven miles. The time for the alternate linkup was 7 A.M. Friday. Swanson would need the next seven hours to get there. That meant no sleep tonight.

The team already was beginning to feel the wear and tear of the first three miles. North Carolina weather was fickle in February. One day could be springlike, the next day snow would be on the ground. The afternoon before, the temperature was in the high 60s, now it was in the 30s and dropping quickly. Weapons quickly became too cold to carry with bare hands. The team had to pack more "snivel gear" as they called it, cold weather parkas and liners, which added weight to loads.

Weight was a Green Beret's nemesis. With few resupply drops on missions, he must live off what he carried. Each man on Swanson's team had to pack: a spare set of boots and clothes plus extra socks because the first set would inevitably become wet; enough rations to survive for a week; two quarts of water; the Army's cold-weather sleeping bag, which weighed twice as much as civilian bags; ponchos to serve as "hooches" (military slang for the place where soldiers slept); and an assortment of insulated liners and pads. On top of that was the team equipment: demolition charges, batteries, radios, medical supplies, generators, ammunition, entrenching tools, thick ropes for bridges, two heavy machine guns. Equally distributed, each man's load weighed eighty to 100 pounds.

Packing and carrying a rucksack was a science a soldier learned after miles of painful marching. The indigestible Meals Ready-to-Eat, which the Army had spent years researching to replace the bulkier C rations of Vietnam, still contained too much excess weight and space. The MREs came in thick brown plastic bags, which the team members ripped open to redistribute their contents. Excess items and cardboard containers were thrown away and plastic-wrapped meals were repackaged. In doing so, a dozen meals could be crammed into four MRE bags and the weight reduced by one third.

Equipment like radios could be centered in the bag so the weight fell more squarely on the back. Styrofoam padding taped to the shoulder straps could make the load more bearable. Special Forces and Rangers had long discarded the infantryman's clunky leather boots. Green Berets could be found wearing lightweight black Adidas, which looked like high-top basketball shoes and were less punishing on the ankles and soles. On long marches in cold weather, soldiers dressed lightly, wearing only camouflaged fatigues and thin polypropylene liners that breathed. If they dressed too warmly, they overheated, then became chilled when they stopped. If it rained, they slipped on lightweight Gortex jackets.

But for all the careful packing, the marches were physically punishing. Green Berets, Rangers, and Navy SEALs usually retired with back and leg problems, like professional football players, because of the years of carrying heavy loads.

The U.S. Army has been marching for more than 200 years and it still has not developed a backpack that makes sense. The current Army version the Green Beret students use is called the Alice Pack, which is little more than a large green nylon bag with side pockets and flaps. It attaches to a lightweight aluminum back brace with a kidney pad at the bottom to rest against the hips.

The physics of the Alice Pack work against the body. Civilian backpacks distribute the load up and down the back, with the pack sometimes several feet above the camper's head. Green Berets don't like those kind of packs because the tops become hung up in low branches. The load of the Alice Pack, or rucksack, is distributed away from the back—as much as three feet away. That causes the pack straps to tug more at the shoulders and the kidney pad to push harder into the hips. The pressure from the straps can rub shoulders raw and cut circulation to the arms. Soldiers call it "The Big Green Wart."

The wart was already beginning to hurt as the team fought its way now through the woods. The knees were the first to become sore from the load. Emerging from patches of forest, the team came across freshly plowed fields, the furrows more than two-feet high. The pace was increased to make up for lost time. But the soft red clay was punishing on ankles turned and twisted from the furrows.

At short stops, the students would bend over as if in a formal bow to rest the weight of the rucksacks directly on their backs instead of their sore shoulders. Straps were shifted and tightened and loosened, anything to move the weight of the rucksack from one part of a shoulder bone to another. The hips began to ache from the pressure of the kidney pad. At longer stops, which came after every grueling mile, the students not on perimeter guard would simply fall back and roll to one side to relieve the load. It was called the "rucksack roll." But now the stops were not rejuvenating—only temporary relief from the pain of the ruck.

At a rest stop halfway to Riverside Church, George Seemann, one of the team medics, moved from man to man asking if any had foot problems. To some, he gave 800-milligram tablets of Motrin to kill the pain. They looked like red horse pills. They were nicknamed "Ranger candy" because Rangers popped them regularly on long marches.

A thirty-year-old Floridian, Seemann joined the Army intent on becoming a Green Beret. But he was waylaid in the Rangers for a little over four years. A hulk of a man with tattoos on both arms—he weighed 220 pounds and was six feet four inches tall—Seemann loved to joke and carry on with the other team members. But he was a conscientious medic, busy all the time, it seemed, during the exercise. It was in the Rangers where Seemann learned that a medic had to be always interrogating the men in his squad on their condition, or they would end up out of action without warning. A Ranger considered it unmanly to volunteer that he had a medical problem. Too much time in a dispensary was frowned on by superiors. So Rangers tried to hide their aches and pains.

Seemann was doing the same himself. Green Beret medic training had taken him two years. During a small-unit tactics exercise in the Q course, Seemann had broken his right ankle. He had to be recycled back four months in the Q course while it remained in a cast. When the cast was removed, the doctors told him he needed an operation to reattach the torn ligaments. But that would mean being recycled again.

No way. Seemann postponed the operation until after Robin Sage and continued the course with his ankle wrapped in a tight brace. Now the pain in the ankle was excruciating from stumbling through the plowed fields. On top of that, he still had a stomach virus from the week of isolation. He had already vomited twice on the march. He drank water so he wouldn't dehydrate, swallowed another Motrin, but kept his condition secret. He was too close to the end to stop now.*

_____

*Seemann was worried about my being on the march. Though my rucksack did not weigh the eighty to 100 pounds each of the other men carried, it did tip the scales at about sixty. To cover the Robin Sage exercise, I had to carry in most of what I would live off of the next two weeks. Seemann did not know what kind of shape I was in, so he quietly passed the word to the other students to keep a close eye on

Finally at 4:30 A.M., the team halted, exhausted and sweaty from the march, their eyes burning from lack of sleep. Riverside Church, the alternate linkup point, was 500 yards to the southeast.

Swanson moved out again with a two-man recon party to check out the church graveyard, where he would meet his guerrilla contact. The route to the church was fairly clear and took less time to reach than he had expected. They were ahead of schedule. Swanson ordered sentries posted and let the rest of the men sleep for an hour and a half until they had to move out for the linkup.

Too hot from the grueling march, most of the men decided not to unpack their sleeping bags. They simply wrapped themselves in poncho liners and fell instantly asleep.

But the cold would rouse them before the hour and a half was up. The temperature had dropped to 20 degrees. The men woke up shivering. Even worse, their overheated muscles had stiffened from the frigid temperature. They had calf and thigh cramps. It took some as long as five minutes just to prop themselves first on their knees, then stand. The rucksacks would have to come later.

6:30 A.M., FRIDAY, FEBRUARY 21

Moran had walked ahead, to the rear of Riverside Church. The team had done well since he gave them the initial chewing out. Their infiltration techniques were sound. Now Moran wanted to watch how Swanson would link up with his guerrilla contact.

The linkup wasn't simply a matter of two people walking up to each other and shaking hands. Certain rules of tradecraft had to be followed or Swanson could end up getting his team or himself shot. The young captain crawled up to the wood line bordering the church cemetery

_____
me. I jog regularly and consider myself in reasonably good condition. But I discovered that night that forty-two-year-old reporters should think twice before they pretend to be young Green Berets. I made it through the infiltration, but could barely move the next day.

to watch for the next half hour, making sure no enemy forces were lurking to spring a trap. The rest of the team remained several hundred yards to the rear. By prearrangement, the contact was to walk up to a gravestone that bore a name each side knew in advance.

Moran waited to see if Swanson sneaked into the graveyard to first find the right headstone where he would meet the guerrilla later. That was important. Anyone could walk into the graveyard to pay their respects at any headstone. Swanson didn't want to make contact with the wrong person.

Swanson knew what to do. He checked the headstones until he found the right one. Then he retreated to the wood line.

At 7 A.M., Keith Phillips, the guerrilla band's sergeant major, emerged from a stand of pine trees on the other side of the road wearing jungle fatigues with no insignias on them. Trailing him was a large mongrel dog, half Labrador retriever half German shepherd, named Hank.

Phillips was a sergeant first class in the 7th Special Forces Group, on temporary assignment for the Robin Sage exercise. Although he played the part of the guerrilla band's sergeant major, its top enlisted man, he would not tell Swanson that until later. For now he was simply a contact. The dog was an unwelcome intruder. Loyal only to his next meal, Hank during the last exercise had led a team of 82nd Airborne counterinsurgents to a guerrilla base camp.

With Hank loping along behind him, Phillips walked up to the designated grave. He peeled off a glove and laid it on the headstone, the signal that it was safe for Swanson to come out.

Crouched with his M-16 rifle at the ready, Swanson walked cautiously up to the headstone and knelt by its side.

"It's too late to pray for him," Swanson whispered the password.

"It's never too late, my son," Phillips answered with the correct response.

Hank walked up and gave Swanson his paw.

The guerrilla base camp was another two miles from

the church. Phillips would take them a way that would make the trip at least three miles. He wanted to confuse the student team on the true location of its base camp—Moran would check the team to see if it became disoriented or kept up with its position on the map—and to wear them down even more before they met the guerrilla chief.

For the next three hours, with the exhausted team trailing him, Phillips zigzagged north and south as he moved west to the base camp. Four times the team had to cross the same creek. They would slide down its five-foot bank on one side, then claw at roots and branches on the other side to climb back up. Like zombies, the students of ODA-941 took one step at a time, turning their minds off to the pain in their legs and backs and shoulders.

The zigzagging stopped when Phillips reached Fork Creek, the base camp's main source of water. Fork Creek was more like a small river, its swift current running over large boulders. If there had been one saving grace from the long march, it had been that the team had managed to remain dry. That would not last for long. Phillips veered south to cross Fork Creek at a point he was sure would leave each student soaked to the knee.

Swanson and one of his sergeants, Clay Ruppenthal, left the rest of the team at the creek bank and trudged—almost in a daze from fatigue—the final 200 yards up a steep hill to the guerrilla base camp. Their boots, filled with water, squished with each step.

10:30 A.M., FRIDAY, FEBRUARY 21

Mark Goode leaned against an oak tree that supported the guerrilla base camp's makeshift command post—bamboo poles and birch branches lashed together in a lean-to with ropes. A corrugated tin roof on top kept out the rain. In the center, a hole had been dug and ringed with large rocks for a fire pit. Goode had an M-16 propped against the tree. The skull of a cow, the command post's symbol of authority, was tied to the top of the oak.

The land Goode used for his base camp belonged to Sherman Hussey, whose cattle and grain farm bordered the forest. For the past five years, the Green Berets had been using Hussey's property, which was located about twenty-five miles south of the small town of Ramseur. A burly man with a gray beard, Hussey liked to wander into the base camp every now and then to sit around the fire pit and chat. He also supplied the students with chickens and goats for their survival training. In return, the students mowed the lawn for Sherm's frail aunt as part of their civil affairs training.

Goode was a thirty-four-year-old sergeant first class in the newly formed 3rd Special Forces Group, also headquartered at Fort Bragg. As an assistant operations sergeant, he had spent twelve years on A-teams serving in remote posts all over the world: Oman, Egypt, Bolivia, Guatemala, Honduras, El Salvador. An outgoing Southerner with jet black hair and mustache, Goode had fallen in love with El Salvador. He had married a Salvadoran woman—many Green Berets married women from the countries in which they serve—and one day planned to retire there on a farm along El Salvador's coast.

For the next two weeks Goode would be in costume: blue jeans, plaid shirt, Oak Trail hiking boots, desert parka, a fluorescent orange baseball cap with "Pineland" and a pine tree (the country's official crest) printed on the front. His men wore orange arm bands with the Pineland seal.

Goode's name in the exercise was Colonel Davis, chief of the guerrilla band Swanson had been sent to train. A dozen young enlisted men from Fort Bragg's 18th Airborne Corps were detailed to Goode to play the guerrillas under his command. Because they wanted guerrillas to be unskilled and unmotivated soldiers the students must train, the Green Beret trainers specifically asked for support troops unaccustomed to infantry life. That way the guerrillas were learning combat skills for the first time, much as an Afghan mujahedeen or Salvadoran campesino would. Female soldiers also were asked to play guerrillas. In his hip pocket Goode carried a thirty-eight-page script titled "Guerrilla Chief Field Training Techniques," which instructed him on how he should act toward Swanson.

Goode planned to play hard to get. He had spent years "on the receiving end," as he put it, working with lazy and suspicious Third World colonels who first had to be convinced that his A-team was qualified to teach them before they would let him in their inner perimeter. So what if they were Americans. That meant nothing in the jungle. In real life it could take a training team as long as a month to gain the confidence of their foreign students.

Moran had walked ahead to Goode's base camp to brief him on the problems the team experienced at the beginning of its infiltration. Colonel Davis would have a reception Swanson would never forget.

A young guerrilla, who had been briefed to treat the student team like the enemy the first day, ordered Swanson and Ruppenthal to halt about twenty yards from where Goode sat. The guerrilla, whose nom de guerre was Smokey, ran up to Goode, saluted, and announced in Spanish that the Americans had arrived.

Goode grunted.

Smokey waved to Swanson and Ruppenthal to come forward.

Swanson, standing at attention, saluted and recited a formal introduction of his detachment.

Goode looked indifferent and spat a wad of tobacco juice toward Swanson's boots.

"So what have you guys got for me," Goode finally said, looking at Swanson as if he were a used-car salesman.

Swanson began to recite the speech he had prepared on how his team was trained in guerrilla warfare, but Goode cut him off.

"You don't understand, Captain," Goode said with a snarl. "I don't care what you can do. What kind of supplies can you give me?"

"Well, we have ammunition and rations and medical supplies," Swanson said, a bit taken aback. He gave Goode a detailed inventory of the team's weapons and number of rounds of ammunition.

"Okay, let me get something straight with you,"

Goode interrupted, giving Swanson a mean look. "Whatever deals my president made with you are not my deals. You understand."

Swanson nodded.

"I make the deals for my guerrillas, not my president, not your president. Now what do you want to teach me?"

"Well, let me look around first," Swanson answered. "I have a group of specialists and if we can get them in here and let them ask some questions, we can tell you how we can help."

Goode laughed, then turned mean again. "I think we're pretty good at it already," he retorted. "Hell, we've been fighting this war for thirteen years. Any of your people been fighting for thirteen years?"

"No," Swanson had to admit.

"So a bunch of goddamn Americans who've never fought a guerrilla war are going to come into my camp and teach me how to fight!" Goode roared.

"At least let my team in to do an assessment of your needs and where we might help," Swanson said, ignoring the insult.

"Well, I don't know about that," Goode said, lifting his cap off to scratch his head. "Like I said, my boys need bullets and rations. You just came out of the woods. If I let you in, for all I know you might just turn around and shoot us!"

Swanson was so exhausted he could have fallen asleep while standing in front of the colonel. His muscles were sore and stiff. His head ached from being up all night. But he kept calm.

They were U.S. soldiers, he said. Goode had nothing to fear from his team. "All I can do is show you my credentials and show you my team," he added wearily.

"You don't need to show me nothing," Goode said impudently. "I'm in charge of this bailiwick. I'll decide whether I can trust you. And as far as the U.S. coming in here to help us. Well shit, it took you this long to give us any aid. You people go into a country and make all these promises. Then every time you bug out. You bugged out of

Nicaragua. You bugged out of Iran. So I don't want to be left high and dry when you decide to bug out of here!"

"Do you have any wounded personnel?" Swanson said, trying to change the subject.

"Wounded?" Goode laughed. The guerrillas around him smirked. "I can't afford to have any wounded. They slow us down too much."

Goode returned to his shopping list. "What have you got in the way of rations and weapons and ammo?" he asked.

Swanson gave him a rough estimate.

Goode sat silent for several minutes, then sent another missile of tobacco juice toward Swanson's feet.

"You let me have 750 rounds of ammunition, two dozen MREs, and your two M-60 machine guns and then we'll talk about your team being allowed in my perimeter," Goode finally said.

Swanson thought about it for a moment.

"The ammunition is no problem and the meals are no problem," he said. "But I can't give you the M-60s."

"And why not?" Goode said indignantly.

"I'm just not authorized."

Goode stood up and looked Swanson squarely in the eye. "What you're saying is you've come here all loaded for bear for yourself, but that doesn't protect me," he said, becoming angrier as he went along.

"We can help you protect yourself," Swanson said, trying to calm him down.

"Does that mean you'll follow my orders and fight for me?"

"Yes and no."

"Yes and no?" Goode asked, mocking Swanson's answer. "What the fuck does that mean?"

"I can't relinquish my command authority over my men." Swanson gave him the school answer.

"So what good are you to me?"

"We can enhance your security."

Goode laughed again, swatting his cap at his side. "Enhance my security! You guys were four kilometers from your linkup point and you woke up every goddamn dog and family in the area. Now you tell me, Captain. What kind of security can you give me?"

Moran had been quietly sitting on the other side of the base camp hooch. He smiled. Goode was following the script perfectly. He hadn't forgotten Moran's briefing about the infiltration problems. Swanson looked like a schoolboy trying to explain a bad report card to his dad.

Goode leaned back against the tree. "Okay, give me a plan," he said finally.

"We can train your auxiliary," Swanson said. The auxiliary were the townsfolk who provided Goode's guerrillas with supplies and warned them of Opforland patrols.

"I'll never let you get close to my auxiliary," Goode said, shaking his head.

"Okay, we can improve your communications security," Swanson continued. "We can help you build an air defense so you aren't ambushed by helicopters."

"And you say you got some doctors?" Goode asked, appearing interested for the first time.

"We have two trained medics who can treat your men and your animals."

"I'll tell you what," Goode said. "You fellas go back. Smokey, you go get their ammunition and food."

"Can we bring our team into the base camp?" Swanson asked.

"Not yet."

Smokey led Swanson and Ruppenthal back down the hill. Goode and Moran huddled to evaluate the captain's performance.

"They weren't bad," Goode said, turning to Moran.

But Moran wasn't pleased that Swanson and Ruppenthal had come up without their weapons.

"My guy told them they couldn't bring them up," Goode said.

Swanson should have insisted on keeping his rifle, Moran said. He could have offered a compromise, like coming up with the weapon unloaded. At least he knew enough not to give away his machine guns.

Goode agreed. Swanson had been a little flustered at first. He could have been a little more tactful about who would be in command.

"But it's good that he didn't give up the authority over his men," Moran said. "That's ironclad. But what he's got to do now is establish some type of rapport with you so that you're both working together."

When Smokey returned, Moran asked him if Swanson left a contingency plan with his team for what they would do if he didn't come back.

He did, Smokey recalled.

"Good, he's learning," Moran said.

A half hour later, Swanson and Ruppenthal returned with the ammunition and MREs.

Goode finally introduced Phillips as his top noncommissioned officer and sergeant major. He explained that his guerrilla band consisted of two patrols.

"You guys got money to pay our guerrillas," Goode said, getting down to business.

"That's correct," answered Swanson.

"How do you plan to do that?"

"First we want them to swear allegiance to Pineland," Swanson said. His briefing books had warned him to pay only guerrillas recognized as part of the resistance army. Otherwise he would be throwing money into a bottomless pit.

But the colonel wasn't buying. "My men owe their allegiance to me, not Pineland," he argued.

"But by swearing allegiance to Pineland, it makes them part of a formal army," Swanson explained. "That way if they're captured they're treated like prisoners of war."

Phillips, the sergeant major, laughed. "The enemy already kills our prisoners," he said.

"If you make us legal now, did that make us illegal before you came?" Goode asked menacingly.

That was too fine a point of international law for Swanson. He continued with his case. "We must make your men fall under the Geneva Convention for their own protection. The only way to do that is make them part of a recognized army."

"I don't want my men swearing allegiance to a country that cuts and runs," Goode retorted.

Swanson ignored the insult and explained that the guerrillas would be swearing allegiance to Pineland, not the United States.

Goode relented—halfway. "We'll take the pay and sign the oath. But my people won't give you their real names."

That posed another problem. Swanson needed some kind of accurate record of who was receiving Pineland dons, which, after all, came from American tax dollars. But Goode was adamant. If the enemy captured Swanson's records it would expose his men.

The whole arrangement was becoming too complicated, Goode complained. "You Americans with all these forms and all these regulations make everything difficult. Then you cut and run," he repeated, "just like you did in Nicaragua." He was better off having nothing to do with the United States.

Things weren't working out the way Swanson expected them to. He set aside the pay dispute for the moment. If he didn't watch out, he may not have any guerrillas to pay.

"Look, what have you got to lose?" the captain said finally, trying to be soothing. "Even if we leave now, you've gotten some food and ammunition from us. So you're already ahead. Why don't you give us a chance?"

So far Ruppenthal had stood silent through the two meetings. A twenty-seven-year-old staff sergeant and weapons specialist, who had spent most of his six years in the Army in a mountain division, Ruppenthal was initially shy and awkward. At first glance he seemed hardly the type to be sent abroad on diplomatic missions. A country boy from a tiny town called Clayton in the northeast corner of New Mexico, he was an outdoorsman, avid gun collector, a patriot. As a kid he loved to visit the cattle auctions with his parents and watch the old cowboys with their dusty hats and leather chaps strutting about or leaning on fence rails eyeing the bulls. They were the real Americans, the real heroes in this country. They represented the way of life he wanted to preserve.

But Clay Ruppenthal was no rube. He was determined to improve himself. A libertarian, he was an environmentalist like Swanson. When not in the field, he had been attending night school to earn a bachelor's degree in history. Maybe he'd teach history in a high school if he tired of the Green Berets, he would say.

Before the students had arrived for their second meeting, Moran had instructed Phillips to grill Ruppenthal to test how well he performed at rapport building.

As Swanson tried to calm down Goode, Phillips turned abruptly to Ruppenthal and asked, "How many combat guys you got?"

Taken aback, Ruppenthal stammered, then calculated that seven of the fifteen men on the team were combat veterans.

"Which wars?" the guerrilla sergeant major pressed.

The Desert Storm war in the Persian Gulf and the Just Cause invasion of Panama, Ruppenthal answered.

The entire guerrilla band began laughing.

"A hundred-hour war and a war that lasted a week," Phillips sneered. "Some combat!"

Ruppenthal stood silent.

Goode finally decided that Swanson's team could move up the hill from the river to his outer perimeter. But the detachment still wouldn't be allowed inside the base camp. This was hardly an auspicious beginning for the young captain. He had hoped to begin training immediately, but he wasn't even on speaking terms with the guerrilla chief. Somehow, he had to get on the colonel's good side. Swanson could not report back that he couldn't get along with the guerrillas.

Goode dismissed the students. After they had left, he dispatched three of his guerrillas to try to sneak up on the detachment to spy on them and steal more of their supplies. Goode wanted to see if the rest of the team was staying awake during Swanson's shuttle diplomacy.

Ruppenthal's first attempt at rapport building had not gone well. It was about to get worse. The three snitches Goode had sent to spy on the team reported back. Phillips, the guerrilla sergeant major, summoned Ruppenthal and began to chew him out. Security around the detachment's perimeter stank.

"My spies went down and saw your men lying around on their rucksacks," Phillips barked. The detachment indeed had practically collapsed after they marched up the hill. "How can you teach us security if your men are so vulnerable there? Your people are down there doing the rucksack flop!"

Ruppenthal tried to make excuses, but Phillips cut him off.

"I don't know if I want my boys around you," he taunted. "They'll pick up bad habits from your men."

Ruppenthal assured him that would not be the case.

Phillips had another surprise for him. "We had been promised 750 rounds of ammunition—you only gave us 340 rounds," he said accusingly.

Ruppenthal was now caught completely off guard. The team had parceled out several boxes and belts of ammunition not bothering to count every single round. After all, this was still just a training exercise. It wouldn't matter, they thought. But Goode had ordered his guerrillas to count every last bullet. Ruppenthal was about to have an important rule of guerrilla warfare drilled into his head: always deliver what you promise.

"How can we trust you if you cheat us on the ammo!" Phillips began ranting and raving. He threatened to hang the entire team. "If you cheat us again I'll have you executed!"

Green Berets constantly faced the problem of American promises like foreign aid not being kept. It didn't take much in the way of unfulfilled promises to jeopardize a mission, as Phillips had discovered serving in Bolivia. Unlike their military counterparts, the Bolivian narcotics police the Green Berets trained could not accept cash bribes. But in return for being honest, the narcotics police were given extra equipment. Phillips almost had a mutiny on his hands when knives promised by a previous mobile training team never were delivered.

Swanson returned to put out this fire. The ammo count was "notional," he said.

"Notional," Goode said, looking at Swanson as if he had just said something totally incomprehensible—which, in a guerrilla's mind, it would be. There was nothing notional about ammo counts.

Moran made a mental note to jump all over Swanson later if he used that rationale anymore.

Goode was becoming angrier by the moment. He badgered Swanson again about his M-60 machine guns. A fine introduction this was. Swanson waltzed into his base camp promising to beef up his security and he wouldn't give the guerrillas two lousy machine guns to do it. "How do we know you won't turn those machine guns around and begin firing on us?" Goode asked menacingly.

If Goode was worried about that, Swanson had a compromise. Goode could take control of his M-60 ammunition.

Goode paused, then smiled like a bazaar merchant who had just fleeced a customer. "Okay," he said quietly. "You have a deal."

Swanson walked back to his base, relieved that this mini-crisis was behind him.

Bugsy Moran rolled his eyes and shook his head. "I'll just bet you that when he tells the team that's the deal he's struck, they'll have him back here in an instant to renege," Moran told Goode. Swanson should never have given up all his M-60 ammunition. That would make the machine guns worthless, "which is what I'm sure his team is explaining to him right now."

Swanson was in a pickle, Moran figured. He'd already shorted Goode on the ammunition. Now he would have to come back and renege on his promise to turn over the M-60 ammo. He could have recovered if he turned over half his M-60 ammo and hid the rest. But Swanson had already told Goode that he brought 1,800 rounds for the machine guns and he knew Goode counted his gifts.

Moran shook his head again. "These guys think they've got Robin Sage figured out," he told Goode. "They think that all they have to do is wait out this harassment and we'll just move on to the next phase of the exercise."

But Moran had something else in store for them. The team had dug itself into this hole. He wasn't going to help them out. Swanson was about to have an important rule of guerrilla warfare drilled into his head: don't promise more than you can deliver.

As Moran had expected, the team objected to Swanson's deal, which pleased the training sergeant. At least the team members were thinking things through. They were backing up their captain, correcting his mistakes. That's the way Green Berets operated.

More shuttle diplomacy. Swanson dispatched Ruppenthal first to try to talk the guerrilla sergeant major into forgetting about the M-60 ammo. No way. "You come up with the ammo now," Phillips ordered. "And my colonel will talk to your leader about it later after he's had his lunch."

Ruppenthal marched back down the hill. The team stalled for time. It was not about to turn over the ammunition, then negotiate to get it back.

Phillips ordered his guerrillas to deploy at the perimeter with their weapons aimed at the A-team. He wanted the guerrillas to act belligerently to see if the team could be goaded into provoking a confrontation.

Green Berets faced this kind of problem in real life all the time. Politicians might decide one country's relations with another, but in the jungle, Phillips knew full well, Green Berets were stuck with establishing their own diplomatic relations with foreign armies. Often the Green Berets were threatened as much by the people they were trying to help as by the enemy.

Swanson returned. Turning over all the M-60 ammunition was out of the question, the captain told Phillips.

"My colonel isn't ready to receive you," Phillips told

him haughtily. For the next meeting, we would meet only with Ruppenthal, the guerrilla sergeant major added.

Another wrinkle in the exercise. Phillips wanted to test Swanson's reaction to the guerrillas trying to strip him of his authority. Swanson must remain in control. But it was not uncommon for foreign officers to make end runs around an A-team leader if the two didn't hit it off and try to deal with a favorite NCO in the Green Beret detachment. The A-team officer must be flexible. To accomplish the mission, he sometimes had to forget his own rank and deal with a foreign officer through one of his team sergeants. The team sergeant became the front man, while the team captain directed from the rear. During the Desert Storm war, some Green Beret sergeants even pinned higher ranks on their collars and claimed to be officers in order to gain the confidence of their foreign counterparts.

But Swanson balked for the moment. His mission plan instructed that the Green Berets as a rule should travel in pairs to every meeting with the guerrillas. Swanson didn't want to give up the lead role so early in the exercise. "Both of us must be here to talk to the colonel," he insisted.

"Fine. If that's the way you want it, none of you can come back," Phillips said stubbornly. "Get out of my camp!"

Moran stretched out in a bed of warm leaves, folded his hands behind his head, and chuckled. He had not walked down to the students' position outside the perimeter and didn't intend to.

"I know if I went down there now they'd be crying to me, 'Oh Sergeant Moran, when's this going to end,'" he said, mocking a child's voice.

Shortly before 1 P.M., Swanson marched back to the guerrilla base camp. He had lost track now of the number of times he'd had to walk up and down that damn hill. His back and legs ached. He had been up thirty-two hours.

But he had to keep a clear head. He had to stay calm. What he said, how he acted now could spell success or failure for his mission. If he didn't watch out, he could end up in a firefight with the very people he was supposed to protect.

Swanson decided to be up front and not mince his words. "I can't give you the M-60 ammo," he told Goode simply.

"You made me a promise and now you're reneging on it?" Goode asked, feigning incredulity.

"I can't jeopardize the security of my team," Swanson said. "I spoke in haste. I made a mistake."

"Nobody makes mistakes here," Goode said, coming to a boil. "If they do they're dead."

"Remember, we're here fighting a common enemy," reminded Ruppenthal, who stood nervously next to Swanson.

"What do we do to people who've made mistakes the last thirteen years?" Phillips asked, turning to Goode.

"I'll show you what we do!" Goode shouted. He grabbed an M-16 armed with blanks, pointed it at Sparky, one of his guerrillas, and fired. The guerrilla fell, sprawled across a workbench.

Swanson and Ruppenthal stood dumbfounded. Goode turned to them, gripping the M-16, his eyes fiery.

"I'm in full control here," he said, choosing his words carefully. "Here's what I can do to my own men. And that's what I can do to you. You've got fifteen minutes. You either come back with that ammunition or get out of my camp!"

Swanson turned around and walked back.

Moran broke into a wide grin. Goode hadn't told him he would shoot the guerrilla. It was a great touch. Swanson would later complain that the shooting was unrealistic. "Just wait until he gets to an A-team," Goode said. "It happens all the time."

The days of Vietnam had long passed, when Green Berets themselves disposed of a Vietcong guerrilla with a bullet. That kind of behavior was now officially outlawed in the force. But in the jungles of Honduras, El Salvador, and Guatemala Green Berets had routinely witnessed summary executions of communist guerrillas. Prisoners were tortured during interrogations. Green Berets were placed in untenable positions. The counterinsurgents they were ordered to train were often no better than hired killers. Some Green Berets rationalized that atrocities happened on both sides, but the press rarely reported torture and killing by the communists. Others found it distasteful, no matter who was committing the crimes. Some even hid the fact that they spoke Spanish to avoid serving in Central America. But few Green Berets ever openly questioned the orders. As one Special Forces soldier privately admitted, "you get so wrapped up with soldiers you're trying to train, those sixteen-year-old draftees you're trying to keep alive through their combat tours, you don't look at what you're doing from any higher level. You just look at it from your level."

Swanson now must come up with a compromise, any compromise, Moran thought. Make up some kind of story if he had to.

A guerrilla spying on the student team ran up to the base camp. Swanson appeared not to be thinking compromise. He had ordered his men to pack up and leave.

"Where the hell are they going to go?" Moran said to himself. If Swanson returned to his forward operating base —which was ten miles away—his superiors would just send him back to negotiate a compromise.

The exercise was beginning to unravel. Moran pulled himself up and walked down to the edge of the perimeter where Swanson's men were loading their rucksacks onto their backs. Moran couldn't tell Swanson what to do to get out of his predicament. But he damn well didn't want them wasting the rest of the day evacuating to their forward operating base.

The students were tense. Moran found one of them, Michael Barnes, prone behind a log ready to fire at the first guerrilla who crossed his path. At thirty-four, Mike Barnes was a fairly senior sergeant to be undertaking Green Beret training. But for thirteen years he had drifted from one infantry job to another and had become bored. So to put some excitement back into his work, he had signed up for a completely different military skill, as a Green Beret medic. Barnes was from Maine, where folks didn't take kindly to outsiders playing games with them. If these guerrillas planned to make trouble he could dish it back with his M-16, Barnes boasted as Moran walked past.

"What happens after you do that?" Moran asked incredulously.

Barnes didn't know. But if he was going to be killed he'd damn sure take a few guerrillas with him.

"Aren't you going to destroy relations between Pineland and the United States with a stunt like that?" Moran asked and walked off, shaking his head. Barnes had a lot to learn about living in a foreign country under someone else's rules, he thought.

Moran found Swanson hurriedly packing his rucksack.

"I just witnessed a war crime," Swanson said excitedly. "I shouldn't be here." Besides, his own men might be the next victims of the colonel's wrath.

"Fine, but what do you do when you go back to your forward operating base?" Moran said calmly. "They'd just tell you that this is the kind of thing that you're supposed to prevent. And remember, you created this problem in the first place."

Besides, "Did you really witness a war crime?" Moran asked. Technically speaking, Goode had shot one of his own men in cold blood, not the enemy.

"But I can't just let it pass," Swanson argued.

"You shouldn't," Moran said. Report it to your higher headquarters—Swanson certainly intended to do that— then let them deal with it.

Swanson paused in his packing. He hated confrontations like this. He wasn't the type of person who enjoyed arguments. He knew Moran wanted him to return to the base camp and make up with the colonel. But he felt uncomfortable about "just shoving the corpse aside" to continue bargaining. Ruppenthal felt the same way. The textbook answer indeed was to report atrocities to higher headquarters, but Ruppenthal knew it would never be that neat and clean a situation when he actually got to the field.

Swanson thought that maybe he should leave for a while until things cooled off. His intelligence briefing before the exercise claimed that this colonel would be glad to have him. Some intelligence. The guerrillas were within minutes of executing him. Swanson shook his head. He had spent hours in classes on guerrilla warfare doctrine. But nothing had prepared him for this mess.

Brad Archer was another quiet type on the team. A college graduate with a degree in political science and business administration, the sergeant had spent eight years in the Army, much of it in a Ranger battalion. Archer didn't ruffle easily. He had a way of smiling and remaining detached from the swirl around him. Now he spoke up. "Why don't we offer one last compromise," he suggested. "Propose joint control of the M-60 ammo." It was as if fifteen lights had been turned on.

At 1:15 P.M., with a minute left to the colonel's deadline, Swanson and Ruppenthal approached the base camp for another round.

"Look, we're both reasonable men," the captain began as Goode stared at him impassively. "We have a common cause here. There's got to be a way to work it out. What about this: you detach a couple of your guys to come down to our camp to serve as assistant gunners on the M-60s. They can watch out for the ammunition along with our guys."

"And at the same time," Ruppenthal interjected, "your guys can be trained by our team as machine gunners."

"What do you say?" Swanson said soothingly. "We have nothing to hide."

Goode sat silent for what seemed like forever to Swanson. "Okay, I'm amenable to this solution," he said finally.

Swanson's shoulders sagged with relief.

"I'm very upset we had to start out this way," Goode said.

"I am too," said the chastened captain.

The two men shook hands. Swanson left to prepare a

training schedule for Goode's men. His engineers began building a lean-to for classes. Maybe now he could get back on track.

Moran was pleased. Swanson was young and terribly inexperienced at this type of warfare. But he was a quick study. And unlike many officers, he wasn't afraid to take advice from his NCOs.

Goode gathered his twelve guerrillas around him. Remember to act like insurgents, he reminded them. "If they ask you questions, challenge them," he instructed. "Ask them if they're spies. If you see any of their gear unattended, try to steal it and bring it to me. Remember, we still don't exactly trust these guys. We'll let them build rapport with us eventually—but not yet."

7:30 A.M., SATURDAY, FEBRUARY 22

Sanjos Rana carefully laid out the pay vouchers and personnel forms on the field table. The night before, Swanson and the twenty-five-year-old lieutenant from Nepal had devised a compromise, which would enable them to pay the guerrillas and still have them listed on a formal roster without violating the colonel's obsession with security. Swanson had taken Rana under his wing to help him adjust to American culture. They had become good friends and Swanson planned one day to visit Rana in Nepal.

Rana had spent hours drawing neat columns for makeshift ledgers. He was nervous about his first assignment in the exercise and wanted his papers organized so the pay call would proceed smoothly.

The Green Berets and SEALs allowed foreign students to take their training, often as not as a goodwill gesture toward the country rather than out of any expectation that these students would graduate with the same skills as the Americans. Because of language barriers and poor military training in their homeland, foreign students often had difficulty keeping up. When the Green Berets discovered that some Third World officers who had failed the Q course were being executed when they returned home for disgracing their country, the training command began shaving points off the grade requirements for foreign officers so they would all pass.

Rana needed no help with his grade, though. He was a member of Nepal's honored warrior caste, under which one son joins the army by tradition. Since he was a boy, Rana knew he would become an officer.

Rana talked little during the training. He worried that he might misspeak, although he spoke perfect Sandhurst English. Yet Swanson thought he learned fast. He adapted well, except to the snakes and the cold, damp North Carolina forests. He despised them both. Nepal was dry.

The pay plan Rana and Swanson devised seemed sound. Each guerrilla would sign a cryptonym on the pay voucher. Then he would fill out a "personal data sheet" that matched his cryptonym with his real name and information on his background. The roster of cryptonyms would be retained at the base camp for the payroll, while the personal data sheets would be airlifted back to the United States.

The colonel, however, had no intention of letting pay call proceed smoothly. Before Rana and Swanson had walked up with their records and cash, Goode had gathered together his guerrillas for their own class. Goode gave several enlisted men instant promotions so the Americans would have to pay them more. No more than three guerrillas would be lined up at Rana's table at any time.

"When you get paid, go back to your tent, change uniforms with someone else and go through the line again," Goode had said. "When you get your dons go to the sergeant major's tent and give him the money."

Pay line scams were a fact of life in guerrilla warfare. A young Green Beret captain could find himself dumped into a Latin American jungle with thousands of dollars in his pocket to pay foreign soldiers. Payroll accounting became more an art than a science. Third World soldiers were routinely shortchanged on pay so their superiors could live in high style. In El Salvador, the officers had become a wealthy class off such practices. Green Berets found it impossible to break the corruption. If they could

keep a Salvadoran officer away from the more objection-
able crimes—such as murder, kidnapping, or running a
protection racket—the Green Berets considered themselves successful. They ignored the petty crime.

Goode formed his guerrillas into two rows. Swanson
led them through a rambling recitation of the Pineland
oath of allegiance. Three men then lined up before Rana,
who was immersed in his records.

Smokey was first in line and began filling out the personal data sheet. He stopped at one entry, which asked him
to list any disciplinary actions filed against him while in
service.

"Disciplinary actions?" Smokey laughed. "What do I
write here? If there's disciplinary action you're shot. I
wouldn't be here filling this out."

"Just write 'nonapplicable,'" Rana said quietly and
began to count out Smokey's dons.

But Smokey balked. "I thought we'd get American
dollars," he griped. "These fucking dons are worthless."

Rana motioned Swanson for help. "We've got a problem here," he told the captain. "They don't want dons.
They want American dollars."

Swanson found Goode. "We only came with dons," he
explained.

"My people prefer dollars," Goode said. "They can
get more goods on the black market with American dollars."

Swanson said he would try to have American dollars
dropped in for the next pay call. That satisfied Goode, who
ordered his men to accept the dons.

Swanson relaxed. Rana continued processing the guerrillas in line, counting out the dons and making sure each
filled out the forms completely. Neither was aware of the
fact that some of the guerrillas were being paid twice and
all were handing their money over to Phillips.

A half hour later, Swanson glanced over Rana's shoul-
der at his paperwork. Eleven men had been paid so far.
"Wait a minute," he said. "Something's wrong here."
Swanson had counted eleven guerrillas in the formation

taking the oath. And there were four guerrillas in line waiting to be paid. The two officers riffled through the paper to try to find the discrepancy.

Swanson called for the guerrilla sergeant major. Phillips now claimed that the four guerrillas had just come in from guard duty and wanted to be paid.

"Something's kind of screwy here," Swanson said, eyeing the signature roster Rana had compiled. "We've got matching handwriting here."

"Matching handwriting?" Phillips asked, feigning ignorance. "Are you some kind of handwriting expert?"

"As a matter of fact I am," Swanson retorted.

"Well, that doesn't mean anything in Pineland," Phillips huffed.

"It looks like your men have been double dipping," Swanson said, irritated. Rana stood mystified. Were they pulling this stunt because I'm a foreign student? he thought for a brief moment.

Another argument broke out. Each side accused the other of lying and bad faith. Goode again ordered his men to train their weapons on the detachment, as Rana and Swanson packed up their vouchers. The morning was barely over and the team was in another tense standoff with the guerrillas.

Bugsy Moran, who was beginning to feel like a labor mediator, buttonholed Swanson. "You should have anticipated this and set up some type of control system for the pay," Moran lectured. "When the guerrillas were lined up in formation for the oath, you should have had Rana right there going down the line with his paperwork and paying each man on the spot. That way the guerrillas couldn't double dip on you."

"Yeah, you're right," Swanson said, a bit grudgingly. "But if I go back and keep paying them they'll think I'm a chump."

But if he didn't find a compromise, Swanson would end up in the same standoff he faced the day before. Again Goode's guerrillas had begun creeping around the forest to encircle his team.

"Don't get frazzled now," Moran warned.

"I'm not," Swanson said calmly. He decided to let things cool down for a while before he returned to the base camp and tried to talk his way out of yet another fix.

The captain finally walked back to Goode's headquarters. "Look, we need to put this behind us," Swanson said.

Goode, who was sitting on a log near the fire pit, stood up slowly.

"Okay, let's walk down the trail," he finally said.

The two men strolled off with Hank, the dog, trailing them wagging his tail. Swanson proposed another compromise. The team would tighten its pay procedures the next time. Meanwhile, Swanson would pay the four privates who were left in the line during the first pay call.

"I can live with that," Goode said. Swanson was starting to pick up the play of the game, he thought. The captain would just have to write off the extra money and juggle his accounts the next month. Green Berets had been doing it for decades.

7 P.M., SATURDAY, FEBRUARY 22

The sun had already set. The night was pitch black. Kelly Albright turned his white pickup truck off Route 2 near Ramseur and into the dirt driveway of a ranch-style brick house. After a day and a half of haggling, the student team on Saturday had finally started training the guerrillas. Classes had begun in the M-60 machine gun, demolitions, setting up perimeter security. Now Swanson was lying facedown and blindfolded in the back of Albright's truck. Beside him in the same position was Klapperich, who had been designated the team sergeant, replacing Ruppenthal. As he was trained to do, Swanson had tried to calculate the miles the truck had driven the past half hour and track its turns in order to have some idea of where he was being taken.

But it was no use. Albright constantly doubled back on the country roads. Near the village of Ramseur, he had stopped at the intersection facing Kildee Church. He made a U-turn, backed up the truck, made a second U-turn, backed up the truck, made a third U-turn, then turned left past the church. Swanson was thoroughly disoriented.

Albright was one of the veterans of the Pineland auxiliary. For nearly thirty years, he had been hauling Green Beret students and picking up rations dumped at resupply drops. A fifty-six-year-old fuel truck driver during the day, Albright had never served in the military. But he knew practically as much about guerrilla warfare as the instructors at Robin Sage. When he died, Kelly Albright wanted the Green Berets to bury him.

He had driven the circuitous route for a reason. Swanson and Klapperich were being taken to the secret hideout of the guerrilla leader most paranoid about his own personal security—Moses, the area commander.

Green Berets, some in uniform, others in blue jeans and parkas wearing baseball caps, guided Albright's truck to a tool shed in back of the house. The tailgate was unhitched and one of the Green Berets, in a surly voice, ordered Swanson and Klapperich to crawl out.

"Lay on the ground," shouted the Green Beret, who was playing the part of a guerrilla.

Swanson and Klapperich, still blindfolded, sprawled facedown on the ground, which by now had become cold and damp. When the two students had left for the area command meeting the sun had not set and the day was still a warm 65 degrees. They had worn only their fatigue blouses and undershirts. But with nightfall, the temperature had quickly plunged to almost freezing. Swanson cursed himself for not wearing a jacket and liner.

Maybe he'd be lucky and finish this meeting with Moses quickly. According to Swanson's intelligence folder, Moses commanded several guerrilla bands that operated in a wide swath of Pineland. If Goode was a colonel, Moses was the equivalent of a general. He was the senior guerrilla officer, whose confidence Swanson must win if his detachment was to remain in this foreign country. The intelligence folder said Moses would be suspicious. But still, it shouldn't be too difficult an assignment, Swanson thought. Moses couldn't possibly be as ornery as the colonel.

"Don't move one fucking inch, or we'll abandon you in these woods," the guerrilla snarled in Swanson's ear.

So much for a pleasant meeting, Swanson thought.

The shades to the house's windows remained drawn during the day. This was one of four safe houses the Green Berets rented to manage the Robin Sage exercise. Inside, they had crammed rucksacks, boxes of MRE rations, field tables piled high with manuals and maps, and canvas cots for instructors who drifted in during the day and night for showers and catnaps. In the entranceway were stacked tactical radios with cryptographic attachments that would scramble the conversation the Green Berets had with guerrilla base camps or the student detachments, so outsiders couldn't listen in.

As Swanson and Klapperich lay shivering on the ground by a tool shack, Moran, Goode, and the instructors from other student detachments huddled with Moses around a Formica-topped table in the kitchen, which served as the conference room.

The area commander was a prized role among the men and women of eastern North Carolina who worked for the Green Berets. The Special Forces trainers carefully screened and trained the civilians who played the part. Area commanders had to act and think like guerrilla chieftains. They had to be quick on their feet, beguiling, mysterious, boisterous one minute, cunning the next, always looking for ways to catch the students off guard yet not become too caught up in the part so that they would lose control and embarrass the trainers.

But if there was a master impresario among the area commanders, it was Moses. Dressed in blue jeans and plaid shirt, with a thick brown beard, hair almost to his shoulders, and dark brown eyes, Moses looked like a cross between Che Guevara and one of the Oak Ridge Boys. His only formal brush with the military was a stint in the Navy. But for twenty-five years, Moses had been making students tremble at area command meetings with his deep voice and piercing stare.

Moses carefully modulated his behavior. He was not

there just to rant and rave. Moses considered himself a teacher. (He asked that only his guerrilla name be used in this book. A local businessman, Moses traveled extensively in the Middle East and other parts of the Third World, where his clients wouldn't look too kindly on him if they knew he worked with special operations forces.)

Tonight, Moses was the center of attraction, attended to by a dozen Green Berets who prepped and primped him like a stage crew fluttering about a Hollywood star. He had his work cut out for him.

Bugsy Moran considered himself lucky. Other instructors now grumbled that they had been stuck with students who bungled the infiltration and officers who had the rapport building skills of Attila the Hun. "Detachments from hell," the instructors called them. Before Swanson and Klapperich would have their turn, the leaders of two other student detachments were marched separately to a nearby tractor shed for their area command meeting with Moses.

The night infiltration by the first student detachment had not gone well. One of the students had dropped a bag of sunflower seeds along the way, which a guerrilla had picked up. Angry, Moses demanded that the detachment's captain pay 5,000 dons to the auxiliary, which had to clean up the trash. The second student leader fared even worse. When Moses demanded that he turn over his M-16 to the guards before the meeting could begin, the young captain stubbornly refused.

Moses flew into a rage. But the captain was adamant. Infantrymen were taught since basic training never to part with their weapons and he was not about to give up his. Moses had the guerrillas drag him back out to the yard to lie on the cold ground for another hour. Just to show the officer that his chivalry was misguided in Pineland—where Moses ruled with an iron fist—the guerrillas hauled one of their guards before the students, who remained facedown on the ground, and pretended to gun him down firing an M-16 with blanks.

That should give the captain something to think about, the Green Beret/guerrillas thought. Holding on to your weapon was fine in combat, but not in this situation. In a foreign country, playing by a foreign military's rules, a Green Beret couldn't be inflexibly wedded to U.S. Army regulations if he was to survive.

But the incident left Bugsy Moran in a quandary. Swanson, though blindfolded, could hear what was going on around him. He had already been upbraided for bargaining away his weapons during his first meeting with Goode. With all the ruckus being raised over the captain's rifle, Swanson might get it in his head that he should hold on to his, Moran worried. They might be stuck here all night if Swanson became as bullheaded as the other captain.

Moran decided to "Santa Claus it," the term the instructors used when they gave students a clue or an answer to solving a problem. He walked out to the backyard and whispered into Swanson's ear to surrender his weapon if asked to do so.

Swanson chuckled to himself. A guerrilla had an M-16 pointed at his back with orders to shoot him if he so much as twitched a muscle. He'd just witnessed his second execution of the exercise. He wasn't about to quibble over a stupid rifle. In fact, he didn't feel like arguing over much of anything.

It was nearly 9:30 P.M. They had been lying on the cold, damp ground with their hands folded under their heads for some two and a half hours, while Moses dealt with the leaders of the first two teams. The earth had sucked practically every calorie of warmth out of their bodies. Klapperich's arms had been asleep for the past hour. Every fifteen minutes Swanson would slowly exercise—so the guard wouldn't notice—each finger of his numb hands to keep the blood circulating. The only thing he could think of—and he repeated it in his mind over and over again—was: "Fuck, it's getting cold out here."

Moran walked back into the safe house to brief Moses on his students. "Slam them on their trick-or-treat infil," Moran began, recounting the bungled start to the infiltration. Next Swanson shorted the guerrillas on the ammunition he offered. So far the team had just been reacting to events, and not doing a particularly good job at that, Goode interjected. They had yet to take the initiative.

Moses nodded and noted the comments in his black book. "Anything else?" he asked.

"Yeah, I need a good way to close this out, provided my captain doesn't go tits up on me," Moran continued. "You should act satisfied in the end, as long as he produces."

"Okay," Moses said, making more notes. He ran through the lines he would deliver, then gathered up his papers and walked out of the safe house to the tractor shed. Moran, Goode, and the other instructors followed.

Inside the corrugated tin shed, at the far end of its pine wood floor, stood a trap door that led down to a dank cinderblock basement. In it, the Green Berets had placed a plywood table with two kerosene lanterns on top.

Moses positioned himself behind the table, took a deep breath like an actor preparing to walk on stage, and sat down in a chair. To his right sat Goode. At the other end of the basement, Moran and the other instructors stood silent. The light above was turned off. The only illumination came from the yellow glow of the two kerosene lamps. When Swanson and Klapperich were led in, their backs would be to the instructor. The only persons they would see would be Moses and Goode, who sat to his right. They wouldn't know that Moran and the other members of the training cadre were standing behind them grading their responses.

Above, Moses could hear the shuffle of feet as Swanson and Klapperich were led blindfolded into the shed. The two willingly gave up their rifles when the guard demanded them.

"Let's don't take forever up there," Moses bellowed. "I don't have all night!"

Guided by the Green Berets, the blindfolded students clumped down the steps into the basement. They stood in front of the table, shaking uncontrollably from the cold, their noses running.

"I want security at one hundred percent out there," Moses called to his guards.

"All secure!" the guards shouted back.

"Take off their blindfolds," Moses ordered.

Swanson thought his eyes would roll out of his head. After almost three hours of being blindfolded, the two kerosene lamps seemed like headlights that had been shone directly at his pupils. He could barely make out some kind of bearded face behind them that seemed to speak in a roar. Swanson squinted to try to focus and adjust to the glare from the lanterns, all made more difficult by the fact that he couldn't stop the trembling in his body.

"I am Moses, the commander of this sector," the guerrilla chief began solemnly.

Swanson managed a wobbly salute and with a voice grown raspy from the cold announced: "Captain Swanson, commander of ODA-941 reporting as ordered."

Moses ignored the introduction and continued in his deep, ominous voice. "There was a debate in my country over whether to allow you here in the first place. We have been fighting this war for thirteen years and you Americans suddenly walk in and claim you can win it for us.

"We thought we were getting your best soldiers," Moses said, his eyes boring in on Swanson, who by now had adjusted to the light. "But we were not prepared for the way you entered our country. We didn't know that you'd make a duck walk from house to house!"

Swanson flushed. The trick-or-treat infiltration. Was he ever going to live that down?

"Now, is this the level of excellence you're preparing to offer us?" Moses asked threateningly.

"It won't happen again," Swanson answered, chastened.

"My men had to abandon the first linkup site because you made so much noise. Do we have a common cause here, you and I?"

"Yes sir. To defeat Opforland."

"Those are just words!" Moses bellowed. "Are we now singing off the same sheet of music?"

"We are, sir," Swanson said quietly.

"What about this training they're supposed to provide us?" Moses asked, turning to Goode.

"I don't know how good it is," Goode answered skeptically. "They've spent most of their time so far insulting me and my men."

Moses turned back to Swanson with an irritated look on his face. "What about munitions?" he asked. "What are you prepared to give us?"

"There's a cache hidden here with supplies from my country," Swanson said, trying to ignore Goode's snide comment and recover the initiative. "When I'm told by my higher headquarters where it's located, I'll be able to provide you with ammunition."

"When can you get the location so I can get my supplies?" Moses pressed.

"In a month," Swanson guessed. That was the wrong answer. It shouldn't take that long. But in case his higher headquarters did not have an arms cache immediately at hand, Swanson wasn't about to make another promise he couldn't keep.

"A month?" Goode snapped. "I can't wait a month. I need that ammunition in a week."

"Okay," Swanson recovered. "At least within a week, I can get a yes or no answer from my higher headquarters on the location of the cache."

"Then how long will it take to distribute the equipment once you find it?" Moses asked.

"It can be given out right away," Swanson answered.

"Okay," Moses said. "You've got a week."

"Anything else?" Moses asked, turning again to Goode.

Goode leaned back in his chair. "Well, they seem to harp on training," he said. "But I'm not sure what they're going to give us."

Moses grilled the two students on what they planned to teach the guerrillas. Klapperich described the training schedule in detail. There would be a field exercise on how to conduct a small raid, a range cleared for firing small arms.

"How combat-motivated are my men?" Moses continued his examination.

"They seem motivated," Swanson answered, although he really didn't know.

"Where are my weak points?"

"We're investigating them."

"What about security?"

"We're improving it."

"What are you prepared to do for me in the long run?"

"We want to recruit more guerrillas, build your force up to battalion strength," Swanson answered, feeling warmer and a bit more assertive. "Instead of striking as a scalpel, we strike as a hammer."

Moses wasn't impressed yet. "Those are cute phrases," he said. "Give me specifics. All you're telling me are nice generalities. I want to know exactly how I win this war."

Swanson took a breath and began again. "We'll conduct more mine warfare. We'll improve medical care to save the lives of more wounded soldiers. That will make them more motivated to fight if they know they have a chance of surviving a battle. We'll provide more pay. We have money to offer for recruiting. We can launch psychological operations."

Moses paused and looked down at his notebook. "I want to meet with you in the future," he said. "I want a detailed plan from you on the operations you want to conduct."

Moses folded the cover of his black book and gave Swanson one last menacing look. "You do understand that I'll accept nothing less than proficiency from you," the area commander said. "Is that understood?"

"Yes, sir," Swanson said.

"Don't foul up again."

The basement was silent for a minute. The instructors in the back did not move or say a word.

Moses broke the silence. "Have security prepare to move out these people," he ordered. "Gentlemen, I apologize but we're going to have to put your blindfolds back on. No one can know my location. Not even you."

Green Berets from the back tied the bandanas around the students' heads and led them up the stairway.

When the trap door was shut after they had left, the lights were turned on. Moses stood up, drained from his performance. Moran, Goode, and the other instructors gathered around the table to evaluate the meeting.

"From my side of the table, the captain was sometimes unsure of himself," Moses offered. "It may have been the incident outside," when he heard the execution.

But as the meeting progressed, the captain and the sergeant appeared to regain their confidence, Moses said. Overall, the session had gone well. The captain and sergeant kept their poise and didn't say anything that might anger the guerrillas. The schoolhouse solution was to be sincere and conciliatory, which Swanson had certainly been. Moran was pleased. Swanson, he felt, would make a good team captain. He wasn't too haughty.

"The captain did a good job of dancing around the question of when we get the supplies from the cache," Moses added.

"He's learned not to overcommit himself," Moran said with a smile.

8:45 A.M., SUNDAY, FEBRUARY 23

George Seemann walked under the tin roof of the ramshackle hooch that Goode called his base camp headquarters. Behind the medic stood the young private the colonel had designated as the guerrilla camp witch doctor. A cold rain had begun to pelt the tin, soaking the base camp and anyone not under cover. For the next three days the combination of rain and chilly temperatures would make life miserable for the students. Barnes, the other medic, had already been busy that morning dispensing medications to his own team. Swanson had a raging chest cold from his three hours on the ground the night before. Two other students had stomach cramps and were throwing up with intestinal flu.

Opening his green canvas medical bag, Seemann was about to give Goode a demonstration of the training his guerrillas were now receiving. Since last evening, Seemann had been showing the witch doctor how to administer an intravenous solution to a patient. The medics had designated a lean-to as the base camp's aid station by hanging a cow bone from a pole.

Administering an IV was one of the most basic emergency medical procedures guerrilla warriors learned. On missions, every Green Beret carried on his back a needle, tubing, and plastic bag filled with intravenous solution that he could administer to a buddy or himself. The IV solution, a combination of sodium, sodium chloride, and lactate, quickly replaced fluids in a body so a wounded soldier did not go into shock. Green Berets also have used it as an emergency source of water. Moran would never forget the time he had been stranded without water in the 110-degree heat of a Saudi desert during a survival exercise before the Persian Gulf War began. The IV solution strapped to his back, called Lactated Ringers, tasted like thick, milky salt water. He could barely keep from retching as he drank it. A packet of grape drink powder he had dumped in didn't make the foul tasting concoction any more palatable. But the solution kept him alive.

Though a routine procedure, administering an IV did have its dangers. Infection was one. Another was a catheter shear. The needle inserted in the vein was encased in a catheter, through which the IV ran from the tube. An inexperienced handler tended to want to probe for the vein if he didn't tap it after puncturing the arm. But once the needle was on its way out of the skin, it should never be pushed back in to hunt for the vein. The catheter might be punctured and broken off. If the catheter had in fact been in the vein all along, the sliver broken off might travel up the vein and cause a stroke.

Then there was the problem of air bubbles in the tube from the IV bag. A bubble more than an inch long in the tube that made its way into the vein could cause an air embolism that would also result in a stroke.

The baby-faced, doe-eyed private who played the witch doctor looked too young to be administering anything, much less an IV. But Phillips, the guerrilla camp's sergeant major, matter-of-factly rolled up his sleeve and offered his arm for the demonstration. Green Berets routinely were guinea pigs. On training assignments in Latin America, Phillips would have to let *campesinos* practice on his arm before they could be convinced that hooking up an IV to their own men was safe.

The young private nervously unwrapped the needle and tubes and pulled the clear plastic bag of intravenous solution.

"Warm up that bag," Phillips ordered. He hated it when cold liquid coursed through his arm, giving him a chill.

The private obeyed, rubbing the bag with his grimy hands. Next he strapped a tourniquet to Phillips's right arm and searched for a vein.

"I've never done this before," the private murmured with a weak smile.

"I know," Phillips said warily.

"You're fine. Do just like I told you," Seemann said with a calm bedside manner. The Army now considered both Seemann and Barnes to be about as skilled as a second-year medical intern, particularly in trauma medicine. They could perform surgery on gunshot wounds. It was not pretty surgery, but enough to keep a patient alive until he could reach a hospital. They were also combination nurses and public health administrators, who could organize preventive medicine and sanitation routines for remote villages. In a guerrilla war, a Green Beret medic would hope to find a real doctor among the insurgents and provide him or her equipment for dealing with more serious cases.

The private swabbed dark orange iodine on a bulging vein.

"There's not going to be any bubble in my arms," Phillips asked, half joking and half making sure the kid had been told about bubbles. "That's all I need is some air gap going to my heart."

Seemann watched over the private's shoulder, talking him through every move. "Don't let his arm get contaminated now," he said quietly.

Fumbling with the tube and bag, the jittery private accidentally dripped IV fluid on his hands.

"Come on now, slow down," Seemann said to reassure him. "Don't get nervous now."

The private, beads of sweat forming on his forehead, gripped the syringe like a screwdriver and removed the protective cap. He lowered it down to Phillips's arm as if he were touching a rattlesnake.

"Draw the skin taught," Seemann reminded him. The private used his free hand to grip the arm.

"Now lower the needle and keep it in line with the vein," Seemann said.

Breathing heavily, the private winced as he punctured the skin with the needle and gingerly pushed it into the vein. Phillips watched every move as Seemann talked the young man through attaching the catheter to the tubing, then checking for bubbles in the tube or swelling above the puncture point.

With the catheter taped to Phillips's arm, the private slumped back exhausted to wait for the IV fluid to drip into the vein. But nothing happened.

"That ain't no good," Seemann finally concluded. The private had hit the vein but had pushed the needle too far, so it poked out the other side. "You'll have to try it again."

The private looked like he had just finished open heart surgery and been told he'd operated on the wrong patient.

"You just missed it, man," Seemann said, calming him down. "It happens."

Phillips rolled up the sleeve on his left arm and the private repeated the procedure. Only this time, after applying the tourniquet, the youngster couldn't find the vein.

"Don't touch the vein with your hand," Seemann cautioned as the private tried to make one bulge with his dirty finger. "Now relax. Remember what I told you."

The private fumbled even more, using the needle to poke at what he thought was a vein.

"That needle's not a pencil," Seemann warned, worried that Phillips's arm might become infected. In this dirty environment, once the needle touched the skin the private had to push it in. He couldn't poke around on the top of the skin with the instrument, or it would pick up germs and be infected before it was inserted.

It was no use. The private could not find a vein, and even Phillips was becoming nervous, with both arms covered in iodine and grime and blood.

"He nailed me the first time," Seemann told Phillips, explaining apologetically that the private had already stuck Seemann earlier in the morning and found a vein.

The private was crestfallen, as if he had lost a patient. But another Green Beret offered his arm. A half hour later, with the second Green Beret's arm covered in iodine and blood, the private finally managed to get the IV fluid flowing into a vein.

1 P.M., SUNDAY, FEBRUARY 23

The Army Meals Ready-to-Eat tasted only marginally better than previous rations. Tiny bottles of Tabasco sauce had been added, which could be poured into the traditionally wretched ham-and-eggs mix to make it a palatable omelet. But cans had been replaced with plastic containers, making the meals more difficult to heat over fires. Real peaches had been replaced with brick-hard dehydrated ones that tasted like sugared Styrofoam even when water was added. And after three days of an MRE diet, which was loaded with concentrated carbohydrates and proteins, a soldier's intestines were so packed a bowel movement felt like going into labor. The student detachment would be consuming the rations for two weeks. But if they were lucky, tonight their dinner would be different.

Swanson led a supply party up to Sherman Hussey's red hay barn. Hussey's farm was situated on the pastureland about a quarter mile away from the guerrillas' hilltop base camp. Hussey allowed the students to draw jugs of water for their canvas water bags at the camp. This afternoon they could have three of his chickens. Hussey had also given them bags of rice, potatoes, and carrots, plus a black iron pot for a gooey chicken stew they would stir over a fire later. But first they had to catch the chickens.

Seemann, Barnes, and Loiselle tiptoed into the barn and began quietly climbing up a wooden ladder to the hay loft, where the chickens still clucked contentedly. As Barnes peeked his head over the loft, one foot still on the ladder, the nervous chickens began clucking louder. They were obviously veterans of other Green Beret ambushes.

The three students raced up the ladders and lunged at the flock nesting in the corner. But the students violated a cardinal rule of covert warfare. Never give your enemy an easy exit—in this case an open barn door. As Swanson, Ruppenthal, Rana, and Robert Bishop (a National Guardsman trying to become a Green Beret) milled about at the entrance, a dozen chickens and roosters came flying or running out, almost knocking them down.

"Aw shit!" Barnes groaned. The fleet-footed fowls were now scattered around the farmyard—their territory. As the three students clambered down from the loft, Klapperich and Rana ran stooped over trying to nab any of the chickens. A rooster sprinted out to the pasture, with Bishop on his tail. But the rooster scooted under a herd of grazing cows. Bishop came to a screeching halt as a bull reared up its head at the intrusion. The smug rooster obviously had pulled this maneuver before.

"Here, I'll show you how to catch a chicken," Swanson said haughtily and laid down the water jug he had been carrying. But these birds were no more intimidated by officers than by enlisted men. Swanson chased one into a pen, but the enclosure was a goat pen, which a billy goat with two-inch-long horns jealously guarded.

A chicken dinner looked more like a distant prospect. The team was winded and the chickens hadn't broken a sweat. Ruppenthal cornered a rooster in an adjoining pen, but couldn't catch the fast bird. Finally Rana jumped into the pen. The Nepalese may not have been the best payroll accountant, but he knew how to corral chickens. The team at least had bagged its first fowl. Twenty minutes later, they had finally grabbed two more and, worn out, walked back to the base camp clutching the flapping hens by their feet.

At the base camp the chickens were dumped in a makeshift pen to await their execution. Seemann pulled out the first victim. As he thought he was supposed to do, Seemann rung the chicken's neck and laid it on the ground. But to his astonishment, the bird stood up, a bit wobbly but still alive, and dashed for the woods. Dumbfounded, Seemann and the rest of the team watched as one third of their chicken stew vanished into the forest, with only a sore neck.

Goode had been watching from his hooch and now walked up chuckling.

"Here, let me show you how to kill a chicken in the field," he said authoritatively.

The guerrilla colonel reached into the pen and grabbed a hen. Gently, he tucked its head under a wing and stroked it for a couple of minutes. That calmed the bird to the point that it no longer jerked in Goode's arms. After finding a twig, Goode laid the hen on the ground and drew a line back and forth from the bird's beak to a point six inches away. After a half dozen of Goode's strokes along the ground, the hen lay motionless, hypnotized by the movement.

Goode placed his boot on the bird's head, gripped its legs and yanked, ripping the head from the neck. The students cringed as Goode held up the jerking body of the hen with a bloody stump for a neck. The execution actually was more humane than a wringing, since the hen had been practically asleep. Besides, it made the meat more tender when cooked because the chicken wasn't excited, with its muscles tight, when it died.

10:10 A.M., MONDAY, FEBRUARY 24

Swanson, his face covered with green and brown camouflage paint, gathered the colonel and his guerrillas around
a makeshift relief map, which he had carved into a patch of
dirt cleared of leaves and roped off with branchcs. The
map, called a "sand table," had white string curving around
mounds of dirt to depict a trail running to the side of a
small ridge. Where the trail bent to the right would be the
spot for that afternoon's ambush.

The ambush would be easy. It was intended that way.
Training Goode's guerrillas was all well and good. But
Swanson had to prove to the colonel that he could produce
better fighters. For that, Swanson had selected what Green
Berets called a "confidence target," a relatively easy operation the guerrillas could conduct, which would demonstrate
that the Special Forces training was worth the trouble and
that the Special Forces soldiers themselves could be
counted on in battle. In this case, the target, according to
intelligence radioed to Swanson the night before from his
headquarters, was several Opfor sentries who regularly
walked down that path.

The ambush was a bread-and-butter mission for Swan-
son. He had spent two years as a Ranger instructor at Fort
Benning, Georgia, teaching classes in raids and ambushes.
He could plan this one in his sleep.

Swanson broke this operation down into a five-paragraph order: situation, mission, execution, service and support, command and communications. The five-paragraph
op order was the standard guide used by soldiers in the
Army—from the squad leader to the division commander
—in order to organize their thoughts on combat.

Reading from a green notebook he clutched along
with a tactical map, Swanson quickly detailed the terrain
for the ambush, using a stick to point out features on the
ground. The ambushers would dig in by 12:30 P.M. "We use
extreme violence in one blast," he said, using Army jargon
for wiping out the sentries. The ambush should last no
more than seven minutes, including the time it would take
to strip everything of value from the bodies.

As Goode and Moran listened in, Swanson covered dozens of details: the infiltration route they would take, the number of open trails that would be crossed exposing the team, the perimeter security during rest stops, the objective rallying point (or ORP) from where the guerrillas would move to the final site for the ambush, the guerrilla sentries to be posted west and east of the road to alert the ambushers of the approaching enemy.

The guerrillas would travel through the forest in a wedge formation. At the ambush site, Swanson would personally position each shooter. Once in position, no talking or eating "and the only thing moving should be your two eyes," he said. Aiming stakes would be pounded in on both sides of the M-60 machine gun, so its field of fire would not rake over friendly forces. "A golden rule," Swanson said. "You start the ambush with your most potent weapon"—in this case the M-60. The cease-fire signal would be a hand grenade Swanson would toss into the kill zone, after which an assault element would rush in looking for stragglers. Lieutenant Rana would remain at the fallback position to account for all the guerrillas during the exfiltration.

No detail was left to chance. When Goode gave the captain a satisfied look, Swanson decided it was time to again reinforce the point that Americans cared for their wounded. "We grab our wounded and our dead," Swanson began, looking at Goode for any reaction. There was none. "You can't leave anyone out there who they can identify later. Leaving behind wounded demoralizes your force. Leaving no wounded or dead lying around demoralizes the enemy. He doesn't know what hit him. We become a phantom force to him."

The colonel pretended to grudgingly accept the logic.

At 11 A.M., after a dress rehearsal on how the ambushers would be positioned, Swanson ordered his force of guerrillas and several of his own team members to move out. The last man in the formation swept the trail so no one would spot their movement. An hour later they had made it to the ambush site west of the base camp.

Shortly before 1 P.M. a team of 82nd Airborne para-

troopers playing the Opfor soldiers sauntered down the
trail. Machine gun fire exploded from the M-60, followed
by short bursts for no more than a minute by the guerrillas'
M-16s. Swanson threw in the grenade simulator to signal
the assault party, which raced out of the woods toward the
bodies of the enemy soldiers. With Swanson hurrying them
along the guerrillas stripped the bodies of their rifles and
web gear and searched through their pockets for documents.

Moran checked his watch. Three minutes. With the
whole world alerted by the gunfire, Moran knew that
Swanson's raiders should be on the target no more than
five minutes before enemy soldiers might close in to investigate the commotion.

"Assault, clear out!" Swanson shouted. There was no
need to whisper after all the noise they had made with the
ambush.

Four minutes, Moran whispered to himself.

"Come on, come on!" Swanson shouted, hurrying the
guerrillas in their search.

As the guerrillas scurried back to the rear staging
area, Swanson counted them off to make sure no one was
missing or wounded. He rattled off their order of march
for the exfiltration and the men faded back into the woods.

"Five minutes," Moran said, pleased. The ambush
went quickly without a hitch. The guerrillas, none of whom
had had much infantry training in their support jobs back
at Fort Bragg, showed enthusiasm and basic combat sense
in the operation. Swanson's team had actually managed to
teach them something. Even Swanson himself felt that he
was now thinking more like an unconventional warrior
than a traditional infantryman.

8 P.M., THURSDAY, FEBRUARY 27

Moses sat behind a metal table with the props he had used
the last time: the two kerosene lanterns. This time, though,
the area command meeting was being held in a wooden
tool shed across the street from Kelly Albright's house.
True to character—Moses was constantly on the run from

Opforland security agents—the area commander always varied the locations for his meetings with the student detachment leaders. A bare light bulb with a tin shade hung from the ceiling. Two large swinging wooden doors were latched together at the other end of the shed. On every wall hung an assortment of farm implements and truck parts.

Moran pulled up a chair to the table as Moses again opened his black notebook to jot down his script for the night. This was the last area command meeting for the students. A week had passed since the first one. One week in the exercise equaled a half year in real life. Now Moses wanted a final progress report on the forces that these students had trained, as the Pineland guerrillas prepared for their final offensive in the war. Depending on a student leader's performance the previous week, this meeting would be used to build him up or tear him down.

The training cadre sergeants and officers hotly debated what approach Moses should take for some of the students. Robin Sage was nearing its end. Several of the team leaders were still bungling operations, violating basic rules of guerrilla warfare tactics and showing no diplomacy with their guerrilla chiefs. The trainers wanted Moses to be brutal with them in the meeting. On the other hand, if the students were salvageable the trainers didn't want Moses going too far and completely humiliating them.

Thank God he didn't have that dilemma, Moran thought to himself as he outlined the script for Moses. Swanson had had a shaky start the first couple of days. It had then rained practically the entire week. The base camp had turned into a swamp with rivulets of muddy water. Clothes were soaked and sleeping bags were cold and damp. The Fort Bragg soldiers playing the guerrillas had become surly. Swanson had contracted tonsillitis and was pumped full of antibiotics. But he and the other students had still managed to train the insurgents into a decent force. Moran wanted the meeting with Moses to be a pleasant one for his charges.

"Sergeant Goode will report that his guerrillas are

trained and expanding their operations and that so far the targets they've hit have been successful," Moran said as Moses nodded and wrote in his notebook. Goode would sit to his right. Another staff officer would sit to his left.

Moran spread out a tactical map on the table to show Moses the final target the students would hit with the guerrilla forces: a bridge four miles northwest of their base camp near the village of Yow Mill.

"Emphasize to them that Swanson's force has to attack the target on time," Moran told Moses. "It has to be done at the hour you've set, because I want to put some time pressure on them."

This attack would support a final conventional force offensive to entrap the Opforland army and defeat it.

Moses leaned over the map to recheck the coordinates he would give Swanson for the bridge assault. "What's the destruction on the target that we want?" he asked.

"Fifty percent," Moran answered. The bridge would be damaged only enough to make it temporarily impassable. The guerrillas would want to rebuild it for their own use later.

Moses sat quietly for several minutes, hunched over his notes, mouthing to himself the lines he would speak.

"Okay, I'm ready," he finally said.

Moses settled back in his metal chair. The room went silent as the cadre again stood in the back out of view of the students. A trainer flipped the switch to kill the overhead light and the room darkened with only a yellow glow from the two lanterns.

Swanson and Klapperich were led in blindfolded. This time the two wore several layers of polypropylene and insulated liners under their jackets so they wouldn't freeze during that godawful wait outside on the ground.

"Remove their blindfolds," Moses ordered.

Swanson and Klapperich blinked their eyes to adjust them to the light from the lanterns and sat down on two metal chairs on the other side of the table.

Moses didn't say a word to either student. He turned to Goode.

"How are the Americans doing?" he asked quietly.

Here it comes, Swanson thought to himself as he held his breath. What am I going to be slammed on this time? Not killing a chicken properly?

"I'm very surprised at how well the Americans have done," Goode said grudgingly. Swanson let out a sigh and relaxed. "With the Americans' help we've made great strides as a combat force."

Moses turned to Swanson with a satisfied look. "Give me your assessment of the guerrilla force's combat capability," he asked the captain.

"We're ready to shut down the flow of materials into your Pineland sector," Swanson said confidently. But he cautioned that like all guerrilla forces Moses's should not be used in any head-to-head confrontation with a conventional army.

Moran, who was standing in the back, smiled. Good answer, he thought to himself.

Moses also liked what he heard. The captain had done his homework.

"We're very pleased that this relationship has been beneficial to both sides," Moses said, the old menacing look in his face now showing a slight hint of appreciation. "Convey that to your men, Captain."

Swanson said he would.

Moses then spread out the tactical map and leaned forward. "Within the next thirty days we think we can drive Opfor to the north of Pineland," he began, pointing to the map as Swanson and Klapperich edged their chairs closer to the table. "But to do that we have to destroy this bridge across Richardson Creek, which Opfor traverses for its supply link to the south.

"You have a tight window to accomplish this mission," Moses continued, his eyes boring holes into Swanson. The bridge had to be knocked out at 8 P.M. on Friday. The attack time could vary no more than two minutes before or after eight.

Moses paused to let the schedule sink in. "So there's no question that you can take out that bridge?" he asked.

"No question," Swanson assured him.

"Can my men do it?" Moses pressed.

"I feel confident that once we leave, even your men can succeed on these kinds of targets without our help," Klapperich interjected.

Moran broke into a wide grin and gave a thumbs-up to the other cadre sergeants standing silently in the back. Klapperich and Swanson were playing this out exactly as they should—confident, in control, winning the area commander's trust.

"Okay," Moses said, turning to the Army staff officer sitting to his left. "Now your SOCCE has instructions for you." SOCCE, pronounced "sock-see," stood for Special Operations Command and Control Element, which in any operation was the Green Berets' rear-echelon detachment that coordinated broad strategy with the guerrilla high command.

The SOCCE officer, played by a staffer from the Special Warfare Center, announced that he had secretly parachuted into Pineland to deliver these instructions. He unfolded his map to brief Swanson on the demobilization plan for the guerrillas.

The demobilization would begin Sunday morning at six. In the Pineland exercise, this was when the guerrillas would be disarmed and sent home, or integrated into the security forces the new government of Pineland would establish after the war. The students would help collect weapons from the colonel's insurgents, then shower them with awards and dons.

The medals and money would be the easy part. Convincing the guerrillas to relinquish their weapons or join the Pineland conventional army would be more difficult. The students would have to be as diplomatic as they were at the beginning of the exercise. But they would succeed. In real life, they probably wouldn't. Demobilizing an insurgent force could be an almost impossible exercise. Guerrilla wars were much easier to start than stop.

"Take your team to grid square 2332 and position them at the Y in the road south of Fork Creek and east of

Reedy Creek for the linkup," the staff officer instructed. "The linkup team will then take you by truck to the demobilization site, which is Coleridge School." Swanson looked at the spot on the map. That was simple enough. The linkup would only be a mile west of his base camp. The school was located about twelve miles north in the town of Coleridge.

"To confirm the bona fides of the driver at the linkup site, walk up to him and ask, 'Are you having truck problems?' " the staff officer continued. "His response should be, 'No, I'm just taking a break.' Now, brief it all back to me."

Swanson repeated the instructions.

"Anything else you men want to bring up?" Moses then asked. The other student leaders who had appeared before him had sat silent, forgetting what they were supposed to say or mumbling something incoherent, because they were still terrified that Moses would blow up at them. Not Swanson.

"Has the post-hostility role of the guerrillas been established?" he asked calmly. It was a tricky question. Moran was pleased that his captain had even raised it. Swanson was thinking two steps ahead. The assault on the bridge was a fairly straightforward commando operation. For the demobilization, Swanson had to feel out Moses on how far he was prepared to go in disarming his men.

"We've been discussing that contingency," Moses said. "Do you have any suggestions?"

"Civil defense, sir," Swanson answered. "Stand the force down and use some of them only to preserve law and order. Or use them as a standing army to protect Pineland." Swanson then went into the mechanics of converting the force.

"Good idea," Moses said.

"We've anticipated the day you'd work your way out of this job and that day has finally arrived," Moses said to wrap up the meeting. "Good work."

Swanson had a smile for the first time.

Klapperich then broke the silence. "You have a large

mosquito on your arm," he said with a sheepish grin, pointing to the bug.

That cocky sonofabitch, Moran thought to himself.

"He's my pet," Moses said with a thin smile.

The blindfolds were reattached and the students were
led out of the shed.

Moran smacked his fist into his hand. "Excellent, excellent," he said, hiking up his belt and strutting about in
the shed like a proud peacock. "That was great, just great."
Klapperich got involved when he didn't have to. Swanson
appeared confident, self-assured. Goode had instructed the
guerrilla informant, whom he had planted in Swanson's
base camp, to tell the captain that the area command
meeting would be Friday. At the last minute on Thursday
evening, Swanson had been handed a blindfold and told
the meeting would be that night to see how he would perform with a change in schedule. But Swanson was already
prepped. The captain walked into the meeting with points
that he wanted to make, instead of just reacting to what
Moses said.

Moran lit up a cigarette and inhaled deeply. "Oh man,
I can't believe my guys did that well," he bragged to the
other team sergeants, some of whom were stuck with problem cases in their student detachments.

"Hey Bugsy, did you feed him that information?" another trainer asked, needling him.

"No, no, he did it all by himself," Moran said laughing, then walked out into the cool night air.

7:55 P.M., FRIDAY, FEBRUARY 28

Moran parked his pickup truck west of the bridge crossing
Richardson Creek and checked his watch. Paul Unti, a demolitions specialist whom Moran had picked to lead the
students' assault on the bridge, was supposed to begin his
attack in five minutes if everything was on schedule. In fact,
Unti's team was already hidden and poised around the
bridge, ready to make its strike. Moran could see 82nd
Airborne soldiers, who were playing the aggressors,
crouched along the side of the bridge to defend it.

Moran checked his watch again: 7:57 P.M. There might be trouble with the locals after this assault, he worried. A woman in a trailer nearby with a snarling German shepherd had complained before about the noise. She probably would not like what she heard in the next three minutes.

Headlights appeared behind Moran and he spun around quickly. One of the locals out for a Friday night drive. Several other civilian cars had crossed the bridge earlier. That's all I need, he thought. One of those cars crosses the bridge when all hell breaks loose and has a wreck. I'll be making little rocks out of big rocks at Leavenworth.

At 8 P.M. on the dot, two M-60 machine guns—one positioned on the side of the road east of the bridge, the other on the west side of Richardson Creek—opened up with a withering crossfire. "Good, they're on time," he said quietly.

Within seconds, the M-60 on the west side of Richardson Creek jammed. That happened all the time when the machine gun was shooting blanks, whose powder would clog the firing mechanism. Moran looked up to see if the assistant gunner who fed the ammo belt into the M-60 immediately picked up his M-16 rifle and continued firing while the gunner tried to unjam the M-60. The assistant gunner, a guerrilla trainee, did just that. Good, Moran noted. They're following standard tactics.

The M-60 team along the road next shifted its fire to the left so an assault force on its right could quickly crawl forward toward the bridge without being hit by friendly bullets from behind. In less than five minutes since the assault began, Unti's team had overwhelmed the defenders.

As the rest of the team formed a defensive perimeter around the bridge, Unti's demolition crew raced underneath the structure and began tying simulated charges of C-4 explosives to five of the support beams. They linked the charges together with detonating wires. Unti pulled out of his breast pocket a grenade simulator he had rigged with a timing device. As the last of the detonating cord tips was plugged into the simulated C-4, Unti gave the handle of the grenade simulator timer a quarter turn counterclockwise and pulled the detonator pin.

"Fire in the hole!" Unti screamed as the crew scrambled up the embankment away from the bridge. With the extended timer Unti had attached to the grenade, they had less than two minutes before it would detonate to signal that the bridge had been blown.

A flash. Boom! Smoke billowed up from the side of the bridge. Dogs from nearby began barking and howling. Moran couldn't tell if one of them was a German shepherd. He checked his watch and was pleased with the time. The assault and destruction of the bridge had taken ten minutes, well under the standard time window for this type of operation.

As the student team and their guerrillas ran north to their rallying point, Moran strolled under the bridge to check the charges and their wiring. All were tied and connected properly and positioned on the right supports. If the demolition had been real, the middle columns would have split and the bridge would have collapsed in the center from its own weight.

"Excellent," Moran murmured to himself. "Excellent, excellent."

8 A.M., SATURDAY, FEBRUARY 29

Moran and Goode walked down to the students' base camp as Swanson finished his "area assessment" for Pineland. The area assessment was an end-of-tour report Green Berets routinely filed that detailed the condition of a guerrilla force, the status of the enemy in a sector, terrain features that might be different from what the maps showed, any bit of intelligence an A-team had picked up. It would be added to file cabinets full of intelligence folders the Green Berets accumulated on countries.

The two trainers asked the students to gather around them. Moran had only minor quibbles about the exercises the night before. Kelly Albright's truck, which had carried part of the team back to the base camp, had not been "sanitized" properly. Albright had found a U.S. government fountain pen in the back. Even that tiny an item might have compromised him at an enemy road checkpoint.

"There isn't a no-go sitting in this bunch," Moran said proudly, as the students around him really relaxed for the first time. "A few of you guys I had some doubts about. But when you hit the ground in the exercise, those doubts went away. And you guys ended on a great note. The area command meeting went great, the combat target went great. My only regret now is I won't have another team as good as you." Later in the day Kelly Albright would drop by with his grandson's Cub Scout den. "They want to look at some big bad Green Berets. So be respectful and watch your language."

Goode next ran through a day-by-day critique of the exercise.

Day one was a disaster, he began, looking at Swanson. "You came up with no specific plan on how you were going to deal with me," Goode said. "Right from the start, you have to have a plan for building rapport. You were good on tactics. But if I had just wanted tactics I could have had a bunch of Rangers in here. It's the rapport-building skills that you have that are valuable."

The guerrilla maneuvers and raids succeeded because the team members led them. "None of my people were in charge," Goode pointed out. "You never let my guerrillas lead anything." This is a natural tendency among American soldiers—even Green Berets—when they're working with foreign armies. Fight the battle for the foreigners because Americans know they can do it better—like in Vietnam.

Not in today's wars, Moran added. On insurgent or counterinsurgent operations, "you'll be the dick walking in the back," he said. On counterdrug training missions in Latin America the Green Beret adviser isn't even allowed to walk with the raiding teams—a regulation the action-oriented Green Berets resent.

"All in all, you did well," Goode concluded. "For a

bunch of guys just out here, I'd be happy to have any one of you on my team."

Now that the trainers had their students' heads swollen to twice their size, Moran thought it time to bring them back to earth. "You guys have got to remember, this is just the beginning," he warned. Graduates left Robin Sage and the long Q course on top of the world, thinking they knew everything. They didn't.

"If you know what's good for you," Moran lectured, "you'll go to your A-teams with your mouths shut and spend your first months listening. It will take several deployments overseas before you feel really comfortable with your job." It's on a foreign deployment—be it a training mission, a clandestine operation, or even guerrilla combat —where a Green Beret really learns to think on his feet, on his own.

"You guys—particularly all you hardheads—are going to find a world out there where nothing is cut-and-dried," Moran continued. Rules and regulations become murky in unconventional warfare. The spit and polish the U.S. Army prides itself on are irrelevant in the jungle. A Green Beret must live off his wits and his inner sense of what is right or wrong.

"You are the ambassadors," Moran said finally. "You are the first Americans these guerrillas often will see. And they'll think you're something out of the movies."

HELL WEEK

The resort town of Coronado had settled down for the evening. A strand jutting just across the bay from San Diego, California, Coronado was the ultimate in exclusivity. The bay bridge connecting it to San Diego charged a dollar a car to discourage the riffraff. All week, yachts competing in the America's Cup trial races had sailed off Point Loma. Now a cool April breeze blew in from the Pacific. The 70-degree nights made the swimming pools a touch too chilly for a morning dip.

Most of the trendy shops and boutiques along Coronado's Orange Avenue were closed. Late diners finished their pricey meals at the historic Hotel Del Coronado, where the movie *Some Like It Hot* with Tony Curtis and Marylin Monroe had been filmed. Retirees from the high-rise condominiums strolled along the Pacific coast beach. The streets off Orange Avenue with their manicured lawns and million-dollar homes were quiet.

It was Sunday, 9 P.M. Another peaceful night.

KABOOOOOOOM! From the south side of the strand came the deafening noise of artillery fire. Machine guns ratatatated. Sirens blared. Piercing screams. KABOOOOOM! More artillery fire. More machine gun fire. More screams. Dessert forks dropped at the Hotel Del. Phones at the Coronado police department began ringing. Lights in the high rises flipped on. Hotel guests thought World War III had started and the Russians were invading the strand. Coronado's old timers knew better.

Hell Week had begun.

South along the strand, the Naval Special Warfare Center, ringed with barbed wire–topped fences and NO TRESPASSING signs, had erupted into a mock battle zone. It signaled the start of the most physically demanding—and carefully choreographed—week of training in the United States military. Hell Week for the U.S. Navy SEALs.

The large, black asphalt courtyard of the Special Warfare Center, nicknamed the "grinder" because SEAL students spend countless hours there each day exercising, had been transformed into a Hollywood set for a war movie. Over the grinder's entrance hung a plaque that read "The Only Easy Day Was Yesterday"—the SEAL motto. A string of glowing, green chemical sticks lined the yard. At the south end, two barrels ringed with sandbags served as grenade pits, in which a hundred artillery simulators were dropped one after another, detonating with the whistling of an incoming round, then an ear-splitting explosion that sent plumes of smoke high into the dark blue sky.

SEAL trainees in green fatigues and caps—an orange string tied each cap to the collar so the student wouldn't lose it—poured into the grinder, then flopped on their bellies and backs like fish as instructors screamed incomprehensible orders into their ears with bullhorns and sprayed cold water on them from heavy hoses.

From the southern two corners of the grinder, fog machines like the ones used in rock concerts belched out billowing smoke, which filled the courtyard with a layer of ground haze that smelled sickeningly sweet, like a tropical fruit punch. John B. Landry, Jr., a SEAL instructor the students had nicknamed "Wild Country," raced around the grinder screaming at the top of his lungs, firing blanks into the air from an M-60 machine gun on his hip. Wild Country was an apt name. Landry seemed almost psychotic during Hell Week. It was all an act. Soft-spoken and shy off duty, it took the thirty-one-year-old Connecticut native almost an hour before his evening shift began to become the maniacal character he wanted to portray.

Atop a podium at the north end of the grinder stood SEAL instructor Joe Valderrama. Gregarious and outgoing, he had jet black hair and a mustache and thick hairy arms. He intimidated students. But Valderrama, a thirty-five-year-old native of San Pedro, California, was fair. His punishments for poor performance were severe, but he did hand out praise.

"On your belly! On your feet! On your backs!" he barked out commands through a megaphone so fast that the students had no hope of keeping up. Some were standing up. Some were on their bellies. Some were on their backs. Some were trying to do all three things at once.

The instructors pretended to be enraged. They walked up and down the rows of students screaming at them as they flailed wildly to keep up. One instructor had a laugh box attached to his bullhorn that blared out a fiendish chuckle. Other trainers carried M-60 machine guns spewing blanks into the air. More tropical fruit fog poured into the courtyard. The students were completely soaked and already chilled from the spraying.

"You better start listening, people," Valderrama roared. His orders came rapid-fire again. "On your belly! On your feet! On your backs!" The students were slightly more in unison, but not much.

The students were ordered back to their barracks just outside the courtyard. Change clothes. Strip off your fatigue shirts. Leave your undershirts on. Be back in five seconds. "Move!" Valderrama roared.

The students stampeded out of the grinder. The first casualty of Hell Week occurred. A student collided with a cinderblock planter as he raced into his barracks and dislocated his shoulder.

Thirty seconds later—Valderrama had timed it on his watch—the students raced back into the grinder out of breath. "You people better hurry up," Valderrama complained as if the students had been lollygagging on a Sunday walk.

Valderrama pretended to be insulted that the students would show up twenty-five seconds late. Again they were sprayed with the hose, sent back to the barracks for another five-second wardrobe change.

Their time was whittled down several seconds. Not good enough. A hosing down. Machine gun fire. The students did "atomic sit-ups" where their knees and feet came up at the same time their torsos did. Back to the barracks for another change.

Fifteen seconds. Not good enough. Back to the barracks. The instructors ranted. The students dashed into the grinder for a third time. A straggler galloped in without his "swim buddy." From the beginning of their training, students had been drilled never to leave the partner they'd been assigned as a swim buddy. There was a reason: in thirty years, Navy SEALs have never left a fellow SEAL behind in combat—dead, wounded, or alive. A Navy SEAL has never been taken prisoner. Never.

Like a pack of dogs, the instructors set upon the student with the missing swim buddy. "What's the matter with you people!" Valderrama yelled into his bullhorn. He ordered them to jump down to the pushup position. Then back up. "Up. Down. Up. Down."

Hell Week was now barely an hour old. The students, already exhausted from the exercise and chilled by the blasts of cold water, had five more days with no letup in the pace. In those five days they would be allowed to sleep just four hours. *Four hours*. That would average out to just forty-eight minutes of sleep a day, for five days. The rest of the time would be spent in agonizing physical drills like the ones they had experienced for the past hour.

From a second-floor balcony Captain Tom Richards, the center's commander and the top officer in charge of SEAL training, silently watched the beginning of Hell Week. A weight-lifting champion in college—he could still bench press 335 pounds at age forty-four—Richards was beefy and compact with a handlebar mustache. Wounded in Vietnam, he could be intimidating around young staff officers. "What a deal," he muttered to himself in mock humor. "Join the Navy and see the world—through your asshole."

Navy SEALs (the abbreviation for Sea, Air, Land) are the most physically fit and ferocious warriors in the American military—and perhaps any military in the world. They specialize in commando assaults, unconventional warfare, counterinsurgency operations, and dangerous reconnaissance or intelligence collection missions that other units turn down. Their forte are waterborne operations: scuba diving, underwater demolitions, coastal raids, riverine combat. But more and more, SEALs have branched out with other capabilities: parachuting, helicopter assaults, psychological operations, Ranger-style small-unit raids on land, counterterrorism.

Their roots are in the Navy frogmen of World War II, whose swimmers surveyed beaches and cleared obstacles for Allied amphibious landings, then left behind signs like "Welcome Marines" for the leathernecks whom the press would praise as the first in battle. After John Kennedy ordered that the services beef up their counterinsurgency units, the Navy in the early 1960s converted many of these underwater demolition teams into Sea, Air, Land teams, which took on the added missions of guerrilla and counterguerrilla warfare.

In the Vietnam War, the Navy SEALs became one of the few special operations forces that the American high command used to fight fire with fire. They were a guerrilla force as terrifying and cunning to the enemy as the Vietcong were to the Americans. The Vietcong called them the "men with green faces" because it seemed that the SEALs could spring up from the ground at any time to grab people. The description was apt. Many a VC guerrilla was awakened in the middle of the night with a gun barrel jammed down his throat and the camouflage-painted face of a SEAL staring from the other end of the weapon.

SEALs accepted some of the most dangerous missions and engaged in some of the most horrific combat in Vietnam. Their decorations in Vietnam totaled three Congressional Medals of Honor, two Navy Crosses, forty-two Silver Stars, 402 Bronze Stars, and several hundred Purple Hearts for combat wounds. The first SEAL to receive the Congressional Medal of Honor later became a U.S. senator from Nebraska. Lieutenant Junior Grade Bob Kerrey had his right leg blown off leading a SEAL raid against VC sappers on an island in Nha Trang Bay in 1969. Immobilized and bleeding profusely, Kerrey still managed to direct the fire of his SEAL squad in a counterattack that wiped out the Vietcong with no more casualties among his own men.

Kerrey's heroism was not uncommon among SEALs. Most SEAL medals for valor were earned for superhuman effort—not necessarily for falling on a grenade or attacking the enemy single-handedly—but rather for rescuing a wounded partner under withering fire or enduring unbearable pain and hardship to accomplish a mission other military men would run from.

Navy SEAL training has been designed to create that kind of warrior. It takes a Navy man more than a year from the time he applies until he becomes a full-fledged SEAL and pins the Trident on his uniform, a gaudy badge designating that branch, which the SEALs have nicknamed the "Budweiser" because it looks a lot like the beer company logo.

Applicants, all of them already physically fit young sailors and officers in their late teens or early twenties, must first go through a seven-week swimming and exercise course just to get in top physical condition to endure SEAL training. Then they attend BUDS, the Basic Underwater Demolition/SEAL Training at the Warfare Center in Coronado.

The first phase of BUDS lasts nine weeks. During the first five weeks, the physical conditioning of the pre-SEAL training continues at a more grueling pace. Swim distances are lengthened, obstacle courses become more demanding, and students learn the basics of small-boat seamanship. Currently, the sixth week of BUDS training is Hell Week.

Hell Week is a sacred rite of passage to becoming a SEAL warrior. A SEAL remembers his Hell Week like a soldier remembers his first day of combat. No SEAL ever forgets the number for his class that went through Hell Week. (The surest way to spot a SEAL wannabe is to ask him his class number and he doesn't know.)

SEALs believe that a man driven to the limits of his endurance during Hell Week—no women are allowed in the force—can withstand the rigors and horrors of SEAL combat. Those who quit during Hell Week—and, often, more than half do—are the ones Navy SEALs believe would quit in their real-world missions.

The men who become SEALs end up in Olympian shape, barrel-chested and muscular from all the swimming. But Navy surveys have found that the applicants who make it through SEAL training are no different physically from the ones who drop out. The difference is in the mind.

Hell Week teaches a commando to turn off pain and focus on his mission. It's a simple concept, but one exceedingly difficult to actually put into practice. Hell Week teaches a commando that pain ultimately resides in the mind. The mind can make the body do things the body never thought possible, like an athlete who breaks a world record. The mind can make a body endure pain and discomfort it never thought could be endured—not by drugs, but by sheer will power.

In Hell Week, a student learns if he can achieve what some SEALs have called the "porthole effect." The real you is only a passenger in your body. In Hell Week a student—his skin chafed and frozen from hours in icy waters, his muscles aching from constant exercise—retreats mentally to the inner safety of his body, looking out through his eyes at the hostile world around him as if he were peering through a porthole. The mind still functions despite the pain and discomfort outside the porthole. Students who don't learn to retreat within the porthole end up quitting Hell Week because they have allowed the physical discomfort to take over their minds.

The porthole effect explains why in Vietnam, SEALs like Kerrey were able to carry on with their missions though gravely wounded.

Over the years, Hell Week (originally called "Motivation Week") has come under attack from journalists, congressional investigators, and Navy bureaucrats, who have accused it of being mindlessly brutal (which it is not).*

_____
*For all the criticism heaped on it over the years, SEALs say that not a single civilian, congressional investigator, or non-SEAL military per-

The SEALs have made cosmetic changes to appease their critics. A student wanting to quit used to have to ring a brass bell and announce that he wanted to "DOR"—drop on request. Navy and congressional officials complained that the bell was demeaning and forced students to remain in Hell Week when they didn't want to be there. The bell ringing stopped. But the humiliation of quitting Hell Week remains. The helmets bearing the names of students who leave are still lined up in a row under the bell, like gravestones. Students who drop out are ostracized by their classmates who have survived the week.

The Special Warfare Center has also modernized its training so Navy men who would make good SEALs aren't needlessly washed out or driven away from the program. Instructors no longer punch students or physically manhandle them. Trainees injured during Hell Week or any other part of SEAL training aren't automatically kicked out of the program, but rather given time to heal their injuries, then are recycled to the beginning of the course to repeat the instruction with a later class. With advances in sports medicine, SEAL trainers now plan exercises that have reduced the number of broken bones among students.

But the hell remains. There has been no letup in the psychological pressure of Hell Week. Three shifts—a half dozen instructors in each shift—are needed to conduct the

---

son has ever watched the entire Hell Week. No doubt it's because the training is nonstop, twenty-four hours a day, for five days and no civilian or military official has bothered to stay up that long. I was the first outsider ever to be permitted to view every minute of Hell Week from beginning to end. During those five days, I slept a total of sixteen hours. That was four times as many hours of sleep as the SEAL students in Hell Week enjoyed. Captain Richards at first was not eager to have a journalist view the entire Hell Week, when the students would have their emotions peeled to the bone. Richards didn't want them observed like animals in a zoo. But the Navy SEAL command had ordered him to accept me for the entire week, and being a good sailor he complied. He did order the trainers to have me dressed in fatigues and a blue and gold instructor's T-shirt so I would not stick out like a sore thumb. Captain Richards and I became friends by the end of Hell Week.

week-long training. SEAL trainers work the BUDS students so hard, the trainers themselves are exhausted after eight hours.

10 P.M., SUNDAY, APRIL 12, 1992

So far, the instructors hadn't seemed too tuckered out to Navy Lieutenant Tom Rancich.

Rancich lay flat on his stomach in the grinder, his hands laced behind his neck, his feet crossed. Valderrama had just taught them whistle drills. If an instructor blew his whistle once, Rancich and the other BUDS students had to dive to the ground, cover the back of their heads with their hands, keep their mouths open, and cross their legs to simulate the position they would take with an incoming artillery round. Two blows of the whistle, the students would begin crawling to whoever was tooting it. Three blows of the whistle, they would stand.

Instructors had been harassing SEAL students with whistle drills for decades. So conditioned did the students become to the drill in Hell Week, that during the Desert Storm war some SEALs instinctively dove to the ground, crossed their legs, and covered their ears when they heard incoming Iraqi artillery rounds.

Valderrama was now driving Rancich crazy with that damned whistle. Up, down, crawl. Up, down, crawl.

Rancich was the leader of BUDS Class 183 now going through Hell Week. At age twenty-nine, he was the senior officer in the class. In fact, he was almost too old for BUDS. After graduating from Syracuse University with a degree in English, Rancich joined the Navy. He then spent the next seven years trying to join the SEALs.

But Navy personnel detailers had procrastinated or mishandled his assignments the three times he applied for the SEALs. He ended up in every other special operations job in the Navy but the SEALs: explosive ordnance disposal officer, diving officer, naval parachutist, special warfare officer. In a year he could make lieutenant commander and be the executive officer of a special minesweeper. If he flunked out of BUDS, it would probably kill his career in the Navy at this stage. He'd have to get out.

Even if he became a SEAL, he was so senior in the Navy that by the time he finished training he might well be commanding the SEAL officers now harassing him as a student—a fact not lost on them. The SEAL officers weren't particularly eager to train someone who might turn around the next day and lead them on commando missions. The harassment was so pervasive in BUDS, it was hard to see how anyone could be singled out for more harsh treatment. But it seemed like for every mistake the class made, Rancich was blamed and paid for it with extra push-ups.

Yet when the detailer had finally given in and offered him a chance to come to BUDS, Rancich wasn't about to pass it up. His father had been a plumbing and heating contractor, worked like a dog all his life, never enjoying the fruits of his labor. His retirement years had been cut short by cancer. Some of his last words to his son: "This was such a raw deal."

Screw the career paths and ticket punching. Rancich would have been miserable if he hadn't grabbed at the chance to become a SEAL.

Rancich had actually started BUDS with the previous class, 182, but two days before Hell Week was to begin he caught pneumonia. He tried to hide it from the doctors, but couldn't. He pleaded up and down the Warfare Center's chain of command to be allowed to go into Hell Week pumped with antibiotics. The instructors refused. Rancich was rolled back to repeat the first part of BUDS training with the next class, 183. He had now spent ten weeks of swimming and push-ups to get to Hell Week, instead of the normal five.

It was getting old fast. His knees ached from running in the sand. His brown hair was nearly bleached from the sun. His lips were chapped and his eyelids drooped over brown eyes bleary from too many exhausting days and sleepless nights. His hands were swollen and rough from clawing over obstacle courses. His voice gravelly from shouting "Hoo-yahs"—the cheer BUDS students yelled to show an exercise hadn't beaten them down.

But the only way Tom Rancich's helmet would be lined up alongside the other dropouts in the grinder was with his head under it.

It was just as well for the instructors that he hadn't quit. Class 183 had started with 104 officers and enlisted men. By Hell Week almost half had dropped out or been rolled back for physical ailments. In the past, the instructors had found that when an officer quit, several enlisted men would follow. Rancich had become the wise old leader of Class 183. If he dropped out, the instructors could expect scores more to abandon Hell Week with him.

The fifty-eight remaining members of Class 183 who began Hell Week had made a pact: no one quits. Class 183 had secret hand signals to keep up morale during the week. But then all classes pledged to have no quitters in Hell Week, and few kept the promise.

"Evolutions." BUDS revolved around the word. All the training to date had been divided into what the instructors called evolutions. An evolution stood for any exercise on the day's training schedule—a trip through the obstacle course, a four-mile run, a long swim, a paddle through the surf. The class had held a Saturday barbecue for the instructors at the beginning of BUDS to try to butter them up with grilled steaks and cases of Heineken. Maybe it would make the evolutions easier.

It hadn't. Monday morning, the first day of BUDS training, the instructors turned on them. They were like professional actors. Off duty, friendly with students. On duty, maniacs, albeit carefully calibrated ones. The students thought the instructors fancied themselves amateur psychologists, who each day seemed to be able to drive them to their mental and physical limits without breaking them. Indeed, the evolutions were scientifically planned. Push people to their limits, then back off. Push people to their limits, then back off.

Each training day began at 5:30 in the morning and ended late in the afternoon. Rancich and the other men of

Class 183 first found that the only way they could endure the rigorous pace was to keep saying to themselves: "If only we can make it through the week." Then came what the training schedule euphemistically called "surf immersion," an evolution that forced the students to run in and out of the 60-degree ocean water. Never in their wildest dreams could the students have imagined that the Pacific Ocean off California's southern coast would be so cold, and that they could stay so wet, for so long. They called it "surf torture."

Run too slowly into the surf and the instructors kept you in the water longer. Slack off on any evolution to conserve your strength, and the instructors were all over you. Have a bad day with slow times on swims or runs, and you were rolled back to the beginning of BUDS.

When they weren't paddling in the surf with their rubber rafts, they were mounting them atop their heads and lugging them across miles of beach. Brand-new, a rubber raft—officially designated IBS for "Inflatable Boat Small" —weighed about 150 pounds. Old and covered with patches, the black raft with its painted yellow trim felt like it weighed a thousand pounds. The SEALs had nicknamed the IBSs "itty bitty ships."

Hell Week was about to begin and the students already felt physically torn down. They popped 800-milligram Motrin tablets to dull the pain. They would talk about their ailments to fellow students who were hospital corpsmen. But they tried to hide aches and sores from the center's medical staff for fear of being rolled back for an injury.

The SEALs give Hell Week a "confidential" security classification, not because it contains any national security secrets, but because the instructors want to keep the students surprised and off balance during the evolutions. The Hell Week Log, a thick book that includes the schedule of evolutions for the week, is kept under lock and key so students won't steal it.

The security measures weren't entirely effective. The students secretly knew every evolution they would face in

Hell Week. They ran a sophisticated spying operation called "SIN," for student intelligence network. Over the years, SIN had even managed to acquire bootleg copies of the secret Hell Week schedule. To keep the students off guard, the instructors varied from the printed schedule. The spy-versus-spy games ultimately mattered little. Nothing could prepare the students for what would happen to them the next week.

Lieutenant Michael Reilly stood atop the berm overlooking the strand's Pacific Coast. At the shoreline, the fifty-seven students of Class 183 lined up in the push-up position facing the Pacific Ocean. Instructors began shooting flares into the clear black sky, lighting up the shoreline and ocean and casting eerie shadows over the students.

Fifty-seven students instead of fifty-eight. Captain Richards had already grilled Reilly about the one student who had dislocated his shoulder running into the barracks planter. Richards watched the dropout rate like a hawk. The morning after Hell Week was never pleasant for the instructors. That was when Richards hauled out the personnel folders for each student who hadn't made it and gave the training cadre the third degree on why he failed. Injuries made the captain particularly surly.

Richards had to produce at least 300 graduates a year to keep the SEAL ranks replenished. In the old days when the SEAL force was small no one cared how many BUDS students washed out. But the SEALs had grown to some 2,500 men in the past decade. Defense dollars were now scarce. Dropouts meant wasted money and training time. As the officer in charge of the entire Hell Week, Reilly was under constant pressure to hold down on the number of dropouts and rollbacks. At the same time, the SEAL teams, to which he'd soon return, didn't want the center graduating trash. Richards also didn't want to see the standards relaxed. Reilly was getting hit from both sides.

A 1986 Naval Academy graduate, he looked much younger than his twenty-seven years. In the Persian Gulf War, he had won a Bronze Star for leading a SEAL platoon on a secret infiltration mission into Kuwait at the beginning of the war.

Reilly grabbed a bullhorn. "Surf torture," he announced.

From the push-up position, the students were ordered to begin a "bear crawl" to the edge of the water. They lumbered forward, bent over on their hands and feet. At the shoreline they were ordered to halt. They stood up. Arm in arm they marched slowly out to the crashing waves. Flares were shot high into the sky above them. The first cold wave hit them in the chest. It took Rancich's breath away. He and the other students staggered back briefly, but continued to march.

Reilly ordered them to halt and sit. More waves knocked them back. With their arms linked, their legs flew up in the air, like Rockettes doing high kicks as the flares above spotlighted them.

The instructors set their watches.

Cold water.

A man could quickly freeze to death in truly icy water. At least it would be a quick death: no more than fifteen to twenty minutes of painful gasping, then he would become giddy and blank out. The longer, more painful torture was to be immersed for extended periods in water that is simply cold. A man wouldn't necessarily die in cold water—not quickly at least—yet the misery and discomfort of being not just cold, but cold and wet, could almost drive him insane.

The danger from being in just cold water was hypothermia, which occurred as the body's normal temperature of 98.6 degrees dropped. At a body temperature of about 93 degrees, a person experienced amnesia and his speech became slurred. At about 91 degrees he became apathetic and clumsy. At about 89 degrees a stupor set in. Below that the more ominous symptoms occurred. At 87 degrees the person stopped shivering. At that stage his heart could stop beating.

Over the years, the SEALs had carefully calibrated surf torture to immerse students in cold water while still avoiding hypothermia. The guidelines they used: if the water was 59 degrees or less, the immersion lasted only ten minutes; 60 to 65 degrees, the students could stay in the water fifteen minutes; above 65 degrees, twenty minutes.

Tonight the water temperature was 63 degrees. (A comfortable range would be at least in the upper 70s.) The students would stay in the surf for fifteen minutes, then come out for five minutes to allow their bodies to warm up.

They would only be slightly warmer after the five minutes. The night air had dipped to 70 degrees and a brisk wind blew from the ocean, which was sure to chill them. Then it was back into the Pacific.

The instructors weren't being sadistic. When the students who made it through the training finally got to SEAL units they would find themselves swimming for hours in frigid waters off Korea or in liquid ice off Alaska. Hell Week was supposed to teach them at least to cope with the madness of cold water.

Ron Cooper, the enlisted shift chief for the evening instructors, brought the bullhorn to his mouth. He began the psychological torture.

"Why put yourself through this, gentlemen," he purred. Cooper and the other instructors would spend the next five days trying to talk the students into quitting, yet secretly hoping none of them did. The role-playing wore him out. A native of California's Bay Area, Cooper was thirty-two years old, tall and lanky. He sported a handlebar mustache and had spent ten years in the SEALs. But after eight hours of acting like a tyrant in front of BUDS students trying to psyche them out, all he wanted to do when he got home was collapse in bed.

Morale was still high in Class 183. Hell Week had just begun. They had only been in the water five minutes.

"Yeah baby!" one student shouted defiantly.

The others cheered as another foamy white wave again knocked them back.

"Look to your right, look to your left," Valderrama chimed in on his bullhorn. "Some of you won't be here by Saturday."

"You people are going to start thinking about how your last job wasn't all that bad," Cooper taunted them.

The minutes in the cold surf passed by like hours.

One of those in the water thinking about his last job was twenty-four-year-old Brett Chappell. He had played baseball for colleges in Colorado, where he'd been a helluva lot drier than he was now. A collision in the outfield and a separated shoulder had ended his chances of a pro ball career. Now, after a little more than a year in the Navy, he was sitting in a puddle of cold water feeling like he was going to shiver his shoulder off.

Fifteen minutes was up. Cooper ordered the class to stand, turn around, and walk out of the surf. The students began to shake from the cold. Their olive drab uniforms and caps were now dark green and sagged on their bodies from being soaked for so long. Their pants had filled with sand that now trickled down from their legs. Their faces, white as sheets in the dark night still lit up by flares, seemed drained of blood. They looked like ghosts, biting their lips, clenching their fists to control the shivering.

Lieutenant Bruce Thomas, one of four Navy doctors monitoring the class around the clock, walked down the line of students with a flashlight. He stopped before each man and shone the light in his face, searching for the early signs of hypothermia: short-term memory loss, slurred speech, clumsiness, a faraway look.

In front of one student Thomas said, "Bell, boat, and oar.

"Now repeat it to me," Thomas told the student.

"Bell, boat, and oar," the student complied, his teeth chattering between words.

Thomas checked the other students down the line. He then returned to the first student he thought might be hypothermic.

"Repeat the three words I told you," Thomas ordered.

"Bell, boat, and oar," the student replied. Good, no hypothermia.

"How do you feel?" Thomas asked.

"Fine," the student lied.

The five minutes out of the water were up. It seemed to the students like just five seconds.

"The water is only 63 degrees, people," Valderrama complained in his bullhorn, pretending to be peeved. "Nobody should be shivering."

"We can't help it, instructor Valderrama," a student shouted defiantly. "We've only been in it once."

Valderrama ordered them back into the surf. They turned around. Arms locked, they marched again into the crashing waves.

"You're wet and you're cold now," Valderrama said through his bullhorn. "You're going to be wet and cold for one whole week. I want to see some laughing."

The students started laughing.

"Keep it up!"

The students howled like hyenas.

"The more you laugh, the more heat you expend," Valderrama said with a chuckle.

The students went silent.

The waves came crashing over them. Some students groaned as the cold became unbearable.

"When I count to three, I want every trainee to disappear in the water," Valderrama ordered. "Get on your backs!"

The students complied. The cold water now washed over them completely.

"Hang on," Rancich kept whispering to himself over and over again. It will end. It will end. Don't think too far ahead. They're not killing me now. I can endure this. Hang on.

"Now go on your bellies," Valderrama ordered.

They went on their bellies.

Dan Greene's knees had been killing him before he started Hell Week. The pain was now deadened from the numbing cold of the water. It was the only bright spot from sitting in the ocean. The twenty-seven-year-old native of Cincinnati had spent four years in college studying economics, but had dropped out before graduating, bored with schoolwork. His brother, a naval aviator, had told him about the SEALs. The idea of being part of an elite group excited him. But it wasn't too exciting just now. He huddled close to the man sitting next to him, desperate for some calorie of warmth the man might share. There was precious little to go around. Some students began urinating in their pants, hoping the warm liquid would bring temporary relief from the cold.

Fifteen minutes. The students were ordered out of the water. Thomas again checked each one of them.

"Remember, this isn't for everybody, gents," Reilly said politely over his bullhorn. "It's voluntary. This is exactly what every day on a SEAL team is like."

Five minutes. The students, linked together like a bedraggled chorus line, were marched back into the ocean for a third sitting.

"Who wants a cup of hot cocoa?" Reilly asked.

"Fuck no!" several students shouted back as a wave rolled over them.

"I've got hot cocoa and a warm blanket in the ambulance," Reilly continued.

It was too much. A student wiggled his arms free from the two men holding them on each side and stood up in the water. Rancich knew immediately what was happening and lunged to grab him. Other students did the same. Too late, he broke free.

The students screamed at him to come back. But he could take no more. 10:45 P.M. The first dropout.

The instructors had set procedures for dealing with quitters. Enlisted men were first sent to the instructor in charge of the evolution for no more than two minutes of counseling, during which the instructor gently probed to see if the student really wanted to quit. The man was then sent to the senior enlisted chief, who had one minute with him before sending him to the shift officer—in this case Reilly. The purpose for the two quick counseling sessions was to see if the student wasn't just suffering from a temporary mental lapse. The instructors called it a "brain fart." If the student snapped back after talking to three instructors and said he wanted to rejoin his comrades, he was allowed one more chance in Hell Week. If he came out a second time, there was no counseling. He was automatically out.

The student sent to Reilly had no doubt in his mind that he wanted to quit.

"Are you going to wake up tomorrow and regret what you've done?" Reilly asked him gently.

"Yes," the young man said, shaking uncontrollably and nearly in tears. "But I can't take five days of the cold."

"Are you sure this is what you want to do?" Reilly quietly pressed him.

The student stood silently for a moment, his arms dangling at his side, his body wiggling all over.

"Yes," he finally said, his head bowed.

"Go back to the barracks," Reilly quietly told him.

Sometimes, students would return to the water if they thought about it. But Reilly found that they usually came back out in ten minutes. It was sad. But he had seen it before. The 20 percent of the class who were unsure of whether they wanted to be SEALs were the first to drop out. They were good sailors. It was too bad they had to endure this final humiliation to realize they wouldn't be good SEALs. But you couldn't have quitters in combat just because it was cold.

A hemorrhage erupted. A second student broke free from the line in the water. This one was an officer. Not a good sign. A third student quit. Then a fourth. A fifth.

The instructors became worried. The 20 percent who were waverers usually lasted at least until late Monday. Panic set in along the line of students as they frantically tried to hold back the quitters.

11:05 P.M. The class—now numbering fifty-two—was ordered out of the surf. Thomas checked them again with the flashlight. Cooper ordered them to count off. Shaking violently, they could barely mouth the numbers.

11:10 P.M. The students locked arms one more time. Valderrama ordered them to prepare for the surf. The thought of another fifteen minutes in the water was too much for a sixth student, who quit. The rest squeezed together in the line desperate for warmth. Hell Week was only about two hours old and their eyes had begun to have a glazed look. They stared vacantly at the ocean, their skin white, like apparitions lighted up in the black night by the flares still shining overhead.

But Valderrama blew the whistle. Startled for a brief second, the students' eyes darted toward him.

Whistle drills, they remembered.

They dove facedown to the sand, hands behind their heads, feet crossed.

Three whistle blows. They jumped up.

Two whistle blows. They began crawling over the sand toward Valderrama. Thank God. Their muscles were stiff and sore from the exercise at the beginning of Hell Week and from spending so much time in the cold water. But at least the crawling would generate some heat in their bodies.

"Back in the water again," Valderrama sang over his bullhorn to the Gene Autrey tune "Back in the Saddle Again." But it was a feint. Though the surf torture evolution was over, Valderrama had the students prepare for another trip into the water. It was a trick the instructors would use throughout Hell Week: order the students to take another dip into the cold water, then watch to see if just the thought of jumping back in would psyche some into quitting.

Cooper singled out one student he thought might be wavering.

"You want to quit?" he asked.

"Fuck no!" the student shouted back.

The hemorrhage had been stanched for the moment.

The flares overhead died out. Valderrama blew his whistle twice. Crawling on their bellies the students followed him inland like ants behind a pied piper, over the berm and toward the entrance to their barracks. In front of the barracks lay the neat row of rubber rafts. The class was divided into five- to seven-men crews for each raft. The number with each raft changed as students dropped out and the boat crews had to be rearranged.

Valderrama began whistle drills with a vengeance. They would do them until they got the drill right, he bellowed. One blow: face down. Two blows: crawl to me. Three blows: stand up. Two blows: crawl to me. One blow: face down. Three blows. One blow. Two blows. Two blows.

The students were hopelessly mixed up. Landry, aka Wild Country, flew into a rage over their ineptitude. As punishment they were ordered to do push-ups. But push-ups in SEAL training were different. They were ordered to drape their feet over the lip of their rubber raft, which stood at least a foot and a half off the ground. That way all the weight of their bodies would be forced on their arms and shoulders.

Twenty-five push-ups. Then the students yelled, "Hoo-ya, instructor Valderrama!" It was the standard cheer after an exercise. They tried the whistle drill again. But still the students couldn't perform it in unison. (Valderrama made sure they couldn't by blowing the whistle too fast.)

The students were ordered to do boat push-ups. They hoisted the rubber rafts on top of their heads and pushed them into the sky. The rafts still felt relatively light. They were filled with paddles and life vests that added extra weight. But Hell Week was still less than three hours old. "Hoo-yah, instructor Valderrama," they chanted after twenty-five boat push-ups.

It was 11:30 P.M. Whistle drills ceased. It was time for barracks inspection. The first floor of one of the center's barracks had been cleared out and cordoned off for the Hell Week class. Only folding cots and each student's duffel bag packed with dry clothes were allowed in the rooms.

Barracks inspection insured that the first floor was truly sanitized. Because the next five days would be so physically punishing, the instructors didn't want the students taking any unprescribed drugs to get them through. Doctors would be monitoring them throughout the week and dispensing antibiotics and Motrin if needed. The students would also be on heavy, but carefully regulated, diets the next five days. The instructors didn't want them sneaking candy or junk food that might send their bodies into dangerous sugar highs at the wrong time.

Valderrama, Cooper, and Landry set their megaphones on an ear-splitting high whine that reverberated through the barracks. Reilly scoured each room, emptying duffel bags, turning over cots and banging them on the floor to see if pills fell out of their metal supports.

"If you have it, bring it out right now or every man pays," Reilly warned.

Reilly darted into the room where Rancich's boat crew stood at attention.

"Where are you hiding food and Motrin?" he shouted into Rancich's face, which was completely covered with sand. "Any drugs, Lieutenant Rancich?"

"No sir," Rancich shouted back.

Reilly dropped them for fifty push-ups anyway. "Hooyah, Lieutenant Reilly!" the crew shouted when they were done.

The only contraband turned up was one Motrin vial and a box of crackers in another room. Reilly planted the crackers box in Rancich's room and blamed him for hiding the food. It wasn't being cruel. During Hell Week, instructors constantly blamed boat crews and students for things they didn't do, just to test their reaction to unfair stress. After all, combat wasn't fair.

"I knew we would find something, gents," Reilly said proudly. Rancich rolled his eyes.

Valderrama roared into his bullhorn. "It's surf torture again. If you're cold now, you're going to be colder on the next evolution. You're going to freeze your balls off!"

MIDNIGHT, SUNDAY, APRIL 12

Valderrama's surf threat was a ruse, for the moment. The students were to face something even more fearsome.

The night shift.

Valderrama, Cooper, Reilly, Wild Country . . . they were all noise and cold and push-ups, yet at least so far it had been short and bearable.

But the long dark night awaited the students. And the

night belonged to the nocturnal SEALs who now stood outside with their arms folded and a certain look on their faces as the students piled out of the barracks.

The students stood at rigid attention by their boats—or as rigid as they could with the shivers lingering from the surf torture. The night shift stalked them silently—like Darth Vaders, growling out commands occasionally, swarming around boat crews that showed the slightest sign of weakness, snarling at them, then dropping them for push-ups. The menacing glares never leaving their faces.

Lieutenant Jeff Cassidy, the night shift officer, scanned the Hell Week log checking off the students who had so far dropped out. He noted their absence impassively. In fact his expression rarely changed during Hell Week. Tall, muscular, his chest and arms bulging under his tight-fitting blue T-shirt, his fatigue cap cocked low over his brow, Cassidy had a handsome face, with a pointed nose and dark piercing eyes. Cassidy rarely spoke to the students except to order more push-ups or bark out a command. His very presence was intimidating, in keeping with the other princes of darkness.

It was mostly an act. Cassidy was soft-spoken and reserved in private, and sort of brainy. He wanted to be a doctor and specialize in diving medicine for the SEALs. Though it wasn't uncommon for instructors to spend twelve hours a day at the center, BUDS was considered light duty for SEALs compared to operational units where they might be deployed at sea six months out of the year. At the Warfare Center, SEALs had a chance to decompress, reintroduce themselves to their families, and catch up on college courses for advanced degrees. Every night after the regular daytime instruction at BUDS, Cassidy ate dinner with his wife, then studied organic chemistry and physiology for his premed classes before falling asleep.

Ken Taylor, one of the instructors on the night shift, was the first to grab a bullhorn. Short, compactly built with a Greco-Roman face, Taylor announced soothingly from his bullhorn: "Remember, gentlemen, hot cocoa and donuts in the ambulance." Taylor would be night shift's

Tokyo Rose, its Baghdad Betty, the instructor who would try to break the students' morale with soft words and veiled threats and grueling evolutions.

Taylor gave them three minutes to don their life vests, fasten and tie the straps—under the legs or around their waists exactly as the regulations prescribed—and be back at attention. With their hands stiff and still shaking from the cold water, there was no way the students could hitch up the bulky vests in that amount of time. Swim buddies helped each other with the straps. A glowing green chemical light stick was attached to each vest so the students would be spotted in the dark. Still they were late.

Taylor ordered them to hoist the rafts over their heads for boat push-ups.

"I will be your nightmare tonight," Taylor warned. It wasn't far from true.

The students were sent out for another round of surf torture as punishment for not putting on their life vests fast enough. The instructors this time parked their trucks atop the berm and shined the headlights on the black ocean. The students rolled in the cold surf for another fifteen minutes. The water temperature had dipped slightly to 61 degrees. When they emerged, they were given just twenty seconds to don their life vests. They failed again, but this time were ordered back to their barracks. Their next evolution had not really begun. This was just their wake-up call to the night shift.

Before they could begin their next evolution, they faced another painful exercise: walking out of the Special Warfare Center, across Silver Strand Highway, to the Naval Amphibious Base on the other side.

It didn't seem like much. But getting to the amphibious base, where the Navy kept amphibious landing craft and headquartered many of the small-boat units that the SEAL teams used, was a punishing exercise for the students. The base mess hall, where the class would gorge its meals during Hell Week, was a mile-and-a-quarter walk from the student barracks. To the other end of the base, which fronted San Diego Bay, was at least two and a half miles. That is, if the instructors took the direct route—which they didn't always.

And the students wouldn't just walk. They had to carry their 150-pound rubber rafts on top of their heads with all the ropes and their wooden paddles inside.

During BUDS training, the students performed special neck exercises so they could withstand the constant bouncing of the heavy raft on their heads. But it still felt like a jackhammer was pounding the top of their skulls. There was no way the load of the heavy raft could be carried smoothly or distributed equitably among the crew. The front and rear men bore the brunt of the load. The bouncing was less for the center men depending on their position and height and how well inflated the raft was. A tall man would be stuck bearing more of the load than a short man. The students could find some relief by using their hands to push the raft above their heads, but the bulky life vests made that difficult. And even their arms quickly gave in to the heavy load. The raft would come bouncing back down on their heads and the best they could do was hang on to the side straps above to guide it. Instructors had seen students with bald spots on the tops of their heads from the constant bouncing and scraping of the raft.

Walking was made more difficult because the pace could never be coordinated among the half dozen men under the raft. Students tripped and stumbled over the men in front of them or bumped into one another from sudden stops and starts. They looked like crippled crabs walking down the road.

Adding to the awkward movement was the instructors' demand that there be no space between the boats as they moved in line to the amphibious base. The bow of one raft had to nearly touch the stern of the raft in front as the line moved, or the instructors harangued the students and beat on the rafts with wooden paddles.

An accordion effect was inevitable as the line moved. The rafts in the rear spread out as the rafts up front picked up the pace, so students at the end of the line had to run to catch up with students in the front.

The instructors added one more twist. One trainer drove a gray pickup truck with a flashing red light at the front of the convoy to block traffic when the men crossed Silver Strand Highway. Another instructor drove an ambulance truck behind the students. Taylor led the procession out, but walked at such a fast pace the students in the rear had to practically run to keep the accordion from expanding. They cursed and groaned as the rubber rafts bounced on their heads.

"Bow to stern!" the other instructors on foot screamed through their bullhorns. It was the command to tighten up the line. The students in the rear ran and grunted to catch up, the bouncing rafts flattening their soggy caps over their foreheads.

"Bow to stern!" The instructors wouldn't let up. Some trainers shoved the boats forward to force the students to pick up the pace. It would only cause the students to stumble and trip more and lose control of the inflatable boats.

Taylor would make sudden stops. The boats would come crashing together.

Taylor would take off. The line would spread out.

"Bow to stern!" the instructors shouted, shoving the boats along.

Out of breath, their heads and necks aching from the bouncing rafts, the stops and starts, the bullhorns screeching in their ears, the students finally made it to the other end of the amphibious base facing San Diego Bay. The strand encircled the bay. They slid the boats off their heads and let them fall to the concrete below, their tired arms barely able to hold on to the rafts' ropes on the side.

They were standing on a helicopter pad. Behind them was Turner Field. Their next evolution: "Lyon's lope."

Wally Graves, a tall SEAL medic with a Southern accent, stood before the class to explain the rules of Lyon's lope. Graves, a thirty-year-old Floridian, was also taking premed classes, hoping to become a doctor.

Lyon's lope was a boat crew competition. The members of each raft would run the race as a crew. The crew could only be as fast as its slowest member. On Graves's command, the students would grab their rafts, drag them across the street in front of them and down the steep bank into San Diego Bay. They would paddle out about 250 yards beyond a row of pylons in the bay, jump into the water, turn the rafts over to simulate dumping out water, upright the boats, then climb aboard and paddle them to shore. The good news was that San Diego Bay was about 7 degrees warmer than the Pacific Ocean. They wouldn't have to worry about hypothermia. The bad news was that the night air temperature had dropped below 70 degrees. They would be even more chilled once out of the water.

Lyon's lope had the answer for that. Once out of the water, the students had to race back to the helipad and rig their life vests for land travel. The bottom straps laced around the waist, not under the legs. Each boat crew member then had to grab his paddle, run a half mile to the other side of Turner Field, toss the paddle into a waiting pickup truck Lieutenant Cassidy would be driving, then run around the rest of the field back to the bank along San Diego Bay.

At the bank, the students would rerig their orange life vests for the water. Bottom straps under the legs instead of around the waist. Each crew would run into the water and sit down in a line with the men's backs facing the bay. Each man would link up with the person in front of him by wrapping his legs around the person's waist. The crew would then use its hands to paddle thirty yards out into the bay like a caterpillar. Next, the crew would turn left, paddle down the bay 400 yards, then head for shore climbing up a wall of rocks and boulders that covered the steep bank at that point.

The crews would then run up the road 600 yards, meet Taylor in the parked truck where they would grab their paddles, run back to the bay, down the rock bank, into the water, caterpillar-paddle 400 yards back to their original position at the helipad, race up the bank, grab their boats, drag them down the bank into the water, again paddle out 250 yards, turn the raft over, then right it back up, paddle the raft back, and drag it up the bank to the helipad.

It was a bewilderingly complex game. But the students had rehearsed it before Hell Week and understood the directions. Just to add another twist, Graves said that before a boat crew could consider the race finished it had to repeat a ditty to him at the end. Graves whispered it to each boat crew leader. It was obscene. "Eat, fuck, suck. Nibble, gobble, chew. I'm a fucking boat crew, who the fuck are you." But the problem the bleary-eyed students would have with it was that it was a tongue-twister and difficult to remember after the grueling Lyon's lope.

Boat crews were now competing in Hell Week. Graves announced that the crew that won Lyon's lope would not have to undergo the next evolution as a reward. (Or so the crews thought.)

The race began. Students scrambled to strap on their life vests and haul the rafts to the bank. "Stroke, stroke, stroke," they shouted in unison, paddling in the bay. They grunted and groaned, shouting commands and directions, dragging the rafts back up the bank to the helipad, fumbling with their life vests to rehitch the straps, beginning the run around Turner Field.

Dumping off their paddles on the other side of the field became another headache. Cassidy lurched the truck forward every time the crews drew near, making it impossible for them to throw in their paddles. The students had to run wind sprints to catch up. Cassidy repeated this four times, before finally stopping the truck and allowing them to toss their paddles into the back and continue the race.

Cassidy stood outside as the last crew dumped its paddles. As the last man in the crew ran by him, Cassidy grabbed him and cupped his hand over the student's mouth. In the confusion of combat, a SEAL team leader can lose track of his people if he's not careful. Cassidy wanted to see if the boat crew was paying attention. The crew was. Several steps down the road, it stopped, realizing it was missing a man.

More than an hour later, Taylor sat in the truck, which he had now parked along the other road. He waited for the crews to climb up the rocky part of the bank after the caterpillar swim and run the 600 yards to his position to pick up their paddles. Thirty years old, a nine-year SEAL veteran, Taylor was a stickler for detail. Students sloppy on the tiniest items in evolutions were the ones who cost lives on real missions as SEALs, he reasoned.

SEALs were just as obsessive about teamwork. New SEAL members had to fit in. Unit cohesion depended on personalities willing to work together. People who were self-centered couldn't be relied upon to rescue buddies in combat. A SEAL team performed only as well as its weakest member. The tradition must be upheld: a SEAL must never be left behind.

Students rarely quit on the Lyon's lope evolution. They would only if they had to go through it a second time. Taylor would test them on that later. For now he watched and listened, as the boat crews, huffing and puffing, ran up to him to retrieve their paddles. The crews whose members were cranky or argued among themselves were the weak ones, the ones the instructors would pounce on later to weed out of Hell Week. They likely wouldn't make good team members in the SEALs.

Rancich and his boat crew, which included Greene and Chappell, were the first to arrive at Taylor's truck to pick up their paddles. They were silent. They had determined looks on their faces. Rancich even managed a smile.

Taylor was impressed. The front-running boat crews usually didn't fall apart. Rancich wasn't a brain surgeon, he thought. But for an old guy, he had grit. Back in Class 182 Rancich had shaved "182" on the side of his head. He was stubborn as a mule. In Class 183, Rancich wasn't afraid to chew out fellow students who were slacking up on the evolutions. Taylor found that the students respected him for it. So far, he seemed like a fairly good leader who could fire up his men.

Rancich's boat crew won Lyon's lope. Out of breath, their chests heaving, they plopped down beside their raft, scrunched up, and leaned on one another to share what little warmth remained in their bodies.

"Weee're weeeners," Antony Hajiantoniou, another

of Rancich's crew members, said exultantly. He was too out of breath to say much more.

Hajiantoniou was a senior chief petty officer in the Greek Navy. He was the one foreign student in the class. Like the Green Berets, the SEALs also trained foreign students, although the instructors privately preferred not to. SEAL training was arduous enough without a foreigner also having to adapt to another language and an unfamiliar American Navy culture. At twenty-nine, Hajiantoniou had been to practically every special operations school in the Greek Navy. His leg muscles and knees ached. He had trouble now running fast in the sand—running fast at all, for that matter. But he couldn't quit. To do so would mean a plane ticket back to Athens, disgraced.

Three minutes of precious rest would be all the reward Rancich's crew would get for winning Lyon's lope. The leaders of other boat crews straggling in sneaked up to Rancich to ask him to repeat the ditty they had forgotten. He whispered it to them. The last-place crew was forced to do push-ups with their feet hanging from the lip of the raft. Rancich's men got to watch the first round of push-ups. But not the second.

Taylor marched up to the class with a bullhorn. "I was just talking to the instructors and they aren't happy one bit," he said in mock outrage. "Some of you cheated on the turns!"

They hadn't. But the instructors wanted to test the students' reaction to the prospect of repeating Lyon's lope. Taylor ordered the students—Rancich's crew included—to lift the rafts over their heads and begin the agonizing boat push-ups. The students now were more wobbly with the push-ups. Up, down, up, down, up, down.

Taylor finally stopped them. "Well, the only way we're going to get this evolution right is to do it all over again," he announced. "The night is young, gentlemen. We'll do this until we see the sun rise. To the surf!"

The students looked crestfallen. It took a full hour to complete the first Lyon's lope race. Taylor now heard more crews griping among themselves as they scrambled again down the bank.

Shortly before 4 A.M., the instructors cut short the second round of Lyon's lope and called the students in. No one was quitting. Cassidy ordered the class to the center of Turner Field and turned on its sprinkler system, whose water was colder than the bay's.

After five minutes of whistle drills in the sprinklers, still no defections. The boat crews were now as cold as they were after Pacific surf torture. The instructors halted the exercise for the first water break of Hell Week. Graves and the other medics in the shifts would pay close attention to keeping the students hydrated throughout the week. The students waddled up like penguins to the drink dispensers. The insides of their legs already were beginning to chafe from the hours in the sea and the rubbing against wet, sandy uniforms. Each gulped down a cup of water and a cup of Exceed, a Gatorade-like mixture. They would need the liquids for the next evolution: the base tour.

4 A.M., MONDAY, APRIL 13

The base tour was deceptively punishing: just walk around the nearly empty amphibious base in the dead of night with the instructors serving as tour guides. Only the students had to carry the rafts on their heads. And the tour lasted an hour and a half.

Graves, at the front of the line of rubber rafts, moved out. With his lanky legs he had a stride that seemed five feet long. He walked quickly. It was like following a race horse.

Three blocks later, Graves stopped at the first building and announced: "Explosive Ordnance Disposal Mobile Unit Three." That was what the sign read in the front of the building. The students were required to repeat a cheer. Though they didn't tell the students, the instructors expected them to memorize each spot they would visit during the base tour. It would be important for a later evolution.

"Explosive Ordnance Disposal Mobile Unit Three!"

the students shouted as loud as they could. "Hoo-yah, EOD Three!"

The next building on the tour was four blocks away. The line of crabs came to a jerky halt, the rafts banging into one another. Graves ordered them to cheer softly. "Amphibious Construction Battalion One Bachelor's Quarters," he announced. The SEALs had had complaints before from sailors and officers on the base being awakened in the middle of the night with these damned student cheers.

"Hoo-yah, Amphibious Construction Battalion One Bachelor's Quarters," the students said, but only in a dull roar, and then laughed. Thankfully no lights flipped on.

Graves picked up the pace. Next stop: the Naval Amphibious Base Car Wash. Same cheer. Then the headquarters for the Commander Naval Surface Force, Pacific Fleet. Then the Main Gate for the amphibious base.

The students groaned and cursed the pain in their necks and heads. Graves walked like he was racing in the Olympics. The human accordion expanded and contracted as he stopped and started. The instructors constantly shouted, "Bow to stern!" But the students had no hope of keeping the line together. They stumbled and tripped over one another, struggling to keep up the loads. They shifted men under the boats to redistribute the weights. Their faces were laced with pain. Some crews began arguing among themselves. Men grunted and screamed with exhaustion.

At 5:30 A.M., Graves halted the line at the ball park next to Turner Field. The students were no longer cold. They were dripping with sweat. They slid the boats off their heads and dropped them to the ground. Even Graves was perspiring from the brisk walk. The instructors would often get a quitter during the base tour. None this time. The students were doing well, Graves thought. But that would be the last thing he'd tell them at this point. He ordered them to lift the boats back up on their heads.

The students looked at him incredulously, but hoisted up the boats. More boat push-ups. The students huffed and puffed. The instructors held a competition to see how long the crews could keep the boats over their heads with their arms extended up like weight lifters. The crews that dropped the boat on their heads had to continue with boat push-ups.

"This is so shitty!" a student under the boat screamed in desperation.

Rafts slammed on heads before the time was up.

"Sunday night and they're already broken," Graves sighed into his bullhorn, intentionally misstating the time to make the students think—as other instructors would do —that Hell Week was lasting longer than it really was.

The instructors now prowled through the lines to make sure none of those standing at attention drifted off to sleep. When he was tired enough, any soldier or sailor could sleep standing up.

"Bingo! I've got someone over here," Graves shouted, shining a flashlight at a student rubbing his eyes. Graves began whistle drills.

"It only takes one to screw up things for everyone," he lectured again. "Not just on this but in a mission. One guy screws up a mission and everyone suffers." The SEALs by tradition viewed battle casualties not as the inevitable result of war but rather because mistakes were made in combat. They were uncompromising on this point. If a SEAL died or was wounded on an operation, it happened because somebody on the team screwed up.

Six A.M. Dawn broke. The push-ups and whistle drills stopped. The students walked to the mess hall three blocks away for their first meal in nine hours of Hell Week—the rafts, of course, atop their heads as they walked.

The instructors fed the students four times a day: breakfast, lunch, dinner, and a midnight ration called midrats. The meals were heavy, loaded with carbohydrates, proteins, and fats. The students were urged to eat as much as they wanted. Food meant energy. Food compensated for lack of sleep. Food replaced warmth.

The students were ravenous. They heaped the plates on their trays with scrambled eggs, stacks of pancakes, sausage, bacon, grits, cereal. Every free space of every tray was covered with food, the sides lined with mugs of milk and hot coffee and cocoa.

Cassidy sat in the back of the mess hall as the students hurried to the tables to begin wolfing down their meals. He leaned back and took off his cap. Even he was worn out from the night shift. For the first time a thin smile crept across his face as he spied Rancich sitting down to begin his breakfast.

Rancich had too grim a look on his face for this early in Hell Week, Cassidy thought. He was getting that thousand-miles-away stare that Cassidy had seen before in students who were about to break.

Rancich had no intention of doing any such thing. His neck was stiff and his spine ached from the constant banging on his head. Sand filled his ears so he had difficulty hearing. Other students had lost the feeling in their hands from pushing the raft up for so long. But once you get into the week you have a better chance of making it, Rancich reasoned. He was determined not to let the screaming and mind games get to him. He had dismantled enough bombs as an explosive ordnance disposal officer to be conditioned to high stress. He just had to keep his anger in check over the petty harassments the officers were dishing out. Instead of looking at the five days he faced, he tried to make himself concentrate on the four evolutions he had just completed.

The students ate silently. Talking was forbidden, but hardly a word would have been spoken anyway. They were sullen, like men condemned to prison. The excitement of beginning Hell Week had long passed. Now the grim realization had set in that ahead of them was a long nightmare.

Graves, the shift's medic, called out students' names who were on his medication list to receive prescription drugs for assorted aches and infections contracted before Hell Week. He dispensed Motrin tablets to others who complained of sore joints.

At precisely 7 A.M., they all marched out of the mess hall. Breakfast hadn't reinvigorated Rancich. It had only been a break in the physical and mental punishment. The students climbed back into their life vests, slung the rafts back on their heads, and marched briskly out of the amphibious base, across Silver Strand Highway, back to their barracks.

As they passed the fence in front of their barracks, Class 182, the class before them that had already completed Hell Week, marched by in their olive drab T-shirts. Before Hell Week, BUDS students wore white T-shirts under their fatigue blouses. After Hell Week they switched to the green undershirts, a badge of honor designating that they had completed their rite of passage.

"Hoo-yah, Class 183!" the students of 182 roared as they passed by, raising their clenched fists in the air as a show of solidarity.

"Hoo-yah," Class 183 shouted back, but their voices were not as strong. From a second-floor balcony, a half dozen students glanced furtively down at the Hell Week class, their eyes trying to avoid looking directly into any of the faces below. They were the students who had quit the night before. They stood on the balcony only briefly. Their heads hung down. They walked back into their rooms.

7:30 A.M., MONDAY, APRIL 13

Back at the barracks, Cassidy huddled over his Hell Week log with Lieutenant Pete Oswald, the officer in charge of the morning shift. Oswald had been a 255-pound center for the Naval Academy football team. He had since trimmed down to 200 pounds. After four years of dull sea duty aboard a Navy minesweeper, Oswald had jumped at the chance to become a SEAL, where the next four years had been more physical and certainly more exciting than hunting mines.

A thirty-one-year-old native of Bellingham, Washington, Oswald had been a BUDS instructor for only six months. He had a pleasant smile and an easygoing manner. Oswald ran his shift like a benevolent overseer, keeping close watch on the evolutions for safety violations, quietly consulting his shift chiefs on the schedule. Rarely did he shout at the students or harass them.

Oswald didn't have to. The morning shift had the most dreaded combination in all of Hell Week: Jaco, McCarthy, and Instructor Blah.

Mike Jaco was the morning shift's enlisted chief. Thirty-one years old, a native of Columbia, South Carolina, his face was tanned with sharp features. His biceps and shoulders bulged from eleven years in the SEALs. His legs were powerful and muscular. On long marches over beaches and berms Jaco could run students into the ground without breaking a sweat himself.

Mike McCarthy had a gentle face. At thirty-one years old, his hair was prematurely gray. Amid his hulky companions he looked bookish and reserved, almost out of place. But he was the terror of Hell Week. The students had nicknamed him "the antichrist." A senior chief petty officer and the shift's medic, McCarthy was obsessed with perfection. From the minute he began his shift until it ended eight hours later, McCarthy was all over the students, correcting, directing, harassing, intimidating, probing, watching, looking for errors or trainees slacking up. His bullhorn was never turned off. McCarthy didn't miss a trick. BUDS instructors were officially tasked with preparing students to be SEALs and McCarthy didn't waste a second of the training day to carry out those orders. He never let up. When his own Hell Week class was on a rare break, McCarthy would find students from other classes just walking by and run them through push-ups. Even his fellow SEAL instructors marveled that he was the most intense individual they had ever met.

Instructor Blah was the nickname for Ivan Trent, a thirty-three-year-old Hawaiian who had served in the SEALs for fifteen years. Trent was a master of megaphone warfare, a psychological operator who played straight man to the tortures Jaco and McCarthy could dish out.

Soaked and shivering again from the surf, the students ran back to the barracks.

Blah awaited them with his bullhorn. "Class, meet

Chief Softy and Chief Nice Guy," Blah said, making the introductions for Jaco and McCarthy.

Jaco and McCarthy stood motionless with their legs spread, hands on their hips, and scowls on their faces. Eight o'clock. It was time to go to work.

Jaco warmed them up with whistle drills. Up. Down. Crawl. Up. Down. Crawl. Then he ordered the boats hoisted up over their heads and marched them out to the berms.

Along the strand in front of the Special Warfare Center stood a series of thirty-foot-high sand berms that prevented waves from washing away the shore. It was difficult scaling the berms on foot because of the loose sand. Jaco now marched his line of crabs up and down the berms in figure eights to tire out the students for the next evolution. McCarthy walked behind methodically shoveling sand into the rafts to make them heavier on the students' heads. After four times up and down the berms, Jaco stopped.

McCarthy began "sugar cookie drills," a combination of surf torture and whistle drills that left them with sand over every inch of their bodies. It was all preparation—if you could call it that—for the next evolution: the four-mile run up and down the beach. Thankfully, the students wouldn't have to carry their boats. But the marching over the berms had made their legs rubbery, and the sugar cookie drills had turned their wet uniforms into sandpaper that was already scraping their skin raw in spots.

The students had to finish the four miles in fifteen minutes. Actually it didn't matter when they finished. They could break a world record and it wouldn't satisfy the instructors, who intended to build on their frustration after the race by complaining that they were too slow.

McCarthy hopped in the ambulance as the students began their run and followed them. He hooked his bullhorn to the side mirror and attached a laugh box to it to harangue them along the way. McCarthy also used the ride to look at each man carefully to spot injuries.

Condominium dwellers and tourists from the Hotel Del strolled along the beach in their brightly colored bathing suits and straw hats as the green clumps of bedraggled students ran past them. It was an incongruous sight. McCarthy considered the civilians a distraction to Hell Week. But there was no way to get around them, he thought.

He pulled the ambulance up beside one boat crew running together and reached for his bullhorn. The four-mile run was supposed to be a crew competition. The students didn't know it, but the instructors weren't particularly interested in what place each crew finished, only that they did their best and stuck together. McCarthy began testing that cohesion.

"Do your best, don't stay with your team," he taunted over the megaphone to students in the last place crew. Then he spotted the problem.

Lieutenant Junior Grade Tom Walsh, a twenty-six-year-old Chicagoan and the boat crew's leader, was limping as he ran.

"One man's going to slow the whole boat crew down," McCarthy continued taunting. "You can't lead from the rear, Lieutenant Walsh. There's no such thing as a bad team, just a bad leader."

Walsh ignored the taunts. But his face began to give him away. He was in pain as he ran.

Some students pestered the medics with every scratch, McCarthy had found. Others wouldn't come forward unless their legs were falling off. Walsh was the latter type. He had begun to feel a pain in his right leg on the last run the students took before Hell Week began but had kept the ailment hidden from the doctors.

McCarthy again tried to talk the crew into running ahead and abandoning Walsh. The crew refused even though it was falling further behind the pack. Walsh's face was covered with sand and sweat. His eyes squinted. He gritted his teeth. The pain in his leg was becoming unbearable.

McCarthy couldn't tell what the problem was. Walsh gripped his right hip with his hand now, as if trying to hold his leg to its socket. His crew mates formed a cocoon around him as they ran to protect him from McCarthy's taunts.

McCarthy was impressed. Walsh must be popular among his crew members. If they didn't like him they would have dumped him. The crew was performing exactly as it should. McCarthy didn't care if it finished in last place. That's where he had been most of his Hell Week. He wasn't looking for Olympians here. As long as they were motivated the entire crew could stay in last place for the rest of Hell Week, as far as he was concerned.

McCarthy wheeled the ambulance around and drove back to the starting line where Lieutenant Oswald stood.

"Walsh doesn't look good," McCarthy told him. "He may have to be pulled."

"What is it?" Oswald asked.

"I think he has a hip flexor injury," McCarthy said, although there was no way to tell until Walsh stopped and he could examine him. A problem with the hip flexor was muscular, not skeletal. Walsh could conceivably hobble through Hell Week without doing permanent damage to himself, McCarthy said—that is, if the doctors let him and he could stand the pain. All Walsh had to do was continue hobbling along, no matter how slow he became. As long as he showed that drive, the instructors wouldn't pull him— although the instructors would never tell him that.

McCarthy climbed back into the ambulance and drove to the last-place crew. It had made the second loop around the beach in front of the Hotel Del and was heading back for the last leg. The crew continued to encircle Walsh, but miraculously it had closed the gap with the crew in front.

McCarthy attached a laugh box to his megaphone. It chortled fiendishly. Walsh continued to ignore it, gripping his hip with his right hand. The other students around him urged him on.

"They're laughing at you, Mr. Walsh," McCarthy continued.

McCarthy tried to entice the crew's second in command to take over. He refused. McCarthy reattached the laugh box to the bullhorn.

The tourists along the beach stared bewildered at the ambulance blaring laugh tracks and following what to them must have looked like castaways washed up from the sea.

"Forever, forever," McCarthy intoned in the megaphone in a singsong voice. "How long are you going to run? Forever. How long are you going to be in last place? Forever."

"How long are we going to stay fired up?" the students shouted back obstinately and laughed. "Forever!"

"You guys are going to get tired of being in last place," McCarthy answered back, not letting up. "Put it to them, Mr. Walsh. Put it to them. It's going to be a long week, Mr. Walsh. Forever."

Walsh's crew finally made it to the finish line. Jaco ordered the class into the surf. Two crew mates now had to carry Walsh under their arms. The lieutenant said nothing, but his face showed that he was wracked with pain. The cold water numbed his sore leg. But the respite was only brief.

Jaco ordered the class out of the surf. Walsh had to be carried to the shoreline. McCarthy pulled him aside to the ambulance to check his leg, with Oswald looking over his shoulder.

Walsh pleaded with McCarthy to let him rejoin his crew. He could tough it out, Walsh insisted. But McCarthy suspected something was wrong with the bone. Walsh would be sent back to the barracks for the doctor to check him.

Walsh turned away. In a rage, he slammed his fist against the side of the ambulance.

McCarthy was all over him for the outburst. "What are you, mad at me, Mr. Walsh?" McCarthy began chewing him out. "Do you want me to let you be injured for life? Is that what you want?"

Walsh regained his composure. No, that's not what he wanted, he said quietly.

"I'm not lying to you," McCarthy said, looking Walsh directly in the eye. "If the doc says you're okay, you can come back out here."

"Okay," Walsh said resignedly and climbed into the cab of the ambulance.

He would not return. The doctors found that his leg had a stress fracture. He would be on crutches shortly.

1:30 P.M., MONDAY, APRIL 13

The afternoon began at the Warfare Center's UDT/SEAL Obstacle Course, one of the toughest in the U.S. military. Again the students were competing as boat crews—although Rancich grumbled to himself that so far it hadn't paid to be a winner. His crew had just won the "Mad Max" evolution—another complex game that combined rowing, running, and breaching the surf with the rafts—and their reward had been only twenty push-ups because McCarthy had spotted Greene's life vest collar turned the wrong way.

For the obstacle course, each crew would be as fast as its slowest man. But first McCarthy and Jaco sent the students to the surf for another dunking, then a roll down the berms so their uniforms would be sticky and sandy as they climbed over the obstacles. Each obstacle had a strange name, like "Burma Bridge" (a seventy-five-foot-long rope bridge the students had to tightrope over) or the "Weaver" (wooden poles the students had to climb over and under). For an hour, Rancich's crew helped one another over logs and up the ropes. They clawed walls to climb over, balanced on beams where one slip would mean a long drop to the sand and a broken ankle.

Allyson Rancich leaned against her car along Silver Strand Highway, which paralleled the obstacle course about a hundred yards away. She strained to catch a glimpse of her husband. Tom had left her a handwritten schedule of when he might be marching to the mess hall and the times he thought he might be near the highway when the two could see each other—if only from a distance. The instructors strictly forbade any friends or relatives from hanging around the students. A student would face all sorts of punishments for an infraction.

But Rancich didn't know if he could survive Hell

Week without these stolen moments. He had confided his fears and doubts to Allyson before Hell Week.

"You can doubt yourself, but I don't," she had told him. "And if you fail, we'll try something else." Allyson was strong. He admired that quality in her. He had to see her warm smile, that long brown hair.

They had met six years ago in Guam. She was a diving instructor at a local scuba equipment store. He was a dashing young naval officer. They fell in love and married a year later. Allyson had followed him from duty station to duty station, enduring the long separations while he was at sea. She had learned to become independent. They had a fourteen-month-old son named Blair. BUDS training offered little time off, but Rancich was determined to keep the family together. Allyson had locked up their beach house in Virginia Beach and flown with Blair to Coronado, where they rented an apartment off base.

Allyson finally picked Tom out of the crowd of green figures slumped and wrapped up in their orange life vests. She cried. He looked awful. They all reminded her of a chain gang.

Rancich saw her. He managed a weak smile. He hoped she had seen it. He sneaked a short wave. He hoped the instructors hadn't spotted it or they would be all over him. For the first time in Hell Week a warm feeling came over him. He'd make it, he thought.

Allyson wiped her tears and smiled bravely. She didn't want him to see her worried. She lifted her hand slowly and gave him a slight wave. She also hoped the instructors wouldn't notice it.

6:15 P.M., MONDAY, APRIL 13

Captain Richards perched a leg on the tailgate of a truck and looked grimly at the line of students shivering half naked along the beach. They had just come from the mess hall. Two hours before, they had been allowed to change into dry fatigues for the first time. It had felt luxurious. But now they were stripped to their shorts and just the sight of the surf and the thought of returning to the cold water made their bodies again shake all over. Richards had seen that fear take over the bodies of students before. In his own Hell Week class, he saw students drop out after one dinner just at the thought of again having to take their boats and crash them against the cold surf.

The students were now lined up for a hygiene inspection, where doctors examined each one closely for injuries or ailments. The instructors often had dropouts during hygiene inspection. Shivering in their underwear after having eaten a hot meal in dry clothes, with time now to think about what hurt and about the fact that the week had really just begun . . . it all becomes too much for some students and they quit. Valderrama had the students dunk in the surf once in their underwear just in case they had forgotten how cold it was.

Dropouts were on Richard's mind at the moment. He wasn't pleased with the Hell Week roster that had landed on his desk that afternoon, by now with the names of fourteen students who had quit or been dropped for injuries. A second hemorrhage had occurred earlier that afternoon during the evolution called "Log PT" (for physical training). Their teeth chattering, students had lain in shallow seawater doing situps with telephone poles on their stomachs or were forced to push them over their heads from one shoulder to another. One of the latest quitters had been from Rancich's crew. Instead of five crew mates to help him hoist the log he now had four: Hajiantoniou, Greene, Chappell, and Lance Dettman, a nineteen-year-old Southerner from Mandeville, Louisiana, who had joined their crew after another student had earlier dropped out. Secretly, Rancich and some of the other student officers didn't mind the class size being whittled. Despite all the bravado about no dropouts, they were grateful Hell Week was weeding out students they considered mediocre.

Richards made a point of attending all the medical inspections of the students. It was a good opportunity to see the physical toll the training was having on the students and to interrogate the instructors while the doctors were busy with their patients.

He motioned Reilly over.

"Where the fuck did the fourteen go to?" Richards asked in a quiet growl. He hated losing this many people so early in Hell Week.

The cold has driven many of them away, Reilly answered nervously. But the water wasn't really that cold, the lieutenant explained. Hell Week classes in the winter endured much colder surf.

"Well it's obvious, there's a perception out there among the students that it's cold," Richards retorted. "They don't know that it really isn't cold. But they think it is. So lighten up on the water a bit."

Reilly argued against it. Hell Week would lose some of its realism.

Richards wasn't about to overrule his junior officer by ordering that the water time be cut back. Reilly was in charge and Richards believed in delegating authority and not reaching down to grab the reins. But he left Reilly with a not so subtle warning.

"Well," Richards said, somewhat sarcastically. "Use your God-given judgment in deciding how long they should be in the surf."

Richards walked down the line of students to watch the doctors. Reilly got the message. But he would alter the times in water only slightly.

The doctors began their medical exams. SEAL medicine had come a long way since 1970 when Richards was a BUDS trainee going through Hell Week. When he complained to a corpsman about a swollen leg he was chewed out for malingering and ordered back into the line. Within a day, surgeons were cutting open his bloated leg to drain it of fluid because of cellulitis. Cellulitis occurred when the skin and the tissue below it became severely infected from the countless cuts and gashes students incurred during Hell Week. Richards, who then had to be rolled back to another class, wanted to kill the corpsman who had ignored his first complaint. If he had been treated early he might have made it through his first Hell Week. Today the medics and doctors monitored the students closely for adverse symptoms.

There were three types of injuries students commonly incurred during SEAL training. The first and most prevalent was iliotibial band tendinitis, an inflammation of the tendon that connected from the upper leg through the knee to the lower leg. With constant running, the tendon became inflamed from rubbing over the bone. The students called it "BUDS knee." The pain alone often forced them to stop, although rarely did they have to drop out of the program. The best remedy for most cases was three days' rest on crutches.

The next most prevalent sports injury was patellar femoral pain syndrome, an inflammation of the cartilage under the kneecap. Rest and Motrin usually cured it, although some students were dropped from the program if the inflammation became severe.

The final injury was a stress fracture. Students were rolled back—some even dropped—because of it. The constant pounding from running on loose sand could cause a microfracture in the leg that didn't show up on X rays. The student might run with it for four to six weeks, complaining only of a sore limb, before the stress fracture grew to the point that an X ray revealed it. By then the fracture usually became too painful to endure and the limping student had to stop training until it healed.

There were other ailments for which the doctors checked. Lack of sleep combined with massive amounts of exercise caused the students' resistance to drop and be susceptible to lung and skin infections.

Lieutenant Scott Flinn pressed his stethoscope against chests, poked and probed knees, and peppered the students quietly with questions about how they felt. None would admit to any problems. Any weakness, the students feared, would get them dropped from Hell Week. Flinn had to play detective and find out for himself.

Curt Swanson, a twenty-four-year-old Texan with a round, freckled face and sandy blond hair, walked up to

Flinn trying to hide a limp. Cooper, one of the instructors, signaled to the doctor that Swanson had a bad knee.

Flinn began probing for what might be wrong. Swanson tried to evade the questions, but Flinn was persistent.

"I don't want to quit," Swanson finally said, near tears, and pointed to his knee. The stinging pain shot up his leg.

Flinn led him to the back of the truck and ordered him to stretch out on the cold tailgate. He massaged the knee, felt all over the joint. Swanson gritted his teeth from the pain.

Flinn poked at a tender spot. Swanson cried out.

It was iliotibial band tendinitis—BUDS knee. Swanson claimed it became painful the previous night. Flinn knew he was lying. But Swanson couldn't afford three days' rest to heal it. He'd be dropped from Hell Week and forced to start training all over again with the next class.

Flinn agreed to allow Swanson to continue. The injury wouldn't cause permanent damage if he continued to walk. Flinn prescribed 800-milligram tablets of Motrin. He'd probably get a phone call on Swanson later that night, Flinn thought. The pain would be too much. He'd never last.

Swanson gulped down the pills, determined to prove him wrong.

MIDNIGHT, MONDAY, APRIL 13

The students looked like soldiers from Valley Forge as they shuffled stoop-shouldered out of the mess hall. One student's boot heel was about to fall off from the wear and tear of the surf and sand. One shoulder slumped lower than the other on some students because of carrying the boats so long. The night had been spent on a boring but painful four-mile swim and run. Another student dropped out because of pulled quadriceps in his thigh. It was a freak injury. The students now became nervous—like professional football players who live through each season dreading that an injury might kill their careers.

The mess stewards had long gone home for the night, so Reilly and the other instructors had stood behind the serving aisle to dish out the midnight rations the cooks had prepared—a carbohydrate- and protein-high diet of spaghetti, ravioli, pancakes, bacon, grits, and eggs. The students had asked for it all, piled on their plates, trays, anywhere.

The night shift—the princes of darkness—had now taken over, but the students were too exhausted to be afraid of them any longer. Cassidy and the other instructors now had to shout at the top of their lungs clear, crisp commands to the students. They were so dazed, they wouldn't respond to anything else.

Cassidy ordered the students to lift the boats over their heads. But with arms and shoulders so stiff, some of the boats fell down to the parking lot.

The instructors flew into a rage. If the students refused to lift the rafts, they would have to do push-ups on the ground. Their feet hanging off the edges of the rafts, the students began the push-ups. But their backs sagged and they could barely bend their elbows.

The instructors knew the students had no exercise left in them, for the moment. The evolutions were calibrated not to try to break the students too early. Cassidy ordered more painful whistle drills where the students had to crawl on the parking lot. But the next evolution—thankfully, for the students—would not be too physical.

Rather, the students would return to their other nemesis: the cold. With the boats finally on their heads, the students marched to the north side of the amphibious base for "drown proofing."

The students were herded onto a pier where small boats and barges were docked. Their next exercise was one every sailor in the Navy had done many times—staying afloat in the water without a life preserver. The students would be required to jump into the bay—which again was about 5 degrees warmer than the Pacific—take off their boots and socks, then strip down to their underwear. They would tie the calf legs of their pants, zip up the pants, then blow into them to make a flotation device. They would do the same thing with their shirts, tying the sleeves and buttoning them up.

That would be the easy part for the next three hours. The hard part would be coping once more with the cold.

The students were led to two large, floating steel docks lashed by chains and ropes to the pier. They climbed on them. Cassidy hooked up a hose and began spraying them with a thin stream of icy water that stung as it hit their skin. The students began shaking uncontrollably.

Taylor had set up a stand with hot coffee and donuts to lure the quitters. The instructors expected some tonight.

"We hate donuts. They suck!" the students shouted with what little defiance they could muster. Cassidy continued to hose them down.

Taylor ordered them into the bay. The students began treading water.

"At this time every man will go down and get a sample of the bottom and put it on your head," Taylor ordered. The students dove under and did as they were told.

Next they wrestled off their boots and socks, puffing and sputtering water, then slung their boots with the laces tied around their necks. Two doctors were posted on the floating steel dock scanning the students for hypothermia cases.

After they removed their boots, the crews were ordered to climb back onto the gray steel deck, which Cassidy had now sprayed with cold water from the hose, then crawl across it to form rows. A cool breeze now whipped across the cold steel as the students sat facing one another shivering. Rancich checked his boots and discovered one of the socks he had stuffed in them was missing. It must have been lost in the bay. He would now have to last until morning with a bare blistered foot in a wet boot.

The doctors shone flashlights on students' faces looking for hypothermia. They found none so far.

Taylor ordered the students to lie on their backs, then take off their blouses. "Once you've unbuttoned your blouses, hold your hands above your chest," he continued.

The students' arms shook wildly in the air because of the cold.

"Don't think about the steel sucking up the heat from your body," Taylor harangued.

It was all they could think about. Some students shook so badly they began to whimper. Hip flexors became sore from the shivering. The instructors began talking to one another over their bullhorns about snow, Alaska, the Arctic, ice water, ice skating rinks.

The students were ordered to crawl across the steel deck back into the bay. They moved gingerly over the deck's hard ridges and protruding bolts, which were painful to their bruised knees and elbows. In the water the students had to make flotation devices out of their blouses. Those who finished had to climb back onto the steel deck, to be doused with more water from Cassidy's hose. Again they were ordered to hold their arms up while lying on their backs. The arms flailed at the sky.

The drill was repeated; this time students inflated their pants. The steel deck was becoming unbearably cold. They came out of the water in just their undershorts. Their bare backs now lay on the steel. Cassidy gathered the trousers, shirts, and boots lying beside each man and dumped them into one big pile.

"If somebody can get a hard-on now, we'll stop this evolution," an instructor joked over his bullhorn. "You get a woody and we'll secure. But you can't use your hand."

The students laughed between shivers.

It was nearly 2 A.M. "I'll give you five minutes to get your clothes back on," Taylor announced. "If you finish in five minutes, we'll secure this evolution."

The students frantically rooted through the pile of clothes to find what belonged to them. Graves sprayed them with the hose as they dressed. Eight minutes passed. Students were still dressing.

Taylor ordered the evolution repeated. He had planned to do it all along.

The students crawled back into the bay, this time with their clothes on.

"We're going to be here all night, ha, ha, ha!" Taylor said, laughing into his bullhorn. "Asshole. That's my middle name. Remember, if you go back to the barracks now there's still time to order Domino's pizza."

No takers. Rancich was so tired, he had finally managed to tune out the taunting and key his ears only to the directions he needed to hear.

"Okay, everybody out of the water, out of the water," Taylor ordered several minutes later, cutting short the evolution when the threat of another hour in the bay wasn't going to prompt defections. "There are too many people dicking around enjoying the bay."

Some students managed a weak laugh.

"I'm going to give you five minutes to get all your clothes off," Taylor announced. The instructors sprayed them with water as they undressed.

"If we could get one quitter, we'll make the rest of you guys warm," Taylor promised.

No volunteers. The instructors were surprised. They usually got at least one.

"The lucky guy who quits gets to go in the back of the ambulance with a warm blanket," Graves chimed in. "Just one guy. One person can make the rest of the class happy."

Rancich and two other students who had undressed quickly were allowed to put their wet clothes back on as a reward. Some reward.

The students were ordered onto their backs with their shaking hands up into the air. The wind picked up. The instructors buttoned up their nylon jackets with the chill. The students looked like tent revivalists with their arms shaking in the air. Some held their hands to try to stop the jitters.

Shortly before 3 A.M., Taylor announced that he would give the students seven and a half minutes to dress or he'd send them on a swim in the Pacific. The students shook and shivered, but somehow managed to get their clothes back on in time. They hobbled across the deck stiffly as if rigor mortis was setting in. Rancich found he could only walk with his arms extended like Frankenstein.

They went for a swim in the Pacific anyway. After a short base tour with the boats on top of their heads to get the circulation running, the students were marched back into the 61-degree ocean for two more hours of swimming and surf laundry.

The cold finally drove two students practically insane. They quit. The class was down to 41. At 5:25 A.M., Cassidy threatened the class with one more round of surf laundry to see if there would be more dropouts. There were none. The students were allowed to return to the barracks to go to the bathroom and change into dry socks and boots.

Five minutes later they shuffled out of the barracks to line up by their boats. Greene and Chappell walked like penguins, their knees stiff, the inside of their thighs chafed raw. They looked at each other, but "cold" was all they could utter from their mouths. Never in their entire lives had they been so cold for so long. Monday had been the worst night.

Or was it Monday? Chappell had begun to lose track of time. He had been shivering so long, it seemed as if his memory had been shaken out of his brain. Rancich also found himself forgetting things.

Cassidy had them do more push-ups with their feet hanging off the boats. Their backs bowed just to stay off the ground.

"You'll do push-ups until your backs break," Cassidy barked over a megaphone. But the students had no push-ups left in them. They could just move their heads down, faking the exercise.

"This is just the beginning, gentlemen," Graves warned. "We'll be back tomorrow night."

6:30 A.M., TUESDAY, APRIL 14

Ensign Travis Schweizer sat at the mess hall table cradling a mug of steaming hot water. A twenty-three-year-old northern Californian who had joined the Navy after graduating from UCLA, Schweizer now headed the boat crew that Walsh had been forced to leave. The hot mug had now become a ritual. For several minutes he simply stared at it, his rough hands cupped around it. He let its warmth seep into his hands. He was losing feeling in his fingers and thumbs from the boat push-ups. Then slowly he sipped the water to warm his insides.

Sitting at the long tables, the students struggled to keep their eyes open through the meal. They fumbled with their forks because their hands were too stiff to form a fist. They rolled their aching necks to bring some circulation to them. They stared vacantly. If they waited too long between bites, they nodded off. The instructors still did not have to enforce the no-talking rule.

Rancich pulled out the chair beside Schweizer and set down his tray. On it he had chipped beef on toast, scrambled eggs, French toast, two bowls of cereal, toast, grits, a chocolate donut, cocoa, grape juice, and a glass of water. He polished it all off in a half hour.

Everything about Hell Week seemed to be getting worse for Rancich. He was becoming more irritated. The painkillers weren't helping his knees. The raft was feeling heavier. San Diego Bay was colder than the night before. The mile-and-a-quarter walk to the mess hall was now a death march. He wanted to grab that hose the instructors were using to spray him and hang them all with it. The night shift was the meanest of the three.

An instructor shouted, "Feet!"—the command for the students to stand at attention in front of their tables. Rancich bolted up, then grabbed his chocolate donut and stuffed it in his mouth in case they didn't let him finish breakfast.

They did. He went back to eating and thinking of everything else that was miserable about the week. His eyelids drooped. He found himself falling asleep in mid-conversation. He looked over at Schweizer. The ensign was gripping his mug, his chin leaning over it, snoring.

After breakfast, the students lined up outside the mess hall and prepared to hoist their rafts. Class 182 ran by on the way to the mess hall. "Hoo-yah, Class 183," they shouted in tribute. Class 183 stared at them vacantly and said nothing. One student vomited part of his breakfast, then tried to scatter the vomit so the instructors wouldn't see.

A student from another boat crew turned to Rancich and whispered, "I think I'm going to quit."

"Why?" Rancich asked in a whisper himself.

"The cold. I hate it," the student said.

"I hate it, too," Rancich answered.

"No, I really hate it," the student said emphatically.

"I really hate it, too," Rancich said. What does he think—that the water's warmer around me, Rancich thought. "Stick it out until tomorrow."

The student turned and said nothing more.

Jeffrey Burgess, a twenty-six-year-old hospital corpsman from the backwoods of Kentucky, walked stiffly up to Graves.

"It's ma knees, instructor Graves," Burgess complained in a Southern drawl and rolled up his pant leg. He was worried. Had he done permanent damage? Should he see the doctor? Burgess was thin to begin with, but now he looked emaciated.

Graves, the night shift's medic, examined the joint and pressed it with his forefinger. "You're okay, get back in line," he said brusquely. Burgess gave him a sorrowful look and returned to his crew.

"There's no inflammation that I can see," Graves explained later. "He's just got sore knees, nothing more than what the other students have. This happens a lot with students who are hospital corpsmen. They've worked in hospitals and they've seen all these ailments. When they get to BUDS and something flares up they start diagnosing themselves and thinking they have a serious problem. A regular seaman who doesn't know anything about medicine will ignore a symptom until in fact it does become severe." The SEALs have always had a problem with hospital corpsman dropping out because they thought they were more injured than they really were. Graves hoped Burgess didn't do the same. The SEALs were always short of good medics.

Back at the barracks, the fearsome threesome—Jaco, McCarthy, and Instructor Blah—waited for the students.

The instructors intentionally increased the pace when they first began the shift—for two reasons. The instructors from the last shift were usually worn out and had slacked up, so the new shift wanted to wake up the students with a fast round of exercises. Also, shift changes meant breaks in the action that allowed time for the students to think. The more they thought about Hell Week the more they tended to drop out. Better to keep them busy.

Tuesday was the make or break night. Most of the remaining defections occurred Tuesday night. After that, students rarely quit. They achieved that state—the porthole effect by some accounts—when nothing the instructors did to them would force them out. But first there was all day Tuesday to finish. Jaco, McCarthy, and Instructor Blah would not make it easy.

Jaco began with whistle drills—up, down, crawl. He began walking up the concrete steps of the barracks. The students had to follow, crawling on their bellies. Next came thirty minutes of boat push-ups. Jaco then set out for the thirty-foot berms, zigzagging up and down them as McCarthy trailed them with his monotonous "forever, forever" on the bullhorn.

The first evolution of the morning seemed simple. The sky was bright blue with only flecks of clouds. The students must take their rafts beyond the surf breakers, then paddle south down the strand and come ashore at a demolition pit. But getting past the breakers this morning proved difficult. The waves were high, crashing both at the shore and far out at sea because it was high tide.

Jaco ordered the boats out but many didn't make it too far. High waves slammed into the rafts so hard they knocked the students out. They clambered back aboard as the instructors barked out orders from their bullhorns on shore. The officers tried desperately to organize a cadence to the paddling but arms were too weak to battle the mighty surf. Three boats managed to slip past the breakers during a lull, but the others were shoved back to the shore. A huge wave tipped over one boat. The students tried desperately to right it, but gave up and dragged it back to dry land to try once more.

"You guys got one minute to get off my beach," Ivan Trent (Instructor Blah) shouted through his bullhorn, showing no sympathy. The students paddled furiously, but another wave almost swamped their boat and they had to flip it over to empty the water.

There was actually a science to making it past the breakers. SEALs divided the surf's wave into three types. First there were the spilling waves, the gentlest to traverse with just quick rowing.

Then there were the surging waves that could swamp a rubber raft if the SEAL team wasn't careful. The two bowmen at the front of the raft were key to overcoming a surging wave. When the wave rose in front of them, the two bowmen had to dig their paddles into it and attack the wave so the rubber boat could leap over. If the bowmen didn't punch through the wave, it would come crashing down on the boat and fill it up with water.

The plunging waves were the ones that arched over a boat forming a tunnel like what a surfer often faces. Plunging waves came crashing down on the boat. There was no way to punch through them. The only way to handle plungers was to avoid them. That's where the coxswain who steered the raft from the rear was key. The coxswain, usually the boat crew leader, tried to regulate the paddling and guide the boat away so it avoided plungers. Finally, all seven boat crews that were left in Hell Week made it past the breakers and began paddling the mile and a half south to the demolition pit.

The demolition pit was actually a mud pit, oblong, about 100 feet long and twenty-five feet deep, filled regularly by hose with seawater, which was allowed to settle into a dark slime in the hot sun. Around the large hole were dug about a dozen grenade pits into which the instructors threw explosive simulators. Strung across it were two heavy, three-inch-thick ropes anchored by telephone poles on both sides. The entire pit was encircled by a barbed wire–topped fence. Leading up to the pit from the front and back entrances were crisscrossed strands of barbed wire no more than a foot off the dusty ground, which trainees had to crawl under to get to the hole. The grenade pits, ropes, and barbed wire obstacle course would be used for a later evolution. This morning the students were to spend the next three hours rolling in the mud. Jaco and McCarthy began with whistle drills in the two-foot-high pool of water. When the whistle was blown twice, the students had to hold their breath and bury their faces in the muck.

Then began the Sunday picnic races. Students started at one end of the pit and somersaulted through the black water to the other end, climbed up the bank, then bear-crawled or bunny-hopped around the hole—it was torture for their sore knees—in order to begin the next race. Students waiting in line for the race did sit-ups or push-ups. While Oswald watched the spectacle from a ridge on one side of the demolition pit, Jaco, McCarthy, Blah, and the other instructors posted themselves around the hole with bullhorns directing traffic.

It was a circus. No one was idle. Through the black water the students did wheelbarrow races (a man walked on his hands, his nose barely above the water, while the other man held his legs), then Eskimo rolls (a man lay on his back, grabbed the legs of the man over him, who grabbed the bottom man's legs, and they rolled forward, the bottom man gasping for air as he came out of the water).

Noise filled the hole. When the instructors weren't barking out orders they had their megaphones tuned to a high whine. They set each megaphone's whine at different pitches. It all sounded like a hard-rock concert.

Shortly before 10 A.M., the instructors lined the students around the bottom of the pit with their bodies immersed in the water and their heads sprouting out and resting on the muddy bank. They were ordered to close their eyes but not go to sleep. Blah patrolled the rim with a shovelful of dirt to throw on any face that appeared to be sleeping. While the ring of bodies shivered below in the water, two students walked around the top of the pit as town criers, chanting: "All's well with Class 183's mud pit in southern California."

The instructors began quizzing them. A wrong answer sent a student running to the Pacific for a chilly roll in the surf.

"Do you know what the most useless thing in a woman is?" McCarthy asked a student, who seemed mystified as if he had been presented the most difficult question in the world.

"A Marine," McCarthy answered and sent him to the surf.

At 10:35 A.M., the students, still in the muddy water from their chests down, were ordered to roll over onto their stomachs. They were warned again: keep your eyes closed, but no sleeping. Instructor Blah laid four bullhorns down on the upper rim of the pit, and tuned them all to different pitches of the loud, high whine. Civilians would have had to wear earplugs. The students pressed the palms of their hands against their ears. It was like being in the middle of a bunch of air raid sirens. All the instructors left the pit except McCarthy, who continued to occasionally splash them with water and mud.

The students' first sleep period had begun—although they didn't know it.

Though they had been told not to sleep, the instructors wanted to test the students' ability to steal it under the worst conditions. It was a skill SEALs and other special operators must learn. During an international crisis, they might be summoned to anyplace in the world. They could spend fourteen hours in a bumpy, noisy transport plane, then be expected to jump out alert and ready for combat. They might be expected to run nonstop operations for several days. Or, as SEALs, sit neck-deep in water for hours waiting on a jungle ambush. They had to learn to replenish their bodies with sleep when others couldn't.

Some students, still taking the instructors' orders literally, tried to stay awake and elbowed the men next to them not to nod off. Other students snored and shivered at the same time.

Some twitched as if suffering from spasms. Sleep normally is a slow passage over eight hours from drowsiness to NREM (nonrapid eye movement) sleep to REM (rapid eye movement) sleep. Hell Week students jumped immediately into what the instructors called "instant REM" sleep with its jerky eyeball movements, body twitches, and irregular heart rates and breathing.

At 11 A.M., the bullhorns were turned off. "Feel the goodness," McCarthy said to the students, soothingly. They now began what the instructors called their hour of "good sleep"—their legs remained in the water but there was no noise. Blah now shoveled dirt and weeds on the back of each man for insulation.

Outside the demolition pit compound, Oswald spotted a middle-aged man several hundred yards away next to a parked car on Silver Strand Highway. He held up binoculars. The lieutenant walked over to investigate. The man was the father of one of the students in the mud pit. He had driven by to see how his son was doing.

"But I'm not going to tell you who he is," the father said to Oswald. "I don't want you harassing him."

Oswald walked back to the pit chuckling to himself. How could we harass the kid any more than we already are, he wondered.

5:45 P.M., TUESDAY, APRIL 14

The students were crammed into a stuffy, first-floor classroom off the grinder. Walking in, a visitor was almost knocked over by the odor. The room smelled like the bottom of a swamp. The combination of three days of body sweat, open sores, grimy mildewed uniforms soaked in seawater twenty-four hours a day, plus urine from the students to keep warm, was overpowering. Instructors didn't want to get nearer than two feet to any student or they would almost have to gag.

Cooper stood at the front of the class trying to hold his breath because of the smell and gamely gave a safety class on the next evolution. The class was important. The next evolution was the most dangerous in Hell Week: "rock portage."

One of the skills a SEAL must learn was to land his raft anywhere, including jagged rocks off a coast. That type of landing, called rock portage, was the most difficult of all. Crashing waves would whipsaw the rafts into the rocks, breaking bones and even crushing backs if the paddlers weren't careful. At night—the only time the SEALs ever infiltrated onto a coast—the ride in could be terrifying with the almost deafening noise of the waves slamming against the rocks and with the boat crew being hurled at breakneck speeds as if on a roller coaster.

The rocks the SEALs used for training during BUDS and Hell Week were the black behemoths in front of the Hotel Del. The sharp-edged boulders stood thirty feet high and protruded out some seventy-five feet from the shore. They made an ideal wall for rock portage evolutions. The students had to land against the rocks, then, with the waves crashing around them, scale the boulders, lugging their rafts along to the clear pond on the other side fronting the hotel.

The evolution gave the students nightmares. The Del's rocks had already claimed three casualties the month before: a cracked rib, a torn knee ligament, and a sprained ankle. The joke among the students: it used to be one big rock at the Del, but it had been broken up into boulders by successive BUDS classes slamming against it.

The students had to pay attention now to the instructions. The trainers perched on the rocks would signal them with arm waves and flashlights for when they should paddle their rafts to the jagged boulders, at what point they should aim the boats on the final surge in or abort because the landing would be too dangerous. Doctors would be stationed to treat casualties.

The class size was now forty. Another trainee had quit since lunch. Because the students had been standing for so many days, when they lay down to rest for the first time Tuesday morning their body fluids had shifted, causing all their joints to swell, making them even more stiff. Reilly patrolled the room with a cup of ice water to dump on sleepers.

"You people are groggy and you may not be thinking straight," Cooper warned in a loud voice. "It's time to pull your head out of your ass now or you won't be in Hell Week long." It was no idle threat. The instructors expected injuries from rock portage.

As they waited for dusk, the instructors ate up time with a retirement ceremony. Inflatable Boat Small number VI had finally succumbed to pounding surf and being slammed against the ground. A seam on the raft had a gaping hole that could not be patched. Landry gathered the students together to brief them on the complicated protocol (which he had just made up) for IBS-VI's decommissioning.

The students stood at attention in two long lines, their paddles on their shoulders at port arms. Rancich, as the class leader, walked solemnly to the front of the formation to deliver the eulogy.

"Distinguished guests and honored personnel," he began, half smiling, in a voice grown raspy from four days of screaming. "We are here today in celebration of a distinguished career of a fine naval vessel—IBS number six, which never faltered in duty, which saw many personnel through high seas and rough surf. It is a great honor that I retire her today."

Pretending to fire their paddles into the air, the students gave the raft a forty-gun salute.

The five-man boat crew of IBS-VI then tilted the raft up and hoisted it so the bow pointed to the sky, to be received by some sea god. They couldn't remember which.

Everybody sang the national anthem.

Then Hajiantoniou sang the Greek national anthem. The others hummed.

The offering to the sea god didn't make it through the second national anthem. The boat swayed in the air and slammed to the ground because the crew could no longer hold it up.

"About face," Rancich commanded. The students marched into the water for a commemorative round of surf torture.

As decommissioning ceremonies go, IBS-VI's was about as solemn as a rubber boat deserved.

Shortly before 7 P.M., the students clipped glowing green chemical sticks to the sides of their rafts. The instructors wanted to be able to see the rafts as they approached the rocks that night.

"Is there anyone who wants to drop out now?" Cooper asked over his bullhorn before the students shoved their boats into the water.

"Fuck no, instructor Cooper," the students shouted back, in a bit of false bravado.

"Very well," Cooper said, beginning with a sigh. "Be prepared to meet your maker. Hit the surf!"

The armada of rafts with its green lights steamed slowly south the one mile to the rocks at the Hotel Del. The students were in no hurry to get there.

By the time the rafts had reached just north of the rocks, night had fallen. The green lights lingered several hundred yards off the rocks. The instructors signaled the boats to approach, but the green lights moved slowly.

What the instructors didn't know was that SIN, the student intelligence network, had launched its first covert operation of Hell Week. Students from another class had secretly swum out to the boats with sealed plastic bags full of cookies and candy for the Hell Week class. The contraband tasted wonderful, all the more so because it was forbidden and the swimmers had risked getting kicked out of BUDS for sneaking it to them.

The Hell Week class would need all the energy it could draw from the goodies. The tide had risen, adding to the velocity of the waves, some four and five feet tall, which were crashing into the rocks.

Cooper and Valderrama positioned themselves on the rocks to guide in the boats. Cooper, at the front where the rocks jutted into the ocean, signaled with a red flashlight. Valderrama, about forty feet behind him, signaled with a green light. The first two boats moved tentatively toward the rocks. The instructors joked that out in the dark ocean they could see green dots (from the chemical sticks) and white dots—the students' eyes wide open.

The first boat went speeding to Valderrama's position. Each paddler kept one leg hung over the lip of the rubber raft as he stroked furiously to control the vessel in the fast current approaching the rocks. A wave tossed the boat high into the air. The paddlers yanked up their legs as the wave sent the boat crashing against the rocks. A second wave beat the boat against a low rock another time. The man at the front clutching a bowline attached to the raft leaped for the rock, clawing at its slippery surface to climb up.

The trick for the man leaping with the bowline was not to get caught between a rock and the 150-pound raft. A wave could come in and crush him. In real SEAL operations the boats would be loaded down with weapons and equipment and would weigh even more.

While the bowline man scrambled up the rock, the other paddlers stroked with all their might to keep the boat from being driven away by another wave and yanking the man off the rocks back into the ocean.

A wave reared up over them.

"Water, water!" the paddlers screamed and braced for a thunderous crash over them.

The bowline man hung on for dear life. The jerk from the line felt like it almost pulled his arms out of their sockets. He screamed from pain and fear.

The secret now was for the bowline man to wrap the rope around his waist and wedge himself between the boulders.

"Take a bite! Take a bite!" Valderrama shouted over the roar of the surf. It was the command for wedging into the rocks.

The bowline man stood up to try to pull the boat in. Valderrama screamed bloody murder and slammed the young man back into the wedge. A major blunder. Never stand up in the rocks. The next wave would always yank you away and you would be swept away into the ocean with your crew mates.

While the bowline man stayed put in the wedge, the stern line from the back of the boat was tossed to him. The other crewmen hopped into the ocean, steering clear of the rocks, and tossed the paddles onto the boulder near the bowline man. One by one they clawed their way up the rocks, then helped the bowline man pull the boat up to begin lifting it over the jagged edges. Crashing waves battered the raft as the students struggled to lift it over the boulders. Elbows were bruised, shins and knees scraped, ankles turned as the crashing surf knocked them and the boat off balance.

They pulled with all their might to hoist the boat over the ridge of slippery rocks. "Up, heave, up, heave!" they shouted, as they inched the boat across.

At the top they could breathe easier. But the trip down the other side of the ridge to the calm pool off the beach had another discomfort. The west side of the rocks facing the hotel was the dry side. On it sat billions of gnats who now stirred up in a huge dark cloud as the students inched down the ridge carrying the boats. The gnats were everywhere. Out of breath, the students blinked and spat and sputtered. They felt like they were swallowing hundreds of the tiny insects.

By its very nature, rock portage was a chaotic operation: the noise, the confusion, the darkness, the boats battered about helplessly by tons of water. But boats could be landed by a skillful crew that coordinated its strokes and commands.

The coxswain, the person in charge of the crew, had to approach the rocks with a plan to overcome them. He had to keep a clear head in the confusion and be the only one issuing commands. He had to carefully pace the approach in so the boat wouldn't be tossed off course by a wave. The crew had to respond to his orders as a team. There was no room for freelancers or flailing paddlers. Each man had to know the routine for securing the boat and follow orders instantly.

But no sleep, weak arms, and lack of experience took its toll that night. Some boats slammed into the rocks with the crewmen paddling wildly. "Row, row," the crewmen all said at the same time, but the boat moved in no particular direction.

A raft flipped over, tossing out the students, who had to clamber back aboard. They circled and came back for another try. The bowline on another raft broke, sending the raft careening down the rocks and into the nearby shore, where Landry stood ready to scold them.

Another student groping for a lost paddle in the foamy water narrowly missed having his head slammed into a rock when the wave hit. Hell Week could have ended for him in a split second.

Valderrama became really enraged. The students were making stupid mistakes. They seemed to be daydreaming, allowing their boats to be hurled by the waves, forgetting all their training on how to negotiate the rocks. They acted like they were doing this the first time.

"I'm going to beat you in the fucking head until you get some common sense!" he raged at one hapless crew, trying to shake them out of their daze.

He screamed at another officer, overcome by the chaos, who froze with indecision and did nothing as the waves battered the crew. "Lieutenant, do something!" he yelled at the top of his lungs. Don't hesitate. Start giving an order. The order might not be the best one but at least the crew would be struggling in the right direction.

A bowline man didn't have a good bite in the rocks. "Get your butt down!" Valderrama screamed.

Too late. The next wave flung the student across a sharp boulder, into the ocean, scraping his arms and legs. Valderrama reached into the ocean, grabbed the man by the collar of his life vest and yanked him back onto the rock, shouting into his ear to get a better bite. But it was like holding on to the line of a bolting horse. The next waves came before the bowline man had a chance to wrap the rope around his waist.

"Fuck! Fuck!" the student screamed in desperation. He couldn't hold on to the rope. His boat washed away.

All the boats were sent out for a second try at the rocks. "Make it work, guys, make it work," Valderrama shouted as the boats circled to approach the rocks one more time. Some boats flipped, sending students into the swirling and crashing surf. But others made it to the boulders and over the ridge.

Rancich's boat, on its second trip, was hurled into the rocks. Pain and fear were wiped out of his mind at the moment. All he could think of was survival. A second wave crashed over them in an explosion of noise and white foam. Chappell and Greene were knocked out of the raft.

"Do something, Lieutenant!" Valderrama yelled at Rancich as he had at most of the other officers. Dettman crawled to a rock, quickly wrapped the rope around his waist, and braced himself for the next wave. He held firm. The stern line came. He wrapped it around his waist. The paddles were next out. The raft was hoisted. The crew climbed up the first couple of rocks.

"Get this boat out of here," Valderrama said tersely. That was all the praise Rancich's crew would get for doing the job correctly. Valderrama was still frustrated with the overall performance. These were not rough seas, he explained later. They would face larger waves as SEALs. But too many of the boat crews seemed paralyzed with fear and lost their sense of the basics. Rock portage had neverthe-less taken its toll: two more students forced to drop out because of injuries when waves slammed them against the rocks. The class was now down to 38.

A crowd of curious spectators from the Hotel Del had accumulated at the rocks to watch all the commotion at sea. Hidden in it was Allyson Rancich with Blair straddled on her hip. As the boats came crashing into the rocks, Allyson found herself explaining the evolution to the tour-ists around her, remembering what Rancich had told her about it, and telling them proudly that her husband was in one of those rafts.

When Rancich came up with the crew's boat after the

first round, Allyson sneaked up to the front of the crowd. She smiled, but said nothing, worried that the instructors nearby would spot her.

Rancich saw her. "I'm fine," was all he could whisper before the instructors ordered his boat back out for the second round. It was a lie.

Now as he dragged the boat across the lagoon after the second round, his whisper was more honest when the instructors weren't looking. "This sucks," he said.

"Yeah, it does," was all Allyson could think to say.

An elderly couple from the Hotel Del, with whom she had been talking in the crowd before, now came up to her. The husband pressed two twenty-dollar bills into the palm of her hand.

"We want you to take your husband out to dinner when they finish," the husband told her and they left.

Allyson thanked them and wiped away her tears.

MIDNIGHT, TUESDAY, APRIL 14

Hell Week was becoming weird for the students. Rancich's eyes were playing tricks on him. Shiny objects suddenly had intricate designs like crystals.

Greene found himself blanking out mentally while walking under the boat. He was now sitting at the dining table in the mess hall with his midnight rations and he didn't know how he got there.

Schweizer was losing his toenails. His feet were becoming so swollen in his boots, the skin was pushing the nails off.

Chappell felt like he was in a dream. He couldn't rid himself of the chills, even out of water. He hadn't slept in the mud pit because of the shivers.

The cold was driving them all batty. Rancich now began shivering just at the thought of going into the ocean. He drank a glass of cold milk and it caused him to shake. Schweizer had shivered so much he felt like the joints in his hip were coming apart.

The instructors ignored the no talking rule and some

of the students began whispering to one another. Their conversations became almost childlike.

"Why do we piss them off at the beginning of each shift?" Schweizer asked as if posing an unsolvable riddle. "Moody sons of bitches aren't they?"

"How do they stay married?" Rancich wondered out loud.

At mealtimes, fatigue was beginning to hit Schweizer like a ton of bricks. He fell asleep in the middle of conversations.

Landry shoved a copy of *The Military Press* newspaper under Schweizer's nose and ordered him to read from an article on Joint STARS, a sophisticated new military airborne surveillance plane.

"Joint STARS was a surveillance concept still being tested when Iraqi armored columns overran tiny Kuwait in August 1990," Schweizer droned on, barely able to focus his eyes on the newsprint. "Joint STARS stands for the Joint Surveillance and Target Attack Radar System, which can detect and identify an object the size of an automobile. . . ."

Schweizer was putting the rest of the class—and even himself—to sleep with the dull article.

Landry cured that. He ordered Hajiantoniou to stand up and pick up where Schweizer had left off. If a student did not pick up the story at the right place, Landry threatened to haul them all out into the parking lot for boat push-ups. Now they all had to stay awake and pay attention.

"De Joint STARS system . . . haaaad been . . . eeenstalled . . . een toooo aircraft . . . at de start of . . . de war in Aoooogust 1990," Hajiantoniou began in broken English.

"Stop!" Landry interrupted and ordered another student to stand and pick up the story.

The student got through two more sentences.

"Stop!" Landry shouted. "Mr. Rancich."

Rancich laid down his fork. "I knew he was going to

call on me," he grumbled under his breath, and read several more sentences.

"Stop!" Landry ordered. "Burgess, get up there."

Burgess decided to have some fun. With his best hillbilly accent, he began to read the article like a tent preacher.

"The first twooooo Joint STARS underwent exhaustive testin' in the United States, brothers and sisters—exhaustive testin'," Burgess said, shaking the paper in the air like a Bible. The students perked up. The instructors had wary smiles.

"Then they were sent to Euuuuurope—yes Euuuuurope—in the Autumn of 1990 to test their ground surveillance capabilities."

"Say it, brother!" a student shouted.

The instructors ordered them all to sing "Amazing Grace."

Burgess continued with a gospel choir now backing him up.

"And Lord, when the emergency call came to shift to Saudi Araaaaaabia, the two test aircraft did so without a hitch."

"Hallelujah!" another student wailed.

"The Joint STARS system employs a multilode sidelooking radar system, brothers and sisters."

"Lord be praised!"

"It has a range of 155 miles."

"He's the way!"

"And it uses a synthetic aperture radar."

"And for only $10,000, you can see Jesus with it!"

The students roared with laughter. The instructors applauded. Burgess sat down, grinning from ear to ear. For a brief moment he didn't feel the pain in his knees.

The next evolution was "around the world." Actually it was a boat paddle around the strand. It only seemed like they were paddling around the world. Shortly before 1 A.M., Wednesday, the students launched their boats from Foxtrot Beach at the Naval Amphibious Base and paddled northwest up the bay, under the tall bridge connecting San

Diego to Coronado. Instructors posted themselves at checkpoints along the way to make sure the boat crews didn't cheat. The armada continued northwest around the aircraft carrier piers and around the North Island Naval Air Station. The water was peaceful in San Diego Bay.

But full of demons.

Sailors at sea on lonely night watches sometimes see them. Apparitions. Mirages. The sea at night can play tricks with sleepy eyes. Hell Week students, by midweek, would hallucinate even more in the ocean. Some saw Indian totem poles sticking up out of the water. Others saw automobiles on top of rubber boats.

Class 183's strange visions came in the early-morning hours of Wednesday as they paddled along San Diego Bay. Sky Cervantes, a twenty-one-year-old student from St. Louis, saw a beautiful girl walking down a staircase into the baywater. He sat back in his raft and rubbed his eyes. He felt like his own body had become a body of water with waves pouring out of his arms. Other students heard voices talking to them as they paddled. Some fell asleep as they paddled. Others screamed, terrified that dolphins were following them.

Rancich's crew began seeing parking signs, stoplights, and picket fences around garages whose doors rolled up and down. The crew swerved the raft to one side to avoid hitting what they thought was a YIELD sign in the water.

1:15 P.M., WEDNESDAY, APRIL 15

The students' second sleep period began. Jaco had mercifully slowed the pace on the march to and from the mess hall. The instructors had intentionally ramped down the activity in the evolutions. Physical punishment did no good at this point. Few students dropped out after Wednesday. Delirious with exhaustion, their minds were on autopilot. Nothing the instructors did would now force them to quit. The psychological harassment would continue, but from Wednesday on, the evolutions simply kept the students moving, cold, and awake.

After more than three days of Hell Week, Rancich's

crew—although it was too exhausted to realize it at the time—was operating truly as a team. Bickering and quarreling had stopped. They had begun to think like SEALs.

They would now be given one hour and forty-five minutes of uninterrupted and noiseless sleep. Rancich and his crew mates sat on their cots in the first-floor barracks room, unlacing their boots and unbuttoning their blouses in slow motion. They said nothing to one another. Rancich stared at his hands. They were peeling. The skin on his feet was shriveled and white.

Kevin Connolly, a nineteen-year-old from Madison, Wisconsin, who was now part of Rancich's boat crew, leaned back on his cot and was asleep within one second.

Rancich was asleep in the next second. Chappell, Haji-antoniou, and Dettman quickly followed. But Greene sat at the end of his cot, staring vacantly at the walls. He lay back and gazed at the ceiling, then propped a leg up on a ledge. A minute later his eyes closed but the leg remained perched on the ledge.

Within five minutes, Connolly began to twitch in his sleep. Instant REM. Chappell's legs twitched and his breath became heavy and quick as if his body was racing to catch up with the unbearable fatigue. Ten minutes later, Hajiantoniou bolted up from his cot, his eyes wide open. He lay back and returned to his deep slumber. Students from other classes tiptoed in to check on the crew. One gently moved Greene's leg from the ledge and laid it on the cot.

The hour and forty-five minutes raced by. At 3 p.m., Oswald and the five other instructors of the day shift filled Super Soaker 50 squirt guns full of cold water. It was wakeup time.

With sirens blaring and bullhorns whining, they barged into the rooms of the sleeping students and began squirting them. The instructors had to watch themselves at this wakeup. Hell Week students would often jump out of bed completely disoriented and start swinging their fists.

Waking up from the hour-and-forty-five-minute nap was hideous for Rancich. He felt like he had only been asleep five minutes. His body desperately wanted to remain lying flat and sleeping in the cot. Now it shook—repulsed by the stinging shots of cold from the water guns. It was like going from zero to sixty miles per hour in a split second. One moment he was motionless in a deep trance. The next moment: instant activity.

Before he could clear his head he found himself in the front of the barracks with bullhorns barking into his ears and Jaco hosing him down with more cold water.

"What's the muster, Mr. Rancich, what's the muster!" McCarthy screamed into his ear. The muster was the number of students presently in the class.

Rancich didn't know what universe he was in, much less how many trainees were left in Hell Week.

"Thirty-nine," he blurted out. He was over, by one. The boat crews scrambled, bumping into one another to assemble a formation for an accurate count. Thirty-eight, Rancich finally told the trainers.

Too late. They were ordered into the surf for not keeping track of their men.

For the next hour, Trent (Instructor Blah) put the students through light exercises—or at least what the instructors considered light. Jumping jacks, wind sprints, chin-ups, crawls across the beach, wheelbarrow races. The winners could sit out the next race.

Blah had an ingenious push-up. The students lined up head to foot in the push-up position. Each student then draped his ankles over the shoulders of the student behind him to form one long push-up chain held up only by the students' arms. The chain managed only two push-ups before collapsing on the sand.

After dinner that evening, the students lined up in front of the exercise room on the first floor of the barracks. They were completely naked, this time for their second hygiene inspection. Captain Richards stood in a corner to watch the exams. There would be more ailments and hidden injuries to ferret out this time. The doctors had no pain meter they could attach to the students to determine their true condition. The students were determined not to reveal any problems that might force them to quit. Richards had seen it before among students at this stage of Hell Week. He had seen it before among SEALs on grueling missions. Normally the body served the brain and the brain reacted when the body hurt. But after days of physical stress the brain got to the point where it no longer cared about the condition of the body. As long as the brain could continue to function properly, it became separated from the body.

Concerned about the body, however, the doctors grilled the students more closely.

Burgess now would not admit that his swollen knees hurt. He could smell the finish line. Dr. Thomas suspected it was bursitis and prescribed antibiotics.

Thomas had Connolly, who was already on antibiotics, repeat the letter E three times—a test for pneumonia. When the lungs filled with fluids because of the pneumonia, the E sounded more like a bleated A.

Simple gravity was causing students' legs and feet to swell. In the normal course of a day, the human body reclined for some eight hours during sleep, which allowed for the even distribution of blood and fluids from head to toe. But because the students were constantly standing up and moving during Hell Week, fluids settled to the legs and feet. It was called dependent edema.

Dettman's body was covered in a rash, but he lied and claimed it wasn't bothering him.

Another student tried to sneak by with a limp. Cooper stopped him and ordered him back for a recheck by the doctor.

Rancich had sores all over his body. His feet were white. He didn't mention sore knees. They let him pass.

Schweizer was already on penicillin for strep throat. The problem now was with his right leg. The pain was excruciating from his knee to his ankle. He had a raging case of tendinitis in his ankle. For the moment, it didn't appear that the inflammation would cause permanent damage if he continued, Thomas advised. But whether Schweizer could last the two remaining days of Hell Week depended on how much pain he could withstand. His teeth clenched, he tried to lace his boot up tightly over the swollen ankle.

MIDNIGHT, WEDNESDAY, APRIL 15

The base tour the students took during the early hours of Monday was now back to haunt them. Although they weren't told then, they were expected to memorize the buildings on Graves's tour. On the next evolution, Graves expected them to demonstrate what they had remembered. It was called the "treasure hunt."

The crabs fanned out across the Naval Amphibious Base. Taylor was assigned to Rancich's boat crew. Rancich walked up to the instructor, who was sitting in the cab of his truck.

"Here's your clue," Taylor said. "Babe."

"Babe?" Rancich asked quizzically.

"Babe," Taylor repeated.

Rancich had one minute to confer with crew mates and decide what building or landmark on the base the clue matched. The students then had to lift the boat over their heads and shuffle off to that spot. If they picked the wrong place, they received another clue, but it meant more walking with the boat to find the spot. The students had a set number of points they had to reach in the treasure hunt. More mistakes meant more walking.

Rancich huddled with his crew.

"Babe?" Chappell asked, mystified.

"Babe," Rancich repeated.

"Is this serious?" Greene asked, becoming somewhat irritated.

"That's the clue," Rancich said, shrugging his shoulders.

They decided that "Babe" was a movie at the base theater, a good guess since a movie had just come out on the life of the famous Yankee ball player, Babe Ruth.

Rancich walked back to Taylor. "We think it's the base theater," he said, tentatively.

"Go ahead, have a good time," Taylor said with a smile. "I'll meet you there." He drove off in the truck.

The crew shuffled to the theater five blocks away. Without the instructors following them, they were free to talk as they huffed and puffed with the boat bouncing on their heads. They talked about the only thing really on their minds. The aches and pain.

Rancich was becoming irritated with birds that he heard chirping in the early morning. The noise reminded him of whistle drills.

"What's all this talk that I'm not supposed to feel anything by Wednesday," Dettman griped. "I feel everything and it hurts. This boat is about to pound my neck out of alignment."

They arrived at the theater and looked up at the marquee. No "Babe."

Taylor pulled up in his truck.

Rancich walked up to him. "That wasn't it," Rancich said.

"Here's your second clue," Taylor said. It was: "That was one strike. You get two more and you're out."

Rancich conferred with his colleagues.

"Turner Field's baseball diamond," he told Taylor.

"Okay, I'll see you there," Taylor said and drove off.

The crew shuffled off to the field, their feet dragging on the pavement. They began grumbling again.

The water and the whine of the bullhorns were driving them bananas.

"This is just totally fucking miscrable," Chappell said, acting amazed at what he had endured so far. "I'm never ever taking anything for granted again—like warm showers and dry socks."

"What pisses me off is that pap about being a winner," Rancich groused. "Where's the reward?"

"If they ever made me go through Hell Week again," Dettman promised, "I'd shave my nuts." Maybe that wouldn't make his crotch so raw.

The baseball field was correct. The crew's next clue: "The venue for Navy Olympians."

That was easy. The track field nearby, Rancich answered.

Taylor drove away. Over the walkie-talkie in his truck came a bulletin on SIN. Two students from another class were nabbed trying to slip candy to the boats wandering about the base on the treasure hunt. Taylor shook his head and laughed just imagining what the instructors would do with the two POWs.

The students never fooled the instructors, Taylor thought. Before every meal, the trainers ran their hands under the tables at the mess hall to feel for Motrin bottles other students had taped underneath for the Hell Week class. The instructors knew every trick in the book.

Well, not every trick.

Three stops later, Taylor gave the crew its next clue: "Smile." Rancich conferred with the crew.

"We're going to the dental clinic," he told Taylor.

"Okay, I'll see you there," Taylor said and drove off.

Along the way, Rancich made a detour to the base's bachelor officers' quarters. Rancich had lived in the BOQ before Allyson joined him in Coronado. He still kept a room there. They had arranged before Hell Week that she and Blair would sleep in the room Wednesday on the chance that he might be able to sneak in himself during the treasure hunt.

As the officers of the BOQ slept soundly, six BUDS students with a rubber raft on their heads tiptoed into the courtyard of the BOQ. The crew stashed the raft behind a row of bushes and crouched near picnic tables. Rancich bounded up the stairs to his room on the third floor.

It was after 1 A.M. when Allyson heard the gentle tapping on the front door. She opened it and Rancich rushed in.

Allyson had gone to a delicatessen in Coronado and bought stacks of cold cuts for sandwiches. She had also baked a bagful of chocolate chip cookies and packed candy in clear plastic bags, one for each crewman. They didn't have time to eat the sandwiches and everyone was getting caught with candy, Rancich said.

"Just give me the cookies," he said. "I've got to get out of here."

He rushed out the door. Allyson thought he smelled like a fish that had been sitting out in the sun for a week.

Down in the courtyard, Rancich distributed the chocolate chip cookies to his men, four of whom were sprawled on the picnic benches snoring when he returned.

They groaned with pleasure as they savored the cookies. They were sinfully delicious. They sat around the picnic table stuffing one cookie after another into their mouths.

But now the crew had precious minutes to make up. They slung the boat back on top of their heads and scurried out of the courtyard taking a shortcut to the dental clinic.

Taylor waited impatiently in his truck, which was parked in front of the clinic. The crew ambled up with its boat, trying to act innocent even though what was supposed to have been a five-minute walk had lasted twenty minutes.

"What the hell took you so long?" he asked suspiciously.

"Mr. Waller had a rock in his boot and we had to stop to let him empty it," Rancich said with a straight face.

Taylor shot me a look that asked, Are you going to back up this cock-and-bull story?

I gave him a sheepish smile and nodded my head.

Taylor decided to let it pass.

Back at the grinder, the instructors meted out punishment to the two students from SIN who had been nabbed smuggling candy to the Hell Week class. They were ordered to eat the contraband they planned to distribute, gulp down Diet Cokes, then run wind sprints across the courtyard until they threw it all up.

7:30 A.M., THURSDAY, APRIL 16

Travis Schweizer pulled his right pant leg up and untied the laces to his soggy boot. He couldn't bring himself to pull the boot off his swollen ankle. The only time he did not think about it was when the boat was bouncing on his head, which was just as painful. He leaned back in the sand and covered his eyes while another student gingerly took off the boot. His leg up to his knee was bloated—a combination of the fluids that had collected and the tendinitis.

McCarthy, the morning shift's medic, turned the ankle sideways to inspect. Schweizer now could not move it up and down.

"Keep your boot on laced up all the time," was all the advice McCarthy could give him. "It will help you with support."

Oswald looked on, worried. He did not want to lose Schweizer. He was a good officer. From the grit he'd shown in Hell Week so far, the instructors knew he would be a good SEAL.

A student helped Schweizer on with his boot. Dragging his leg like a useless limb, he walked back to his boat crew lined up again at the obstacle course.

Though the students could sense that the physical pace of Hell Week had slackened, the instructors wanted to maintain the intensity of the psychological pressure. The instructors also weren't adverse to injecting spurts of physical pressure into the remaining schedule—just to remind the students how bad Hell Week could be. The next evolution would be one example.

Three times the students had had to climb and crawl over the obstacle course. Now they had to lug their rubber boats over and under the barriers.

"This will be your most severe test," Instructor Blah announced with a devilish smile. "You have a week to go in Hell Week," he lied. More mind games. "The next evolution decides who's not a team player. You've had a cakewalk the last four days." Laughter rippled through the student ranks. They had had their last hour-and-a-half sleep period earlier that morning. It would be all they would get for the rest of Hell Week.

"This is a bigger challenge," Blah continued. "This is teamwork, gents. T-E-A-M."

Rancich's team had the benefit of watching the three crews in front of them struggle and in some cases fail to get the heavy rafts over the obstacles. Just to make it interesting, McCarthy had shoveled sand into the boats to weight them more.

The first obstacle would be the toughest: a half dozen telephone pole stumps, spaced about four feet apart in a staggered line, which the students must walk across to reach a solid wooden wall twelve feet high. Rancich devised a plan in his head.

The crew shuffled to the wooden wall, turned the boat around, backed it up so it stood stern to bow parallel to the wall. Using the straps, handles, and ridges of the raft as steps, Dettman deftly climbed up the boat to the ledge of the wall. He flipped the bowline over and jumped down to the other side. Connolly followed him up the raft and straddled the wall.

Dettman wrapped the line around his waist and started walking away from the wall. Connolly pulled the bow from his position on top of the wall. Rancich, Chappell, Greene, and Hajiantoniou pushed the stern up from the other end. Slowly they hefted the boat up so it teetered like a seesaw on top of the wall. Greene and Rancich then scaled the wall and jumped to the other side to catch the boat as they tipped the bow over and it fell to the ground. Chappell and Hajiantoniou followed over the wall.

Rancich's crew worked like a creaky, but still functional, machine—wobbling across a telephone pole set up as a balance beam with the boat on their heads, dragging the raft under barbed wire, shoving it over log barriers using their oars as supports. An hour later, sweaty and sandy, they staggered to the finish line in first place again. They were rewarded with being allowed to sit by their boats until the other crews finished.

6:15 P.M., THURSDAY, APRIL 16

The students lined up naked in the barracks for their third and final hygiene inspection. After the obstacle course, the rest of the day had been spent crawling under barbed wire and through the black murky water of the demolition pit with simulated artillery rounds exploding around them. It was almost impossible now for the students to function individually. Arms were slung over one another's shoulders for support. A student's good leg became a crutch for another's bad leg. It was as if each boat crew was pooling the parts of each body that still worked into the collective body of the crew to keep it moving.

There was no use hiding injuries at this point; by now their symptoms were too pronounced and the doctors could easily spot them. Blisters had become ulcers. Necks and shoulder blades were rubbed raw from the life vests. Chafing had inflamed testicles. Cellulitis grew from infections. The question the medical team now had to answer for each student: could he make it for another day of Hell Week without doing serious damage to his body?

Burgess's knees were infected. But the infection was still on the surface. It hadn't moved to the joints where it could cause more serious damage. He was allowed to pass.

Dettman's buttocks were covered with a bright red rash.

Both of Chappell's feet were so swollen he had taken the insoles out of his boots to relieve some of the pressure.

Chappell now thought he had hydrophobia. He would start shivering just thinking of water.

The doctors gave Greene Motrin for the pain that was shooting up and down his right calf to his knee and pumped him full of antibiotics to guard against cellulitis.

Rancich had welts inside his thighs. His feet were swollen. His toes felt like they were falling off. A gash on his left calf festered.

Swanson, pockmarked with scars, limped up with the iliotibial band tendinitis in his knee. Flinn, the doctor who checked him during the first hygiene inspection, marveled that he had endured the pain so long. The cold water helped deaden it, Swanson explained and hobbled on.

Schweizer now had to drag his swollen right leg with his hands in order to walk. The doctors laid him down on the floor. He could not extend his leg. His knee felt hot. He couldn't bend his ankle. The pain was excruciating.

The doctors went to the corner of the room to confer

with Richards and Reilly. Schweizer stared at them intently. He could feel a rush of fear sweep his body. Was it going to end here? This close?

Bursitis was swelling Schweizer's calf, the doctors whispered to Richards and Reilly. There was also cellulitis in his leg. A lot of bad things could happen to the young man if he were allowed to continue. He had to be pulled.

Richards and Reilly huddled by themselves. Another student, Graham Allen, a twenty-three-year-old San Diegan, sat in a corner. He had been pulled from the line after the doctors had examined him. His testicles were dangerously swollen.

Reilly motioned Schweizer and Allen over to where he and Richards were standing. Schweizer could feel his heart pounding.

"You'll both be rolled forward with the class," Reilly told them quietly. Schweizer let out a sigh.

"No problem," Reilly explained. "It happens every Hell Week." Students injured after Thursday are often allowed to cut Hell Week a day short and continue with their class to the next phase of BUDS training, particularly if they were good students and the instructors wanted them as SEALs. Schweizer and Allen were. Another day of Hell Week would make no difference for them. They wouldn't quit despite their injuries and they wouldn't get any more out of the week except permanent damage to their bodies.

"Go back to your rooms, get a shower, and do not communicate with the rest of the class for the remaining two days," Richards instructed.

Travis Schweizer stood under the shower head and allowed the hot spray to beat against his body. The shower didn't feel as good as he thought it would. It stung. The cracks and crevices of his skin were all tender from the sand and seawater. But he desperately needed the warmth under his skin.

He felt both sad and elated. Sad that he wouldn't see Hell Week to its end. Elated that it was ending for him.

Rancich popped his head into the shower stall and shook Schweizer's hand.

"I'll see you tomorrow," Schweizer said.

"Sure," Rancich said with a smile. "Give my wife a call."

"I will," Schweizer said. Rancich ran off to join his crew.

11 P.M., THURSDAY, APRIL 16

The students had paddled for four hours up and down the Pacific coast and had finally landed south along the strand at midnight. Hell Week was nearing its end. Lieutenant Cassidy and the princes of darkness would just try to keep the students awake and occasionally cold during their shift.

The students used their paddles to dig a large fire pit in the sand. MREs were passed out for the midnight rations. The instructors peppered the students with questions to keep their eyes open.

"What's the difference between a paddle and an oar?" Nobody knew. Nobody cared.

A full moon was blurred by the hazy sky. The students collected driftwood and broke up abandoned crates to start a roaring bonfire. They stuck their paddles in the sand to form a fence around the fire pit, then huddled around the edge of the blaze, soaking in its warmth and clawing at the MRE bags.

"The night of the living dead," Reilly joked as he handed Cassidy the Hell Week log book for the shift change.

The students were drawn to the licking flames like moths. The instructors had to drag several back because they were singeing their clothes and boots.

The instructors ordered them to perform an Indian rain dance around the fire so the students wouldn't stiffen up in the cold night air. The students would be kept dry for the night except for the ones the instructors caught nodding off—who were sent to the surf for a roll.

Graves made them memorize the four rules of life for a Navy SEAL:

1. Don't play poker with a man whose first name begins with a city.
2. Don't date a girl with a dagger for a tattoo.
3. Don't get less than 12 hours sleep a night.
4. When sky diving, always pull your rip cord.

The students widened the fire pit with their paddles, singing dirty sailor songs as they shoveled to pass the time.

> The first mate, the first mate,
> He had a mighty big 'un.
> He wrapped it around his waist
> And saved the rest for riggin.'

Like prisoners on a rock pit, they sang refrain after refrain, shoveling sand to make the fire pit wider. Taylor ordered a staircase carved in the sand for the entrance to the pit.

"Listen up," Taylor said. "When the fire erupts I want a great big 'Ooooh' out of you. Now rehearse it."

"Oooooh," the students said obediently. They felt like trained seals.

Taylor poured gasoline on the fire to reignite it. A ball of flame shot up into the air.

"Oooooh," the students said on cue. Then they sang "Come on baby, light my fire" and sat with their legs crossed around the blaze. They moved in slow motion. Some stared absentmindedly at their chapped hands and swollen legs as if it was the first time they had ever seen the limbs.

The next evolution was life stories. Each student had to stand up and give his biography plus describe the most significant event in his life. The students stood up to brag about their sexual exploits. Most of the stories weren't true. The instructors laughed and sent the students with the most outrageous yarns to the surf.

Burgess got up with one of the few true tales. "I was born in a hospital with two doctors," he said in his Kentucky twang. "There were eighty-four people in ma' high school. And I started workin' in the saw mill when I was fourteen. I joined the Navy because they had better food. The greatest day of ma' life was when I got married. She was good to me. And I'm good to her. That's the greatest day of my life."

The instructors laughed and heckled and booed. They liked the sex stories better.

Tell us about the times you've been in trouble, the instructors ordered. (The stories became wilder and more fictitious.)

Tell us what drugs you've tried. (Separating fact from fiction here was difficult.)

Tell us who's your least favorite instructor. (They weren't about to tell.)

5:20 A.M., FRIDAY, APRIL 17
After campfire stories, the students were ordered to rehearse commando exercises and escape and evasion techniques. It was a slow walk-through of the maneuvers. There was no point in ordering any exercise. The students had reached their physical limit. The instructors just wanted to keep them awake.

The students now gathered again around the glowing embers that remained from the bonfire. MREs were passed out once more for the breakfast meal. Chappell, his blond hair bleached from the sun, leaned on his paddle and stared vacantly, first up into the sky where a foggy dawn had begun to break, then down at his swollen feet. He now couldn't walk without help from a crew mate.

Connolly squatted in the sand looking at his MRE bag. His hands ached so much he couldn't open it.

Rancich now had Connolly issue orders to his crew. His voice was too hoarse. During the night, Rancich's eyes kept playing tricks on him. He kept seeing students wearing red flannel shirts.

"It's Monday; you have a long way to go," Graves said. But the mind games no longer had any effect. Students clustered around instructors, desperate to catch a glimpse of their watches so they could calculate the hours and minutes they had left in Hell Week.

The instructors now kept their distance from the students—out of a healthy respect for their medical condition. After five days of Hell Week, the students had become human incubators for every respiratory infection in the book. Seasoned instructors knew not to get too close or they would contract what had come to be known as the "Hell Week grunge." Some trainers were already hacking and coughing.*

The students shoveled sand on the remaining embers and dragged their boats out to the surf for the paddle north to the barracks.

The surf was rough. The weak students barely made it past the breakers. A swift current ran against them. An hour later they had made little headway up the coast. Jaco signaled them to return to shore. The students would have to travel on land.

Again they shook uncontrollably. Every face was grim. Words were spoken sparingly, only enough to function. The slightest step, every movement was painful.

His feet now badly swollen from cellulitis, Chappell had to be carried ashore by Dettman and Hajiantoniou, who set him gently down on the sand beside their boat.

Cellulitis was settling into Dettman's hands. Bronchitis had already kicked in. His lips were blistered.

Jaco ordered boats on heads. He moved out at a mercifully slow pace. Hajiantoniou slipped on a clump of seaweed and fell. The other students practically walked over him. They were too dazed to stop. He lifted himself to his knees, stood up, then hobbled to catch up.

Chappell now hung on to the boat straps, letting his crew mates drag him along.

"You're not pulling your load," McCarthy told him.

"Yes he is," Rancich said, his raspy voice barely audi-

---

*I caught the grunge. After a week of interviewing students closeup, I flew home with a miserable case of bronchitis that took me two weeks to shake off.

ble. With the boat still bouncing on his head, Rancich wrapped his left arm around Chappell's waist to help him along. But he knew Chappell was not going to make it much further.

A mile down the beach, Rancich's boat and crew were ordered to peel off from the line and stop at the instructors' parked pickup truck.

Oswald ordered them to the surf, then ten more push-ups.

They took several steps.

He stopped them.

"Do you think you can catch up with the rest of the men?" Oswald asked.

"No," was all Rancich could manage to say, pointing to Chappell's leg.

"Okay," Oswald said with a smile. "You guys are secure."

They stood motionless and stunned. The words took a while to be processed by their brains.

For five days they had been winning most of the crew competitions and grumbling that there had been no reward for coming in first. They finally got their reward. They were permitted to finish Hell Week several hours earlier than the rest of the class.

The words finally sunk in. They attempted a "Hoo-yah" but it came out cracked and raspy. Slowly the six men hobbled together and wrapped their arms around one another in a giant hug, like survivors of a shipwreck rejoicing to be found alive.

"Good job, Lieutenant Rancich," Oswald said.

"Thanks," Rancich said, his voice barely a whisper.

They unhitched their life vests and climbed into the back of the truck.

Back at the Special Warfare Center, staffers from the training command crowded along the second-floor balcony of the classrooms fronting the grinder to watch the first returning victors of Hell Week. They stood in deferential silence as Rancich and his five crew mates walked to the courtyard.

The crew had to be closely baby-sat at this point. They were in no condition to make any decision for themselves. Kevin James, an instructor and the class proctor, took over.

"Go get a shower now," he said, making sure they all paid attention to everything he said. "Don't fall asleep first. If you did, you'd never wake up. After you've showered, put on your green T-shirts."

They smiled.

"Don't put your boots back on. Wear flip-flops or sneakers. Stick with your swim buddy. Don't let anybody wander off. We don't want anybody going to sleep and injuring themselves in the shower or falling into the john."

Students from another class had cleaned their rooms and picked up their clothes. Anything the crew needed—food, prescriptions, toiletries—the other students would bring. Later, when the crew was allowed to sleep, these students would watch over them. In the first twenty-four hours after Hell Week an arm or leg dangling from a cot would swell up with fluids. The students would be there around the clock to keep them tucked in. The crew members would also find themselves waking up in the middle of the night soaked in sweat. The body would be readjusting to normal temperatures outside and the slower pace.

The Hell Week class would have to remain in the barracks for twenty-four hours of observation. It was dangerous for them to be out in the civilian world just now. If they were in an automobile accident or slipped and fell on a sidewalk, which could easily happen in their condition, they could be badly injured. If they were rushed to an emergency room, the doctors would have no idea what had happened to the physical wreck in front of them and might accidentally mistreat an injury.

The crew sat in the barracks room, slumped in chairs and on the edges of cots. A student unbuckled Haji-antoniou's belt. His fingers were too stiff. Another student brought crutches for Chappell and unbuttoned his shirt.

"I never want to go through this again," Connolly mumbled to himself. "I'm afraid to take off my socks."

Greene's neck felt like it had been screwed into his

shoulders from the constant pounding of the boat on his head.

Two students helped Chappell remove his boots and peel off his socks. Chappell looked down at his blistered and hideously bloated feet in disbelief. "Oh my God," he gasped. "They look awful." The students carried him to the shower.

By the next day, they would all have what students called "grapefruit knees."

Thirty-eight students from Class 183 (counting Schweizer and Allen, who had been rolled forward) had made it. The next week, five of them would be laid up with post-Hell Week injuries that delayed their graduation.

The remaining thirty-three members of Class 183 had really just begun their SEAL training. They had ten more weeks of physical training and scuba diving instruction. Then they would head to nearby San Clemente Island for nine weeks of light infantry tactics and commando training. Afterward, they would be packed off to the Army for parachute training and Ranger School.

Before they could be officially designated SEALs, they would have to spend another six-month probationary period on an operational team to test their proficiency and compatibility with other commandos. The instructors said the Navy would be lucky if just twenty-four students from Class 183 completed all the training the first time around and didn't have to drop out or be recycled.

The graduates who would finally be allowed to pin the Trident on their uniforms could hardly be faulted for a feeling of superiority. Even if they never became SEALs, the survivors of that dreadful week in April had at least endured what few others could.

THE COWBOYS

At Hurlburt Field, an out-of-the-way Air Force base along the Florida panhandle, the pilots of the 20th Special Operations Squadron downed tequila shooters in a ramshackle bar called the "Hooch." They wore red scarves under their flight suits. Their radio call sign during flights was Cowboy. They were the Air Force's elite special operations helicopter pilots. And when they partied by themselves, they became almost weepy when a jukebox blasted out their unit song, "Wanted Dead or Alive," by Bon Jovi.

> I'm a cowboy, on a steel horse I ride
> And I'm wanted dead or alive
> Wanted dead or alive
> I walk these streets, a loaded six-string on my back
> I play for keeps, 'cause I might not make it back

The men of the Green Hornets Squadron are the techno-warriors of special operations. The steel horse they ride is a $40 million Pave Low, the most sophisticated helicopter in the world. It is a twenty-one-ton behemoth that looks like a giant black cockroach with propellers, a high-tech bus that can fly combat troops 600 miles on a tank of gas; if they need to go further, it can refuel in the air and fly them hundreds of miles more.

The chopper is so technologically advanced it takes six crewmen to fly. Officially designated the MH-53J, the Pave Low is crammed with some of the most exotic space-age navigational aids in the Air Force inventory, plus top secret electronic countermeasure devices, radar warning devices, flare and chaff dispensers, and jammers to help the aircraft evade enemy air defenses and fool antiaircraft missiles. Encased in armor plating and bristling with 7.62-millimeter miniguns and .50-caliber machine guns, it is the Battlestar Galactica of helicopters—so complex, an onboard mission computer with 256,000 bits of memory has to sort the navigational information for the pilots.

In the world of special operations, getting to work has always been a problem. Commandos can't rescue hostages, assault terrorist hideouts, or train guerrillas if they can't reach them. Over the years, one of the weakest links in American special operations forces has been the transportation. To make it to the battle, commandos need sophisticated helicopters like the Pave Low, which can fly hundreds of miles at night in bad weather that would ground other planes, dodge enemy radars and surface-to-air missiles by traveling at low altitudes, and put teams exactly on their designated targets.

A cargo plane pilot simply has to navigate to a well-lit airstrip. A jet fighter pilot can see the large bridge he bombs from the sky. A Pave Low driver must find needles in haystacks. He must fly hundreds of miles to a Latin American jungle and pluck out a lonely Green Beret in the middle of the night. He must helicopter a Delta Force team to a nondescript apartment building in an Arab city where a hostage is being held. There is no room for error, no time to wander about looking for the right rooftop.

Regular military helicopters—special operators call them "vanilla" planes—will travel set routes to haul troops and cargo. They'll avoid bad weather or flying too close to the ground. The pilot will rely on dead reckoning and simple navigational aids to get him fairly near his target. A Pave Low will fly at treetop level or zigzag through mountain ranges on rapidly changing missions in adverse weather. Its pilot will depend on about a dozen complex navigations systems so the chopper can land on a dime a thousand miles away.

Cowboy may be their call sign, but that's hardly what they are. A Pave Low pilot must be part daredevil, part computer nerd, part nitpicker, part organization man. (No women, as of this writing, fly the plane because of combat exclusion rules.) He must be able to concentrate despite millions of distractions. He must have the sense of direction of an Indian tracker. On the sticks and controls he must have the delicate touch of a surgeon. To manipulate the dizzying array of gizmos in combat he must have the muscle memory of an aerospace engineer. And he must be able to calmly fly almost blindfolded 150 miles an hour, 100 feet off the ground, depending on nothing more than the glowing green Pac-Man displays of his cockpit computers.

It has taken decades for this Pave Low pilot to evolve. Yet he almost didn't. Air Force special operations squadrons were born during World War II when the First Air Commando Group, a ragtag collection of maverick pilots, airlifted supplies to Wingate's Raiders, the famed British commandos who harassed the Japanese in Burma (now Myanmar). After the war, the First Air Commando Group was mothballed. Tactical jet fighters that could travel at the speed of sound and long-range strategic bombers that could drop atomic warheads on the Soviet Union became the glamour aircraft of the new Air Force. Air commando units were patched back together briefly during the Vietnam War. Cargo planes refitted with side-firing cannons, nicknamed "Puff the Magic Dragons," attacked Vietcong strongholds. Huey and Jolly Green Giant helicopters rescued downed pilots and ferried Green Beret commando teams on secret missions, such as the unsuccessful Son Tay prison camp raid in 1970.

The failed 1980 rescue of American hostages in Iran demonstrated that the Defense Department did not have long-range special operations helicopters to insert commandos into Tehran. An embarrassed Pentagon ordered the Air Force to rebuild its 20th Special Operations Squadron with a new and improved version of the C/HH-53 Super Jolly Green Giant called the Pave Low helicopter. But the Air Force refused to buy many of the new helicopters. In 1983, the Pave Low pilots were left behind in the Grenada invasion even though their long-range night-flying skills could have been put to good use. A year later, the Air Force in a secret deal tried to give the Pave Lows and their mission to the Army, whose helicopter fleet had grown to 5,000. But Congress blocked the move and forced the Air Force to buy more Pave Lows for its special operations units.

Gradually the Pave Low pilots were assigned more missions: chasing drug traffickers in the Caribbean, helicoptering SEALs and Green Berets on clandestine training operations, conducting secret rescues in Central America. During the Panama invasion Pave Lows were dispatched to help rescue hostages being held at Torrijos-Tocumen Airport and the Marriott Hotel in Panama City. They assaulted Panamanian Defense Force strongholds and evacuated American wounded. They rushed Delta Force commandos around the capital city hunting for Noriega and dodged bullets to drop Army Rangers into the besieged U.S. embassy compound.

Today the Pave Lows are part of a growing Air Force Special Operations Command that Congress forced on the service. Their pilots are fiercely loyal—so much so that the Air Force doesn't offer them the flight pay bonuses given to other aviators to keep them from deserting to the airlines.

The larger special ops organization with its forty air units has afforded the Pave Low some bureaucratic cover from the Army, which is still doggedly trying to take over the helicopter's mission. Air Force special operations units are now based not only at Hurlburt, but also in Europe and Asia. In addition to the Pave Lows, the force has MH-60G Pave Hawk armed escort helicopters, specially equipped MC-130E and H Combat Talon cargo planes that can fly parachuting commandos on secret infiltration missions or refuel helicopters, and AC-130H Spectre gunships, which are flying artillery batteries providing pinpoint accurate air cover (as was done for U.N. peacekeepers in Somalia).

Outside of Albuquerque, New Mexico, at Kirtland Air Force Base, the service has built a multimillion-dollar complex full of computers and fancy simulators to train its fixed-wing and helicopter pilots. For future Pave Low cowboys, Kirtland is the graduate school of special ops helicopter flying.

The squadron briefing room was cramped, with faded tan walls and gray metal chairs. For the training flight they would take that night, the two student pilots, Dave Dubuque and Neil Billings, spread out maps, navigation logs, and weather charts on the center table.

"Time hack," Dubuque said and began fingering the setting on his watch. "Five, four, three, two, one. Hack."

All the watches in the room were now set exactly by Dubuque's at 4:30 P.M. It was a minor item on their preflight briefing checklist, but one that their instructor, Captain Joe Becker, watched carefully. Everything about Pave Low flying revolved around being on time on the target—in plus or minus ten seconds.

At thirty years old, Joe Becker was one of the youngest Pave Low instructors at Kirtland. But he had a surprisingly seasoned career in the helicopter. Reared in California, he had skipped a year in grade school and enrolled in San Diego State University early. He had hoped to become a professional baseball player after college and had even landed a tryout with the San Diego Padres as a first baseman.

But he hit like a shortstop and ran like a catcher. By age twenty-one, Becker was a second lieutenant in the Air Force. Three years later, he had maneuvered his way into the Pave Low squadron even though he was short on flying hours. Five years later, he was helping plan secret snatch missions with Army commandos to capture Manuel Noriega during the Just Cause invasion.

Becker liked the tension and secrecy of special ops. For any world crisis—a coup in Haiti, an emergency in North Africa, a hostage standoff in the Middle East—the 1st Special Operations Wing would immediately form a secret planning staff to respond. The television in the squadron ready room was always tuned to CNN. The pilots would scramble with every international news bulletin, like beat reporters chasing ambulances.

Becker found Kirtland a slow-motion sabbatical. It had taken him a while to adjust to the decompression of training schedules instead of strip alerts. When he arrived three months ago, it was all he could do to keep from grabbing the controls in the cockpit and flying the Pave Low when a student made a mistake. He was now getting used to what amounted to university life in the helicopter. Laid back and reserved by nature, Becker even came to enjoy working with the students.

If he taught them nothing else, he wanted the students to leave Kirtland thinking like special operators. Working the sticks and flipping the switches weren't enough. They had to develop a special operations frame of mind—almost a lifestyle. You could pull anyone off the street and make him a conventional helicopter pilot, Becker thought. But to be a special operator the pilot had to have that mind-set to accomplish a mission no matter the hazards. The Pave Low instructors had to instill that type of thinking in the students. It wouldn't come to them automatically.

A conventional transport pilot would fly by the book, err on the side of safety, ground his plane if the weather was too bad, and not be particularly concerned about making his destination exactly on time. The special operator had to be obsessed with accomplishing the flight on time. He would look at bad weather and hostile terrain as obstacles to work through, not mission show stoppers. He would push his helicopter to the limit to meet a pickup.

The stopwatch approach to the mission had to be inculcated in the special operations pilot from beginning to end. It meant that Dubuque's time hack to synchronize the watches occurred exactly at 4:30 P.M. It meant walking out to the helicopter and climbing into the cockpit seat exactly at 6:50 P.M., then starting the engines at 7 P.M. so the crew wouldn't be rushed through the preflight checks. Rotor blades would turn at 7:05 P.M. A few minutes late and it could even throw off the schedule for the rest of the flight.

Dubuque and Billings cross-checked the route they would fly before giving the coordinates for the way points to their flight engineer. Both Air Force captains, they were about to take their second flight in the final Pave Low phase of their training.

To become a Pave Low pilot took eight months of mentally rigorous training at Kirtland. Some 100 Air Force aviators were picked each year for the highly prized slots. Most of the students were seasoned captains who had already completed conventional helicopter training on a loan program with the Army. At Kirtland, they divided their time between weeks in intense classroom training, simulated flights in a $175 million computer complex the pilots nicknamed "Wally World," and real rides in the helicopter.

In the beginning, Dubuque and Billings had spent almost two months just sitting in a classroom with the 439-page flight manual nicknamed the "Dash-One" plus stacks of computer disks with video lessons, trying to fathom the Pave Low's complex systems. It was like drinking from a fire hose. All that technical information and jargon.

They had spent another four months just learning the basics of flying the helicopter during the night and day. That in itself took practice. Handling the huge Pave Low was like piloting the *QE 2*. The monster helicopter took much more airspace to bring to a stop over a landing zone. Student pilots constantly overshot their targets. In the cockpit of most choppers, a pilot could see all around, including the ground on which he was landing. In the Pave Low he was so high up in the aircraft he couldn't see a thing. Just to hover and land this elephant, the pilot had to have three crewmen in the plane talk him down until he felt the thump of the helicopter's wheels on the dirt.

Dubuque was still getting used to what for a pilot was an unnatural act of flying so low to the ground and not being able to see what was outside. A thirty-year-old Connecticut native, he had a thick mustache and blond hair brushed back. He had traveled south to the University of South Carolina to play football as a walk-on. He didn't make the team, but graduated with a business degree. Dubuque joined the Air Force with no desire whatsoever to be part of its jet fighter mafia. Air Force culture considered helicopter pilots second-stringers, aviators not good enough for the glamour jets. But the thought of sucking oxygen from a tube, having your face plastered back with Gs, and spinning in a cockpit until you puked never seemed appealing to Dubuque. This slow-moving, flying video game was more fun, and more than enough to handle.

Billings, a twenty-eight-year-old Los Angeles native, had graduated from the Air Force Academy. But less than 20-20 vision kept him out of jet fighters so he ended up in Hueys. He soon became bored with the routine and sent in his application for the Pave Lows. He had a jaunty air. In private, though, Billings was the first to admit that the self-assuredness was mostly a front. It had taken him six years before he really felt comfortable flying Hueys. He didn't know when he'd feel comfortable handling this electronic monster. The instructors at first had thought Billings was too cocky to be a Pave Low pilot. The force shunned showboaters. But during the training he had proved that he had the flying skills. Billings would calm down when he got to an operational unit and realized he was just a rookie, Becker thought.

Up to now Dubuque and Billings had been flying the helicopter at night as conventional pilots would, using night vision goggles and a few comparatively simple navigation systems. Now they were learning to "pave." That was when the students mastered the precision navigation systems that enabled the helicopter to fly undetected for hundreds of miles at treetop level during the night or in bad weather—and be able to place commando teams on target on time.

At the heart of the Pave Low was its "Enhanced Navigation System"—which was military-speak for twenty of the fanciest navigating aids in aircraft technology. All the gizmos tried to tell the pilot exactly where he was on earth at any time plus where he was heading. It was the ultimate in redundant systems, everything to make sure that if a gadget failed, the pilot didn't get lost.

The ENS included the inertial navigation system with its ring laser gyro, a delicate nonmechanical gyroscope that operated with laser light beams and mirrors to sense the slightest movement of the helicopter over the earth's surface. The ring laser gyro then fed those readings to a computer, which used them to calculate the helicopter's exact position, its air speed, and the direction of flight. The calculations were repeated almost instantly every time the pilot jostled the sticks to change the pitch and roll of the plane.

The pilot could always cross-check that reading with the onboard magnetic compass, or the automatic direction finder, or the attitude director indicators, or the radar altimeter. Even more backup came from the Global Positioning System, a sophisticated receiver and antenna that updated the helicopter's position with eighteen satellites orbiting the earth 10,000 miles up in space.

Still another backup was the Doppler Navigation System. A nineteenth-century Austrian physicist named Christian Johann Doppler had discovered that the frequency of sound and light waves increased or decreased depending on the length between the source of the waves and their observer. The best example is a train whistle, whose pitch rises as the train approaches a person, then drops as it whizzes by. The military has been able to apply the Doppler effect to a radar that measures velocity. A Doppler transmitter and sensor under the Pave Low's belly shot four beams of frequency-modulated radar energy to the ground below, then fed the readings to a navigation computer, which spewed out continuous speed and position updates.

And finally, near the copilot's right knee in the cockpit was a circular screen called a Projected Map Display that looked like something out of a James Bond movie. Aerial maps of the land the Pave Low would fly over on a mission were reproduced on 35-millimeter filmstrip cassettes. When a cassette was loaded into the PMD and calibrated with the mission computer, the screen showed the movement of the helicopter across the map as it flew.

To keep the Pave Low from crashing into the ground or the sides of mountains during low-level night flights the pilot depended on two other systems. The first one, the terrain following/terrain avoidance radar, shot out a beam from a large gray bulb in the nose of the helicopter that swept in front of the plane as it traveled, like a blind man with a cane. Inside the cockpit, the pilots could look at a round radar scope, on which an electronic corridor was displayed. If they maneuvered the helicopter through the corridor they wouldn't hit anything. The terrain following/ terrain avoidance radar also generated climb and dive commands, which the pilots followed as they flew.

The second system was the forward-looking infrared detection set, or "fleer" as the pilots called it after its acronym, FLIR. Using a cryogenically cooled sensor in the helicopter's front turret, the FLIR picked up the infrared energy emitted from the ground and projected it on small green cockpit screens in front of the two pilots. The pilots might only be able to see pitch black from their cockpit windows, but their FLIR video monitors would give them a bright green television picture of what was outside.

Piloting off the terrain avoidance/terrain following radar scope and the FLIR video was a mental endurance test. Think about an airline pilot who has to fly on instruments alone to get through stormy weather so he can land on the runway. The airline pilot will spend about four minutes of intense concentration as he guides the jet through the rainy clouds and depends only on the instrument panels in his cockpit to tell him how far he is from the ground. A Pave Low pilot will spend hours flying blind with nothing but the screens in front of him to keep him from crashing into the dark jungles or mountains several hundred feet away.

A powerful mission computer sorted and combined the positioning information all the radars, gyros, compasses, and electronic maps churned out every second in order to give the pilot the best estimate from the helicopter's collective brain on exactly where the aircraft was. Still, the flood of information coming from the cockpit systems was too much for one human brain to absorb.

Simply steering the helicopter and making sure it

didn't hit the ground kept the pilot busy. His eyes stared at the radar scope and FLIR video monitor to follow the climb and dive commands. He cross-checked their readings with the attitude indicator. His left hand gripped the collective pitch lever that moved the chopper up and down. His right hand gripped the cyclic stick between his legs to move the craft forward and bank to the right or left. And his feet manipulated the pedals on the floor to control the tail rotor so the helicopter could yaw right or left.

The copilot meanwhile became a touch typist flipping toggles and tweaking knobs so fast he had to take classes in the simulator in what military people call "switchology"— the art of finding the right buttons in the cluttered cockpit. Between the pilot and the copilot an enlisted flight engineer sat in a jump seat helping the two to manipulate the different navigation systems and read all their signals.

The navigating was made even more complicated by the fact that the Pave Low's control panels were not laid out with the human being in mind. Climb into an Air Force F-16 jet fighter cockpit and you find it is ergonomically designed with all the controls conveniently at the pilot's fingertips. Not so in the Pave Low.

The chopper was designed to combat the crew. To save money, the new avionics for the helicopter, whose body was still the old Jolly Green Giant's, were slapped into the plane wherever room could be found, not where one pilot could easily reach them. The cockpit was crammed with more than 860 control panels, gauges, screens, toggles, knobs, switches, dials, lights, sticks, levers, and pedals. They were spread out in front of the pilot, over his head, even behind his seat. Further back on the left wall of the chopper's main cabin were two metal shelves bolted to the deck of the helicopter where about a dozen of the overflow computer modules, videotapes, radios, electronic warfare black boxes, and avionics interface units were stacked. The pilots called it the "pizza rack."

What it all meant was that there had to be three sets of hands on the steering wheel just to drive the car. The Air Force officially called it the "crew concept" of flying. It divided the thought process for piloting the plane among different crew members. Since one person couldn't handle —much less reach—all the switches, throttles, and knobs to keep the Pave Low moving, under the crew concept the job had to be parceled out to three people. That cut down on pilot overload and mistakes and crashes.

Since one pilot couldn't see all the controls and their readouts, the other two sets of eyes had to tell him what they said. On top of that, the Pave Low's three other crew members in the back of the aircraft had to lean out the chopper's side hatches and rear ramp to act as scanners and tell the pilot in the cockpit what they saw outside.

Visual information had to be converted into voice information. For the Pave Low pilot, it was like flying blind with five back-seat drivers constantly telling him what to do. That took some getting used to. And on top of the chatter from his crew, he had a half dozen radio frequencies to monitor for communications from the outside. F-16 pilots who've taken a spin in the Pave Low walk away afterward with headaches from all the noise.

To cope with cockpit stress—or "task saturation" as the flight manuals euphemistically term it—pilots developed filters in their ears to tune in and out of the radio chatter. Like fathers reading newspapers with screaming kids running around them, the pilots mentally sifted and sorted the important information they needed during flight. Away from the aircraft, many Pave Low pilots worked out at gyms instead of hitting the bars to relieve the stress.

Dubuque and Billings had spent practically the entire day planning the mission. There were a million details and contingencies to consider. Fuel consumption had to be calculated based on airspeed, altitude, and the times the helicopter would be surging, cruising, or hovering. If they would be refueling aerially they had to plan the refueling points at spots where, if the tanker didn't show up, they would still have enough gas left to land at a ground refueling point and not be stranded on the mission.

Conventional pilots would fly the most direct route to

a point. A Pave Low pilot must find the most covert route, navigating mountains and valleys to mask his helicopter from enemy radars and planes. Emergency landings and escape routes had to be considered. Antiaircraft batteries and radars had to be avoided.

For this run, their helicopter would fly north from Albuquerque through the jagged Jemez Mountains with their snow-capped peaks. The aircraft would loop west, then head south to the stepped mesas of the Zia and Laguna Indian reservations in order to reach its infiltration point two hours later.

How well the plane's multimillion-dollar navigation system performed ultimately depended on the pilot's skills with a paper map, a clear plastic ruler, and a sharp pencil point.

In order to hit a target dead-on hundreds of miles off, a Pave Low pilot had to use way points along the way to make sure he was on track and to update the enhanced navigation system, whose radars and gyros could drift off course. The best way points were any terrain feature that stood out on his map, like a road crossing, and that he could also spot from the air visually or through his radars.

The pilot fed the way point coordinates into the helicopter's mission computer. That computer could handle up to ninety-nine way points. Dubuque had plotted sixteen for his flight. The mission computer used the way point coordinates to calculate the airspeed and direction for the chopper so it would arrive at each landmark—and eventually the target—on time.

The computer was sophisticated enough that it could do that. But the key was making sure that the computer had the right coordinates for way points. The slightest error could spell disaster for an infiltration mission. If the pilot inadvertently transposed two numbers on the coordinates he punched into the mission computer he could send the aircraft hundreds of miles off course. Latitude and longitude coordinates had to be figured down to the degree, minute, and one hundredth of a minute if the pilot was to land on top of his target. Flying just one degree off course for sixty miles would put him one mile off his target. The width of a pencil line on a map translated into a thirty-yard margin of error on the ground—often unacceptable in clandestine pickups where the helicopter had to be within yards of its target. The pilot had to plot latitude and longitude coordinates as if he was engraving a dollar bill. Some refused to allow their crews to leave the ready room before a mission until the way point coordinates had been cross-checked by two people on the map.

Dubuque ticked off the other items on his checklist for the preflight briefing of the crew. There were many: antihijacking security while the helicopter was parked, emergency procedures for engine failure or a crash landing, survival equipment each crew member would carry. There were no loose ends.

Chuck Dean, a thirty-six-year-old technical sergeant from Greenville, South Carolina, who was the crew's student flight engineer, delivered the threat briefing. Flight engineers in vanilla choppers more or less went along for the ride, keeping the back end of the helicopter orderly and attending to minor equipment repairs. In the Pave Low, the flight engineer became practically a full-fledged copilot who monitored the enhanced navigation system and talked the pilot through the entire flight. In this scenario the threat was Soviet surface-to-air missiles. Dean went over the secret defensive maneuvers the helicopter would undertake to evade them. Against enemy jets, the Pave Low's best defense would be to hide in the mountains.

On a real operation, a Pave Low would fly through mountains at just 100 feet off the ground. For safety reasons, Becker kept the student flights at 200 feet. Even so, there were risks at that level. It was dangerous anytime a helicopter flew low at night through mountains and landed in remote areas on dusty, uneven terrain. The danger was compounded by the fact that these airmen were inexperienced students. Also, the aircraft's 3,900-horsepower turbo engines had to perform at peak power at the altitude it was flying. Through the mountains it averaged 9,000 feet above sea level. The air was thin at that level, creating less lift for the chopper. These flights always made Becker nervous. On training flights the instructor sat in the copilot's seat (which in a helicopter was on the left), acting as both teacher and safety officer as the student put the chopper through its paces. This low to the ground Becker's hand never strayed far from the cyclic—just in case something happened and he had to take control of the aircraft's steering.

Dean gathered up Dubuque's navigation log with the way points and headed out to the Pave Low parked on the tarmac so he could punch their coordinates into the control display unit. The CDU was the keyboard and rectangular screen on the cockpit's center console that fed the mission computer on board the craft. Dean would also spend the next two hours testing and calibrating the enhanced navigation system's radars and sensors so their readings would be accurate in flight. He was still amazed at how incredibly busy it kept him.

Easygoing with a Southern accent, Dean was at the midway point in his career in the Air Force. Twelve of his seventeen years in the service had been spent as a gunner on a B-52. It wasn't a mentally taxing assignment. He spent most of the B-52 flights merely as a passenger. The best thing that ever happened to him was when they eliminated his job on the bomber the year before. That gave him a good excuse to pack up his wife and two kids and head to Kirtland to start over as a Pave Low engineer.

Now seven months later, he was practically an aviator himself. It was a bit intimidating. He still had to keep the two-inch-thick plastic checklist book on his knee as he sat in his cockpit seat to prompt him on all the switches.

The pilots walked to the supply room to fetch their helmets, night vision goggles, and survival vests, which contained rations, first-aid kits, and pocket radios. They twisted the rings off their fingers. The cockpit had so many hooks and switches, in an emergency a ring could get caught and pull off a finger.

They would be wearing one of the most sophisticated

of the NVGs that the military had produced, officially designated the Aviator's Night Vision Imaging System AN/AVS-6(V)1. It consisted of a small battery pack with a toggle switch that was attached with Velcro to the back of the pilot's helmet. Battery wires snaked around to the front of the helmet and connected to the night vision goggles themselves, which were clipped to the front of the helmet visor.

When a pilot wanted to look through the NVGs, he turned the battery toggle switch in the back and flipped down the binoculars, which enhanced the available light around him. Dubuque and Billings looked like brain surgeons in an operating room with the binoculars protruding from their eyes.

At 6:50 P.M. on the dot, Dubuque climbed into the pilot's right seat to begin his checklist for starting the engines. Billings would sit in the back for the first half of the flight. He would have his turn at the controls later.

The sky was quickly becoming pitch black. There would be no moon out tonight, perfect weather for a clandestine flight. Behind the Pave Low, an MH-60G Pave Hawk was parked and going through the same preflight checks. Major George Selix, a Pave Hawk instructor, sat in its copilot seat. He was taking up another student pilot for a training run: following the Pave Low as an armed escort during its flight through the Jemez Mountains.

A computer junkie, the thirty-five-year-old Selix had a clipped way of speaking and a quick sense of humor. Guys from New Jersey were like that, he would say with a laugh. It was April Fool's Day. His wife had written "I'm pregnant" on the napkin in his lunch bag. Some joke. He hoped there wouldn't be any April Fool's surprises following the Pave Low tonight. Student pilots could be hellions on the controls, speeding up, slowing down. For the Pave Hawk following in the back it was like being the last man on a Roller Derby line. Only in this case you were barreling through mountain passes with precious little clearance on either side.

At 7:05 P.M., the rotor blades began turning as the Pave Low's two General Electric turbo-shaft engines began to whine. The helicopter began rocking with the vibration of the engines. Scanners in the back of the chopper began adjusting controls for the avionics in the pizza rack and hooking up intercom lines. Everyone was preoccupied with his own set of tasks to ready the complicated machine for flight. The rear cabin's gray metal walls and ceiling were covered with a spaghetti maze of wires and tubes and hoses and small motors. Litters were strapped to the left rear wall to carry wounded. Lashed to the right rear wall was a forest penetrator, a raft that looked like a giant bullet. Attached to the end of the hoist line, the penetrator could poke through thick forests, then fold out its seats to hoist up commandos.

The scanners slipped on fire-retardant Nomex gloves and green flight jackets. They would keep the hatches and rear ramp open during the entire night flight and lean out from them to watch for obstacles the aircraft could hit, such as power lines, trees, radio towers, or even other planes. Wind already whipped in from the wash of the rotors. The cabin would become even colder in the crisp chilly night air of the Jemez Mountains.

The otherwise dimmed cockpit glowed with the green light from the FLIR screen. With his checklist book on his lap Dean used a green, chemical light stick to illuminate the dimmed switchboards as his fingers skittered across the controls and knobs. Leaning over his shoulder was David Robinson, a thirty-year-old Air Force staff sergeant from Dallas, Texas, who was Dean's instructor for the flight. A veteran Pave Low engineer, Robinson prodded Dean to speed up the checklist or they would fall behind on the time they were supposed to begin taxiing down the runway. The plane hadn't moved an inch and already Dean felt like he was having to catch up.

The whine and engine rumble now reached a deafening roar as the motors revved. The crew wore earplugs under their helmets to filter some of the noise. The intercom that connected the crew members through their helmet mikes and earphones now crackled with nonstop chatter from Becker, Dubuque, Dean, and the scanners in the back. The radio net sounded like a roomful of auctioneers rattling off the checklist.

"Number one engine?" Dean said.

"Started," he answered himself.

"Caution and advisory panels," Dean continued. "Checked." He pointed his chemical light to check the reading.

The checklist went on and on.

"Number one throttle one hundred percent.

"Flat pitch torque and engine overspeed protection.

"Checked.

"Engine overspeed protection.

"Check.

"Throttles.

"Set.

"Fuel control levers.

"Open."

Every part of the helicopter's movement was scripted. With the "engine start" checklist completed, the crew began the "before taxiing" checklist.

Ground crews pulled the blocks from under the helicopter's wheels.

The aircraft began moving slowly down the taxiway. Becker checked his watch: 7:20 P.M. They were two minutes late. Dean never caught up with the checklist and Dubuque never prodded him to hurry.

Becker made a mental note for his post-flight critique. Never start a mission late, even if only by two minutes.

As the Pave Low creeped down the taxiway, Dean read off the wind speed and direction. The rear scanner alerted Dubuque that the MH-60G Pave Hawk was also pulling out of its parking space.

The right, left, and rear scanners in the back of the helicopter began a round-robin of commands. They were the pilot's eyes behind and on the sides of the chopper. They would warn him of danger he couldn't see.

"Right secure," the right scanner called out.

"Left secure," the left scanner said next.

"Tail secure," said the tail scanner.

Robinson next showed Dean how to aim the enhanced navigation system's radars and other sensors to a spot on the runway. In effect, that spot was the helicopter's first way point. Surveyors had already plotted its exact position on the map.

Keeping the cyclic and pedals steady, Dubuque gently pulled back the collective stick.

The three scanners in staccato radio transmissions warned the pilot as he lifted the aircraft.

"Clear right."

"Left."

"Tail."

The helicopter lifted off the ground.

Dubuque inched the hovering chopper over to the survey mark at the end of the runway. While he checked the engine and transmission instruments and watched the flight controls, Dean for the next five minutes trained the Doppler and other sensors on that spot on the runway. The projected map display and inertial navigation system were also calibrated to the spot. Now the Pave Low's navigation system knew the exact point on earth from which it was starting. Using that point as a reference, the radars and computers would monitor the helicopter's every movement to calculate its exact location throughout the flight.

"Everyone up on goggles," Dubuque ordered.

Night vision goggles were flipped down over helmet visors. Lights were blacked out in the cabin.

The crew checked off in cadence that it was now looking through the goggles.

"Right side up."

"Left side up."

"Tail up."

Dubuque also flipped down his goggles. He would shortly be flipping them back up when he began flying the helicopter solely off the radars. Enhancing the available light, the goggles produced a monochromatic green image. Pilots found that it was like looking through two toilet roll tubes with green cellophane at the ends. The landscape was reproduced in sparkling shades of green. It looked like a grainy black-and-white movie, only all in green. The lights from Albuquerque sparkled bright like Christmas tree lights—all green.

The takeoff checks had to be accomplished lightning fast for the helicopter to make its launch time for the mission. Dean again fell behind.

"Keep up with your checklist," Robinson snapped. "Right now you're back at the tail of the plane." It was an expression the instructors often used. Whenever a student was too slow in reciting the rapid-fire flight procedures he was "behind the airplane" or "back with the tail scanner."

Dubuque began a power check of the helicopter's engines. Dean watched the gauge monitoring the engines' revolutions per minute to calculate whether they had the power to take the helicopter through the high mountains during the flight. Better to make sure now that the engines had the horsepower rather than up in the mountains when it would be too late to correct the problem. If Dubuque didn't have 100 percent power, he'd have to quickly plan a route where the air was thicker and would give him more lift. Or he'd have to dump equipment to lighten the helicopter's load.

He had the power for the flight through the mountains.

Next came the hover coupler check. Keeping a helicopter hovering stationary in flight over a target was one of the most difficult chores for the crew. To help control the helicopter in this delicate maneuver, the pilot could grip a special hover trim control stick near his left knee. That activated the hover coupler, a handy device that when mated with his Doppler radar and altimeter could automatically keep the helicopter steady in a hover over a target on the ground. But the pilots had to know before the mission began whether the hover coupler worked.

Dubuque lifted the Pave Low to 100 feet off the runway and grabbed the hover trim control stick to his right.

First he brought the chopper to a hover manually. The chopper shook and rattled but held steady. The wind from the rotor wash whipped back up from the ground. The tail yawed only slightly.

Dubuque wiggled the hover trim stick to make sure he could move the aircraft right, left, forward, and back to adjust his hover over a target. The stick worked.

"Okay, stick to the rear," Becker said. That was the command for shifting control of the hover to the scanner at the right front door of the helicopter under the hoist. At that door was another hover trim control stick. When the helicopter was hovering over commandos on the ground to pull them up on the hoist, the scanner manning the hoist would grip the rear hover control stick in order to position the hovering aircraft exactly over the soldiers below. During this maneuver the pilot, in effect, gave up control of the helicopter to the right scanner in the back, who—unlike the pilot—could actually see the men being hoisted up.

The rear hover trim stick worked. The scanner then passed back to Dubuque the control of the chopper.

"Okay, now hold us down at fifty feet," Becker ordered. The lower the helicopter hovered the more dangerous it was, because there was less space between the aircraft and the ground to correct for mistakes if the coupler, working in combination with the Doppler, failed. Though his hands never strayed far from the sticks Becker made a point of keeping calm in front of the students. The "back-enders"—the nickname for the scanners behind the cockpit—could sense danger or uncertainty just from a pilot's voice. It was important for the pilot to project an air of command and control.

The hover at fifty feet was steady as a rock.

"Coupler off," Dubuque said and took control of the aircraft with the cyclic and collective sticks. The Pave Low hadn't even begun the mission, and he was already sweating inside his flight suit from just making sure that everything worked.

"Okay, bring the nose around clear for takeoff," Becker quietly ordered. "Take it nice and easy with the 60 on the ground." The 60 was the MH-60G Pave Hawk, which was just about to lift off from the runway.

"Sixty's on the go," the tail scanner announced. The Pave Hawk was now completing its power checks and drawing near to the Pave Low. The Pave Low climbed to 200 feet and cruised slowly at forty-five miles an hour so the Pave Hawk wouldn't be left too far behind.

The cockpit chatter never let up. There were dozens of commands and checks to be issued every minute. Anyone listening in would find the babble mind-boggling, but it was the only way the corporate flying could be accomplished in a plane so complex.

If the intercom wasn't noisy enough, now the control tower back at Kirtland broke in with the warning that a civilian Beechcraft plane was closing in on the Pave Low at eleven o'clock. The scanners leaned out the windows and picked up the plane on their night vision goggles. It veered away. They relaxed.

The lights of Albuquerque passed below as the Pave Low snaked north up the Rio Grande River toward the dark forbidding Jemez Mountains off in the horizon.

Dubuque was seven minutes from his second way point, the Jemez Canyon Dam.

"Reinitialize your Doppler," Robinson reminded Dean. Dean punched commands into the keyboard of the Doppler Control/Display Unit on the cockpit's center console to center the steering command for the radar.

"Okay, crew, we're going to do a roll check here," Dubuque announced. He began pitching and rolling the helicopter to make sure its terrain-following radar transmitter and FLIR sensor still remained pointed steady along the aircraft's flight path regardless of how the chopper pitched and rolled. If the radar and sensor instead swerved or flared up following the helicopter's movements the screens in the cockpit would go blank.

They never did. The transmitter and sensor remained correctly aligned as they were supposed to.

Dubuque could see the Jemez Canyon Dam ahead on the glowing green FLIR screen in front of him. He was still getting used to interpreting the shades of green from the infrared picture in order to identify terrain features. He radioed back to his crew that the helicopter was about to pass the dam. The scanners leaned out their hatches and called out as the Pave Low neared it.

"Five, four, three, two, one," one of the scanners said as they approached the way point.

"Mark," the scanner said to signal the exact time when the helicopter crossed the way point.

Dean quickly pushed buttons on the enhanced navigation system and the Doppler. Seconds later, a row of numbers flashed up on a computer screen in front of him.

The ENS and Doppler had calculated their best estimates of exactly where the helicopter was when it was lined up over the way point. Dean compared the "deltas" for the three sets of coordinates.

The deltas were the differences among the ENS's reading, the Doppler's reading, and the coordinates that he knew from his navigation log to be the correct ones for the Jemez Canyon Dam way point. If there were large differences among the three sets of coordinates for the way point, that meant the ENS or Doppler were misaligned and Dean would have to adjust them.

The deltas were tiny. The ENS and Doppler didn't need updating.

"Okay, crew, we're on the system," Dubuque said and flipped up his night vision goggles. To simulate adverse weather outside, Becker required the student pilot to turn up his night vision goggles so he saw only pitch black outside and was forced to use the radar screen. From now on he would be paving, flying solely off the enhanced navigation system and the terrain-following radars and sensors. The FLIR and terrain-following radar screens would be his windows to the outside world. He would remain hunched over responding to their every command as the rest of the crew poured directions and readings into his ears for the helicopter's other systems that he couldn't see.

The FLIR screen was busy—so busy in fact that the flight engineer had to help the pilot read all its symbols and images. In the lower left corner of the screen Dubuque saw "3"—the number for the flight's next way point fed to the

FLIR from the onboard computer. Along the right side, a white bar bobbed up and down showing the altitude of the aircraft. In the upper right corner, numbers ticked off the time and distance to the next way point. A strip at the top gave him his compass heading—one of three compass readings on the control panel that he could read if he chose to. In the upper left was his ground speed.

Swaying around in the center of the screen were a series of parallel white lines that represented the attitude indicator reflecting the helicopter's axis in relation to the horizon. The FLIR also issued climb and dive commands. To stay on course to the next way point, Dubuque manipulated the cyclic and collective sticks so a white dot matched up with the white cross hairs in the center of the FLIR screen. Finally, behind all the symbols on the cluttered screen was the infrared picture of the terrain outside.

Dubuque's eyes also constantly darted right to the terrain-following radar scope on his front console, which depicted the mountain peaks to his left and right as he flew into the Jemez. As long as he maneuvered the helicopter so the apex at the bottom of the scope stayed within the light green corridor, he wasn't going to hit anything. The scope depicted a corridor 1,500 feet wide and just over a mile in front of him. With the helicopter moving so fast it was like steering a motorcycle down a narrow short hallway and trying not to hit the walls.

The Pave Low flew so close to the sides of mountains that Dubuque had to watch the terrain-following scope as closely as he did the FLIR screen. The consequences of an error were stark. If the terrain strayed into the apex of the scope, he'd kill himself and his crew.

The Pave Low passed its next way point at the tip of the Santa Ana Mesa on time and banked northeast into the Jemez Mountains. Dubuque struggled to keep the aircraft speed at 110 knots. The radars worked best within the range of eighty to 120 knots. But at times his speed dipped down to sixty knots. He accelerated the helicopter.

Becker smiled and made another mental note for his critique. A Pave Low pilot wanted to maintain a steady ride, or the choppers in the back of the formation, which had to race and brake to keep up, would start squawking. Selix was probably griping in his cockpit, Becker thought to himself, chuckling.

Becker was right. Selix wasn't any too pleased with the stops and starts.

Dean, the student flight engineer, flipped the switches to begin the fuel transfer that emptied one of the wing tanks into the helicopter's main tanks that fed the engines. Among his many duties during the flight, he was responsible for making sure there was a constant flow of fuel into the mainframe tanks.

As the Pave Low neared its next way point—a windmill at the mouth of Bland Canyon—Dean was still falling behind in his calls. The flight engineer had to constantly stay ahead of the pilot, tracking the projected map display and watching the FLIR screen to warn of obstacles and dangers ahead. But Dean felt as if he could never catch up in the flight.

It was because he was new to this, Robinson realized. It would take many more flights before he really felt comfortable with the commands and could call them out from memory.

Dubuque also was becoming too preoccupied with the radar screens. That was understandable considering how nerve-racking it was to fly through mountains and not be able to look outside. But it was just as nerve-wracking for the crewmen in the back, and Dubuque wasn't warning them on what was ahead in the flight. When the helicopter lurched up and down over the mountains and ridges, Becker knew that the backenders would become edgy if the pilot didn't keep them informed.

Outside, as the Pave Low raced northwest through Bland Canyon, the dark mountains of the Jemez, with bright white snow capping their peaks, rose up on both sides of the helicopter. An icy wind whipped through the rear cabin. Even through the grainy green picture of the night vision goggles, the view was breathtaking—and somewhat scary. The Pave Low seemed perilously close to the sides of the mountains. Peering through their NVGs the scanners felt that they could almost reach out and grab a pine cone off the trees.

The night vision goggles made the mountains seem closer than they really were. Even so, they were hardly far off. Becker calculated that the mountains often were only about 700 feet away on each side of the aircraft. At that distance and with the Pave Low's current speed, the helicopter could crash into the side of a mountain in about four seconds if it was off course to the right or left.

Becker decided to add to the pressure on Dubuque. He turned off the FLIR screen to simulate a system failure. Dubuque and Dean now had to look at four other screens and radar indicators to keep a fix on their course. The helicopter wobbled as Dubuque and Dean adjusted to flying with degraded navigation systems.

Becker then switched off all of the screens for the enhanced navigation system to simulate total system failure.

"TF fail," Dubuque radioed back to his crew to warn the scanners that the terrain-following radar was down.

"Okay, flight engineer, you have to call out all the readings and become a human navigator indicator," Becker told Dean.

Dean began rattling off the climb and dive commands. He began sweating inside his flight suit.

Overcompensating, Dubuque began jerking the sticks up and down. Peering through his night vision goggles, Becker kept a close watch out the cockpit windows during the simulated system failure.

Alerted that the screens were now blank, the scanners leaned out the hatches and the ramp to call out their estimates of altitude and distance from the mountain sides. The scanners had been through this drill many times before and gave surprisingly accurate estimates. They had to. Their lives depended on how well they eyeballed the distances.

Becker turned back on the radar screens. Dubuque

readjusted the altitude and course to resume terrain following off the FLIR and radar scope.

"The 60 behind us must be wondering what the hell we're doing," Becker said with a laugh.

Selix was.

The Pave Low had been flying for about an hour. Dubuque's wrist had begun to cramp from gripping the cyclic stick between his legs so tightly. Becker took over the controls as Dubuque twisted his right wrist to work out the cramp. Flying the helicopter was physically exhausting.

While he took a break, Dubuque flipped down his night vision goggles to peek outside for the first time.

Only then did it dawn on him that he was really flying a helicopter and not just crouched over some fancy Nintendo game trying to keep a tiny circle lined up on cross hairs.

"Boy, this is realistic," he said, almost in awe over what he was doing in these dark, forbidding mountains.

Dubuque flipped up his night vision goggles and went back to piloting off the screens.

He missed his eighth way point. His mission plan called for him to fly through the valley west of Cerro del Medio, a mountain peak over 9,000 feet high. Instead he looped the aircraft east around the mountain.

The error was a minor one. On the FLIR screen it was easy to mistake one mountain pass for another. Dean would need more experience in the flight engineer's seat before he would be able to juggle watching the pilot's FLIR screen and the projected map display to ensure that the aircraft followed the correct landmarks.

Dubuque found the ninth way point at the San Antonio Valley to the north and managed to make up the lost time with the remaining benchmarks.

At 8:35 P.M., the Pave Low finally flew out of the Jemez mountain range. The helicopter banked to the south over the arid mesas and flatlands of the Zia and Laguna Indian reservations and sped toward its final infiltration point, where in the scenario it was to drop off a commando team.

Dubuque and Dean made another power check of the engines. The air temperature and pressure were different. They wanted to ensure that the helicopter engines still had power for the hover over the commandos' landing zone.

Three miles from the landing zone, a barren dusty plain on the Laguna reservation, Dubuque flipped down his night vision goggles. He would fly visually the rest of the way.

Dubuque and Dean ran through the landing checks. Dubuque peered outside the cockpit window hunting for the landing site, comparing what he saw with the reading from his Doppler radars.

He banked left.

"The LZ is coming off the right nose," Becker said, helping him out.

The cockpit chatter picked up.

Each scanner began calling out what he saw outside the plane. The scanners now became more important to Dubuque. At this close range, they often spotted obstacles on the ground faster than the radars.

There was a cadence to the chatter between the flight engineer and the scanners as Dubuque closed in on the target. As the helicopter made its final approach Dean called out the altitude, airspeed, and rate of descent. The scanners then chimed in to warn Dubuque of any obstacle they saw outside with which the helicopter might collide.

No obstacles were in the way. The helicopter sped forward.

"Two hundred feet, fifty knots," Dean said, calling out the altitude and speed.

The helicopter neared telephone lines along a gravel road. Each scanner called out as the aircraft crossed. The pilot always wanted to know about phone lines—the bane of low-level flying.

"One hundred feet, fifty knots," Dean continued.

When the helicopter neared the target at fifty feet off the ground, Dean stopped making the altitude and speed calls. The scanners now took over.

Craning their necks out the hatches, they watched for

any trees or high bushes that might catch the helicopter blades and talked the aircraft to the ground. The right scanner took the lead, giving Dubuque a constant foot-by-foot alert on his altitude and guiding him slowly down.

The Pave Low's wheel thumped on the rocky plain: 8:50 P.M. Dubuque had hit his target on time. If a commando team had been on board it would have raced out the rear ramp.

The dusty cold wind from the rotor blades' wash whipped into the rear cabin.

The tail scanner announced when Selix's Pave Hawk landed a short distance away.

The Pave Low remained on the ground for two minutes, its rotor blades still whirling and kicking up a cloud of dust. The MH-60G Pave Hawk, which had parked directly behind the Pave Low, blinked its exterior lights to signal that it was ready to leave.

Dubuque increased power and pulled back the collective stick.

The right and left scanners leaned out the hatches to watch for obstacles and announce that all was clear.

Dean rattled off the engine power, rate of climb, altitude, airspeed, and steering.

The tail scanner watched out the rear ramp to make sure the Pave Hawk was following. It was.

The Pave Low then went LZ hopping. For the next forty-five minutes, Dubuque practiced flying and landing at different points around the mesas to simulate dropping off and picking up ground teams.

At 9:36 P.M., the Pave Low had landed at its fifth infiltration point. Billings, the other student aviator, climbed into the pilot's seat for the last half of the training mission. A Pave Low instructor who had to recertify in mountain flying replaced Dean as the flight engineer.

Dean couldn't remember when he had worked so hard. At least in the simulator he could stop the action if he fell too far behind in the cockpit scramble. Not in a real flight. He was so busy he never caught up. He seemed to be

behind the entire flight instead of ahead of the pilot anticipating the navigation checks.

Dubuque felt totally drained. He had been so consumed by flying the helicopter and concentrating on the
screens that he hadn't even had time to pay attention to
the danger of the night flight. He slumped into a bucket
seat in the rear cabin and leaned back to collect his wits.
The night air was freezing cold, but he was dripping wet
under his flight suit.

Billings took off for the north to practice "TOTs"—
time on targets, where the helicopter would try to hit various infiltration points within seconds of the designated
time. To reach a valley in the north, the Pave Low wedged
through a tall canyon, again with the mountains uncom-
fortably close. The right and left scanners peered out of
their hatches nervously and called out the distances to the
mountain edge. With a delicate touch at the sticks, Billings
guided the aircraft through smoothly.

His hover at one landing zone, however, was not as
picture perfect. Bringing the heavy Pave Low to a hover for
a drop-off point required a gradual deceleration to the target. Above all, the pilot could not slow down too fast at the
last minute. The helicopter would simply overshoot the target. The rule of thumb was that for every one tenth of a
mile that the helicopter traveled on the approach, it should
reduce its ground speed by ten knots.

The pilot had to calculate in his head how far away he
should begin decelerating so that he was at a slow enough
speed near the end to engage the hover coupler, which
guided him in to a final stop. As the helicopter neared the
ground to its pickup point, its speed had to be no more
than thirty knots when the pilot engaged the coupler. If it
was more than thirty knots, the coupler would try to rapidly
decelerate the aircraft by flaring the nose, like a horse rearing up when it comes to a quick stop.

Billings was flying too fast into his landing zone. To
help him slow down he engaged the hover coupler. But the
aircraft was traveling at over thirty knots. The coupler
forced the nose of the helicopter to flare. The effect was

deceiving to Billings. Flying off the video screens, he didn't realize that his chopper had come almost to a dead stop and its nose was rearing up about 600 feet off the ground.

For the crew in the back, the lurch up was frightening.

With a roar of its engines the helicopter shuddered as the nose rose up and the tail dipped down. The crew could look out the rear ramp and see the ground below instead of the horizon. It was like being in a cereal box with someone shaking them out of the top into a bowl.

In this case the helicopter's rearing up could be deadly for the entire crew. If the aircraft remained flared for too long with its nose up, it would lose the lift from its blades and fall back to the ground, crashing first on its tail.

Becker, who had his night vision goggles flipped down and could see what was happening, quickly grabbed the controls and yanked the chopper out of its automatic hover. The Pave Low leveled off.

Becker took a deep breath to keep calm. It was the third time in a week that he had had to grab the controls from students to prevent a serious accident.

Becker handed the controls back to Billings. The student pilot made a sweep around the valley and took another try at the hover. The second time he was successful.

After the hover, Billings banked the helicopter into a circle and headed south, back toward Albuquerque.

The Pave Low neared the runway at Kirtland shortly after 11 P.M. Billings and Becker quickly calculated their "bingo"—aviation slang for the amount of fuel needed to reach the airport with the 900 pounds of reserve that Air Force regulations required them to have when they landed.

They had enough fuel for still another twenty minutes of flight. Becker let Billings practice more hovers over the runway, during which the tail scanner would unfurl a rope ladder out the back of the helicopter to simulate a Green Beret team climbing out.

The Pave Low finally made its last landing at 11:23 P.M. Becker flipped up his night vision goggles and relaxed for the first time that night.

Billings taxied the helicopter with its rotor blades still

whirling to a tanker truck. The final exercise of the night was "hot gas."

Normally the helicopter engines were shut down for refueling, which could take up to forty minutes. But in emergencies or fast-moving operations the Pave Low could be refueled in ten minutes by keeping the engine running and the blades whirling.

But a hot refueling could be dangerous. When the helicopter was operating, it built up a static charge, which could create a spark, igniting the jet fuel or its vapors.

Billings shut off the radios and navigation system to reduce the chance of a static charge. A fire guard was posted with an extinguisher ten feet from the helicopter.

The crewmen dragged the tanker hose to the helicopter and fastened its nozzle to the coupler on the chopper's skin. Dean checked the connection to make sure the fit was tight.

Another crewman crouched on the tarmac near the tanker clutching the "dead man valve." If there was an accident and the fuel the tanker was pumping caught fire at the nozzle, he could shut off the flow immediately at the other end of the hose near the tanker so it didn't blow up.

The hot refueling went off without a hitch. The hose's nozzle was disconnected and the Pave Low lumbered forward to its final parking space on the tarmac.

It was midnight before Dubuque, Billings, and Dean gathered in the ready room with the instructors for their debriefing. A case of beer in the training squadron's refrigerator was ripped open and they passed around the cans.

They laughed and joked and let the cold beer wash down their parched throats.

Selix walked in carrying a hand saw and laughing.

"Who was flying that first route?" he roared, pretending to be sawing off a head.

Dubuque ducked into a side room. Selix chased after him.

They all laughed even more as Selix ribbed Dubuque about his erratic flying.

"We did go from seventy to 180 a couple times," Dubuque said sheepishly.

"A couple timês!" Selix howled.

"Hey, that's why I'm a student," Dubuque kidded back. "If I did everything perfect I'd be teaching you guys."

Becker settled everyone down and began his critique of the Pave Low flight. He was good-natured about it. He wanted it to be a learning experience for the students. This wasn't going to be any ass-chewing session.

"Okay, first thing," Becker began quietly. "We were behind the power curve on the checklist for the taxi."

Dean had had problems keeping up with the cockpit calls. He was reacting to events in the flight rather than anticipating them and directing the pilot. But that was to be expected at this point in his training. He'd speed up with experience.

Dubuque came down the wrong valley to one of the way points in the Jemez Mountains. "But it was no big deal." He made up the time at later way points.

Both pilots were too aggressive on the sticks. The secret to paving at night was to keep the helicopter level and at a steady speed as it weaved through the mountains and bobbed up and down over peaks and ridges. A smooth ride made it easier to hit the way points on time and kept the formation of choppers behind the Pave Low tight.

Dubuque's flying improved as the flight progressed. But he needed to talk to the crew more. Let them know what was happening during the flight. This was corporate flying. No one could be left in the dark.

As for Billings's first hover when Becker had to grab the stick . . .

"It was horrible," Billings admitted.

"Well, it was interesting," Becker said with a smile. Billings was a good pilot. Becker knew he wouldn't repeat that mistake.

Becker spent the next twenty minutes running through minor points in the flight: approaches that needed an extra thirty seconds of deceleration, ground speeds that varied too much along the way, moments when the apex in the terrain-following radar scope brushed too close to the electronic corridor and the student pilot had to bank the helicopter away too abruptly. Flying the Pave Low was like an intricate choreography. Every motion, every movement had to be perfect, or fatal.

At 1:30 A.M., Becker, Dubuque, and Billings pulled up to a table at Milton's, an all-night diner in Albuquerque. It was kind of a ritual after a night flight that the Pave Low instructors went out for an early breakfast with the students to continue talking about the training. They were so keyed up after the four hours in the aircraft they couldn't sleep anyway. This was the ultimate in high-tech helicopter aviation. Whether they were returning from training or real-life combat, they would always feel this way after an operation. It was exciting. It was exhilarating. It was the most physically and mentally demanding flying they had ever experienced.

And they were ravenous. The three pilots ordered eggs and bacon and pancakes.

"It's basically playing a video game up there," Dubuque said as he wolfed down his pancakes. "I never once thought I had hills ahead of me. I was so busy concentrating on the screen and so consumed by the controls and the system I never had time to think about hitting the hills.

"Besides, this is such a crew airplane, you know they won't let you fly into a mountain," he added with a laugh.

They joked about the mistakes they had made during the flight—the "manly" takeoffs and landings, as Billings put it. Covert infiltrations were supposed to be daring missions—at least that's the way the movies portrayed them. Yet flying them in the Pave Low required a delicate and graceful touch, like swans gliding over hills and landing softly on a lake.

Though their call sign was Cowboy, these Pave Low pilots had to perform like skilled technicians. From the start, they had to accept the fact that they couldn't fly the aircraft alone. In the macho world of military aviation, where the single-seat fighter jockey was revered as the ultimate top gun, corporate flying could be a cultural shock. "In this airplane, you're a much smaller part of the picture," Dubuque still marveled.

Becker mostly sat quietly and smiled as the students swapped war stories about the flight. Dubuque and Billings handled themselves well in the cockpit, he thought. More importantly, they were both hungry to get into a Pave Low squadron. You had to desperately want this kind of life to be good at special ops flying. The work was too dangerous and all-consuming for the ambivalent.

It was nearly 3 A.M. when the three pilots had finished their breakfasts and run out of anything else to say about the flight. Fatigue was finally beginning to set in. They stood up and trudged wearily to their cars for the drive home.

Tomorrow night they would be back in their cockpit, staring at their glowing green screens with the radio chatter in their ears as they paved through the dark mountains of the Jemez.

1. Captain Ken Swanson *(left)* chats with his Green Beret instructor, Sergeant First Class Dan Moran, during the two-week Robin Sage guerrilla warfare exercises.

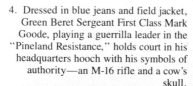

2. Captain Swanson *(center, seated)* plans an ambush operation to gain the confidence of the guerrillas he has trained.

3. After days of indigestible Army Meals Ready to Eat (MREs), Green Beret students *(left to right)* Steven Stankus, George Seemann, and Clay Ruppenthal finally catch chickens for dinner.

4. Dressed in blue jeans and field jacket, Green Beret Sergeant First Class Mark Goode, playing a guerrilla leader in the "Pineland Resistance," holds court in his headquarters hooch with his symbols of authority—an M-16 rifle and a cow's skull.

5. Navy seamen from Class 183 roll heavy logs through a mud pit during Hell Week, the grueling rite of passage to becoming a SEAL.

6. SEAL students must carry on their heads 150-pound rubber rafts nicknamed "itty bitty ships." Lieutenant Tom Rancich *(left, front)* and crew push it up as an instructor shovels in sand to weigh down the raft.

7. Not only do SEAL students have to negotiate a daunting obstacle course, but their rubber rafts must come with them.

8. Lieutenant Rancich and his crew strain to push up a telephone pole.

9. During what SEAL instructors consider a light workout, students do push-ups in a long chain.

10. Boat Crew Five moments after being told it has successfully completed Hell Week. From left to right: Kevin Connolly, Antony Hajiantoniou, Rancich, Brett Chappell, Lance Dettman, and Dan Greene.

11. The $40 million MH-53J Pave Low helicopter, the most sophisticated military helicopter in the world, according to the Air Force.

12. Student pilots *(left to right)* Captain Neil Billings and Captain Dave Dubuque meet with their instructor, Captain Joe Becker, before a Pave Low night flight through New Mexico's Jemez Mountains.

13. Before a night flight, Technical Sergeant Chuck Dean *(left)* and Captain Dubuque check the rear cabin's "pizza rack," crammed with electronic equipment.

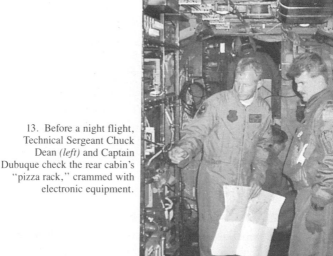

14. General H. Norman Schwarzkopf, commander of the allied coalition in Desert Storm, distrusted special operations forces and kept them under tight rein.

15. General Carl Stiner, chief of the U.S. Special Operations Command, lobbied Schwarzkopf to set up a secret commando force in the Persian Gulf to launch clandestine missions in Iraq and Kuwait.

16. Major Bob Leonik piloted one of the Pave Lows that led a helicopter raid on two Iraqi early warning radars to begin Desert Storm.

17. Lieutenant Colonel Rich Comer, the 20th Special Operations Squadron commander, led the Pave Lows in the attack on the Iraqi radars.

18. "In peace we will always remain hand in hand."
During Desert Storm, the Army's 4th Psychological Operations Groups
dumped twenty-nine million leaflets on Iraqi soldiers. This one was
nicknamed "love and kisses" because it stressed Arab brotherhood.

**19. "I crossed 'Shatt Al-Arab' as you wished, and I obeyed your
orders. I feel death is knocking on the door whenever we go on the
offensive and I feel I am on my last breath."**
Leaflets dropped later in the war were more hard-hitting, blaming Saddam
Hussein for putting troops in danger.

20. **"If you want to save yourself comply with the following:**
   - **Remove the magazine from your weapon.**
   - **Carry the weapon on your left shoulder, pointing the barrel downward.**
   - **To assure us of your sincere desire to save yourself, please put both hands above your head.**
   - **When approaching our locations, do so slowly; any person ahead of the group raises this leaflet above his head.**
   - **This will affirm your desire for safety.**
   - **You will be transferred into the hands of your Arab brothers as soon as possible. Welcome."**

Some leaflets showed Iraqi soldiers how to surrender.

21. **"This is your first and last warning! Tomorrow, the 28th Inf. Div. will be bombed! Flee this location now!"**

At Schwarzkopf's suggestion, psyops officers dropped leaflets warning Iraqi soldiers that B-52s would bomb them. After several such attacks, the infantrymen clambered out of their bunkers to grab the latest leaflets.

22. Parodying the movie *Dr. Stangelove,* Major Skip Davenport sits atop the 15,000-pound BLU-82 bomb that his Combat Talon air crew dropped during the war as a psychological weapon.

23. After each BLU-82 attack, these psyops leaflets were dropped on Iraqi soldiers.

اهربوا وحافظوا على الحياة او ابقوا ولقوا مصرعكم

لقد تكبدتم خسائر هائلة
نتيجة استخدامنا
أقوى قنبلة تقليدية في هذه الحرب
وهي أقوى من عشرين صاروخ
اسكود من حيث قوة التفجير
أحذروا !
سوف نقصف مواقعكم مرة أخرى
سوف يتم تحرير الكويت
من إعتداء صدام العراق
أسرعوا بالانضمام الى
اخوتكم في الجنوب
سنعاملكم بكل الحب والاحترام
أتركوا هذا الموقع فلن
يحقق لكم الامان

Above left: "Flee and Live, or Stay and Die!"
Above right: "You have just experienced the most powerful conventional bomb dropped in the war. It has more explosive power than 20 SCUD missiles. You will be bombed again soon. Kuwait will be free from aggression. Flee south and you will be treated fairly. You cannot hide."

24. Chief Warrant Officer Chad "Bulldog" Balwanz practices digging a hide site for his reconnaissance mission deep inside Iraq.

25. Chad Balwanz's Green Beret team posed for this photo just before beginning its secret infiltration into Iraq. Standing left to right: Terry Harris, Dan Kostrzebski, Rob Gardner, Balwanz, Charlie Hopkins, Jim-Bo Hovermale. Kneeling left to right: James Weatherford and Robert DeGroff.

26. Colonel Jim Kraus, who sent Green Berets deep into Iraq before the ground war began, stands hatless watching the fighting unfold.

27. Master Sergeant Jeffrey Sims' team poses with the crew of *Lady Godiva,* the MH-60 Black Hawk helicopter that rescued them. Standing left to right is the air crew: Richard Detrick, James "Monk" Crisafulli, Randy "Beastman" Stephens, Todd Diffendorfer, Bruce Willard, and Gordon Hopple. Kneeling left to right is the Green Beret team: Sims, Ron Tabron, and Richard Torbett.

28. Chief Warrant Officer Richard Detrick aboard an MH-60 Black Hawk preparing to fly a rescue mission during Desert Storm.

29 and 30. Green Berets experiment with designs for camouflaged hide sites that would be dug in western Iraq.

31. Lieutenant Tom Deitz stands at the bow of one of the three speedboats the Navy SEALs used to fake an amphibious landing along the coast of Kuwait at the beginning of the ground war.

32. Captain Ray Smith, who led Navy SEALs during Desert Storm, addresses his men at a base along Kuwait's coast.

DELTA FORCE

The imposing compound is tucked away in a remote corner of the vast Fort Bragg, North Carolina, military reservation, hidden by pine trees and carved out of what used to be called Range 19 with its red clay and sandy soil. Two tall fences, each topped with barbed wire and laced with electronic sensors, stretch more than six miles around the compound. Unmarked patrol cars drive slowly on the outer perimeter, their drivers inside watching warily for any vehicles straying near on the gravel roads that approach the facility.

Inside, tall grassy berms have been erected to hide the sniper ranges and obstacle courses from prying eyes. (During the Cold War the compound was a favorite intelligence target for Soviet spies who hung around Fort Bragg.) Behind the berms sit tall buildings that look like Swiss chalets with beige walls and red gabled roofs. At one time, a blue sign was posted at the compound's main gate with an innocuous-sounding identification for what is going on inside: "Security Operations Training Facility."

The "facility" is the home of Delta Force, one of the best counterterrorism and assault forces in the world. The Pentagon still refuses to publicly acknowledge that Delta Force even exists. It's a somewhat silly subterfuge. The force has been depicted and idolized in at least a dozen movies and books, some of which have been written by former Delta operatives. A visitor can walk into offices of the U.S. Special Operations Command at Tampa and find coffee mugs sporting the secret Delta Force logo: a kelly green triangle inlaid with a white dagger and another gold triangle.

Nevertheless, Delta remains one of the most secretive

special operations units in the United States military. Little is known about how the unit actually works. Journalists have never been allowed to set foot in the compound. And only reluctantly do Delta operatives let visiting government VIPs from Washington have a peek at what goes on inside.

One of the gawkers was George Bush, who as vice president once watched a Delta exercise when the unit was still located in the old Fort Bragg stockade in the middle of the post. To give him a taste of what the force could do, Delta operatives wanted to have Bush sit in a chair in one of the shooting house rooms with goggles and earphones. A commando team would burst in and spray the targets around him with bullets to simulate a hostage takedown. Delta operatives had found that the rubberneckers would usually leave with their pants wet and never bother the unit again.

Horrified, the Secret Service protecting Bush insisted that blanks be used. No way, said the operatives. A compromise was struck. Bush was placed behind bulletproof glass with two armed Secret Service agents on each side. A four-man Delta team blew open the door and "double tapped" the posters of Arab terrorists surrounding the veep. Double tapping, as they explained to him later, meant two shots were fired: the first to disable, the second in the next instant to kill. Bush bounded out of the glass shield all smiles and nervously shook the hands of the assault team.

Delta moved out of the stockade and into its new $75 million complex at Range 19 in 1987. It is the ultimate counterterrorism training center. Commandos practice hostage rescues in a three-story shooting house nicknamed the "house of horrors," where rooms are filled with pop-up posters and moving robots. In some rooms panels can be shifted to change their configuration for a living room, dining room, or office. Slide projectors can flash images of terrorists or hostages on walls and ceilings, which are specially made with bullet traps to absorb and mark the rounds fired. Computers score the hits. Delta is even experimenting with three-dimensional holograms of terrorists and hostages. To sharpen their shooting skills, commandos in one room can voice-activate an image of a bouncing ball with the command "up." The video stops when a round hits the ball.

In the aircraft room of the shooting house, a portion of a wide-bodied airliner is suspended by steel cables from the ceiling. Seats with mannequins posing as passengers are inside. Shooters slap ladders to the side of the airliner and practice opening the cabin doors to assault hijackers. Other parts of the shooting house have elevator shafts and stairwells to rehearse clearing operations.

No expense has been spared. The compound has an Olympic-sized pool, sauna, three racquetball courts, a fully equipped gymnasium and basketball court, Nautilus weight room, and tall swimming tank for drown-proofing exercises. In another building a three-story-high climbing wall has been constructed where mountain teams practice scaling and rappeling from cliffs. On some hallways squadrons have boards with sixty different locks displayed so operators can practice picking them. The paneled commander's conference room has such elaborate video equipment, the Pentagon once investigated it because the trappings were nicer than what the Joint Chiefs of Staff were afforded.

Outside are a series of ranges. Range 19 Alpha has the demolitions range where explosives are tested. There's a jungle lane along which commandos can walk and fire at pop-up targets. Range 19 Bravo is the sniper range, where the "long guns," as the snipers are called, practice dropping targets from as far as 642 yards away; 19 Charlie is the range for the "short guns," the door kickers and room clearers who fire at targets closer than fifty-three yards; 19 Delta is the pistol, submachine gun, and shotgun range. The moving-target range is 19 Echo, where commandos learn to fire from fast cars or to shoot at them. On still another range is constructed a "skid pad," a strip of road that commandos use to practice driving maneuvers to evade terrorist ambushes.

The compound is self-contained. There is a cafeteria and bedrooms in which operators can sleep when they must go into isolation for a mission. Each squadron even has its own bar, where commandos can socialize off duty.

Delta Force, which draws its operatives from the U.S. Army, is one of three American counterterrorist outfits. SEAL Team-6, based in Norfolk, Virginia, is the Navy's version of Delta and specializes in counterterrorist assaults at sea or near the coast. The FBI has a Hostage Response Team (HRT) with jurisdiction over terrorist attacks or hostage taking inside the United States. All three forces share tactics and collaborate on training.

Delta Force commandos have been made larger than life in Chuck Norris and Lee Marvin films. The real operator is much less colorful. The average Delta commando is thirty-one years, has spent at least ten years in the Army as a sergeant before he joined the force, boasts an IQ of 123, and is married with children. (Wives are given cover names for anyone who asks what Army unit their husbands are in.) Hardly any commandos smoke. Many are teetotalers. They wear their hair long and grow beards when working undercover. They keep low profiles in their neighborhoods and avoid carousing among Fayetteville's nightclubs. That might attract attention. And they are intensely patriotic. At private Delta parties the favorite song is "God Bless the USA," a country-western ballad by Lee Greenwood.

On counterterrorist assaults to clear out a room, Delta commandos wear black fire-retardant jump suits with Nomex ski masks, black rubber-soled boots, bulletproof body armor, black helmets, earphones, and throat microphones. They may carry a German-made, 9-millimeter, Heckler and Koch MP-5-series machine gun, with a white light or laser to illuminate targets. They can be calmly and methodically violent. "A qualified Delta operator will not miss what he shoots at and will only hit what he intends to shoot at," explains a former Delta commando. "He is a man capable of killing, but someone who doesn't enjoy it."

Delta Force began in 1977, after the Carter administration realized it was woefully behind its European allies in developing a military force to combat the burgeoning terrorist threat. An eccentric Army colonel named Charles

"Chargin' Charlie" Beckwith was given the assignment to piece together in two years a secret counterterrorist unit that could respond anywhere in the world. Beckwith organized Delta Force along the lines of the British SAS, the famed Special Air Service commando force with its four-man patrols, sixteen-man troops, and larger squadrons. Setting up shop in the stockade, he also borrowed heavily from SAS's selection procedures and training program in order to choose and instruct his new commandos.

The early Delta training consisted of experimenting with an eclectic patchwork of counterterrorist techniques Beckwith and his staff officers culled from commando units all over the world. At the heart of the training program was —and still is—shooting. Delta's operators set out to become the best marksmen in the world. Shooting came first. An operator could get out of daily practice firing only if he was in the hospital and near dead.

Shooting skills were parsed and perfected down to the tiniest movement. Many of the techniques are still kept secret. The critical skill Delta's commandos had to learn was the ability to walk into any room and shoot terrorists before they could kill hostages. An infantryman is taught to lay down a hail of gunfire to cut down anything in front of him. A sniper has time to aim and fire from long distance. A Delta commando has a split second to aim, fire, and kill the terrorist but not the hostage.

For this kind of close-quarters combat, fought three to seven yards away from the target, the operators first learned "instinctive firing," a technique perfected by Southeast Asian police who had to be quick and deadly with a pistol when they patrolled back alleys and slums. British SAS commandos who had adopted instinctive firing for their squadrons flew to Fort Bragg to teach Delta.

Instinctive firing was a quick-shot procedure for when the commando didn't have time to take careful aim. The shooter stands facing the target with arms extended and the weapon clasped in both hands. Both eyes are kept open. The shooter looks out over the top of the pistol, rifle, or machine gun and zeros in on any distinctive spot on the target like a pen or necktie. For a distance of seven yards, the shooter picks up the target on the front sight. At first, Delta commandos used the standard Colt .45 pistol or a modified World War II M-3 grease gun—a heavy, simple, yet highly accurate machine gun. The .45-caliber round in both weapons could knock a man down as well as kill him. Later they would shift to the more sophisticated Heckler and Koch MP-5 machine gun and a variety of 9-millimeter pistols.

As more operatives with gun savvy joined Delta, the commandos drifted away from instinctive firing and perfected their own version of what was called "rapid aim fire." Delta brought in Secret Service agents and sharpshooters from the Los Angeles Police Department and U.S. Border Patrol to serve as consultants. Instead of looking over the top of the weapons, rapid aim fire had the commando—in the millisecond he lifted his weapon to shoot—pick up his target on the front sight and center it on the rear sight. Delta operatives discovered they could fire just as quickly as with instinctive shooting and the fire was more accurate.

They also altered their stance. Instinctive firing called for an "isosceles stance" where the shooter's two legs were spread apart as he held the weapon in front of him. City cops preferred twisting their bodies so they fired over a braced right arm that acted almost as a rifle butt to steady the weapon hand. The stance also made them less of a target to the criminal. Delta combined the best of both and came up with a "practical shooting stance," which enabled the commando to be more relaxed and ready to spring for cover.

Delta operators still spend hours each day perfecting both instinctive shooting and rapid aim fire. Both techniques are taught in the force's training curriculum. The commandos fire as many as 500 rounds daily. They shoot so much their trigger fingers cramp.

But counterterrorism commandos have to be able to think and shoot. Theirs is a combat like no other in the world. The enemy hides behind innocent civilians and never fights fairly. Appearances are deceiving. The difference between a terrorist and a hostage might be the look in an eye. Beckwith wanted the service's nonconformists for his force, soldiers who chafed under regular military regime, who thought for themselves, not just by the book.

To develop that kind of person—commandos who were inquisitive, resourceful, and imaginative enough to cope with this new form of combat, who could operate as precision parts of a killing machine in one second and as freethinking mavericks on their own in the next second—an unorthodox training program has been established. Operators are sent to airports across the country to learn aircraft repair, baggage handling, and cabin cleaning so they can pose as maintenance crews during hijackings. After aircraft workers leave for home at night, the hangar doors at Miami's International Airport are locked and Delta operatives practice storming a plane or studying its compartments.

Others take classes in the morphology of buildings they might have to assault, learning how to read blueprints or trace heating and air conditioning ducts. In one exercise, Delta commandos were allowed to use an abandoned Los Angeles jail where they tested flash-bang grenades, breaching steel doors, and firing through smoke with machine guns fitted with lights or laser scopes.

Commandos learn urban survival skills like breaking into buildings, making bootlegger turns in speeding cars, and ramming through roadblocks. In one drill, an operator is stripped of his wallet, driver's license, and all other forms of identification. He is given five dollars and told to find some way to travel from Fort Bragg to Washington, D.C., without getting arrested. Other commandos have been dumped in European cities to fend for themselves.

Delta trainers devised what some operators nicknamed "buffoonery drills" to get commandos used to the unexpected. Evaluators pasted paper targets on ceilings in the shooting house to see if the door busters would think to look up when they cleared a room. One team blasted the door to a room only to find every piece of its furniture stacked at the front.

In another exercise, a Delta team was told to spirit a hostage away to the third-story room of a nearby building. Only in this case the hostage was a goat. And the team wasn't allowed to lead the goat up the stairs. After dragging the bleating and kicking animal up the side of the building to the third floor, the team was told to evacuate the goat—again not using the stairs.

Delta Force perfected its counterterrorism tactics after much trial and error, some of it comical. One early attempt at using an explosive to disable a bus sent its roof flying into a stand of trees.

An important technique that had to be learned was blowing down doors so a commando team could storm a room. In the early attempts, operatives found they were picking splinters out of their chests when the door blew. To keep the charge attached to the door they tried smearing the plastic explosive with sticky axle grease. But the grease ignited in the explosion and produced a fireball that practically blinded the first commando storming through and singed the eyebrows off the others.

In another exercise, Delta's demolitions team was secretly testing explosive charges on abandoned barracks at an Army post in Virginia. As night fell, the team decided to practice blowing through a wall. They argued among themselves over whether the charge was too weak or too powerful. It turned out to be too powerful. The blast sheared a telephone pole. As the smoke cleared, the team watched the lights on the Army post slowly blink off. The commando who had argued for the heavier charge was left behind to explain the blackout to angry housing officers.

After years of research, sophisticated breaching techniques eventually were perfected in a top secret "Breaching Manual." The size of blasting charges was calculated down to the last milligram so explosions didn't injure the hostages inside or the commandos storming through the door. Delta demolitions experts now paste I- and H-shaped charges to doors using special adhesives. Or large thin sheets of explosives can be slapped on a door. Special timing devices ensure that the top of the sheet is ignited a microsecond before the bottom. That way the blast drives the door down and the commandos run over it. If the bottom ignites first, the door flips end over end injuring hostages inside.

Other breaching charges have been developed to blast through walls, tear down barred windows, or punch holes through roofs without injuring hostages inside. (Delta commandos had planned to blow a hole through the roof of the American embassy in Teheran to rescue the hostages there. They had perfected a charge to blast open the solid steel gate to the soccer stadium next to the embassy. Helicopters had planned to land on the soccer field to evacuate the hostages.) Delta also learned to disable cars and buses with special explosives that did not ignite the gas tank or injure the passengers.

The training exercises also became more elaborate. To test whether his commandos would actually pull their triggers and take a life, Beckwith ordered one troop assembled for what he told them was a real hostage crisis in Quebec. French separatists were holding an American consul in a cabin and negotiations were going nowhere. CIA agents were drafted to play the part of Canadian officials and mounties. Agency prop artists built a cabin at Camp Perry, Virginia, the CIA's training facility known as the "farm." The commandos were told they were being flown to Quebec to stand by. Landing at an isolated part of Camp Perry, they were hustled off to a staging area where fake Canadian newspapers with reports on the crisis had been printed.

Delta trainers in disguise played the part of terrorists. CIA cosmetologists even made up one of them as a female terrorist. A CIA operative impersonating the voice of Jimmy Carter's national security adviser, Zbigniew Brzezinski, finally gave the order over a SATCOM radio for the Delta troop to storm the cabin. Delta trainers in the cabin slipped under trap doors, and movable mannequins popped up in their place.

Beckwith almost had a brawl on his hands after the furious Delta commandos who busted down the doors to the cabin discovered they were gunning down dummies. But the exercise had a more important consequence. Back at their Fort Bragg compound after everyone had had a chance to cool down, a committee of operators organized itself for a heart-to-heart talk with Beckwith.

Boss, we're learning the wrong lesson with those kind of exercises, the group told their colonel, who could be muleheaded when it came to how the commandos should be trained. The British SAS training program, which Beckwith swore by, placed a considerable amount of emphasis on finding out whether its commandos would actually kill people in a showdown. Hell, Americans have never been as squeamish as the Brits about that, the committee told Beckwith. They always shoot first and ask questions later. You could get any Ranger to kick down a door and hose a room with bullets.

The quality Beckwith had to test with an American commando was whether he wouldn't shoot, the committee told him. Was his trigger finger too itchy? Would he gun down the terrorist, but hold his fire to avoid hitting the hostage?

Beckwith saw the point. From then on, more shoot/no shoot exercises were inserted into the training. The shooting house was filled with more of a mix of targets—posters depicting not only fierce-looking terrorists, but also mothers clutching babies, plain-dressed businessmen, teenagers who might or might not be a threat. The commandos now practiced "discriminate shooting"—not killing the innocent.

Delta Force's first hostage rescue operation ended in failure. After spending almost six months preparing to rescue Americans held hostage in the embassy in Tehran, Beckwith was forced to abort the mission at Desert One. It was a heart-wrenching failure. The United States had a world-class counterterrorism unit that had been grounded on its first operation because of bureaucratic bungling, faulty transportation, and no broad military strategy for combating terrorism.

Future rescues may be few and far between. In the last couple of years hostage holding overseas has become almost an extinct terrorist tactic. Diplomatic red tape tends to hamstring Delta's foreign operations. It is barred by law from rescuing hostages inside the United States. Though Delta operators have served as security advisers when the Olympic games have been held in the United States, the FBI and its hostage rescue team has jurisdiction over domestic terrorist attacks.

Overseas, Delta teams have had trouble catching up with their targets. Operatives were dispatched to the Middle East to rescue Americans held in Beirut, but the team ended up cooling its heels in Cyprus because American and Israeli intelligence couldn't pinpoint the hostages' location. In other cases, foreign governments have blocked missions. During the TWA 847 hijacking in 1985, Algerian authorities refused to allow a Delta team to assault the airliner when terrorists forced it to land in Algiers. Foreign countries also have developed their own counterterrorism units, which are just as capable of rescuing hostages and which their leaders understandably prefer to use over Delta.

Delta has had a number of mini-missions. Its commandos have been sent around the world as advisers to help foreign countries deal with hostage crises. Delta teams were secretly dispatched to Honduras and Peru to advise local militaries combating terrorists. Delta operators went to El Salvador to help President José Napoleón Duarte retrieve his kidnapped daughter and to Somalia to hunt for renegade warlord Mohammed Farah Aidid.

Delta's most recent daring hostage rescue came during the American invasion of Panama on December 20, 1989. Delta in fact had begun its own clandestine operations in Panama long before the Just Cause invasion was launched. But they proved to be largely frustrating experiences.

After Panamanian dictator General Manuel Antonio

Noriega stole local elections in May 1989, President George Bush ordered about 1,900 Army and Marine troops sent to Panama as a show of force. Delta and SEAL Team-6 commandos were secretly deployed with the soldiers in Operation Nimrod Dancer. The U.S. Southern Command headquartered in Panama had been ordered to begin moving military convoys on Panamanian roads to exercise American rights under the Panama Canal Treaty. Delta and the SEAL teams were dispatched to respond in case Panamanian Defense Force soldiers blocked any of the convoys or took American GIs hostage. But the PDF backed down. Except for a few forays into Panama City to check future targets for the invasion, the Delta Force commandos sat in a hangar at Howard Air Force Base, wilting in the oppressive heat.

Three months later, the FBI received a tip from an informant that Pablo Escobar Gaviria, the billionaire leader of the Medellín cartel, had secretly flown to Panama, possibly to relocate his operation there. The Defense Intelligence Agency cabled the U.S. Special Operations Command with an urgent, top secret message: Escobar was holed up perhaps with Noriega at Bocas del Toro, an island hacienda off Panama's Pacific coast. The Justice Department had just ruled that the FBI could abduct fugitives in foreign countries.

Delta Force and SEAL Team-6 were scrambled again for an operation code-named "Pokeweed." American law officers would actually arrest Escobar, and if they were lucky, Noriega. Delta and the SEALs would scout out the hacienda first, lead in the officers, then be available for backup. Delta was plunked back into the hangar at Howard. Army special operations helicopters flew to Panama to ferry Delta in for the strike. Air Force special operations Pave Low helicopters flew secretly to the USS *Forrestal* aircraft carrier parked off Aruba to pick up SEAL Team-6.

The assault was set. Bush signed a secret finding allowing the Special Operations Command to dispatch a Delta reconnaissance team to the island to check out the hacienda before the attack. But the hacienda turned out to be an abandoned cinderblock shack. There was no Escobar, only squealing pigs in a farm behind the shack.

At the Special Operations Command a joke started making the rounds. There were four kinds of intelligence: signal intelligence, imagery intelligence, human intelligence, and "DIA rumor intelligence." At Delta Force the raid became known as the "pig farm operation."

But it wouldn't be the last false alarm. In late November, a Colombian informant walked into the U.S. embassy in Panama City claiming that he worked for the Medellín cartel, which he said was planning to ram American military installations with ten car bombs. General Maxwell Thurman, the hard-charging new commander of the Southern Command, had been secretly organizing a hemispheric-wide assault on drug traffickers. The cartel planned to retaliate, the informant told the embassy. One of the car bombs was aimed at Thurman.

The Southern Command went on full alert. Delta again was flown to the Howard hangar with two missions: to protect Thurman from a cartel attack, and, if one occurred, to possibly snatch Noriega in retaliation. Delta, however, never had to consider the possibility. The informant's information proved to be bogus. Delta commandos were now running a pool to see how long they could sit in the hangar at Howard before going stir-crazy.

On December 14, less than a week before the invasion, Delta Force held an elaborate secret dress rehearsal of its two most important missions in Just Cause: the capture of Manuel Noriega and the rescue of an American businessman named Kurt Muse. Air Force special operations Pave Low helicopters took off from Florida's Hurlburt Field with a contingent of Delta Force commandos and flew 250 miles west to a deserted Army range in Louisiana. Two hundred and fifty miles would be the distance Delta would fly from Panama City to La Escondida, a mountain retreat that Noriega also used as an alternate command post along the Costa Rican border. At the Army range in Louisiana was a full-scale mock-up of the mountain home Delta would assault.

At Eglin Air Force Base, which is located next to Hurlburt Field, guards blocked off access to a remote corner of the facility. During the previous month, construction crews had trucked in plywood, two-by-fours, and building supplies. They hammered day and night with intelligence agents directing them in the work. When they had finished, the crews had constructed what amounted to a Hollywood set—full-scale replicas of every home or hideout Noriega might occupy the night of the invasion. The builders used overhead satellite photos. The CIA supplied blueprints and drawings of the structures' insides.

No pertinent detail was left out: door hinges and locks in the right places, the width of steps exactly to specifications, bars on windows. The Delta planners also spaced out the mock-ups exactly as the real buildings were spaced out in Panama. Some were built in southern Mississippi, others further south in Florida.

The centerpiece was a full-scale mock-up of the three-story Cárcel Modelo prison in Panama City, where the Panamanian Defense Force had jailed Kurt Muse. Muse had been arrested in April for running a CIA-supplied clandestine radio station in Panama that made anti-Noriega broadcasts. PDF guards were under orders to shoot Muse if the Americans tried to rescue him. In an operation code-named "Acid Gambit," one of the Delta teams would blast its way through a cupola on the roof of the prison, race down to Muse's second-floor jail cell, and free him.

General Jim Lindsay, the leader of the U.S. Special Operations Command, watched the final rehearsal as a black MH-6 "Little Bird" helicopter swooped down on the roof and a Delta team piled out. The quiet-running Little Bird lifted off within seconds. The team raced toward the cupola. Sentries crouched around it for security while a Delta demolitions expert carefully laced the steel door with breaching explosives.

The demolitions expert stopped for an instant. He stripped off the plastic explosives, reached into his harness, and pulled out a pair of bolt cutters. He snapped the lock off with the cutters.

"Shit," Lindsay muttered to himself. The Delta commando was supposed to quickly blow the door to stun the guards and begin the assault. Switching to the bolt cutters had wasted precious seconds, Lindsay worried. This operation already was complicated enough. When little things go wrong big things go wrong.

After the exercise, the Delta commando tossed Lindsay the padlock and explained the switch. Other Delta operators had been playing the part of PDF guards in the prison. As the demolitions expert prepared to ignite the breaching charge he had spied the pretend guard through a crack in the door. The guard on the other side was standing too close to the door and might have been injured in the blast. As a safety measure, the demolitions expert cut the lock instead.

Lindsay smiled. The commandos were thinking on their feet. It was a good sign. For that matter, the entire rehearsal had gone off without a single hitch.

Delta Force commandos raided all of Noriega's homes and hideouts the night of the Panama invasion but turned up nothing. Intelligence agents who had been tracking Noriega the day before had lost him. He had secretly driven to Torrijos/Tocumen airport where he spent the night of the invasion at a hotel with a prostitute. As Army Rangers parachuted into the airport, Noriega escaped in a waiting van, leaving his uniform behind. After the initial assault, Delta scrambled every time a phone call came into the U.S. Southern Command from someone who thought they had seen the fugitive dictator. Several times Delta missed him at a friend's house or villa by less than an hour. Noriega finally sought asylum in the papal nunciature in Panama City on Christmas Eve, then surrendered to American forces on January 3.

The rescue of Kurt Muse, however, went off about as flawlessly as the rehearsal. The operation actually began several days before the invasion. Secret Delta Force doctors, stationed at military hospitals around the country, quietly slipped away from their duties and flew to Panama. Patrick Hurley, a senior Delta Force sergeant, led a sniper team to a clump of jungle off the road leading to Cárcel Modelo prison and waited. Several minutes before the invasion began at 12:45 P.M. on December 19, Hurley's team picked off PDF guards posted in front of the prison. An armored personnel carrier with a Delta ground team inside raced up the road to the entrance.

At about the same time, the Little Bird helicopter landed on top of the roof. Four commandos wearing black uniforms, night vision goggles, black helmets, and carrying MP-5 Heckler and Koch machine guns with laser scopes jumped off. This time they blew the metal door to the cupola, then another door, and raced down to the second floor.

Muse had been asleep in his stuffy, hot cell when he was rudely awakened by the sound of machine gun fire and explosions. He quickly grabbed his clothes, put them on, and lay on the floor.

For Muse, the next two minutes were a blur of smoke, flashes, and machine guns rattling. Then all was quiet. On the other side of his cell door, he heard a voice.

"Moose, you okay?" a Delta commando whispered.

"Yo!" Muse called back.

"Lay down," the commando ordered. "We're blowing down the door."

Muse did as he was told. The door flew open in a cloud of smoke. The commando rushed in, slapped a Kevlar helmet and bulletproof vest on Muse, and calmly told him they would be heading for the roof. Just follow him.

As they passed the end of the hall where Muse's guard had sat—the one with orders to execute him if there was a rescue attempt—Muse saw only a desk overturned and the rear wall covered with bullet holes. The Delta commandos had shot their way in, dropping most of the guards before they could even reach for their weapons. Muse saw at least five bodies as he ran up the stairs. But not all were killed. One guard had cowered in a fetal position as the commandos stormed down the stairway. The assault team had handcuffed him to the railing. Muse marveled at the commandos' self-control as he passed the manacled and terrified guard.

The commandos and Muse climbed aboard the helicopter on the roof. Muse was told to sit in the middle seat between two operators. Three commandos jumped on each of the two pods outside Little Bird.

The chopper took off. But about ten feet airborne Muse felt what he would recall later as a "big jolt": rifle fire from the nearby comandancia.

The aircraft plunged to the street just past the prison wall. The pilot then literally drove it down the street, bouncing along, and turned left into a parking lot. The pilot tried to get the chopper aloft again, but the plane didn't reach past two stories high when it was again met by a hail of gunfire from the comandancia a block away and dropped to the ground like a stone.

The helicopter's left pod crushed on impact, injuring the three commandos who were hanging from it. A fourth Delta commando was wounded. The others reverted to standard infantry tactics, forming a perimeter around the fallen craft to protect Muse. An armored personnel carrier arrived minutes later to rescue them. Muse escaped unharmed.

With its hostage rescue mission possibly shrinking, Delta over the past few years has broadened its portfolio. No longer is it simply a counter-terrorist unit. It has evolved into a versatile clandestine commando force—which happened to be what Beckwith wanted all along. Operators can be packed and ready to fly out of Fort Bragg within an hour to infiltrate undercover anywhere in the world for precision assaults in a hostile city or deep behind enemy lines.

Delta has come a long way since its early period when Beckwith could count on about 100 door-busters and shooters. Today the force is made up of some 800 people, many with highly specialized skills.

How Delta is organized remains classified. The names of its members are never publicly acknowledged. The cutting edge of the force is a senior Delta staff and three assault squadrons, designated A, B, and C. The force is commanded by an Army colonel with a lieutenant colonel for a deputy. Under them are more lieutenant colonels commanding various staff directorates for administration, intelligence, operations, and logistics.

Each of the three assault squadrons has about seventy-five commandos, also headed up by a lieutenant colonel. A squadron is made up of troops consisting of fifteen to twenty-one men led by a captain or major plus a senior sergeant major. The troops are further divided into four-to six-man teams of operators, all of whom are senior Army sergeants. Each troop has a mixture of snipers and assaulters. About one third are long-range marksmen, while the rest specialize in close-quarter, door-busting combat. The teams can also be organized by specialty. One may be a water or air team skilled in scuba diving or high-altitude parachuting. Another may be a mountain team with climbers. Another may be a mobility team that specializes in getaway cars or racing across deserts in dune buggies.

In 1989, Delta added an aviation squadron, which is secretly headquartered at a base in Virginia. The unit has about a dozen AH-6 attack and MH-6 transport helicopters divided into red, blue, and green platoons. Delta still depends on the Air Force Special Operations Command and the Army's 160th Aviation Regiment for its longer-range transportation. But it uses its own aviation squadron for quick, covert assaults. In the past, the squadron has also flown CIA operatives on secret infiltrations into the Middle East.

The choppers are Delta's undercover transportation. The helicopters are painted with civilian colors and have fake tail numbers. Gun packages can be hidden inside the choppers for clandestine infiltrations, then strapped on the outside when the aircraft become combat assault planes.

The fifth squadron in Delta is the support squadron, many of whose members are not commandos, but are nevertheless some of the force's most skilled specialists. In the support squadron are the administrative, finance, logistics, and operations detachments that keep the entire organization functioning. A selection and training detachment screens and trains new operators. A medical detachment supervises the Army doctors who are secretly on call at Fort Bragg or posts around the country for when commandos go on missions. A research-and-development detachment is the skunk works for new weapons. A technical and electronics detachment develops exotic eavesdropping devices and surveillance equipment. In a hostage standoff, T&E can plant bugs to listen in on terrorists' conversations or microvideo recorders that can be slipped into hallways and heating ducts to tape their movements.

One of the more unorthodox detachments is nicknamed the "Funny Platoon." It is the intelligence detachment. The Funny Platoon was born out of a long-running dispute Delta has had with the Intelligence Support Activity, the Army's super-secret spy unit that places undercover operatives overseas to scout targets for the military. Delta has always wanted to train and vet the ISA agents who slip into a country to provide Delta commandos with intelligence in advance of an operation. But ISA, whose agents are mostly ex-Green Berets who have already gone through rigorous screening and training, has resisted being gobbled up by the commandos.

So Delta organized its own detachment of intelligence operatives who could sneak into a country ahead of a commando team and radio back last-minute information on a target. A cover support element in the detachment prints up phony documents and travel orders for operatives sent abroad. Other intelligence officers also monitor the world with computer terminals patched into the CIA and Defense Intelligence Agency.

The Funny Platoon is also unusual because it is the only unit in Delta that has women. Special operations is practically an all-male profession. Women have been barred by combat-exclusion laws from serving as commandos in Army, Navy, and Air Force special operations forces. In the early 1980s, however, Delta secretly experimented with bringing women in as operatives. Delta officers wanted male and female operators to be able to infiltrate countries under a husband-and-wife cover. The women, who were not part of the assault teams, would recon targets for the shooters.

Four women made it through a modified selection and assessment course. But the mixing of sexes didn't work. The male operators weren't yet ready for liberated teams and the women soon left the force.

The idea was secretly resurrected in 1990. Five women from the Army again endured a modified Delta selection and assessment course and are now working in the Funny Platoon. As of this writing, the women had not been used in real operations. But one day they will, Delta officers believe. The females are trained as undercover agents who, for example, can pose as airline stewardesses to case a plane being held by hijackers.

Delta's selection of commandos is shrouded in mystery. For the people going through it, selection and assessment, as it's formally known, can be creepy.

Twice a year, Delta's administrative staff makes a secret visit to St. Louis, Missouri, to pore over military records at the Army's main personnel center. The staff first looks for outstanding Army captains and sergeants among the Green Berets and Rangers. Then, depending on what special skills are needed in the unit at the moment, the Delta screeners review the files of soldiers from other branches, such as explosive ordnance or communications.

From the records review, Delta draws up a target list. The soldiers on the list receive a letter, which says Delta is interested in them. If the soldier is also interested there's a telephone number to call. If he isn't, he's told to throw away the letter.

For the soldiers who telephone, a Delta staffer is sent for a preliminary interview to check them out. That further shrinks the lists of prospects. Delta officers now fan out to different duty stations for the applicants in order to give them a tough PT test, whose standards are 20 percent higher than the regular Army's, and a swim test. Those not yet qualified to parachute out of planes are sent to airborne school.

After passing the physical test and being certified as a parachutist, the applicant goes to Camp Dawson, a nearly empty Army National Guard post in West Virginia's rugged Appalachian Mountains, where he begins a one-month selection and assessment course.

Selection and assessment is ruthless in weeding out soldiers not fit for Delta. Trainers consider it extraordinary if twelve out of 100 applicants pass. In some classes all the applicants wash out.

The trainers use a combination of land navigation, psychological tests, and enforced isolation to thin the ranks. Before the formal selection course even begins, each applicant is run through about a week of more PT and swim tests, plus map reading and patrolling instruction to brush up on infantry skills.

Then he pays his first visit to Delta's team of psychiatrists. The applicant takes a battery of psychological tests and answers hundreds of questions from the doctors: What's your family like? How do they feel about you joining Delta Force? How do you feel about going to foreign countries? Do you have a drinking problem? Do you ever feel that you're being followed? Do you feel ugly? The questions are asked over and over again as the psychiatrists try to assemble a psychological profile on each man.

The doctors are looking for a stable individual, someone with an anchor in his life, whether it's religion, his family, or his own self-confidence. Lone wolves, immature soldiers, those with a criminal bent are sent packing. A delicate psychological balance must be found in a Delta shooter. "The psychiatrists want to make sure you're not too willing to pull the trigger, but at the same time you're not too hesitant," said a former Delta trainer. The shooter must be a man capable of bursts of calculated killing "but not someone who will go berserk in a Texas tower."

At the end of the psychological evaluation each student must write an autobiography.

In the second week of the preselection phase, applicants are worn down physically by long, forced marches with heavy rucksacks. The week ends with a grueling eighteen-mile march beginning at night through dense forests. The trainers want applicants to begin the next eighteen days of formal selection and assessment already exhausted.

During the eighteen-day formal selection course, the students experience information deprivation. American GIs thrive off the military's buddy system. They're happiest when their leaders are talking to them. No matter how hellish the combat, having a comrade in the foxhole makes it more bearable. Everything a Delta applicant has done in the military up to this point he's done as part of a team. But in this stress phase of selection and assessment he is tested on how well he operates completely alone.

The experience can be unnerving. Applicants are identified only by a number and color. The color designates the squad, the number designates the individual. They cannot talk to one another to compare how they are doing. Delta testers say nothing to them, nor give them any clue on how well they are doing. The trainers don't shout at the applicants, but they don't praise them. They don't frown, but they don't smile. The applicants feel like they're being ordered about by robots.

A typical day: No one sounds reveille. The applicants are told to wake themselves up by 6 A.M. In their barracks room is a blackboard with the day's instruction written on it. "Pack a forty-pound rucksack and don't be light."

Rucksack loads vary by day, from forty to fifty to seventy pounds including water. Sometimes the evaluators even change rucksack weights during the day's march. If a student is caught along the march with a light rucksack—it often happens when he drinks too much water, which lightens his load—the evaluators give him a "BFR"—a big fucking rock to increase the weight.

The applicants assemble silently outside the renovated World War II barracks, then are trucked to a drop-off point where they are fed. They will normally receive a hot meal in the morning and at night.

After breakfast, the truck drops them off in groups of four onto back roads. Evaluators assign them different points on the map that they have to reach quickly. It's a timed test. How fast do they have to get there, the students usually ask.

"Just do your best," the evaluator always says.

With an M-16 in one hand, a compass in the other, and the rucksacks on their backs, the students march off by themselves, clawing their way through the dense forest. Four hours later, scratched, bruised, and blistered from the march, the applicants reach their first rendezvous point.

The evaluator says nothing. The student doesn't know if he has passed or failed, whether he is doing well or poorly. The evaluator, his face impassive, makes a mark in a notebook and calls out the student's number and color.

"Okay Green-19, your next coordinates are here," the evaluator says mechanically, pointing to the map. "The standard is the best you can do. Have a nice day."

The cross-country marching continues all day and into the night. At the last rendezvous point, the applicant's duffel bag is waiting for him. He sets up camp, eats, and crawls into his sleeping bag.

"You need to be ready to go at seven in the morning," is all the evaluator tells him. Nobody wakes him up the next morning. If he's still in his sleeping bag when the truck arrives to take the class to the next starting point he's left behind.

The exercise varies to keep the applicants off balance. One day he will be given three MRE packets and the marching is cut short in the early afternoon. The next day the marching lasts eighteen hours and he is given only one MRE packet. If he didn't think to save a ration from the previous day he goes hungry. One day a student is Orange-36. The next day he's placed in another squad and given a new number. He's now Yellow-5.

Psychiatrists roam among the applicants to observe their behavior and see how they react when their mental and physical defenses are down. Graders secretly watch the applicants marching through the forests. Hiding behind bushes and trees, they use cameras with telephoto lenses to photograph applicants to make sure they are plowing through the underbrush and not cheating by walking on roads or cleared paths. The first time a student is caught on a road he is warned. The second time he's out.

Students are constantly on the clock. But they never know if they are meeting their times. Some invariably get lost in the forest or miss their rendezvous points.

A grader will walk up. "What's your color and number?" will be all he asks. The grader will pull out a notebook, scribble a notation and walk off, leaving the applicant behind bewildered.

For many candidates, the combination of physical stress and isolation becomes too much. They quit. Applicants are allowed only so many bad days when they fall behind on a march—although they never know when they are falling behind. Some applicants are pulled out early for poor performance. Others who have failed are allowed to stay in the course as red herrings to disorient the remaining candidates on the true performance standards.

Delta tries to ease the humiliation for the applicant who is being dropped. A grader will pull him aside and say quietly: "Son, you're an excellent soldier. You're a credit to the Army and your unit. But you're not what we're looking for in Delta." A flowery letter will be sent to his parent unit commending his performance.

But the applicant will be whisked away. The others will never know why. Every morning fewer people simply show up for the truck taking them to the drop-off point.

By the eighteenth day of the stress phase, about three fourths of the applicants usually have quit or been dismissed. The ones remaining must now march forty miles in two days. This time they can walk along the winding but open Appalachian Trail. Now they are racing against time to see how fast they can complete the forty miles in the two days allotted.

At the end of the forty miles, the handful of students

left, bloodied and blistered from forty-eight hours of non-stop marching, are trucked off to a barracks for a shower and the final phase of selection and assessment.

A couple of military books, like Lawrence of Arabia's *Seven Pillars of Wisdom*, are dumped in an applicant's lap. He now has eighteen hours to read the books and write a detailed report on each one. The evaluators want to measure his mental alertness when he's physically exhausted and has not slept for forty-eight hours.

After the book report, the candidates spend a second session on the couch with the psychiatrist. They are given another battery of tests, some of which were developed by the CIA or the British Special Air Service. Another favorite psychological test given is one that was administered to OSS agents during World War II. The same interview questions are asked again. By this time the applicant is so physically wasted he spills his guts out to the psychiatrists. Past lies are admitted, the times he cheated on tests in grade school, family problems.

The final hurdle is the commanders' board. Each applicant is brought separately into a room and placed in a chair. In a circle around him sit Delta's commander and the five squadron leaders who leaf through the stacks of psychiatric reports and personality profiles that have been compiled on him.

The commanders grill the applicant often for hours. Impossible questions are asked:

You're behind enemy lines and a little girl picking flowers spots you. Are you willing to strangle her to continue your mission?

An informant offers you critically important intelligence that will tremendously affect the national security of your country. But he'll give it to you only if you perform a homosexual act with him. Will you do it?

You are ordered by the national command authority to Los Angeles to assassinate three known terrorists as they leave a hotel. Will you carry out the hit or question whether it is a lawful order?

There are no correct answers. The commander and his

staff are conducting one final test to see how the applicant stands up under pressure. Does he get flustered by the questions? Will he be flappable overseas in front of diplomats or with terrorists in a standoff?

The squadron commanders can be brutally honest. Some play Mutt and Jeff routines. One will stand up and shout: "I don't want this student in my squadron. He slacked up on the marches and he complained the whole time." Sometimes an applicant will be asked if he cheated and took the trails instead of wading through the underbrush. If he lies, the commander will toss in front of him the photo surreptitiously taken of the violation. The applicant will be dismissed.

After the interrogation, the senior Delta officers meet privately. Graders will still watch each applicant through one-way windows in a holding room as he waits for the results, reporting back to the commanders on his behavior.

The senior Delta officers sometimes argue over candidates. One squadron commander will want a man. Another won't. The psychiatrist and head of the selection and training detachment will appear before the board with their evaluations.

The decision to accept an applicant is made by majority vote of the board. The Delta commander can overrule that decision, but he rarely does. Lingering questions about reliability and intelligence are usually what prompt rejections at this point.

If a candidate is accepted, his selection and assessment records are sealed forever. Neither he nor anyone else in Delta is ever allowed to see the scores or what the minimum standards were for passing. The mystery of selection and assessment is preserved.

The next step is the Operators Training Course—six months of instruction in commando assaults and covert operations. Much of the training documents consist of classified handouts. Delta tries to avoid publishing manuals that might slip out of the unit and be pirated by urban SWAT teams or foreign armies.

A typical training schedule has students spending more than 1,100 hours during the six months in the shooting house, on the firing ranges, or in exotic field exercises. The students first begin with an administrative block of instruction, during which they receive classes, for example, in "memory training" (how to quickly memorize documents pilfered on clandestine operations) and "image projection" (how to dress so you don't stand out in a crowd overseas). Delta's psychiatrists give a two-hour class on stress reduction and relaxation. Students spend three days at the Charlotte Motor Speedway or on racetracks in California to learn riding motorcycles and driving to escape an attack.

The next five weeks are spent reviewing the basics of rifle marksmanship, logging countless hours on the range, and learning instinctive and rapid aim firing for close-quarter combat. Another six weeks are spent studying advanced light infantry skills, emergency medicine, and communications equipment for covert operations.

Then the students plunge into what makes Delta training unique: nine weeks of "assault and rescue operations." A week is spent in the shooting house on two- and four-man room assaults. The students learn to climb and enter buildings. They practice crawling from window to window four stories up. They learn the "SWAT handshake" (a grip over the thumb to pull a man up), the "sling climb" (scaling up the side of a building using ropes), and the "shoulder assist" (a way to climb onto roofs where a student braces himself on the knee and shoulder of another student).

They learn how to "basket climb," to move from window to window up the side of a building. One operator braces himself out of a window with his hands and legs forming a basket, while the next operator uses the first man's thighs and shoulders as a ladder to climb up to the next story.

On sharply peaked roofs students learn to walk sideways in pairs, grabbing each other's arms for balance on each side of the peak. Coming down the side of a building students practice the "spider fall," a safer and quieter way to slip off a roof than by simply jumping. The operator drapes his right leg over the roof and hangs on to the ledge by his left hand and foot. With his body pressed flat against the wall like a spider, he falls with his right hand gripping his pistol ready to shoot.

The sight of commandos jumping from helicopters onto rooftops makes for exciting videos on the evening news. But the operation can be nerve-wracking for the chopper pilots and commandos. It becomes even more dangerous in the dark. Delta Force spent eight years developing air assault tactics. A Black Hawk helicopter piloted by the Army's 160th Special Operations Regiment soars down to a rooftop. The aircraft quickly flares up so it doesn't hit the side of the building, then hovers closely so the commandos can jump off.

During the hover, the pilot must cope with unstable air drafts because half the time his rotors are over the roof and the other half they're over the ground below. If the pilot doesn't delicately compensate with the cyclic and collective sticks he can send the aircraft crashing into the building. The commandos in turn must learn to link hands and hug the roof after they jump from the aircraft so they aren't blown off the building by the rotor wash when the chopper flies away. They practice fast-roping onto rooftops by sliding down specially woven, thick ropes wearing heavy gloves.

In another exercise, students straddling the landing struts on each side of an MH-6 Little Bird swoop down into a city street with machine guns blazing to surround a getaway car. The students learn how to shoot hanging from the side of the helicopter so the spent brass shells don't come flying back into the pilot's face causing a crash.

The students spend another three weeks learning to be bodyguards. Using training manuals and instructors from the Secret Service, they study how to guard diplomats and generals, protect motorcades, and spot concealed weapons, assassins, and ambushes.

For still another three weeks, the students learn how

to be spies. There are tradecraft classes in surveillance, photography, and casing a building. Students are sent to cities to practice trailing people. They learn how to operate clandestinely through cutouts, work dead-letter drops to retrieve information from agents, and practice car tosses to throw out bags to operatives from speeding vehicles. The CIA provides manuals and officers for this instruction.

At the end, the students are run through a week-long "tradecraft FTX"—a field training exercise, where they are dumped into cities like Houston and Chicago to rehearse cloak-and-dagger techniques. With Delta trainers secretly watching and filming them from nearby buildings, students are given envelopes full of cash with instructions for exchanges at drop sites. Directions are left in caches, the times for rendezvous are taped under phone booths.

The FTX can have its unexpected surprises. During one dead drop exercise at a shopping mall in Raleigh, North Carolina, Delta students discovered a local drug dealer was using the same potted plant for his deliveries. The students tipped off the police and changed their drop.

At another FTX in nearby Charlotte, a student was supposed to retrieve a message from a bus stop ledge in front of a used-car dealership. But reaching into the cinderblock wall he accidentally shoved the dead drop message through the slats. Panicking, he began dismantling the wall. Evaluators filming the student eventually stopped him because he was attracting too much attention from passers-by curious about why he was tearing apart the bus stop.

The operators training course offers just the basics. New commandos are assigned to operational teams where they will spend hundreds more hours in the house of horrors. Operators are expected to be jacks of all trades, and masters of them as well. A Delta commando is considered a rookie until he has been in the unit at least five years.

Special skills are nurtured among the operators. If a commando likes to tinker with cars, he's encouraged to become an expert in hot wiring. If he is scientifically inclined, he might become an expert in explosives. The force accommodates, even encourages, different personalities within its ranks. "They're like a bunch of mustangs," says a former senior Delta officer. "But the unifying ethic among them all is a high standard of performance. Nobody's going to break the standard in the brotherhood."

Part II

DESERT STORM

THE ROAD TO WAR

August 2, 1990. General Carl Stiner, head of the U.S. Special Operations Command, sat in the CIA's headquarters building in Langley, Virginia, putting the finishing touches on a training operation his command was running with the agency. A CIA aide rushed in with a bulletin from the agency's operations center. At 2 A.M. that morning, Iraqi armored divisions rumbled across the border into Kuwait. Stiner was not surprised. The CIA had assured the White House that Saddam Hussein's Iraqi forces massing at the Kuwaiti border were doing so only to intimidate the Kuwaitis as part of a festering dispute over OPEC oil prices. But the month before, Stiner's own intelligence staff had warned him that Saddam may be launching more than just a show of force.

His intelligence officers watched the world closely for potential hot spots, to which American special operations forces might be summoned. They were convinced that Kuwait would be the next crisis. So was Stiner, who had a considerable amount of Middle East experience himself. By the end of July he had already begun turning over in his mind the battle roster of special operators who should be immediately detailed to the U.S. Central Command (CENTCOM), which was responsible for the Middle East. CENTCOM's special operations staff was thin. It would need beefing up. Stiner also ordered his senior officers to start thinking about what they would do if the Special Operations Command "goes to a crisis level." There was the threat of terrorism, he worried. If Saddam invaded and the United States responded militarily there were bound to be terrorist attacks in retaliation.

Stiner cut short his meeting at Langley and hopped

aboard his Air Force Learjet to fly back to the Special
Operations Command headquarters at MacDill. A crisis
action team had already been formed when he arrived.

In the southeast corner of Pope Air Force Base next to
Fort Bragg, Major General Wayne Downing sat at a conference table in the Joint Special Operations Command's
closely guarded headquarters. Across the table was a group
of senior Israeli special operations officers. Downing commanded JSOC (the operators called it "jaysock"), the organization under the U.S. Special Operations Command that
controlled the Pentagon's top secret counterterrorist units
such as Delta Force and SEAL Team-6. Over the years
Israeli special operations units had formed a close relationship with JSOC. Operators from the two forces met regularly to swap intelligence and tactics.

As the officers proceeded through the agenda for their
meeting, an aide slipped into the room to relay the bulletin
on the Iraqi invasion that had just flashed on CNN. The
meeting stopped.

The operators set aside the agenda items. The subject
immediately shifted to Iraq. No explanations were needed.
The American and Israeli operators realized instinctively
that JSOC would be grappling with Iraq for months to
come.

The Israelis knew the country well. They had contingency plans to block an Iraqi ground invasion through Jordan by launching commando raids into western Iraq to
slow the advance. Other commando teams were specially
trained to hunt and destroy Baghdad's Scud missile launchers deployed in the western desert.

The Israeli operators began telling the Americans
what they knew about Iraq. Downing and his officers took
copious notes. The Israelis had valuable insights on the
urban and rural environment in Iraq, the lay of the land on
which JSOC's forces might fight. The Israeli commandos
reviewed the capabilities of the Iraqi army, its elite Repub-
lican Guard, and the security services in Baghdad.

Sensitive subjects, but ones critical in JSOC's line of

work, were broached. How vulnerable was the U.S. embassy in Baghdad? Could a rescue be launched? Saddam Hussein himself was discussed—the bodyguards who surrounded him, his vulnerabilities, the weak points in the security cordons, his patterns of movement, points where he might be attacked. All contingencies—including targeting Saddam for assassination—had to be considered. The option was not openly discussed. But the Israeli operators were professionals. They knew the Americans were too. JSOC would appreciate any intelligence they might have if a hit had to be planned.

The JSOC officers found the coincidence uncanny. JSOC had just completed a secret exercise in the barren deserts of Texas and New Mexico. It was a major test of the outfit's deep-strike capability. Delta Force, Army Rangers, helicopters from the Army's 160th Special Operations Aviation Regiment, and aerial tankers from Air Force special operations squadrons had all participated. In the desert scenario the JSOC commandos were attacking a hidden strategic target deep within a fictional Middle Eastern country. The exercise would prove valuable—that is, if JSOC was invited to the war.

The Pentagon would not flash an execution order to its major commands for another two days, but the commanders-in-chief of its major commands, the CinC's (pronounced "sinks"), were already making private plans to deploy American forces to Saudi Arabia. Stiner was one of them. He ordered a "self alert" for the Special Operations Command. As a CinC he had the authority to scramble his own troops before he received any warning order from the Pentagon. Stiner's staff had long ago prepared contingency plans for the special ops units that would be assigned to the Central Command for a crisis in the Middle East. He began mulling over what special operations units should be sent early.

Stiner soon found out it would be none. The U.S. Central Command was headquartered at MacDill along with the Special Operations Command. But relations between the two headquarters were chilly. The special operators considered CENTCOM a Sleepy Hollow command whose staff practically broke down MacDill's main gate to get away early from work every afternoon. CENTCOM's staff had an even lower opinion of the commandos.

No one nurtured the animosity more than CENTCOM's commander, General H. Norman Schwarzkopf III. "Stormin' Norman" Schwarzkopf despised special operators. In an Army now giddy over light divisions and paratroopers, Schwarzkopf was somewhat of an anachronism—a tank officer whose first love was heavy armored units. Schwarzkopf had earned a reputation in the Pentagon for being overbearing and undiplomatic (his other nickname, which he preferred over Stormin' Norman, was "the Bear"). At the Central Command, he was quick-tempered and intimidating with subordinates, a four-star who paid close attention to his press clippings and who could be hypersensitive about criticism. Officers in the Special Operations Command considered him a meat-and-potatoes thinker, a pompous, plodding tactician who knew little about unconventional warfare and didn't care to learn much more.

The criticism was hardly fair. Grunt soldiers worshipped Schwarzkopf, who could speak their language and who would come close to tears at the thought of military casualties. He had won two Silver Stars in Vietnam rescuing fallen comrades. An opera buff who spoke fluent French and German, he had immersed himself in Middle Eastern politics and regularly shuttled in regional experts for personal briefings. And now, as the possibility of having to block an Iraqi invasion of Saudi Arabia stared him in the face, Schwarzkopf was thinking tanks, artillery, and men—and plenty of the three. Lightly armed Green Berets and SEALs were the last thing on his mind.

Schwarzkopf and Stiner got along well, or about as well as could be expected for a couple of hard-charging, four-star generals stuck together on a tiny base in Florida. But Stiner could be just as stubborn as Schwarzkopf. The biggest war since Vietnam was about to break loose and his command was not going to be left on the sidelines. For the next five months he set out to change Schwarzkopf's mind about special operations.

The leader of the daring invasion of Panama, Stiner had taken over the Special Operations Command only three months earlier after its first leader, General Jim Lindsay, had retired. Both men had commanded the 82nd Airborne Division and its parent unit, the 18th Airborne Corps. Lindsay respected Stiner's military genius and had pushed the Pentagon to nominate him as his replacement at the special ops command.

Stiner had never wanted to be anything but a soldier. He was born in La Follette, Tennessee, just northwest of Knoxville. La Follette was a tiny town where patriotism abounded and military service was expected of the able-bodied. Stiner would never forget as a boy, watching all the young men of the town, many of them still teenagers, line up at a dusty bus stop, going off to fight in World War II. One day he would take that same bus to join the Army. He did so right after graduating from college, entering the infantry as a brand-new second lieutenant and thinking he'd be lucky if he retired as a captain.

Stiner's paratroopers at the 82nd ate up his down-home style. With his shaggy brown hair and craggy features, he looked like Fess Parker and could play an even more convincing Davy Crockett. The division nicknamed him "Uncle Carl." Around his men he turned up the Tennessee twang and salted his language with country sayings. The 82nd staff even kept a private notebook of "Stiner-isms." After one grueling exercise when Army testers had second-guessed his division's performance, Stiner cracked: "Well, ah'll tell you fellas. Everybody's got twenty-twenty hindsight through his asshole."

Senior Pentagon officers accused him of being a swell-head. But for a general, he had a knack for becoming quickly intimate with enlisted men. After four sentences he would know more about a soldier than his own company commander did. But he didn't coddle his troops. A compulsive note-taker during staff briefings, Stiner could recall the tiniest details of an operation. In a war room over the map board, the Southern drawl quickly went away.

Congress had been skittish about confirming Stiner as the nation's top commando. It was ironic. Military reformers on Capitol Hill had long bemoaned the fact that the Pentagon did not have enough aggressive warriors in its top command slots. But they quivered now when they got one. The fear was unfounded. A Vietnam veteran who had been wounded in combat, Stiner was aggressive yet steely calm under pressure. He had made waves in the military because the Pentagon brass had used him as a troubleshooter to jump into international hot spots. In 1983 as a young brigadier general, he was flown secretly to Beirut by the joint chiefs to be their eyes on the ground as the Marines became embroiled in the Lebanese civil war. The U.S. European Command, which had jurisdiction over Lebanon, was furious because it had not been notified of the trip.

Two years later as JSOC commander, Stiner almost got into a gunfight with Italian troops at the Sigonella Air Force Base in Sicily because his Delta commandos, who had surrounded an Egyptian airliner, were blocked by the Italians from capturing the *Achille Lauro* cruise ship hijackers inside. But Stiner kept his cool. Delta backed down and allowed the plane to fly to Rome with the hijackers. Stiner enraged Italian authorities when his commandos hopped in their own plane to shadow the airliner; but even that was done with Pentagon approval.

In 1989, General Max Thurman, head of the U.S. Southern Command, named Stiner to be his ground commander for the invasion of Panama. By then a lieutenant general, Stiner was in charge of the 18th Airborne Corps, whose 82nd Airborne Division was on constant alert to respond to international crises. Thurman gave Stiner a free hand to plan and run the entire invasion while he attended to the other duties of a CinC. It was an unprecedented delegation of authority on Thurman's part. But Stiner was the best fast-attack general in the Pentagon and Thurman wanted a quick takedown of the Noriega regime. A former

Green Beret, Stiner shelved the previous plans for a piece-meal takeover of Panama and launched a surprise night invasion using mostly special operations forces. Like Thurman, Stiner believed in applying overwhelming combat power to defeat an enemy quickly and ruthlessly. It would save American lives and even hold down enemy casualties. That proved to be the case in Just Cause.

The Stiner solution to Saddam Hussein would be much bolder than anything Norm Schwarzkopf ever envisioned.

A week after the Iraqi invasion of Kuwait, the Bear faced a terrifying mission. The first spy satellite photos handed to him of Iraqi T-72 tanks that had rolled through Kuwait showed they were heading south to the Saudi border along with mobile artillery. Schwarzkopf and Joint Chiefs Chairman General Colin Powell believed that American combat divisions had to be rushed to Saudi Arabia if the U.S. was going to preempt a second invasion. Bush agreed. A massive deployment was ordered to protect Saudi Arabia and eventually to retake Kuwait.

Stiner had a more daring plan to halt an Iraqi invasion of Saudi Arabia and possibly even force Baghdad's army out of Kuwait: pinprick Saddam's rear. The Special Operations Command's intelligence officers were convinced that Iraq was ripe for resistance movements. The Green Berets had already assembled secret "area studies" of the region that identified potential dissidents. Kurdish rebels in the northern mountain provinces of Iraq had been unsuccessfully battling the regime for decades. Fundamentalist Muslim Shiites, who made up more than half of the country's population and lived in the marshes and river plains of the south, had long chafed under the dictatorial rule of Saddam and his Sunni Muslims in Baghdad. Many rank-and-file Iraqi army officers privately opposed Saddam.

Occupied Kuwait was even more fertile ground for guerrillas. At least four separate resistance groups quickly formed after the invasion. Kuwait's interior ministry controlled one, the defense ministry another, while the CIA and Saudi intelligence service each controlled two others.

But none of the groups was working with any of the others and the guerrillas were getting precious little support from professionals outside the country who would know how to organize them.

While Schwarzkopf scrambled to build a wall of tanks and guns to blunt an invasion of Saudi Arabia, Stiner proposed to organize a covert war in Iraq and Kuwait. Green Beret "pilot teams" would secretly infiltrate into southern and northern Iraq to survey the dissidents who might be organized into armed resistance groups. Brigadier General Richard Potter, Jr., a former Delta Force commando and the take-charge chief of American special operations forces in Europe, had already secretly flown to Turkey with a small pilot team of Green Berets and Air Force officers. The visit's cover story: Potter was in Turkey to set up a search-and-rescue operation to aid downed American pilots if the United States and Iraq went to war. His real mission, both Stiner and Potter secretly agreed, was to scout out the guerrilla potential of the Kurds.

The Special Operations Command would coordinate the different guerrilla factions in Kuwait so they would fight as one force. Green Berets and SEALs would infiltrate into the country to train insurgents and help lead them on raids. Delta Force commandos would slip in undercover to carry out delicate operations, such as assassinating senior Iraqi military officers who were part of the occupying army.

The Special Operations Command was convinced that the covert war would disrupt Saddam's game plan. If the Iraqi dictator had any designs on Saudi Arabia, the guerrilla operations in Kuwait or his own backyard were sure to divert his forces and buy time until Schwarzkopf had assembled a powerful enough ground force to repel any invasion. At the very least the Iraqi occupiers would be immobilized in Kuwait. Who knew, the Green Berets and SEALs might be able to create enough havoc that Saddam would decide Kuwait wasn't worth it and withdraw his army. War might be avoided.

Excitement swept through the headquarters at

MacDill. But the command had to move fast. It was already picking up intelligence that bands of Kurds in northern Iraq and Shiites in the south were taking advantage of Saddam's preoccupation with Kuwait by launching sporadic raids on military vehicles and communications outposts. The Saudi-Kuwaiti border was still porous. If an operation was to be launched, Green Beret, SEAL, Delta, and British SAS commando teams had to be slipped in before the Iraqi army built up its defenses and nothing could get across. A week into the occupation and the guerrillas had already managed what amounted to a spontaneous uprising by several thousand insurgents. Kuwaitis were sneaking out valuable intelligence for the Pentagon on the Iraqi military buildup at the Saudi border plus videotapes of the pillaging in Kuwait City. Iraqi convoys were being ambushed. Bombs were being planted in battalion command posts and staff cars.

But they were lash-out attacks. There was no cohesion to the guerrilla warfare, still no coordination among the different rebel groups. Weapons were scarce. The insurgents were poorly trained. No underground support structure was in place to back up the guerrillas, no secret cells or front organizations to compartmentalize operations, no escape routes or safe houses to hide the rebels. In the small confines of Kuwait City guerrillas would return home after an operation and be arrested on the spot.

American special operations teams could whip the guerrillas into shape, back them up with an underground, mold them into an effective fighting force. The logic of the operation seemed overwhelming to Stiner's staff. All they needed now was an invitation.

Stiner began lobbying Powell and Schwarzkopf. Powell wasn't enthusiastic. At age fifty-two, he had become the youngest officer and first African-American to hold the nation's top military job. He ended up being one of the most influential officers to occupy the position. But Powell had private misgivings about the American military buildup in the Persian Gulf and had argued unsuccessfully for giving the economic embargo more time to force Saddam's army out of Kuwait. Stiner was light years ahead of him with all this talk about a guerrilla war in Saddam's rear. If Powell had his way, there would be no war at all.

Schwarzkopf had other things on his mind besides Green Berets. His Central Command headquarters had become a "pressure cooker," as he would later write in his memoirs. Never before had he dealt with problems so complex, for which decisions had to be made so quickly. He was in charge of the largest military deployment since the Normandy invasion of World War II. But Eisenhower had twelve months to plan Normandy. Desert Shield was planned in less than a week. If Iraqi tank divisions massing at the Saudi border decided to attack before he was ready to defend, a bunch of Green Berets speaking Arabic weren't going to stop them. Schwarzkopf needed tanks and tank killers fast.

Stiner's staff quickly discovered that its plan faced other roadblocks. The Special Operations Command's intelligence officers had a rough idea of what potential dissident groups existed in Iraq. But they didn't have details. To operate clandestinely in Iraq, Green Berets would need much more than the intelligence in their area studies. They would need the nuts and bolts of any potential resistance. But the CIA—which had spent the Cold War years spying on the Kremlin, not recruiting penetration agents in the Iraqi army or cultivating guerrilla leaders—did not have that kind of detailed intelligence in its files. And the agency balked at turning over to Stiner's command the few spies it did have in Iraq so the Green Berets could develop an underground guerrilla network.

The Central Command staff also wanted no part of Stiner's covert action plan. Neither did the White House. They didn't think there was much of a resistance movement in Iraq worth organizing. Schwarzkopf had the same intelligence files that Stiner had. Dissent within the Iraqi army seemed pretty amorphous. The CIA had found dissidents galore outside of Iraq, but hardly any residual opposition in place within the police state. The conservative Saudi princes, who are Sunni Muslims, were aghast at the thought of arming and organizing fundamentalist Shiites in southern Iraq, who might end up allies one day with the radical and anti-Riyadh mullahs in Iran.

Potter had already sounded out both the Turks and CENTCOM on organizing the Kurds. By the end of September, he had almost half the 10th Special Forces Group stationed in Turkey—ostensibly for future search-and-rescue missions—and had secretly drafted a plan to carve out northern Iraq for Green Beret teams. But the Turks were nervous over the prospect of armed and unified Kurds. Ankara had been fighting a counterguerrilla war almost as long as Baghdad to suppress Kurdish enclaves that lapped over into southeastern Turkey. There was no way Schwarzkopf was going to cede northern Iraq so some brigadier general could have a playground for his Green Berets.

Besides, Schwarzkopf's aides complained, was he supposed to stir up a revolution in Iraq? His job, for the moment, was keeping the Iraqis out of Saudi Arabia. Once he accomplished that, his next mission would be to kick them out of Kuwait. Nowhere in his marching orders were there instructions to have rebel groups, many of them radical, balkanize Iraq—an outcome that horrified the State Department.

Even some special operations officers privately questioned whether the Green Berets were being overly romantic about organizing a resistance movement. After all, occupied Kuwait was not occupied France. It could take years to put together a truly effective underground in either Kuwait or Iraq. In the war Schwarzkopf planned, an underground wouldn't make much of a difference. In four months, he would have enough tanks, planes, and artillery in Saudi Arabia to simply steamroll through Kuwait. Nothing the Green Berets could do with the insurgents in that short amount of time would have any appreciable effect on the outcome of the war. They would only be an unnecessary distraction for CENTCOM.

Schwarzkopf believed they could be a dangerous headache as well. He was afraid of anything kicking off the battle before he had his forces in place. The last thing he wanted was some Green Beret team being policed up by the Iraqis in Kuwait or their own country and that serving as a provocation for a preemptive attack on Saudi Arabia. No commandos would cross the border early, he decreed.

A gloom hung over the headquarters at MacDill. The Green Berets hotly disputed that it would take so long to organize the resistance. Stiner's senior aides questioned all these dire warnings that Saddam would invade and Washington should do nothing to spark a preemptive strike. The satellite photos on their desks showed that the Iraqis by mid-September were digging in to defend Kuwait, not to attack Saudi Arabia.

The command's intelligence officers had other photos and videotapes that sickened them. Washington never took the Kuwaiti guerrillas seriously, but Baghdad had. Shaken by the unusually fierce guerrilla resistance his troops were meeting in Kuwait, Saddam by the middle of September cracked down. Curelly and systematically, Iraqi occupiers dismantled the young guerrilla movement. With no underground set up, no safe houses or escape routes established, resistance fighters by the hundreds were rounded up and executed. Iraqi death squads moved house to house rounding up weapons and suspects. Bloated bodies hung from cranes and lamp posts as warnings to anyone who now dared resist. Scores of suspected guerrillas were tortured to tell all they knew about the resistance. With no compartmentalized cells set up to protect underground networks, Iraqi security services easily penetrated the rebel units and decimated many.

Stiner pleaded with Powell and Schwarzkopf (now in Riyadh) to be allowed to send teams in to save the Kuwaitis. Powell continued to defer to Schwarzkopf. The Central Command stuck to its rigid rule: no allied forces crossed the border. By the end of October the brave Kuwaiti resistance was no longer a problem for the occupation army. Those who were left could only manage to secretly radio intelligence to Saudi Arabia on Iraqi military positions that might be attacked when the allies finally invaded.

The CIA's Special Operations Group did send Arab nationals on its payroll secretly across the border and into Kuwait City to join agents who had remained behind during the invasion. Schwarzkopf bent his no crossing rule to allow the agency's Arab assets to infiltrate. If they were captured, it wouldn't be so obvious that they were working for the Americans as it would be if a Westerner was nabbed.

Those operations didn't amount to much. The Arab agents who were sneaked in supplied Kuwaiti guerrillas with radios and organized them for surveillance operations and as targeters for allied bombers. The 5th Special Forces Group was eventually allowed to train—in Saudi Arabia—a ragtag group of fifty Kuwaitis the CIA had recruited who would infiltrate back into their country to set up escape and evasion routes for allied pilots shot down. It was hardly worth the effort. Of the fifty, the Green Berets guessed that only three would be militarily proficient enough to be of much use to the downed pilots.

The CIA also organized about 100 Arab operatives to infiltrate into the western part of Iraq to help rescue downed pilots. But Air Force planners would later complain that the Arab operatives ended up not doing much of anything in the way of helping pilots.

To this day many of Stiner's aides still privately seethe over the missed opportunities in Kuwait and Iraq. It was scandalous, as far as they were concerned. The "rape of Kuwait" was allowed to happen because of small-mindedness and parochialism in Washington and the U.S. Central Command. An organized resistance movement would have made it too dangerous for Saddam to set on fire every oil well in Kuwait during the war and empty millions of barrels of oil into the Persian Gulf. An environmental disaster might have been avoided. After the war, timid leaders in Washington who had raised the Shiites' hopes that they might be freed turned their back on them for fear that to help would give Iran a foothold in the south. Eighteen months after the war, the Bush Administration, realizing that its worry about a fundamentalist partitioning of southern Iraq might be groundless, established a no-fly zone over the south that prevented Iraqi warplanes from bombing the Shiites.

Postwar pictures of freezing and starving Kurds fleeing Saddam's army in the northern mountains of Iraq eventually became too much for the White House. A little more than a month after the cease-fire, General Potter and about 2,800 special operations soldiers joined Marines to establish an enclave in northern Iraq to feed and protect the Kurds. Potter's Green Berets also used Operation Provide Comfort as a cover to begin secretly organizing and training the Kurdish guerrillas. The Green Berets, however, were under tight reins. Special Forces teams were allowed to teach Kurdish guerrillas "soft subjects," such as surviving in the field and setting up medical aid stations. But they were barred by the White House from arming the Kurds or teaching them offensive tactics, such as ambushes and raids. The White House had promised the Turks that Provide Comfort would not increase the threat to them from the Kurds.

Potter's men fattened their dossiers and made important contacts among the Kurdish rebel bands. The contacts would be valuable if Green Berets ever had to return to organize the rebels in a real guerrilla war against Saddam. But the Green Berets were ordered to leave northern Iraq three months later. The mission they wanted to perform—arming and leading the Kurds in a guerrilla war to topple Saddam—was left unfulfilled. It was the same old story, they complained.

Stiner was more subdued than the angry Green Beret officers on his staff. He wasn't as fixated as they were on organizing a guerrilla war in the Persian Gulf. Stiner had a more important plan he was hatching in his mind—getting JSOC and himself inserted into the war.

Wayne Downing, the commander of the Joint Special Operations Command, was mulling over the same ideas. A handsome young general with red hair and a chestful of medals from two combat tours in Vietnam, Downing had risen through the ranks quickly. He had two qualities other generals in the Pentagon liked. He was a well-rounded warrior, having commanded a Ranger regiment, an armored brigade, and now the Joint Special Operations Command. He also handled himself smoothly in Washington's bureaucratic snake pit.

In the first week of August, Downing had ordered his staff to begin planning possible rescue operations for Americans trapped in Iraq and Kuwait. His intelligence officers went further and began investigating strategic targets in Baghdad that might be hit by clandestine commando teams from JSOC.

Stiner hopped aboard his personal jet and flew up to Fort Bragg. The two men cloistered themselves in Downing's office in the JSOC compound. Downing had an easel with butcher block paper hung on it. He began sketching out ideas with a felt-tip marker. It was a brainstorming session. Ideas for raids inside Iraq were batted back and forth. Downing and Stiner were good friends. They had followed the same career path. Both had commanded JSOC. During the Just Cause invasion of Panama, Downing had served under Stiner as his joint special operations task force commander. The two men thought along the same lines.

The heavy oak door was hidden off a second-floor corridor in the Pentagon. A combination lock kept it secured. Only a small wooden plaque identified it as the entrance to the Special Operations Division for the Joint Chiefs of Staff. A video camera mounted on a stand above swiveled back and forth so guards inside could watch anyone approaching. As Schwarzkopf assembled his army in Saudi Arabia during the month of August, a small planning cell took shape within the division. At Stiner's urging, Powell had ordered that it be formed. Its work would be highly compartmentalized, classified Top Secret-SI. Special Intelligence. Its participants would be sworn to secrecy.

Quiet calls went out to the Pentagon's top commandos around the country. Drop what you're doing and fly to

Washington. The men were not told why they were summoned to the capital. Delta officers attending the War College at nearby Fort McNair quietly slipped away from their classes. Planning officers from JSOC flew up from Fort Bragg. Stiner detailed one of his senior aides to the group. Officers were picked for specialties—commando operations, tradecraft, intelligence—not because of what organization they belonged to. Ability counted the most. The planning cell wanted only the best. The work was too important to let the usual interservice rivalries get in the way. They would be reporting directly to Powell.

For the next five months the tiny cell in the Special Operations Division would formulate deep strike missions for American commandos inside Iraq. In military parlance it was called attacking Iraq's "centers of gravity"—targets that if hit would throw the regime off balance and bring a quick end to the war. One mission would never be discussed in any forum outside the cell: the assassination of Saddam Hussein.

Special Operations Command intelligence officers made discreet trips to Washington to hold private seminars with academics who were experts on the regime in Baghdad and Saddam Hussein. The intelligence officers wanted more than what they were getting in the CIA files. Who were Saddam's closest associates? What kind of men surrounded him? What were the political power centers in Baghdad? Where were the weak points, which if hit by surgical strikes might cause the regime to collapse? Who was or wasn't loyal in the army? What kind of security services surrounded Saddam? What were his social habits?

It was no use sending a Delta team into Baghdad for the hit, the planners soon realized. Saddam was impregnable there. Layers of security men surrounded him constantly. But there was one place where Saddam was vulnerable. At least once a month, the dictator secretly traveled to Kuwait City to inspect the booty he had claimed as Iraq's nineteenth province. The planning cell began formulating what some at the Special Operations Command nicknamed "the Yamamoto strategy." Isoroku Yamamoto was the World War II Japanese admiral who died when American fighter planes intercepted his transport aircraft and shot it down.

The planning cell considered the same type of ambush for Saddam. It would be a difficult operation. Saddam rarely talked on a military radio, whose transmissions the United States could intercept. The regime telephoned its command post in Kuwait City over buried fiber optic cables to alert them when the dictator planned a visit. A wiretap on the cable was not feasible, the planning cell concluded. The commandos would likely have to rely on spy satellites to alert them when Saddam traveled south.

American intelligence analysts had detected what they believed was an interesting pattern to his movements. Saddam had more than ten motor homes spread out in parking lots in Baghdad, the southeastern Iraqi city of Basra, and Kuwait City. Each motor home was equipped to be a command post so he could stay in touch with his generals. American spy satellites routinely passed over the motor homes. The pictures they took were quickly sent back to the planning team.

His movements would vary some, but generally Saddam took a helicopter from Baghdad to Basra. The chopper would land at a military airport near Basra and Saddam would hop into one of the motor homes and be driven along one of two highways south to Kuwait City. Along the way he might switch to another motor home.

The planning cell left open the possibility that Saddam would be captured alive in a commando attack. But the cell's planners suspected that if the Pentagon gave the green light and an operation was actually launched, Saddam would be killed. Washington's cover story would be that the raid had been intended just to capture the dictator, but things had gone wrong and he had accidentally died in the assault.

A Delta team could ambush Saddam in the mobile home or on the helicopter. But he was probably easiest to target on the helicopter ride from Baghdad to Basra, the planning cell determined. Alerted by the spy satellites that

Saddam had boarded the aircraft, Delta or SEAL Team-6 commandos would be secretly put on the ground in southern Iraq or northern Kuwait astride the air route over which the helicopter would fly. Alerted by SATCOM radio of the approaching aircraft, the ground team would shoot it down with shoulder-fired Stinger missiles.

Powell was intrigued by the idea of some type of American force targeting Saddam. So were Defense Secretary Dick Cheney, Bush, and senior aides at the White House. Powell had already made sure that the Air Force also was collecting its own intelligence on the dictator's movements and hideouts so that American jets could attack him if an air war began. The Army's early computer runs projected as many as 20,000 American casualties if divisions had to be sent in to dislodge Saddam's forces entrenched in Kuwait. If Saddam were captured or killed ahead of time, perhaps a costly ground war could be averted. Powell allowed the cell to keep refining its plans.

Schwarzkopf thought the planning cell's scheme to have special operations forces ambush Saddam was harebrained. The commando team might be compromised. Then he would have to send in a huge force to rescue them. Again, it might spark a war when he was not ready. Just because the Pentagon had intelligence now that Saddam had flown and driven several times to Kuwait City didn't necessarily mean that the dictator would continue to do so in the future. He certainly wouldn't make the same number of trips once the air war started.

By the third week of October, the cell had progressed as far as what was called "concept planning" in military jargon. A rough outline of how the operation would be conducted and its feasibility was put together. If approved by Powell, more detailed "operational planning" would have been the next step, where the mechanics of the hit would be fleshed out. It would be a delicate operation, but doable, many in the planning cell and the Special Operations Command felt.

The thornier problem was political. An executive order strictly prohibited assassinations of heads of state. Pentagon lawyers advising the planning cell had drafted a legal brief rationalizing the strike. Saddam could just as well be considered a military commander as a political leader. He would be fair game flying to Kuwait in his military uniform.

The legal justification was thin to say the least. Knocking off Saddam, whether he was in a uniform or business suit, would be seen by the American public—and the entire Arab world—as a political assassination plain and simple, which the executive order barred. The Defense Intelligence Agency wanted no part of the operation. After Washington had waffled in supporting the coup attempt against Noriega in October 1989, the CIA had gone to the Justice Department for a legal opinion on the executive order banning assassinations. If the foreign leader also was the military force commander, the Justice Department advised, he could be taken out in a war. But the agency was on shaky legal ground assassinating him before the onset of hostilities, the Justice Department lawyers ruled.

By November, the cell's assassination planning had died a quiet death. Bush and his senior aides had concluded that a land campaign was inevitable. Time had run out for a surgically quick solution, such as capturing or eliminating Saddam.

But the White House gave the Air Force the green light to attack the dictator with as many precision-guided munitions as it wanted. By Washington rules, the approval came in classic backdoor fashion. Senior Air Force officials made it abundantly clear in their late October briefings at the White House that Saddam himself would be one of the targets in the air campaign they planned against Iraq. His homes, his command bunkers, the buildings he might visit would all be bombed. The White House raised no objections to the plan. If one of the bombs was lucky enough to score, Washington would have a plausible cover story that Saddam had simply been an unlucky casualty of war. There would be no way to explain a hit team attacking him from the ground.

The logic of it all left some officers at the Special Operations Command mystified. The Pentagon would be allowed to try to assassinate Saddam with planes that probably wouldn't succeed, but not with commandos who just might. Saddam could be eliminated by a ground team, they vehemently insisted. The regime would collapse and the Iraqi army would likely vacate Kuwait without the allies having to launch a ground war.

Senior Pentagon officials doubted that a commando raid could ever have succeeded. The futile hunt for Noriega during the Just Cause invasion had convinced them that targeting a crafty dictator was easier said than done. Even some of the planning cell's members believed that they never had enough solid information on Saddam's trips to Kuwait to put together a workable ambush. Intelligence agents discovered that some of Saddam's generals and senior party leaders were also using the motor homes. By the time a team was positioned to strike, Saddam would likely be long gone from wherever he had been sighted, some cell members believed. Planning a hit was a waste of time.

The planning cell's attention shifted to rescuing hostages Saddam now held in Kuwait and Iraq. The cell continued to examine other strategic targets in Baghdad, centers of gravity that if struck would unsettle the regime. The Special Operations Command's intelligence section worked with the CIA and Defense Intelligence Agency to pinpoint the Iraqi military's command and control centers and communications nodes that linked Saddam to his generals. Intelligence teams visited private contractors, many of whom had worked in Iraq, to develop blueprints for Iraqi communications nets. Detailed lists of command posts, switching stations, and bunkers were compiled that might be attacked by ground commandos in order to isolate Saddam from his generals. Contingency plans were drawn up for raids that would cripple Iraq's oil facilities. Some of the information was fed to Air Force targeters. Other intelligence developed on the political weak spots in the regime was fed to psychological operations planners.

On the morning of January 15, Bush signed National Security Directive 54. The NSD spelled out the rationale for launching Operation Desert Storm, which was to commence in less than two days. War was being waged to force Saddam's army out of Kuwait and to restore stability in the Persian Gulf.

Tucked away in the top secret document was a section dealing obliquely with the assassination of Saddam Hussein. If the Iraqi dictator used weapons of mass destruction in the conflict, if he launched terrorist attacks against Americans, or if he engaged in environmental terrorism, then it would be "an objective of the United States government" to bring about a "change in the Iraqi leadership." Exactly how that would be done was not explained.

The passage, which was written by White House aides, left Pentagon officials scratching their heads. The Central Command's Air Force planned to target Saddam anyway with aerial bombing, hoping for a lucky strike. As it was, eight days after the war began Saddam violated one of the NSD's conditions: environmental terrorism. Iraqi soldiers sabotaged Kuwait's main supertanker loading pier, which resulted in millions of gallons of crude oil being dumped into the Persian Gulf. Yet no more deliberate attempt to assassinate Saddam was carried out beyond the aerial bombing already planned by the Air Force.

Pentagon aides suspected the passage was the White House's attempt at historical cover-your-ass. Just in case a bomb did kill Saddam, the White House would have some justification for it in the top secret directive.

American bombers spent most of the war trying to attack Saddam from the sky. The Air Force even had a Yamamoto strategy of its own. If U.S. intelligence could catch Saddam flying in an aircraft during the air war, the Central Command was prepared to shoot it down. Pilots flying F-15 Eagles had top secret orders while they were on patrol in the skies over Iraq. If they ever received from their orbiting AWACS control plane the code words "Horner's Buster," they were to fly immediately to whatever enemy aircraft the AWACS designated and shoot it down. No questions asked. The code words were derived from the last name of the commander of U.S. warplanes in the Persian Gulf, Lieutenant General Charles Horner, and the first name of Horner's principal air campaign planner, Brigadier General Buster Glosson.

The F-15 pilots were to hunt down the aircraft and destroy it at all cost. Even if that meant an F-15 ran out of fuel on the way back and the plane had to be ditched, the mission must be accomplished. The Eagle pilot could be rescued later. The target was too important. Horner's Buster were the code words for a mission to attack Saddam if he was caught flying in an aircraft.

In the first week of February, Central Command air war planners thought the Horner's Buster mission might be launched. Intelligence came in that Saddam might fly to his hometown of Tikrit, north of Baghdad. But the dictator never boarded the plane. One other time, Air Force jets strafed a convoy of cars traveling north from Kuwait. Only later would the CIA learn that Saddam had been riding in one of the cars. His vehicle was not hit. The allied air campaign never brought about "a change in the Iraqi leadership."

Back at Fort Bragg, Downing's JSOC staff had begun contingency planning for another covert operation. Its code name would be "Pacific Wind."

In the third week of August, the occupying Iraqi army rounded up hundreds of Americans, Europeans, and Japanese nationals who had been trapped in Kuwait after the invasion. They were packed off to Iraq for "relocation," where they joined thousands of other Westerners who had been denied exit visas. Some of the Westerners were trucked to strategic military and industrial sites where they would serve as human shields if the allied bombing campaign began. Others were jailed and put on diets of stale bread and water. The hostages might be useful as bargaining chips with President Bush.

Back in Kuwait City, Iraqi troops surrounded the American embassy where Ambassador W. Nathaniel Howell and a tiny band of embassy and CIA staffers bravely held out. The Iraqis had cut off water and electric-

ity to the compound, but Howell, who had secretly stock-
piled supplies, refused to take down the American flag and
cede what by international law was U.S. soil to the Iraqis.

Downing and his staff had begun planning for hostage
rescues almost from the minute word had flashed that Iraqi
tanks had crossed the Kuwaiti border. Rescuing all Americans in Iraq was out of the question. This was not Iran.
Delta had had a workable plan for infiltrating into Tehran
during the 1980 rescue attempt. But Teheran was a city in
turmoil. Delta would have slipped in under the cover of
confusion. Plus a discrete number of Americans were being
held in what was a lightly defended embassy. Baghdad was
a well-guarded city on full military alert. There were too
many hostages and they were scattered over the central
part of the country. The travel distance to Baghdad was
long and the line of support to back up the Delta team
would be thin.

But the State Department wanted its senior diplomats
still left in Baghdad to be able to escape if an embassy
takeover was imminent. The CIA, which also had officers
in the embassy, did not want a repeat of Tehran, when
three of its operatives under diplomatic cover were captured. JSOC worked out a secret escape plan. The Americans would slip out of Baghdad and Air Force or Army
special operations helicopters would pick them up at one
of several prearranged evacuation sites.

A rescue at the besieged embassy in Kuwait City was
feasible. Unlike Baghdad, Kuwait City was in turmoil and
near the Persian Gulf, where Delta and SEAL Team-6
commandos would have the American fleet as backup. The
travel distance was much shorter. The American embassy
itself was near the coast, making an escape less dangerous.
At a secret site on Eglin Air Force Base in Florida, JSOC
built a full-scale mockup of the American embassy in Kuwait City, which Delta commandos practiced storming.

By the end of the first week of the invasion, JSOC had
picked three Delta commandos from fifteen volunteers
who would sneak into Kuwait City. The CIA helped select
the three operatives it thought would blend in the best. A

cover was worked out with an international oil company. The three operators, each carrying sophisticated communications devices and electronic beacons so they could be constantly tracked by JSOC, would pose as American businessmen stranded by the invasion. Delta wanted the three operators to be rounded up along with the other Americans.

One of the greatest dangers hostages faced in a rescue attempt was being accidentally shot by the rescuers. Hostages might jump up at the wrong time or get mistaken for hostage-holders. The Delta infiltrators would help guide in the door-busters and shooters, then keep the hostages calm and quiet.

The Delta infiltrators were never sent. Again Schwarzkopf, worried that they might be caught and ignite a conflict, balked at the operation. Cheney, too, was concerned that an early rescue attempt might be misread by Saddam as the beginning of the war and might provoke him to counterattack Saudi Arabia. Schwarzkopf had his doubts that any hostage rescue was feasible in Iraq or Kuwait. Powell and Cheney nevertheless ordered that preparations for one continue.

As it turned out, the operation wasn't needed. In December, Saddam released all his foreign "guests." With no Americans left in Kuwait, Howell and his staff closed down the embassy and evacuated.

After the war, the American embassy staffers who would have been rescued were brought back to the Kuwait City compound and placed in the rooms where they would have been during the operation. The Army's 160th aviation regiment, which would have provided the transportation, then flew in the Delta commandos, who conducted a walkthrough of their rescue. It would have worked, JSOC concluded.

As the Iraqi army entrenched in Kuwait grew to more than 240,000 men during the first few weeks of the occupation, Saddam bared his teeth in a way that quickly unnerved Washington: by the threat of terrorism. Washington was besieged by reports of increased terrorist activity. The CIA had begun tracking some thirty Iraqi hit teams that had fanned out across the world to strike at American and moderate Arab targets. The Iraqi regime publicly called for an Islamic *jihad* (holy war) against Washington and secretly radioed Palestinian terrorist groups urging them to attack the United States. Radical groups began casing American embassies overseas.

At MacDill, Stiner assembled a secret unit that began examining potential flashpoints around the world and calculating Delta's response time. The intelligence community identified some twenty places in the Middle East, Europe, and Asia where terrorists might strike or American forces might be called on to rescue an embassy under attack. Terrorist base camps and enclaves in Iraq and the rest of the Middle East were pinpointed for possible commando assaults.

The American forces in Saudi Arabia were an obvious terrorist target. But Schwarzkopf resisted allowing any experts from Washington or MacDill to meddle in the antiterrorism measures his staff had already formulated. Security had been beefed up around American military command centers. Three thousand Air Force airmen billeted early on in vulnerable high-rise Saudi hotels eventually were moved to makeshift bases more inaccessible to terrorists.

But the Central Command was still nervous. There were several thousand Palestinians living in Saudi Arabia. The command's intelligence staff had been tipped off that as many as a half dozen terrorists were living in the Iraqi embassy, which continued to operate in Riyadh. Schwarzkopf worried that the Abu Nidal organization, whose attacks the past two decades had killed some 300 persons, might strike at his troops in Saudi Arabia. A bus carrying Americans had been shot at in the Red Sea port city of Jidda.

Aides thought Schwarzkopf was somewhat paranoid about his own security. One special operations unit that he did allow into his theater quickly was a team of Delta Force operators who beefed up the regular Army detail already guarding him. Army public relations officers tried to play down Schwarzkopf's growing number of bodyguards. After all, generals in war zones are expected to face the same hazards as the troops in the field.

Schwarzkopf's staff thought all the commandos and military police surrounding him were a bit much. Other senior American generals had refused protective details as an unnecessary bother. It was one thing to have security men around for trips out to the troops. But his staff thought it was ridiculous for Schwarzkopf to keep a pistol strapped on and a phalanx of Delta commandos surrounding him while he walked around inside the Central Command's headquarters building in Riyadh. The headquarters building, which belonged to the Saudi Defense Ministry, was already heavily guarded on the outside. "What the hell did he need those guards for in that building?" one of Schwarzkopf's generals said. "If terrorists had ever gotten down there in our command bunker, we'd have already lost the war."

Schwarzkopf certainly was an important person to protect. His death at the hands of terrorists would have had a devastating effect on the allied war effort. Still, the security around him appeared comical at times. When the general slept at night, a Delta guard sat outside his bedroom on the second floor of the headquarters. During the day, beefy Delta Force commandos toting submachine guns would cram into the headquarters building's elevator with Schwarzkopf while other commandos would race up stairs to meet him at the next floor.

It would be almost two months after the invasion of Kuwait before Stiner would clue in even his own staff on the real operation he wanted to set up in the Persian Gulf. When he did, it took their breath away. Stiner wanted to deploy himself to Saudi Arabia and be the second four-star American general in the theater fighting Iraq. Schwarzkopf would run the conventional war. He would run the covert war.

His plan was audacious. Stiner, along with a thirty-man headquarters staff from the Special Operations Command at MacDill, would fly to Riyadh in order to oversee any counterterrorism missions that might be needed in the region and to launch deep-strike operations in Iraq or Kuwait. Stiner proposed to bring along two generals: Downing, who would run a JSOC contingent, plus a brigadier general from Stiner's staff who would serve as the operations chief.

JSOC would be divided into three packages. Each would have a mix of Delta Force and SEAL Team-6 commandos, plus Air Force and Army special operations helicopters and Rangers for backup. An "A Package," which was the largest of the three, would be deployed under Stiner's command in Saudi Arabia to cover the Middle East and Southwest Asia. The next largest element, a "C Package," would remain at Fort Bragg to keep watch on Asia, Latin America, and Africa. Finally, a "B Package," the smallest of the three, would fly to Europe to be on call for terrorist attacks there.

It would be a replay of Just Cause, when General Max Thurman had summoned Stiner to run his war against Manuel Noriega. Of course in this case, Stiner would only have a piece of the war. But it was a piece that he felt was critically important. While Schwarzkopf was absorbed with getting his heavy combat divisions into the theater and preparing them for battle, Stiner, working as his subordinate, would pay attention to the missions the Central Command could not handle: counterterrorism and striking Saddam's centers of gravity behind the lines.

While Stiner's plan may have had a tactical logic to it, bureaucratically it could not have been more unrealistic. No regional commander-in-chief worth his four stars would let another four-star into his theater to co-lead a war. Even many of Stiner's own aides thought the boss was tilting at windmills. Some commandos also questioned the tactical soundness of moving such a large JSOC and Delta contingent to Saudi Arabia. With the high-speed air transport available, Delta could be in the Persian Gulf within forty-

eight hours of an alert. It would be better for them to
remain at Fort Bragg where all their high-tech training
equipment was located to keep their shooting skills honed.

But the tactical quibbles were beside the point. Having
two four-star American generals run different parts of one
regional war would be somewhat unprecedented—particularly two generals with such healthy egos as Schwarzkopf
and Stiner. Riyadh would freeze over in August before
Stormin' Norman would allow it, Stiner's aides knew.

Stiner was undeterred. He flew to Washington to win over
Powell. Powell knew there wasn't room for two chiefs in
the Persian Gulf. Stiner's plan was unworkable. Cheney
agreed. But Powell didn't kill it. He didn't have to. He'd let
Schwarzkopf do it for him.

If Stiner could get CENTCOM to agree to it, Powell
would go along, he told Stiner. But he was not going to tell
Schwarzkopf how to run his theater. It was the proper response for a chairman to make. A CinC did run his theater,
although Powell could and would overrule Schwarzkopf
many times in the planning and execution of the war. In
this case, though, Powell was going by the book. He knew
Schwarzkopf well enough to be dead certain he'd never
agree to this plan.

Stiner flew to Saudi Arabia in October to woo
Schwarzkopf. The Central Command staff treated his traveling party as if it were a delegation of Iraqi officers. "We
all knew he was going to try to dump forces on us," recalled one senior CENTCOM officer. Schwarzkopf and
Stiner met with only a few top aides present. The two generals dodged and weaved. Stiner again made a pitch for
sending special operations teams into Kuwait to organize
the resistance. He then had Downing outline his hostage
rescue plan for the embassy in Kuwait City. Downing also
outlined JSOC's capabilities to launch surgical commando
strikes deep inside Iraq. Schwarzkopf repeated that he
didn't want anyone or anything accidentally starting his
war. Deep-strike missions were too risky. The two generals

represented different styles of warfare and they were talking past each other.

Schwarzkopf wanted the special operators to support his conventional warfare plan, to be adjuncts to it, to fill in where his own forces could not handle the job. That meant he wanted the Green Berets, not off on some risky raid deep in Iraq, but rather serving as forward scouts for his ground armies or using all that foreign language training they had to make sure the Arabs in his coalition didn't kill one another.

In fact, Green Berets who had finally made it to Saudi Arabia were doing just that. Some Special Forces teams were camped at the northern Saudi border to spy on Iraqi troop movements in Kuwait and act as human trip wires to warn the Central Command if Saddam's army moved south. Others were serving as liaisons with the foreign forces in the coalition. Schwarzkopf didn't trust the Arab units. Green Berets would provide him with "ground truth" on their true fighting capability, which was uneven among outfits. During the war, the Special Forces advisers in some cases ended up being de facto leaders of forces too unfit to battle on their own.

Schwarzkopf needed Navy SEALs to help clear all those mines the Iraqis had seeded in the Persian Gulf. The Air Force's Pave Low pilots could prepare for infiltration missions inside Iraq, but it would be to pick up downed American pilots.

The last thing Schwarzkopf wanted was a gaggle of commando generals running around Saudi Arabia half cocked.

Stiner decided to broach that subject casually.

"Why don't you let me send you a general officer to coordinate the special operations," Stiner asked as if he was offering to deliver him a box of cookies from home.

"I'll think about it," Schwarzkopf replied with a thin smile.

Schwarzkopf may have dug in his heels, but Stiner knew that no issue in Washington ever died. Back from Saudi

Arabia, he tenaciously began making the rounds in the capital.

But it proved futile. Powell refused to overrule Schwarzkopf. Stiner tried an end run at the State Department and White House. They were no help either. Washington simply wasn't interested in what he could do to preclude this war, which now seemed inevitable. No one was thinking beyond two big armies colliding in the desert.

After Christmas, Stiner made a second trip to Riyadh for one last try at changing Schwarzkopf's mind.

Schwarzkopf by now had had his fill of lobbying. "You've got forty-five minutes," Schwarzkopf began brusquely as Stiner walked into his office. Under military protocol, four-star CinCs were normally more genteel with one another.

Unfazed, Stiner quickly got to the point. He laid out his plan in detail: the A Package he wanted to deploy in Saudi Arabia along with a headquarters element, the C Package that would be based in Europe, and the B Package that would remain at Fort Bragg. He would command the Saudi force along with Downing and another special ops general. Colonel Jesse Johnson, the Central Command's ranking special operations officer, could still control the "white" special operations forces who would serve as liaisons with the foreign units and perform the reconnaissance and search-and-rescue missions. Stiner's "black" force would be in charge of counterterrorism and deep-strike missions. "White" was Pentagon jargon for forces that operated overtly. "Black" designated the covert side.

Schwarzkopf sat back in silence. His face completely hid his contempt for Stiner's plan.

"Carl, that is a really good idea," Schwarzkopf said with all the sweet diplomacy he could muster. "I'm going to need time to look at it."

That meant no.

"I'm not sure the Saudis want another American four-star in the theater," Schwarzkopf continued, deciding to pass the buck.

"What about stationing our force in Egypt?" Stiner pressed politely.

"Well, you'd have to get country clearance from Egypt for that," Schwarzkopf deflected. "I don't know if it can be done."

"It was a slow roll," a Stiner aide recalled.

Ultimately 7,705 special operations soldiers would serve in the Desert Storm war, including even Downing and a contingent of Delta commandos. Another 1,049 would stand by in Turkey to rescue downed pilots. The operators would eventually launch daring missions. They would fight bravely.* But Schwarzkopf would allow them to perform no special operations mission unless he personally approved it. They would fight only on his terms and by his rules. Stiner was never allowed into the Persian Gulf to fight his war.

If he had been, would the outcome have been different? There was indeed little time to organize a Kuwaiti resistance before Desert Storm began. Saddam never succeeded in retaliating with terrorist attacks. A punishing, forty-day aerial bombardment reduced the combat power of the Iraqi army hunkered down in Kuwait by almost one half. Cruise missiles and smart bombs in many instances

---

*Though all their Desert Storm missions were secret at the time, the operators did manage to show off once for the media. A small Green Beret team from the 5th Special Forces Group was the first to walk through the American embassy in Kuwait City after the capital had been retaken. They found the compound deserted.

Army officers who spotted the team inside shooed them away. Senior Green Beret officers planned to personally lead another assault team to recapture the embassy. The media had been invited to watch. It wouldn't look good if the embassy were already occupied by American soldiers.

The first Green Beret team to enter the embassy went to a top floor of a nearby hotel to watch the spectacle and laugh. With the network camera crews in place and the videos rolling, helicopters then hovered over the embassy. The senior officers with what turned out to be the second assault force fast-roped down onto the rooftop. They then proceeded to clear the empty embassy for the second time, causing about $5 million worth of damage (according to private Green Beret estimates) from blown-down doors and busted-up furniture.

were as effective as ground commandos for deep strikes, with far less risk to human life. Guerrilla operations would not have affected the ground campaign, which had tanks racing across open desert in only 100 hours of combat.

But Desert Storm left disturbing loose ends. Fearing accusations that they were slaughtering Arabs, Powell and the White House halted the American offensive before Schwarzkopf could finish off Saddam's army in southern Iraq. Saddam quickly reconstituted the remnants that escaped to brutally suppress the Shiites in the south and attack the Kurds in the north. Neither dissident group was organized well enough to fight back effectively. The Air Force's jets were unable to kill Saddam with their smart bombs. His political centers of gravity remained intact. The White House's unstated war aim of toppling Saddam failed. Two years after Desert Storm, he was as politically entrenched and as defiant as before the war.

Stiner was philosophical about the rejection. He appreciated the political and diplomatic restraints under which both the Pentagon and the White House had to operate. But some special operators remained bitter. Many brave Kuwaiti guerrillas could have been saved during the occupation if special ops teams had been sent in early, they argued. Shiite and Kurdish rebels might have been organized to help topple the regime. Even Saddam himself might not have been around if the plans being hatched by the Special Operations Division cell had been realized. Opportunities were tragically missed.

OPERATION EAGER ANVIL

Bob Leonik walked across the airstrip at Al Jouf, a desolate outpost near the northwest corner of Saudi Arabia. It was early afternoon on January 16, 1991. A bitter cold wind swept across the desert and whipped up sand that stung the Air Force major's cheeks. Al Jouf was little more than a secret makeshift airfield about 130 miles south of the Iraqi border. The Royal Saudi Air Force had allowed the Americans to use it as a forward staging base for beginning the air war. Parked on the runway were MH-53J Pave Low helicopters from Leonik's 20th Special Operations Squadron and AH-64 Apaches, tank-killing attack helicopters from the Army's 101st Air Assault Division.

Al Jouf reminded Leonik of some abandoned fertilizer plant he imagined in the southwestern United States. A drab one-story cinderblock building—it might have served as a passable airport terminal if anybody had ever bothered to fix it up—was surrounded by canvas tents and several raunchy trailers. The underground bomb dumps used to store aircraft parts had been infested with snakes the airmen gingerly evicted two days earlier when they had first arrived.

At least the apartment houses in which they were now living represented a step up for Leonik and his crew. The squadron had spent the previous months in tents at King Fahd International Airport, their main base some 720 miles southeast near the Persian Gulf coast. Air Force fighter pilots had clawed and scratched for choice rooms in the high-rise apartments around King Fahd. Lieutenant Colonel Rich Comer, the 20th's commander, believed the squadron's esprit de corps would be better served if his crews lived together in tents. Perhaps. But Leonik had no qualms about giving up the camaraderie for a few luxurious days of carpets, kitchens, and television sets in the Al Jouf apartments.

It never ceased to amaze Leonik how he had ended up as a Pave Low pilot. He hardly fit the mold, if there was one. A Detroit native, he'd grown up with an odd combination of passions. He enrolled in Michigan State University to earn a degree in criminal justice. He wanted to be a cop. But he would have been just as happy playing in a symphony orchestra. He had studied the classical trumpet since he was ten years old.

After college, he joined the Baltimore Police Department, serving on its SWAT team. He then returned to Michigan State to earn a master's degree. But instead of returning to police work he joined the Air Force. After three years of flying Huey helicopters, Leonik began training for fixed-wing aircraft. But his sinuses blew on a high-altitude flight and he was grounded. He felt as if he had hit a dead end in his life. He'd never be allowed to fly fixed-wing planes. Now the Air Force wasn't much interested in keeping him. A friend suggested he try the Pave Low. Special operations could be a career killer, he knew. But he decided to take the gamble.

Now thirty-seven years old, Leonik had found a home with the Pave Low. Flying the sophisticated helicopter demanded intense concentration, the same concentration a musician needed to interpret a complex score. Leonik had most enjoyed the technical precision of classical music. Now he reveled in the precision of this helicopter's enhanced navigation system. A Pave Low pilot was like a symphony conductor, Leonik thought. His instruments now were the gyroscopes, radars, infrared sensors, altimeters, and Dopplers of the aircraft. One navigation system complemented the other. The pilot must modulate the tone and tempo during the entire flight, he discovered. More fortissimo from the infrared radar, allegro from the altimeter, decrescendo in the Doppler. Each crew member was a virtuoso. Like a conductor, the pilot manipulated the men and instruments to achieve harmony in the air.

His men found that Leonik often slipped musical terms into his commands. He demanded clear, crisp calls from his scanners like the staccato of a trumpet. It inculcated a sense of exactness in his crew.

As Leonik strolled across the runway, the top secret mission turned over in his mind. Its code name was "Eager Anvil." The Pave Low crews had been training for it almost five months. Only two weeks ago had they been briefed on what its real targets were. The Pave Lows, which boasted the most sophisticated navigation system in the world, would lead an assault force of Army AH-64 Apaches just across the border inside Iraq to destroy two early-warning radar installations.

The Air Force and Army choppers made a lethal pair. Unlike conventional helicopters, the Pave Low's high-tech sensors, radars, and jammers enabled it to fly stealthily less than 100 feet off the barren desert at night to arrive exactly on target within seconds of its designated time. The $10.5 million Apache was a flying fortress. Each gunship had sixteen Hellfire missiles, seventy-six aerial rockets, four Stinger air-to-air missiles, and 1,200 rounds of 30-millimeter ammunition. Together the aircraft would sneak across the border and pierce a hole in Iraq's vaunted air defense system. That would create an electronic corridor for Air Force warplanes just behind the Pave Lows to slip through undetected. The warplanes would veer west and destroy Scud missiles before Baghdad had a chance to order them fired at Israel.

Two days earlier, the Pave Lows had moved to Al Jouf so if they were ordered to fly the operation they would start closer to the target. Comer thought the order could come any day now. "The road home is through Baghdad," he had kept telling his squadron. War was inevitable.

Leonik had never believed it. For months he had watched the diplomatic roller coaster with Iraq. One day there would be a breakthrough in the negotiations. The next day war seemed imminent. Leonik always suspected that somebody would soon cave in. The Iraqis would capitulate, the Saudis would capitulate, somebody would pull a rabbit out of the hat. Then thankfully the five months they'd spent rehearsing this complex operation would have been a waste of time.

At the airport terminal, Comer sat in the operations office of Colonel Ben Orrell, the deputy commander of the 1st Special Operations Wing. The wing was the parent unit over the 20th Squadron. Orrell was now the forward commander for all the Air Force special operations aircraft based at Al Jouf. A lanky Kansan with a balding head and dark blue eyes, Orrell was a highly decorated veteran of Vietnam, where he had flown as a Jolly Green Giant helicopter pilot. He had the receiver of a secure telephone pressed to his ear. He was talking to the wing's secret command center back at King Fahd.

"Are you serious?" Orrell asked over the phone, not believing what he was hearing from the other end of the line. "Well, I'll be damned."

He hung up the phone and turned to Comer. On his face was the look of both resignation, excitement, and of some fear.

"We go tonight," he said quietly.

"What do you mean?" Comer asked. His brain hadn't processed the sentence. "Where are we going?"

"We're going to Iraq tonight," Orrell said just as quietly. Then a slight smile crept across his face. "Or more accurately, you're going to Iraq."

Comer slumped back in his chair to let the weight of the words sink in. Though he'd told his men that the only way they would ever leave this godforsaken desert was after a war, the news now hit him like a slap in the face.

"Holy shit," he finally said. "Really?"

In less than twelve hours, Comer and his Pave Lows would secretly begin the Desert Storm air war. CNN and the other networks would broadcast across the global village that the bombing campaign began at 3 A.M., January 17. It would actually begin twenty-two minutes earlier with Eager Anvil. Their operation would fire the first shots of the war.

Comer and Orrell walked quickly out of the terminal and hopped into a rental car to alert the crews. Their first stop was out on the tarmac, where Lieutenant Colonel Dick Cody sat in the cockpit of an Apache performing a maintenance check. Cody commanded an Apache aviation battalion in the 101st Division. His eight Apache gunships would provide the firepower to destroy the Iraqi radars.

H-hour was 3 A.M., Orrell told Cody. The mission was on.

"Shit hot, I'm with you!" Cody shouted, slapping Comer on the shoulder. Cody was gung ho. In the early 1980s the Apache had earned a reputation as a hangar queen because its complex systems kept breaking down in the field. The maintenance problems had since been reduced and Cody's battalion had logged the best mission capable rate of any Apache outfit entering the Persian Gulf. Cody was convinced that the Apache was the perfect helicopter for the kind of quick destruction needed at the radar sites. He'd also show the doubters that this chopper was reliable.

Comer smiled and climbed back into the sedan. The two men agreed to confer later that night on the flight. Their personalities could not have been more opposite. Brash and outgoing, Cody had the swagger of a fighter pilot. Born in Vermont, he was a West Point graduate and had spent almost fourteen years in Army helicopters, ten of them as a test pilot.

Comer was more somber and subdued. He had grown up in the small town of Gastonia in western North Carolina and had joined the Air Force simply to try something different, to see the world. Nobody in his family—for that matter, nobody he knew in Gastonia—had ever done any traveling. He had visions of becoming an astronaut.

His first class in mathematics at the Air Force Academy disabused him of that notion. Comer decided to become a Jolly Green Giant pilot. He ignored the academy instructors who sneered that only sissies flew Air Force helicopters. Two years after graduation, he was dodging bullets as a young copilot in the *Mayaguez* operation.

Comer's military career had been far from orthodox. He spent two years earning a master's degree in English (his thesis was twentieth-century American playwrights), then another three years teaching English literature back at the Air Force Academy. He had been flying Pave Lows since 1986 and had taken over command of the 20th Squadron just two months before it had been deployed to Saudi Arabia.

Comer had jet black hair, thick eyebrows, and dark brown eyes—no doubt from his own Middle Eastern background. His family had come from Lebanon. Coincidentally, Cody's family also was Lebanese. How ironic, Comer now thought. Two Arab-Americans would start the Persian Gulf War.

Comer caught up to Leonik on the tarmac.

"We're going to launch tonight," he told him simply. They would meet in the squadron's hooch tent in an hour. There were other people to alert and countless details to attend to until then.

Leonik stood by himself for a moment on the tarmac, thunderstruck by the news. He found he had mixed emotions. He felt proud. Three years ago he had almost washed out of the Air Force. Now he was a secret warrior about to embark on a mission other special ops pilots could only dream about. But he also felt sad. He didn't really want to be the person who started a war.

But there was no time to dwell on that now. Leonik rushed back to the apartment house to brief his crew. The maintenance men had already been alerted and were buzzing around the Pave Lows. His flight crew only needed to gather up their personal gear. They had rehearsed the mission more times than they could remember. The coordinates for the targets and their way points for the flight had all been plotted on navigation logs. Leonik stopped by the intelligence shop for the latest sightings of armed Bedouin bands that might roam under their flight path. The Pave Low was crammed with top secret electronic warfare black boxes to evade enemy air defense systems and was covered in armored plating, but a stray bullet could always hit a weak spot or one of the cockpit windows and kill a pilot.

Leonik next sat down with the two Air Force pararescue specialists who would be on the flight in addition to the six-man crew. Nicknamed PJs (they were originally called pararescue jumpers), these specialists were the next best thing to having flight surgeons on board. They were skilled medics and rescue experts, in tip-top physical condition, who would be on the flight to take care of survivors if any of the choppers were shot down. Leonik hoped they would have a boring ride.

The hour flew by. At 4:30 P.M., the Pave Low squadron convened in Comer's headquarters tent. Comer struggled to hide his emotions. He had to be the calm commander, like they said in all the military manuals. He had to exude confidence in front of the men. He had to convince them that he knew the mission would succeed. (In fact, he was convinced it would, barring some catastrophe.) He couldn't give off any hint that he was about to explode with excitement and even some fear.

Comer took a deep breath and began in an even voice. "The war starts tonight. H-hour is three o'clock in the morning." The Pave Lows would launch at 1 A.M. The airmen who hadn't received the advance warning until then stared in disbelief. There was a scattering of slow whistles. Someone in the back whispered, "Holy cow." No one cheered. That only happened in football locker rooms.

The early-warning sites they were to attack—each a collection of shacks and Soviet-made radars with some mounted atop vans—were parked just across the Iraqi border north of the western Saudi village of Ar Ar. The eastern radar site was about twenty miles inside Iraq. The western radar site was about fifteen miles inside. About thirty miles separated the two. The mission: destroy the two radars almost simultaneously so one could not have time to warn the other that it was under attack or get a message off to Baghdad.

Pentagon and U.S. Central Command intelligence officers had spent months studying the French-designed Kari air defense system in Iraq. The allied air war planners felt that they knew the strengths and weaknesses of the network better than the Iraqis. Technicians with the supersecret National Security Agency had even made three attempts to disrupt the Iraqi telephone and air defense systems with computer viruses. In one operation, CIA agents planned to introduce the virus into the microchip of a French-made computer printer the Iraqis intended to smuggle across the Jordanian border for their air defense computers. But that operation and the other two were aborted. NSA's technology was good, but not good enough to disable a country's air defense system through one printer.

Iraq had the most sophisticated air defenses in the Third World. It divided the country into five sectors, each controlled by a sector operations center, or SOC. Each center was heavily bunkered. All were buried thirty feet in the ground and protected by six-foot reinforced concrete roofs. The SOCs, which were linked to a national air defense operations center in Baghdad, served as the nerve centers that coordinated the air defense. (The Air Force's F-117A Stealth bombers would target all of them with deep penetration bombs the first night in order to create chaos in the entire system.) Feeding into the SOC in each sector were early-warning radars along the border, like the two Comer's team would soon attack. The radars tipped off the SOC when enemy planes crossed into Iraqi territory. The SOC then would feed information on the enemy to underground interceptor operations centers, or IOCs, which would direct fighter jets or Soviet-supplied surface-to-air missiles against the intruders.

But the system had its weaknesses. The radar coverage often did not overlap. In some areas, if one radar site blanked out, a neighboring site could not fill in with coverage. American spy satellites and RC-135 electronic surveillance planes plotting the Iraqi radar coverage had noticed a thin spot in the southwest radar shield. If the Pave Low—Apache team attacked two early-warning radars there, it would create an eight- to thirty-mile-wide hole in the sector. Because the Pave Lows flew close to the ground under the radar's coverage or used terrain to mask their movements, they would not be detected by the early-warning sites when they traveled in for the attack.

But timing was critical. The two early-warning sites had to be destroyed by exactly 2:39 A.M., twenty-one minutes before the first sortie of F-117A Stealth bombers struck targets in Baghdad at 3 A.M., which was H-hour for the start of the air war. The black, batlike F-117As, which were built to evade detection by enemy radars, would also sneak across at other points along the border before H-hour.

At 2:41 A.M., two minutes after the radar sites were to go down, fourteen Air Force F-15E Eagle attack fighters along with an EF-111A Raven radar buster and four Navy F-14 Tomcat interceptors would roar across the border through the corridor created by the Pave Low—Apache attack. It would take the F-15E strike force exactly twenty-one minutes to reach the fixed Scud missile launchers deployed at the H-2 oil pumping stations near the Jordanian border. Satellite photos showed that at least nine Scud missiles there were armed and pointed at Israel.

The F-15Es would attack the missiles at 3:02 A.M., two minutes after H-hour when the F-117As hit key command and communications targets in Baghdad. The Central Command air staff in Riyadh figured that the two-minute interval would not give Baghdad enough time to transmit an order to the western Scud batteries to fire their missiles. In fact the regime would likely be preoccupied with the bombs falling on the capital and pay no attention to western Iraq, where, if all went according to plan, its radar screens would show no allied air activity. The F-15Es would simply slip through the electronic shield at the border, fly west undetected behind the other radars along the border, then destroy the Scud missiles on their fixed launchers.

But everything had to happen on time. If either of the radar sites was hit too early or too late, some Iraqi radio operator still alive might flash a warning to Baghdad. Its air defense system might light up like a Christmas tree. The regime might begin launching its western Scuds against Israel before the American warplanes had arrived to destroy them. And alerted by the attack, surface-to-air missile batteries in western Iraq might pick off F-15Es from the Scud-hunting sortie.

The Pave Low and Apache helicopters, all part of what now was called Task Force Normandy, were divided into two teams. Each team would have two Pave Lows as guides (if one broke down along the way the other would be a backup) and four Apaches, which would destroy the radars. The Red Team would attack the western site; the White Team would hit the eastern site.

Comer read off the names of the crew members who would be flying. Captain Corby Martin and Captain Ben Pulsifer would be the lead pilots for the two Pave Lows in the Red Team attacking the western site. Captain Mike Kingsley would pilot one of the White Team's Pave Lows. Leonik would pilot the other. Comer would hop into the copilot's seat in Leonik's chopper and serve as the mission's overall commander.

Operational security was paramount, Comer warned. The start of the war was one of the most closely guarded secrets in the Central Command. AT&T had hooked up a civilian line to the Al Jouf terminal. "If I catch anybody using that telephone to call home, I'll rip your tongue out and sew it onto your boot so you'll have to walk on it," Comer growled. The pilots laughed. Comer was always coming out with these lurid threats to make his point.

He now turned serious. "You guys are ready," Comer assured the airmen. "You've rehearsed this many times. You are the right guys for the job. I would risk my life for any one of you. I know I can count on you. And I'll try to get you all through this alive."

The crews sat silent for a moment. Then they rose and walked out to their apartments. Although they knew it would be impossible, they would try to catch some sleep the next six hours. It would be a long night.

Leonik lingered in the room, then approached Comer.

"You knew this would happen all along, and you're going to be the squadron commander today," Leonik said, beaming. "I want to congratulate you." He shook Comer's hand.

Comer stared at him blankly. Only Bob Leonik would think of something melodramatic like that, he thought to himself. Comer felt like a 600-pound gorilla was sitting on his shoulders. He'd been over the mission a thousand times in his head. Their last major rehearsal of it six days before had gone off perfectly. Only the unexpected could foul them up now: an enemy listening post moved since the last satellite sweep, a roaming Bedouin band armed with shoulder-fired SAMs (surface-to-air missiles), a Pave Low and its backup broken down.

So much was riding on this mission—not only the start of the war and the lives of his men, but also the very future of his helicopters. Cody wasn't the only one who had something to prove with his Apaches. If this mission failed, it would be a long time before anybody invited the Pave Lows to another war.

Two hours later, Leonik lay in his bunk staring at the ceiling. He had already gathered his crew together after Comer's meeting. Remember, clear, crisp calls in the cockpit, he told them. Don't step on other people's radio transmissions. Stay calm. Leonik had seen combat before. He had flown one of the Pave Lows during the Panama invasion. The experience had not been that much different from a difficult training mission, he told his men. Just keep your wits about you. No John Waynes. No heroes.

Now Leonik could not pry the mission out of his mind so sleep would come. He went over in his head the flight's nine way points, where he would update the navigation system to ensure it was on track. He mentally walked through the mission profile, the sequence of steps and procedures he would carry out during the entire operation. He had memorized countless checklists, contingencies, and backups if the helicopter's engines malfunctioned, if they came under attack and had to alter the flight plan, if they were shot down and had to escape south to the border.

Poison gas was a scary threat. No one had good intelligence on whether the Iraqis would use chemical weapons.

The Pave Low's enhanced navigation system could place the plane within feet of a target hundreds of miles away, within seconds of a designated time. But no sensor or computer ever worked perfectly. A good Pave Low pilot never relied completely on the navigation system. An inner voice told him when things weren't quite right and he wasn't really in the place the computers told him he was. It was called air sense, and Pave Low pilots honed it only after years in the cockpit. The voices now all shouted in Leonik's brain. His eyes remained wide open.

On top of that, he had a raging head cold. He dared not tell Comer for fear he might be pulled from the flight. Only by the grace of God was he flying tonight. He had been scheduled for the "penalty box" during two critical weeks when the mission was being planned. The Pave Low pilots routinely rotated off the flight line to manage the squadron's administrative chores. If he had been serving his time in the penalty box, he wouldn't be flying in the operation. But Kingsley, an old flight school classmate, had demanded that Red Team's second Pave Low be piloted by Leonik and the duty roster was changed. Leonik was lucky to be on this mission. Hell, they all were lucky to be on it, he thought.

The operation would be risky, intense. But as is often the case in the modern military, the bureaucratic battle to get Eager Anvil off the ground had been even more so.

Some four months earlier in the middle of September, Norman Schwarzkopf stood in his office trembling with rage. Air Force Brigadier General Buster Glosson, the top air war planner on Schwarzkopf's staff, and Colonel Jesse Johnson, CENTCOM's senior special operations staffer, had been rousted out of their quarters and now stood before Schwarzkopf as he flew into one of his famous tirades.

In his hand, Schwarzkopf had an equipment request form from the Green Berets asking that all kinds of vehicles, antitank weapons, and portable direction-finding equipment be rushed to Saudi Arabia. They needed the equipment to carry out their part of the air war, Schwarzkopf had been told earlier in the day. Special Forces ground teams would slip across the border in four-wheel-drive Humvee vehicles and destroy the two early-warning radars to open the corridor for the F-15Es.

Who the hell approved Green Berets attacking those radars? Schwarzkopf now shouted at his two senior aides. He had approved knocking out the two radar sites with aircraft—not with Green Berets. If there was to be a war with Iraq, it would begin with aerial bombing. He hadn't okayed any troops being on the ground in Iraq. Goddamnit, he fumed to himself, the minute he dropped his guard those snake eaters were cooking up some operation behind his back.

"I want you to make damn sure that the only person who can commit ground forces is the president of the United States," Schwarzkopf raged at the two men. He wasn't about to put up with freelancers in his command. "The special ops guys work for me!"

Schwarzkopf's aides found that when the CinC had one of these temper tantrums it was best just to wait silently until he finished ranting and raving. This was a pimple of a problem as far as Glosson was concerned. The Air Force brigadier and his strike cell had spent the past month sequestered in a converted storage room of the Royal Saudi Air Force headquarters building planning the nuts and bolts of an air campaign. H-hour would begin with F-117As sneaking in undetected and taking down the entire Iraqi command and control of its air defense system. Then more than 600 allied warplanes would swarm over the country that night to obliterate what was left so the allies would have free reign of the skies. Knocking out two lousy radar sites was only a small part of the steamroller planned for the war's opener.

When the plans were first drawn up, Glosson hadn't even intended to strike the fixed Scuds in western Iraq until several hours after the air war had begun. Only when he received intelligence indicating that Iraq might fire the missiles at Israel did he approve a mission to destroy the two radar sites so F-15Es could slip past and attack the Scuds before Baghdad ordered them launched. Iraq's Scud-B missiles came in two extended-range versions, the Al-Hussein, which traveled 403 miles, and the Al-Abbas, whose range was 559 miles. The two missiles were tactically worthless because they were so inaccurate. But the last thing CENTCOM wanted on the first night of an air war was Israel being provoked into attacking Iraq because Scuds were striking its soil.

The western Scuds had to be attacked when the bombing began. Glosson had approved infiltrating Green Berets across the border to destroy the radar sites. His stealth bombers would be busy with more important targets at H-hour, so none could be spared for this strike. It was no big deal.

A couple days later, Schwarzkopf had cooled off. When Glosson had briefed him earlier on the entire air campaign he had mentioned that special operations forces would be used to knock out the early-warning site. Schwarzkopf then had approved the whole air war plan. But Glosson had not specifically mentioned that Green Berets would lead the attack and Schwarzkopf had not paid close enough attention to that part of the briefing to ask what kind of assault forces would be used.

"Sir, you told me to put together an air campaign for you and I did," Glosson said soothingly. No one was trying to run an operation behind his back. Glosson had assumed he could use anyone in the command to carry out the air war, including the Green Berets.

Schwarzkopf wrapped his thick arm around Glosson's shoulder. "Buster, I got a lot of pressure on me right now," he said apologetically. "I just didn't focus on it in the briefing. Isn't there some other way we can do this without putting people on the ground?"

"I'll see if we can use helicopters," Glosson said.

The Air Force C-21A Learjet with Jesse Johnson inside had just landed at King Fahd International Airport. The

Army colonel had set up his headquarters there to control all the special operations forces in the theater. In the seat beside Johnson was Colonel George Gray III, the commander of the 1st Special Operations Wing, which oversaw the Pave Lows and other Air Force special ops aircraft in the Persian Gulf. Gray's headquarters also was at King Fahd.

A sandy-haired and freckle-faced Floridian, Gray had been a C-130 cargo plane pilot in Vietnam. He later helped configure the aircraft to be used for low-level infiltration missions for the Joint Special Operations Command. Away from work, his passion was rebuilding old cars. For years he had been towing a '47 Chevy, a '52 pickup truck, and a '68 Jaguar XKE from one duty station to another. They were now rusting away in the saltwater air back at his quarters in Hurlburt. His wife, Barbara, was busy enough with four kids without having to attend to three jalopies in the driveway.

The two colonels now racked their brains over how a helicopter attack could be put together to take out the early-warning radars. Schwarzkopf had more or less said not to come back until they had their act together. Then he would reconsider the mission.

Gray believed the Pave Lows would be great pathfinders for the raid. They could fly low to the ground and not crash into a sand dune, as the conventional helicopters had been doing on training flights in the Saudi desert. But the choppers were too lightly armed to destroy the radars within seconds so the radar operators inside could not radio a warning to Baghdad. The colonels had to find heavier firepower.

Gray gazed out the window of the C-21A as it taxied to a stop. A line of Apache helicopters was parked nearby. They belonged to Cody's aviation battalion, which had just moved into King Fahd.

"Hell, Jesse, let's try that," Gray said, nudging Johnson and pointing to the Apaches. Mixing the two services in a joint air operation was always tricky. The Air Force special operations helicopters had never before worked with the conventional Apaches. Their flight procedures were different. But it just might work.

Johnson was willing to give it a try. Cody was brought in on the top secret plan. He jumped at the chance to join the operation. Cody and Comer, who had never met until then, soon became good friends. Comer liked Cody's can-do attitude.

Glosson also liked the idea. Gray and Comer were convinced that the helicopters could destroy both sites almost simultaneously so no one there would have enough time to warn Baghdad. Glosson wasn't so sure about that. No matter how well timed the attack, he believed that one of the two sites or someone nearby was bound to get a call off to Baghdad. But it probably would not matter if that happened, Glosson thought.

During the months leading up to the air campaign, the Central Command planned to fly F-117As, Air Force aerial tankers, and other warplanes close to the Iraqi border almost on a daily basis, just to dull the Iraqis' senses on when an attack might occur. The allied warplanes would edge up near the two radar sites in southwest Iraq to create the impression that these would be the places where the allied air armada would cross to launch its attack on Baghdad.

If one of the two radar sites did get off a transmission that it was under attack, the message would probably be garbled. Whoever received it in Baghdad might ignore it as just another false alarm. If they took it seriously, even that might work to the allies' advantage, Glosson had told Schwarzkopf. Because of the deception campaign the previous months, the Iraqis would think that the force that had crossed the southwest border was headed for Baghdad. They wouldn't know that the F-15Es were flying toward the western Scuds. The air defense system around the capital would come alive and the antiaircraft guns would begin shooting blindly into the empty sky. After several minutes, the gunners would realize there were no enemy planes above and the air defense system would stand down. A few minutes later at H-hour, the F-117As would swoop in and drop their bombs with the Iraqis now off guard.

The mission was practically foolproof, as Glosson saw it. If the radar sites didn't transmit a warning, great. If they did, Baghdad would shoot at shadows. All Glosson really wanted to do was buy a few precious minutes so his F-15Es could fly to those western Scuds undetected.

A week later, Gray unfolded a flip chart in the cramped conference room off Schwarzkopf's office in the Riyadh headquarters. Schwarzkopf sat at the far end of the long table surrounded by several senior aides with his arms folded. He looked like a man about to be given a sales pitch for the Brooklyn Bridge.

Gray pressed ahead with the operation they had in mind. With enough practice, he was convinced the Pave Lows and Apaches could choreograph an attack on the early-warning radars that would instantly blind them and not tip off Baghdad.

Schwarzkopf was still skeptical. He was impressed with the Pave Lows, which had been flying low on the desert during moonless nights and not crashing into the sand dunes. But those special operators were going to get him in trouble. He just knew it.

Schwarzkopf didn't have to commit himself to the mission at this point. All Gray wanted was his blessing to begin rehearsing it. He would come back later with the results of the rehearsals and Schwarzkopf could decide then if the operation should be launched.

"Okay," Schwarzkopf said grudgingly. "But you're not going to be shooting any of my Hellfires during the practice." The damn things cost $42,000 apiece and Schwarzkopf didn't want the operators firing up the small stocks he had accumulated so far in the theater. He would need all of these tank-killer missiles he could lay his hands on if a war started.

"With all due respect, sir, I've got to shoot some of those missiles to make sure they work," Gray said firmly but deferentially. "I can't fake the mission. We need to rehearse this thing as true to form as we can."

Schwarzkopf pondered for a moment. "Well, you're

right," he finally said. "But you call me every time you shoot one of those suckers." He would keep his fingers in this operation every step of the way.

As Gray folded up his flip charts, Schwarzkopf delivered one last order.

"Do not fuck this up," the general said looking at him steely-eyed.

Gray penned those words in his notebook and left.

Comer's Pave Lows and Cody's Apaches began training together over the deserts south of King Fahd Airport. For operational security, only Gray, Comer, and Cody knew the real mission for the first couple of months. The pilots were told only to practice different scenarios. They began with the basics. The two units normally flew in different formations and at different altitudes. They now had to get used to flying together. The Pave Low would bob up and down following the nap of the earth at an altitude of 100 feet or lower. The smaller Apaches had to practice trailing close behind, but not get swept up by the heavier aircraft's rotor wash.

Next they flew together for long stretches at night, as they would on the mission. The Pave Lows practiced hitting way points with the Apaches trailing. The Apache pilots, wearing night vision goggles, learned to key off the tiny infrared signature from the exhaust of the Pave Low's engines.

Each group began concentrating on its part of the mission. Using satellite photos, the Apache pilots built sand tables with models of each radar site and practiced the formations that would be used in the attack. The Pave Low pilots plotted way points for navigation updates and studied weather charts of the prevailing winds in southwest Iraq, which might throw the flights off course.

The mission planning was sharpened to an even finer point. The Pave Low pilots feared that the high-speed Hellfires would crash through one wall of a radar van and out the other before exploding. That fear was put to rest at the first range test. The Hellfire used in the attack soared

1,800 feet into the sky when fired, then dove down through the target's roof and exploded, guaranteeing more complete destruction.

The mission, whose flight times were figured to the second, was broken down into compartments. U-2 spy planes had plotted the coordinates of the radar sites. The Pave Low pilots now plotted their "no-shit coordinates," the exact release points near the radar sights, to which the Apaches would be taken at 2:37 A.M. The Apache pilots calculated that the no-shit coordinates must be no further than five to eight miles from the site. At that point, the Apaches would update their navigation systems and lock in their targeting, then creep up to the radars for direct hits with the Hellfires. Once over the coordinates, it would take the Apache pilots about a minute to acquire and track the targets on their sensors, punch a firing solution into their computers, then close in for the kill. The Hellfires would take about twenty seconds or less to reach the radars.

Choreographing the helicopters at the radar sites became complicated. With their fancy navigation devices, the Pave Lows expected to have no problem getting to the exact drop-off point on time. The trick was positioning the Apaches exactly over that point so they could quickly find their targets. The radar sites might be blacked out at night, so the Apache pilots might not be able to see them eight miles away by just looking out their cockpit windows.

The onboard computers and sensors would have to find the targets. The Apache computers would already know the exact coordinates for the enemy radars. But that was only half the solution to the targeting. The computer also had to know the exact location of its own helicopter when the aircraft tried to lock on to a radar site. Then the computer would simply direct the Apache's infrared sensors to the known target coordinates and the pilots would be able to see the enemy radars through their cockpit video monitors.

But if the helicopter itself was in the wrong spot or the computer did not know where the helicopter was, the pilots would not be able to automatically find the target. The computer would point the infrared sensor to where it thought the target was. But because it didn't have a firm fix on the helicopter's own position, the computer might be miles off target with its directions. The pilots then would have to waste precious seconds slewing the infrared sensor to find the radar sites so the weapons could lock on.

The Pave Lows had to find a way to position the Apaches exactly on their no-shit coordinates. But how? They could talk the Apaches to the spots over the radio. But the Iraqis, who were sure to be monitoring the airwaves, might intercept the transmissions and warn Baghdad.

One of the Apache crewmen came up with an ingeniously simple solution. Chemical light sticks. The Pave Low's tail gunner would tape several of them together in a bundle. When the Pave Low hovered over the drop-off point, the tail gunner would drop the chemical light sticks to the ground to mark the coordinates. The Apache would fly over the glowing sticks and the onboard computer would be able to quickly point the sensors to the target.

The Pave Lows and Apaches tested it out in the Saudi desert. The light sticks worked. For that matter, everything worked at the half dozen dress rehearsals the helicopters conducted. At a graduation night exercise in late November, the Apaches fired $252,000 worth of Hellfires that blasted all their targets (and practically ruined the gunnery range for other planes to use).

It was December when Gray and Johnson returned to Riyadh to win final approval from Schwarzkopf for Operation Eager Anvil. They met in Schwarzkopf's spacious second-floor office. In one corner sat a huge modern desk with a red hotline phone hooked to Washington. Oil portraits of Saudi King Fahd, Crown Prince Abdullah, and Prince Sultan hung from one wall. Across another wall stretched a large picture window. Gray imagined Schwarzkopf pitching him out of it if the mission failed.

Schwarzkopf sat on the edge of an overstuffed couch, his blue eyes fixed on Gray as he began his briefing.

Gray recounted the rehearsals the Pave Lows and Apaches had conducted. They had all gone well. He was confident that the Pave Lows could guide the Apaches to the radar sites so they arrived on time. The second site would be knocked out within seconds of the destruction of the first site. That should not give either installation time to warn Baghdad.

"Show me the targets again," Schwarzkopf ordered.

Gray spread out a map on the carpet in front of the general and got down on the floor on his hands and knees to point to the coordinates. Schwarzkopf crouched over for a closer look.

How would the choppers get there? Schwarzkopf asked.

A small valley called a wadi snaked south of the eastern radar site, Gray explained. The Pave Lows and Apaches would fly low through the small valley to conceal their movement from those radars. The team attacking the other site would fly close enough to the ground and make evasive maneuvers so it wouldn't be detected by the western radars.

Schwarzkopf leaned back in the couch and stared at the map for a moment. Finally he looked up at Gray.

"Are you going to guarantee me one hundred percent success on this mission?" Schwarzkopf asked in an intimidating voice.

What a helluva question for a lowly colonel to get from a four-star general, Gray thought for a brief moment. Sure the rehearsals had gone off without a hitch. The crews were ready—as ready as they'd ever be. The Pave Low had the sensors and radars and navigation gizmos to fly low with pinpoint accuracy. The Apaches had enough armaments on them to level a small town. Every inch along the flight paths and at the radar sites was being photographed and analyzed. But hell, this was still a hairy mission. What if they ran into something out there in the desert that could shoot down the choppers, which they hadn't expected? What if Bedouins with guns or SAMs had moved in after the last satellite sweep? Comer had thought there was a possibility several Apaches would be downed by enemy fire, perhaps even a Pave Low. No plan survived the first shot of battle. Every commander knew that.

Gray took a deep breath.

"Yes, sir," he finally said.

"Okay, colonel," Schwarzkopf said. "Then you can start the war."

Leonik walked quickly to the Pave Lows' operations tent for his final preflight briefing. He cradled his helmet under one arm. His survival vest was buttoned over his flight jacket. A holstered .45 caliber pistol hung from his left shoulder. It was 11:30 P.M., an hour and a half before take-off from Al Jouf and the beginning of Eager Anvil.

In front of the ops tent, Ben Orrell, the 1st Wing's forward commander, sat peacefully in a rocking chair waiting for his pilots to show up.

Leonik liked Orrell. He was sort of a father figure for the pilots in the 20th Squadron. Several months before, Leonik had been flying a long, boring milk run shuttling supplies for the Green Berets. He decided to give his crew something to laugh about and buzzed a tactical operations center on the ground. An angry Army colonel inside, who had about fallen off his chair when the Pave Low swooped low, had complained to the 1st Wing.

Orrell was furious. "Goddamnit, we don't need circus stunts!" he scolded Leonik. But Orrell never held a grudge. Things were back to normal the next day.

Now the Pave Low pilots were about to begin what for them would be as high-stakes a mission as they'd ever get. Orrell had a right to be nervous and to warn them not to screw it up. But he just sat there rocking back and forth as if it were a lazy Sunday afternoon on the porch of his house.

"I'm proud of you," was all Orrell said as Leonik opened the flap to the tent. "Just go do the mission."

Leonik smiled and walked inside.

The pace now picked up. The pilots were tense as they received their final intelligence update on the threat along the flight path. Leonik gathered up the intelligence maps he would need. He handed his navigation log to Dan Sheriff, his flight engineer, who walked out to the tarmac to load the way point coordinates into the control display unit of the Pave Low's powerful mission computer.

A seasoned flight engineer, Sheriff knew the Pave Low's complex navigation hardware like the back of his hand. If something broke down in flight, he usually could be counted on to jerry-rig some kind of fix. Backing him up was the alternate engineer, Bob Rice, who was fairly new to the crew. On this flight, Rice was the right-door gunner and scanner.

At the tail gun was John Summers. A crack shot with a .50-caliber machine gun, Summers also was the crew's scrounger. No one was better at finding extra rations and water for long flights. Mike Pearce stood at the left gun. Another newcomer, Pearce was high-strung and talkative. Leonik could always tell if he was tense by the pitch of his voice on the intercom radio.

The crew worked well together, Leonik thought. Nobody got on anyone's nerves. The backenders were all top-notch scanners. They would call out altitudes and be right within a foot.

By the time Leonik and Comer had climbed into the cockpit, Sheriff had already punched the way point coordinates into the control display unit on the center console. He was now calibrating the forward-looking infrared radar and the other sensors that would enable the helicopter to pave across the desert. Communications specialists crawled into the back of the helicopter to make sure the right cryptographic codes had been entered into the half dozen radios on board so the pilots could communicate on secure frequencies.

Sheriff, Leonik, and Comer began ticking off the hundreds of items on their preflight checklists.

"Chocks are out, ground crew is cleared out," Pearce radioed Comer on the intercom. Wooden blocks were pulled from the wheels of the helicopter. It was several minutes before 1 A.M., January 17. The Pave Lows taxied down the runway.

"Okay crew, we're coming forward," Leonik announced. "Taxi checklist." Sheriff rattled off more lists. The scanners began a round robin of calls to warn of obstacles.

"Clear forward left," said Pearce.

"Right," said Rice.

"Tail," said Summers.

Lights were turned off in the rear cabin. Summers could see the White Team's four Apaches, with their rotor blades whirling, begin to follow the two Pave Lows down the runway. Cody sat in the pilot's seat of one of the White Team's Apaches. Because its radar site was further away, the White Team would take off first. The Red Team would follow seven minutes later.

"Okay crew, we're going to be taking off on a heading at 270," Leonik continued, giving his men the direction of flight. "We'll do the power check first. We're looking for 117 percent power. We'll check out the hover coupler directly after that."

The procedure they followed was boilerplate. The pilots and engineer always checked the rpms at the beginning of the flight to make sure the engines had enough power for the trip. Then they tested the coupler, which helped the pilot keep the aircraft in a steady hover over a target. Leonik willed himself to keep an air of calm to his commands and the running commentary he liked to deliver on what was happening in the flight. When things got tense in the cockpit, he would intentionally slow down his speech to keep the crew from becoming nervous. But with so much going through his mind at the beginning of the mission, it seemed that even the crew was proceeding through the checklists in slow motion.

Leonik's first way point was at the end of the Al Jouf runway, whose coordinates ground surveyors had already plotted. Sheriff aimed the navigation system's radars and sensors at the spot so the Pave Low's computers would know the exact point on earth where the flight was beginning.

With the Apaches in a staggered formation behind them, the two lead Pave Lows tilted forward and sped northwest from the runway at a hundred feet off the ground. The Iraqi border was 130 miles away. For the short twenty-mile flight inside Iraq, the Pave Lows would drop even lower, to fifty feet off the ground. The night was hazy and dark. Kingsley's Pave Low led in front. As the lights from Al Jouf faded behind them, Leonik felt as if he was flying into a black hole.

Everyone in the plane stayed busy. Leonik, in the right cockpit seat, kept his eyes glued to the glowing green FLIR screen in front of him and the smaller terrain following/terrain avoidance radar scope to its right. Following their climb and dive commands plus the readings off the radar altimeter and attitude indicator would keep him from crashing into a sand dune. He went over one more time with the crew the emergency procedures if they had engine problems or had to ditch the aircraft. With their helmets' night vision goggles flipped down, Pearce and Rice leaned over their .50-caliber machine guns and craned out the open door windows on each side of helicopter. Flying this low, they constantly scanned for obstacles like power lines and dunes. Summers, squatting behind the machine gun at the tail, watched the Apaches.

"How's the formation look?" Leonik asked over the intercom microphone that extended from his helmet and was pressed to his lips.

"Staggered left," Summers said. A half hour later, the Apache formation would shift to the right behind the Pave Lows to break the monotony.

Twenty miles northeast of Al Jouf the helicopters were flying over barren desert. "Okay, let's spread out the formation and test fire our weapons," Leonik ordered. Each gunner shot off a half dozen rounds from the ammunition belt that fed into the machine guns. All three worked.

Leonik could tell the crew was nervous just from their voices on the radio.

"How you doing back there?" Leonik asked. "Gun check clear. Everything okay?"

"Roger," said Pearce, his voice now high-pitched.

"Mike, I can smell you," Leonik kidded. "Did you use deodorant tonight?"

"He's gotta go back to Al Jouf for it," Rice said.

"Naw, I'll just move to the tail," Pearce said.

They all laughed.

Comer busied himself with the radios. As the mission commander he kept track of all the helicopters. He was also Task Force Normandy's link to the Central Command through the satellite communications radio on board the Pave Low.

Comer now flipped the switch for the SATCOM.

Something was wrong. The frequency was silent. There should have been all kinds of chatter on the SATCOM frequency tonight. Hell, the war was starting. Comer keyed his mike and spoke. No one answered.

Strange, he thought. They had used their SATCOM radio every night for the last two months and nothing had ever gone wrong. Comer raised Kingsley's Pave Low on a secure short-range radio.

"Do you guys have SATCOM working?" he asked.

They didn't. What the hell was going on? he murmured to himself.

Comer began the standard trouble checks the crew performed when an AN/ARC-164 SATCOM radio went down. Sheriff leaned back and with a glowing chemical stick checked the SATCOM radio set control panel on the flight engineer's console to his left, then the KY-58 secure voice system that would scramble the radio signals. He could find nothing wrong.

Comer, Leonik, and Sheriff looked at one another. They each were thinking the same thing. SATCOM was the only long-range radio they had that could receive a message from the Central Command headquarters. The helicopters were now racing toward the Iraqi border at 110 knots. Unless they could get this radio fixed, the Central Command had no way to re-call them if H-hour was postponed or if there was some diplomatic breakthrough and Desert Storm was canceled.

Comer began fidgeting in his seat. He tried to keep a cool-commander look on his face, but Sheriff could tell when he was agitated inside. And this was one of those times.

It was something about Snickers bars that calmed down Comer in tight spots. He'd tell his men time and again, "If you guys just keep me in Snickers bars I'll be okay."

Rice had had his wife mail a large plastic bag of miniature Snickers bars. The bag now sat at his feet under the machine gun.

Rice reached down pulled one of the pieces of candy out of the bag and poked it in Sheriff's ribs. Sheriff, who was sitting forward in the cockpit between Comer and Leonik, reached behind and grabbed it, then handed the tranquilizer to Comer.

"Thanks," Comer said, unwrapping the chocolate bar and stuffing it in his mouth.

For the next fifteen minutes, Comer tried every procedure he could think of to raise the Central Command on the SATCOM radio. When he became fidgety, Sheriff would stick his hand behind his back. Rice would slap a piece of candy in it.

"You need another Snickers bar, sir?" he asked.

"Yeah, I need another Snickers bar. Pass one up."

Sheriff finally asked what was on his and Leonik's mind. "What are we going to do if we never raise them on SATCOM?"

Comer looked at them both. "We're going to start the war by ourselves," he finally said. "I hope everybody else joins in."

The men flew in silence. The Pave Low streaked across its second way point south of Ar Ar, the border village that lay on Tapline Road, which was the east-west highway stretching across Saudi Arabia.

Suddenly the entire helicopter jolted, like a car running over a speed bump. Sheriff quickly looked down at the center control console between Leonik and Comer where most of the aircraft's navigation panels were located. The numbers on the control display unit, the video screen for the mission computer, had gone screwy.

"It looks like the system has dumped its alignment," Sheriff said, looking back up at Leonik.

"Gentlemen, we've got a slight problem here," Leonik said in a quiet, almost singsong voice.

That was an understatement. The system that had dumped its alignment was the entire enhanced navigation system, which controlled the helicopter's seven navigation computers, sensors, and radars. The entire system had blanked out. The ENS in effect was telling the pilot it was completely lost. It didn't know where the helicopter was on earth.

"It appears we have dropped our alignment, crew," Leonik announced formally on the intercom, as if he were reading a dip in a quarterly sales report. "We will endeavor to do everything we can to bring that back in the most expeditious manner."

For the calamity they faced, Leonik seemed awfully prim and proper. But that was how he always talked on the intercom when the tension mounted, the crew had found. It was Leonik's way of saying something's wrong but the pilots have it under control. He would even correct their grammar and chide them when they used foul language. "How many years will it take to make you a proper speaking person?" Leonik would always say. The crew would laugh and try to put on airs. They found it did relieve the strain.

The left side of the cockpit where Comer sat was beginning to fill up with Snickers bar wrappers. Had gremlins taken over this plane, he wondered. First the SATCOM, now the entire navigation system goes haywire. The SATCOM he could probably live without. The enhanced navigation system he couldn't. Hell, it was the only reason the Pave Lows were on this flight. Without the ENS, the aircraft was no better than any other vanilla chopper with the pilot navigating off a road map. If the ENS blew they might as well land this beast, spread out lawn chairs, and watch the war go by.

"Do we have any lights on in the back?" Comer asked over his intercom.

Pearce, the door gunner, turned around to the pizza rack, the metal shelves on the left side of the rear cabin. They held the electronic control boxes for the navigation subsystems that fed the ENS. If any of the fault lights flashed on the control boxes, it would indicate that one of the navigation computers or sensors that fed the ENS was broken. Pearce looked up and down the rack. No lights. The terrain-following radar monitor panel, mission computer, projected map display SDC, terrain avoidance/terrain following SDC, inertial navigation unit, Doppler radar SDC, bus interface unit, they all seemed to be working.

Maybe there was something wrong with the flight controls, Sheriff said. He began to adjust knobs and dials on the center console. Minutes ticked away. The helicopter neared closer and closer to Ar Ar, which was just thirty-five miles south of the Iraqi border.

Leonik concentrated on flying the plane, using a paper map on his knee as a reference. God, I hope we don't get lost, he kept thinking. Fortunately Leonik could follow Kingsley's Pave Low, which was taking the lead. Comer, who had as good a working knowledge of the complex navigation system as Sheriff, began checking the hardware for each navigation subsystem of the ENS. The Doppler radar that tracked position and helicopter velocity seemed okay. So did the inertial navigation unit with its ring laser gyro. The bus interface unit that converted analog signals to digital for the mission computer and the avionics systems operated fine. No problems with the radars and infrared sensors or the projected map display, which automatically traced the movement of the aircraft across a filmstrip map.

Finally Comer decided nothing was wrong with the ENS hardware. Some unexplained glitch must have brought it down, a stray volt or electron. Maybe a grain of sand from the desert had slipped into one of the circuits, causing a momentary belch in the electronics.

Comer ordered Sheriff to crank up the ENS again. They would perform an airborne alignment of the navigation system. In effect the pilots would tell the computers and sensors where they were on the earth and the system would begin navigating from that point. An airborne alignment while traveling at 110 knots would not be as accurate as when Sheriff did it when the aircraft was parked on the runway at Al Jouf. But for the next twenty-three minutes, the helicopter would be flying level on a straight line. And they had several way points before the Iraqi border, which they could use to correct the errors in their estimated position.

Sheriff began the realignment. Meanwhile, Comer returned to the headache with SATCOM. He was supposed to be a mission commander. Instead he'd become an overworked maintenance man. Surely if they called off the war, somebody would find some way to contact them, he thought. The AWACS flying around Saudi Arabia would figure out how to reach them.

"What do you see out the back?" Comer asked Summers.

Summers scanned the horizon beyond the Apaches with his night vision goggles. He saw clumps of tiny lights from the allied warplanes loitering in the skies south.

"Well, if we're going in unauthorized, there's a whole lot of people back here on their way too," Summers said into his helmet mike.

Yeah, I'm probably being too paranoid, Comer thought. Nothing's stopping this war. Still, he would feel a lot easier if he had that umbilical cord connected to the Central Command headquarters.

Then it dawned on him. The other Pave Low he had radioed also couldn't raise anyone on its SATCOM. It was highly unlikely they both would experience mechanical failure at the same time. They must have begun with the same problem when they took off from Al Jouf. The codes.

The cryptographic codes installed in the SATCOM radio enabled it to link up with the Central Command's secure radio. Maybe the codes had been incorrectly loaded back at Al Jouf. Comer quickly tried reloading the codes on different settings of the KY-58.

One finally worked. Chatter burst from the SATCOM radio. Comer's shoulders sagged and he took a long breath. They were five minutes from the Iraqi border.

What he now heard over the SATCOM frequency sounded surreal. Radio operators in Riyadh gossiped with buddies back at military bases in the United States. Some were using it to call home and have wives mail extra uniforms. Others were sending faxes, whose transmissions snarled up the frequencies. Apparently a lot of people had been kept in the dark on H-hour. He wanted to shout into his microphone and tell them all to shut up. The war was starting.

At 2:12 A.M., their Pave Low crossed the border. Leonik checked the cockpit clock to make sure they had crossed at the right time. They had. The ENS now was aligned tightly and back on course. Several minutes later, Martin's Red Team would pass the border further west.

Leonik ordered the remaining few lights in the cabin doused. They now flew totally blacked out. Pearce, Rice, and Summers scanned the land outside looking for roaming Bedouins, any signs of tracer fire, or the plume of a heat-seeking SAM. The Pave Low's altitude dipped to fifty feet. Ahead, Leonik could see the lights of an Iraqi army listening post. He banked the helicopter right to avoid the post and flew into the Wadi Hamir, which stretched northeast but below the radar site. No rifle fire. The radars showed no SAM threat. They had sneaked across undetected.

"Well we're in Iraq," Comer said matter-of-factly.

More than 700 miles southeast, George Gray and Jesse Johnson stood nervously in the basement of the air terminal at King Fahd. The basement had been converted into a joint operations center to control all the commando forces in the Persian Gulf. Tactical maps and intelligence charts covered the walls. On rows of tables sat SATCOM radios and secure phones that linked the JOC to the Central

Command's headquarters in Riyadh and the command posts for all the special operations units. Gas masks were stacked in piles near the tables. The JOC would also serve as a bunker if there was a Scud attack. In the back, a section was partitioned with Plexiglas, where Johnson, Gray, and the other special ops commanders met privately and kept a hotline telephone linked to Schwarzkopf.

The two colonels looked up at the clocks. Comer had just radioed the code word that Task Force Normandy had crossed the border. There would be no other communications with the helicopter team until after the radars had been destroyed. Then another code word would be sent. That would come in just twenty-six minutes, which, at this moment, seemed like forever.

Leonik also felt as if he was in a slow-motion movie. The Pave Lows streaked through the Wadi Hamir, which ran less than ten miles southeast of the radar site. A one-lane road paralleled the narrow valley. As the wadi bent southeast, the Pave Low banked northwest. The aircraft jumped over the ridge at the elbow and raced across the road. The scanners kept their eyes peeled for vehicles that might be driving down the road and spot the black choppers crossing. None were in sight.

The Pave Lows now moved slowly to just southeast of the radars. Leonik could see blurry square objects on his green FLIR screen in the cockpit.

Kingsley's Pave Lows headed for the no-shit coordinates about ten miles southeast of the radar site. He was dead on target at 2:36 A.M. The tail gunner waved the glowing bundle of chemical sticks out the open rear hatch of the Pave Low so the four Apaches could see the marker.

The bundle fell to the ground and the two Pave Lows pulled back to the south. The shooters took over the operation. The Pave Lows were now the audience, standing by in case any aircraft were shot down and the PJs were needed to rescue the crew.

Cody's Apaches now moved quickly. The gunships flew over the no-shit coordinates at a speed of sixty knots and quickly updated their Doppler navigation systems and fire control computers. Buttons were pushed on target acquisition designation systems, called TADS, and FLIR sensors instantly slewed to the enemy radar sites.

Targets were locked onto at eight miles away. The Apaches crept forward low and slow. FLIR screens began clearly identifying each target for the Hellfires at five miles out.

"I've got the target," Apache pilots said to their copilots over cockpit intercoms.

In a fenced compound almost a mile wide sat seven Soviet-supplied radars: two Flat Face radars, two Spoon Rests, two Squat Eyes, and one Tropo Scatter radar. All had dishes atop their partially buried vans. Power generators sat next to each of them. There were also communications shacks and barracks. Several antiaircraft gun emplacements had been dug around the perimeter.

With the TADS locked on to the enemy radars, the four Apaches closed in like sharks swimming to a kill. Laser beams shot out from the gunships to keep targets in cross hairs for the Hellfires. Each pilot knew what he was supposed to hit. No words were exchanged between Apaches. The pilots had already picked their targets during the sand table exercises.

At about four miles out, Lieutenant Tom Drew, one of the Apache pilots designated the fire team leader, broke radio silence for the first time and calmly announced: "Party in ten." The Hellfires would launch simultaneously in ten seconds.

Pilots in the four Apaches began counting off to themselves. "Ten, nine, eight, seven, six, five, four, three, two, one."

FLIR screens in Apache cockpits flashed "LAUNCH."

Roused by the noise from the helicopters, an Iraqi sentry ran to one of the radar shacks. As he opened the door, the Hellfire bore down on the roof. The shack exploded into a fireball, sending shrapnel scattering for hundreds of feet.

The Apaches continued firing the Hellfires as they closed in for the next two miles. Thirty of the missiles crashed into vans and shacks, causing fiery explosions. Then sixty of the helicopters' Hydra-70 rockets slammed into the antiaircraft emplacements. The razor-sharp fléchettes from the rockets ripped to shreds anyone who stood out in the open. The job was finished by automatic chain gun cannons that spewed out thousands of 30-millimeter rounds at barracks and what remained of the vans.

The destruction unleashed by the Apaches was perfectly timed and cataclysmic. The attack began at 2:38 A.M., H minus 22 minutes. Within thirty seconds the eastern radars had stopped operating. Seven seconds after the eastern site was struck, the Red Team had attacked the western site. Within four minutes, both radar installations had been leveled.

Leonik's crew watched silently as the Apaches methodically went about their violent work.

"They did it!" Leonik finally shouted into his intercom.

"Well, we're at war, guys," Comer said.

"I'm the first person in my family who's ever been in a war," Pearce said into his mike.

"Well, you're in one now," Comer answered, "so let's keep our minds on business and be ready to go in there if somebody gets shot down." The PJs had already strapped on their rescue gear. They could see random tracer fire coming at the Pave Lows. The attack no doubt had awakened anybody within miles of the site.

Comer now waited impatiently for Cody to radio him that the site had been destroyed. The Apaches would then rendezvous with the Pave Low. But Cody was busy accounting for all his Apaches and receiving their damage reports.

Comer finally radioed Cody on a secure channel the two command ships shared.

"Can you confirm California alpha?" Comer asked. "California" was the code word designating that the eastern radar site had been attacked. "Nevada" was the code word for the attack on the western radars. Then there were one of three suffixes with the attack code: "alpha," designating that the target had been completely destroyed; "bravo" that the radars had been put out of action but were repairable; or "charlie," that they were damaged but still working.

Comer waited for the reply.

Cody finally keyed his mike. "Yeah, California alpha," he said. "Target destroyed."

Several minutes later, Comer received the same message from Martin's Red Team: "Nevada alpha." The western radars were completely destroyed as well.

Gray and Johnson looked anxiously up at the clock: 2:39 A.M.

"Goddamn, we better hear California pretty soon," Gray said, leaning over to Johnson in a whisper.

The F-15s destined for the western Scud sites had crossed the border. The two colonels sat in the joint operations center helpless, not knowing if the radar sites had been destroyed, if the F-15s had slipped in undetected, if all the helicopters were safe, if the mission had been successful, or if they had a disaster on their hands.

The hotline phone from Riyadh rang.

Johnson lifted the receiver. Gray could hear Schwarzkopf storming on the other end of the line.

"Goddamnit, where are the code words!" Schwarzkopf barked on the line.

Gray dared not raise Comer on the SATCOM. He would have his hands full out there. Any headquarters commander worth his salt knew not to pester troop leaders when they were fighting.

Still, Schwarzkopf was about to go into orbit. If the operation had gone awry, it would just reinforce his prejudice against special ops units, Gray knew. The clock read 2:42 A.M.

At last, the SATCOM radio began to crackle.

"California alpha, Nevada alpha," came the message from Comer.

Johnson grabbed the hotline receiver and passed the good news on to Riyadh.

"Thank God," Schwarzkopf said on the other end of the line. He hung up the phone and scrawled a note on a yellow pad: "SOF targets destroyed." SOF was military jargon for special operations force.

Pandemonium erupted on the SATCOM. Radio operators from all over Saudi Arabia began speaking at once.

"Are we at war?"

"Tell me that again?"

"Are we really sure we're about to have a war? It doesn't sound like one."

"Don't send any more faxes. We need this frequency."

"Tell me that again."

It seemed like no one back at headquarters believed Comer when he relayed the code words. Every staff officer in Riyadh and King Fahd who had access to a SATCOM radio now wanted their own status report from him on the mission.

"Will you leave us alone out here," a frustrated Comer finally said after delivering the code words for the sixth time. "We're all busy."

"Will everybody get off the radio," a harried female operator at the Central Command's Riyadh headquarters said finally. "We've got a war to fight."

Cody's Apaches and Comer's Pave Lows finally sortied at the rendezvous point south of the radar sites. All six helicopters were accounted for.

The trip back would be even more dangerous. Roaming Bedouin bands armed with SAMs would now be alerted. The White Team would only encounter small-arms fire. But a Bedouin band alerted by the noise fired two SA-7 surface-to-air missiles at Pulsifer's Pave Low in the Red Team after it had left the western site. Alerted by the Pave Low's tail gunner, Pulsifer dispensed flares. The heat-seeking missiles chased the decoys instead of the helicopters.

As he flew south, Leonik glanced up into the sky.

American warplanes streaked overhead through the corridor Task Force Normandy had just created. It looked like an interstate highway at rush hour. For an instant he took his mind off the cockpit as his whole life flashed before him. Three years ago he was grounded because of bad sinuses, practically finished as a pilot. But the Pave Low squadron had taken him in and now he was part of the first air strike of Desert Storm. As the warplanes soared above him and veered west to hunt Scuds, he felt an overwhelming, corny exultation, as if he was on the fifty-yard line of a football game yelling, Go! Go! Go!

In the Central Command headquarters in Riyadh, Glosson stared curiously at the CNN broadcast on the television set.

"The night sky is filled with a hail of bullets from antiaircraft guns," CNN correspondent John Holliman said breathlessly as he peered out the window of his room at the Al-Rashid luxury hotel in downtown Baghdad. Sirens began blaring. The black night filled with starbursts and tracer rounds like a Fourth of July celebration. The city was under attack. The air war had begun.

Glosson looked at his watch. It read 2:43 A.M.

"What the hell are they shooting at?" he mumbled to himself. The Stealth bombers wouldn't be there for another seventeen minutes.

Glosson would later learn that a frantic call from the southwest Iraqi border had made its way to Baghdad. Air Force electronic surveillance planes secretly monitoring Iraqi radio traffic had intercepted the transmission: "We are under a—" Then dead silence. The warning could have come from a border listening post sounding the alarm. But intelligence officers believed the more likely source of the transmission was one of the two radar sites Task Force Normandy had attacked.

But what Glosson had predicted then happened. The Iraqi antiaircraft guns around Baghdad fired wildly into the empty sky for twelve to fifteen minutes. Then they stood down. The capital was eerily quiet.

"Shit, this is great," Glosson said with a wide grin on

his face as he and the other strike cell officers watched CNN. "They're fired out before anybody gets there."

Several minutes later, at 3 A.M., F-117A Stealth planes dropped their 2,000-pound, laser-guided bombs on Baghdad's International Telephone and Telegraph Building, its Tower for Wire and Wireless Communications, the air defense command centers, and the presidential palace. At 3:02 A.M., F15E Eagles began attacking the fixed Scud launchers at the H-2 pumping station near the Jordanian border. They had sneaked to the launchers undetected. None had been fired on by enemy SAM batteries until after the H-2 attack had begun.

After the flight, Leonik was exhausted but too keyed up from the night to go to sleep. He strolled around the Al Jouf compound, breathing in the chilly dry air of the desert, trying to decompress from the mission. Hundreds of thoughts cluttered his mind: the danger of the mission, the excitement, how lucky he was to be alive, how lucky he was to be even flying. He was now with a band of brothers who cared about him, who would give their lives for him, whom he trusted completely with his own life. When men go to war they don't die for their country or a cause, he knew. They die for their friends. Simple friendship made the sacrifices worthwhile. He would never have closer friends than the ones who were in this squadron.

Leonik finally returned to his apartment. There was a surprise on his bed. He had once mentioned to one of the wing's flight surgeons how much he missed hardboiled eggs. Underneath a poncho at the foot of the bed was tucked a dozen of them.

Leonik smiled. It was good to be home.

PSYOPS

Tony Normand packed the few personal effects he had accumulated in his skyscraper office several blocks away from the Central Command's Riyadh headquarters and prepared to fly home. It was December 20. Desert Storm would begin in less than a month. Leaving Riyadh before the war had been the most difficult decision of his life. But it was time for the colonel to relinquish command of the Army's 4th Psychological Operations Group. Normand had taken over the 4th Group in 1988 and had rebuilt it into what he felt was a credible psychological operations unit. The normal two-year tour in that position was up.

A native of Birmingham, Alabama, the Army tours in military and diplomatic posts all over the world had not dulled Normand's thick Southern drawl. Back at his headquarters office in Fort Bragg hung five photos of men who symbolized to him the connecting tissue of a military career: Robert E. Lee, who lost the war but won the peace; Ulysses S. Grant, who won the war but lost the peace; George Armstrong Custer, a failure as a general; Stonewall Jackson, a success; and the actor Harry Morgan, who always kept everything in perspective as the fatherly Colonel Potter in the television series *M*A*S*H*.

But Normand's folksy manner was deceptive. He was not a bashful country bumpkin. A former tank officer and infantry company commander in Vietnam, Normand had drifted into the Army's foreign area officer's program, which trained soldiers to be politico-military diplomats. His specialty was Southeast Asia. Normand could have extended his tour with the 4th Group to see it through the war. But he chose not to. Layton Dunbar, the new colonel scheduled to take over, was an old friend who had already commanded a psyops battalion under the 4th Group. A straight arrow and smart, Dunbar was a fellow Southerner, although almost two decades as a foreign area officer had wiped clean the twang he had been reared with in the South Texas town of McAllen. Now Dunbar had a deep baritone radio voice. He seemed more like a Madison Avenue ad executive than a practitioner of psyops's black arts.

It was time to go, Normand thought. He had had his fifteen minutes in the spotlight during the invasion of Panama, where he had skillfully put together a psychological operation that convinced thousands of Panamanian Defense Force soldiers to surrender. Psyops, which conventional infantry commanders usually disdained, had saved American and Panamanian lives in that one-week war.

Normand had vowed not to leave Saudi Arabia until he had put in place a psychological operations campaign that could be launched if there was war. Some of the unusual operations were under way or about to begin as he now packed his bags. Hundreds of thousands of bumper stickers, with encouraging messages for the Kuwaiti resistance printed on them, had already been sneaked across the border. Kuwait City was covered with them. Cardboard cutouts of Kuwait City's state mosque, a powerful symbol to the Kuwaitis with its distinctive dome and minarets, were slipped in along with small cans of black spray paint. Like a silk screen, the mosque was rendered on thousands of walls. The graffiti buoyed the spirits of the underground and irritated to no end the Iraqi occupiers who futilely tried to wash it off.

Within a week, 12,000 empty plastic jugs—discarded by American GIs who had been gulping down bottled water in Saudi Arabia's 115-degree heat—would begin floating toward the Persian Gulf coast of Kuwait. Normand's operatives had bribed local Arab smugglers who had been sneaking contraband into Kuwait to dump the jugs off the coast when they made their runs. Inside psyops specialists had stuffed leaflets with cartoons showing a Marine amphibious armada crashing onto the Kuwaiti shore like a giant wave. The leaflets helped keep Iraqi divisions tied down along the coast, fearing an amphibious assault.

By the end of December, the "psychological preparation of the battlefield," as it was clinically called in the military, would move into high gear and never let up. Desert Storm would see the largest and most intense psychological operation ever waged by American armed forces. Six hundred and fifty psyops specialists had deployed to Saudi Arabia. By the end of the war, twenty-nine million leaflets had been dumped on Iraqi soldiers in Kuwait. For eighteen hours a day, carefully formatted radio broadcasts had filled their ears with subtle pleas to surrender. Combined with the punishing, round-the-clock allied bombing, the results had been dramatic.

Normand would later feel proud of what his handiwork had accomplished. But not that day in December. He was leaving Riyadh partly in disgust. He had thought that after the 4th Group's success in the Panama invasion the skeptics would have finally been convinced that psychological operations could save both American and enemy lives.

But they hadn't. The lessons of Just Cause had to be relearned in Desert Shield. Normand had spent four frustrating months in Riyadh and Washington browbeating generals and bureaucrats to organize a psychological campaign for the Persian Gulf. Four months frittered away while Saddam Hussein dominated world propaganda. What the allies finally cobbled together came painfully late. And though hugely successful, the psychological operation could have succeeded much earlier. Who knows, Normand thought as he loaded up boxes on his desk, perhaps we could have avoided this whole damned war. If only the bureaucrats in Washington had been thinking creatively. We'd never know. And at that point, he didn't much care. His work was finished in Riyadh. He was going home.

Normand was proud of the analytical staff he had assembled in the 4th Group. Many of the civilian experts on his payroll were Ivy League Ph.D.'s in sociology and anthropology. Most of his officers had master's degrees. They had come a long way from the days of loudspeakers and propaganda leaflets.

Ever since the rulers of the Byzantine Empire used subterfuge against their rivals, nations have dabbled in psychological operations to overcome their enemies short of brute force. Yet Americans have had a historical antipathy to this form of political warfare. Psychological operations, once associated with Tokyo Rose or Goebbels's propaganda machine in Nazi Germany, ran contrary to American notions of straightforwardness and fair play. Americans fought with armies, not words, with the truth on their side, not deception.

The U.S. military has had a love-hate relationship with psychological operations. After Vietnam, the Army's psychological operations capability had shrunk to an understrengthed unit at Fort Bragg, which kept antiquated loudspeakers and printing presses running. The discipline was revived by the Reagan administration during the 1980s. "Public diplomacy" was the new buzzword in the State Department. Diplomats became more aggressive public promoters of the new administration's right-wing agenda. International communications organizations like the U.S. Information Agency, the Voice of America, and Radio Free Liberty were energized to sell anticommunism abroad. Defense Secretary Caspar Weinberger ordered the Pentagon to pump more money into military psychological operations and draw up a master plan that would spell out how the generals would aggressively use psyops in their war plans.

Normand found the discipline intriguing, not necessarily as a black art or a tool for some politician's agenda. (He would boast that during his entire tour as a psychological operator he never once had to tell a lie; the truth was always the better weapon in this kind of warfare.) There was potential here, Normand thought, a chance to delve into foreign governments, to see how they tick, figure out what makes their people do what they do. A good psychological warfare expert, he soon discovered, was no different from a market research executive, except the psyops officer also liked to jump out of planes.

In 1988, Normand took over the 4th Group, still the Pentagon's only major, active-duty psyops unit, but one that was now growing. He began shaking up the organization. Loudspeakers and leaflets represented only a tiny part of psychological operations. More important was the message that provoked or swayed a foreign audience, many of whom might be illiterate. Crafting a simple yet effective message often required months of intensive research. No single leaflet ever convinced an enemy soldier to surrender. Yet an expertly crafted one could start him thinking about it or ease the guilt if he decided to give up. But the 4th's message-crafting capability was flaccid.

Normand toned it up. He sent officers to graduate schools and noncommissioned officers off to U.S. embassies overseas to soak up foreign culture. Civilian analysts who had been churning out fuzzy, thousand-page studies were dispatched to military tactics schools to learn what commanders really needed and ordered to produce memos no longer than three pages.

The Panama invasion became the big test for Normand's rejuvenated organization. Fourth Group experts flew to Miami to begin consulting with Panamanian exiles on messages for leaflets and loudspeaker broadcasts. Panamanian focus groups were assembled to pretest themes. The word "surrender" would never be used on loudspeaker tapes. Sensitive to Latin machismo, the tapes would ask PDF soldiers to "cease hostilities," to make giving up less humiliating.

When Just Cause began, psyops teams parachuted in with Army Rangers and 82nd Airborne soldiers. Loudspeakers were quickly erected around the burning comandancia in Panama City urging PDF officers not to waste their lives for Noriega. Within an hour, Panamanian soldiers began pouring out of garrisons with their hands up.

By the next morning, psyops soldiers had fanned out in Panama City to warn civilians away from the shooting.

Two-man loudspeaker teams on trucks with megaphones on top accompanied American infantry companies rooting out PDF soldiers and paramilitary Dignity Battalion thugs. In many cases the psyops team also talked enemy soldiers out of buildings, thus avoiding firefights. A radio team with Spanish-speaking disc jockeys began broadcasting information on the invasion twenty-four hours a day. Psyops engineers took over a local television station and began broadcasting propaganda commercials showing rows of jewelry and stacks of dollar bills confiscated from Noriega's homes, then cut-aways to the grinding poverty of Panama City's slums.

The campaign was hardly flawless. Psyops teams along with civil affairs units were not in place after the war to try to head off the looting rampage in Panama City that did some $1 billion worth of damage. Still, Normand had demonstrated that his unit could be as effective a weapon as rifles and tanks. Clever marketing could save lives on the battlefield. The skeptics had been convinced, Normand believed. Now the principles that had been proven in Just Cause could be applied to the Desert Shield deployment unfolding in August, or so he thought.

Within a week after the invasion of Kuwait, about a dozen 4th Group officers had flown to the Central Command at MacDill. Loudspeaker teams flew into Saudi Arabia with the first American paratroopers. Back at Fort Bragg, Normand assembled his experts, who, working with the liaisons sent to MacDill, drafted a bold top secret plan for waging psychological warfare against Saddam Hussein. Twenty-six separate psyop campaigns were proposed.

Some were mundane. In Iraq, red crescents were painted on field hospitals and ambulances. If there was to be a war, leaflets would have to be dropped on Iraqi soldiers informing them that a red cross was painted on American medical facilities, hopefully so they wouldn't be attacked. Jordanian or Syrian smugglers doing a booming business across the border could be paid to drop loose boxes of leaflets along the sides of roads in Iraq.

The plan proposed "strategic initiatives" that Washington could take to back up the military campaign in the Persian Gulf with a broader effort targeted against the Iraqi government. Public diplomacy would be coordinated among the White House, State Department, and Pentagon so the administration spoke in unison. Subtle contacts would be made through intermediaries to allies in the region. A State Department official might telephone a colleague in the British foreign ministry, who in turn would urge a friendly Jordanian economist to go on the air in a Middle Eastern broadcast, which could reach Baghdad and spell out the economic hardships Iraq would face from the embargo.

Riskier and more covert propaganda campaigns would try to destabilize the Baghdad regime. Secret broadcasting stations would be set up in the region to beam propaganda into Iraq. Some of the most watched regional television programs in the Middle East were early-evening Egyptian soap operas. Anti-Saddam themes would be slipped into the scripts.

The Central Command did not approve the plan immediately. Its staff had to be lobbied. But when Normand's team finally reached Schwarzkopf with a briefing, he proved to be an easy sell. The CinC may have been unduly prejudiced against special operations, but he immediately saw value in a psyops campaign. It could save lives. Normand, who had deployed to Saudi Arabia in August with Schwarzkopf and his staff, boarded a flight back to the States. Because it involved so many federal agencies, the Bush administration now had to approve the psywar.

Normand quickly discovered that obtaining the Central Command's approval had been a cakewalk compared to Washington. The Pentagon's joint staff, Powell's inner circle of top aides and the jealous guardians of access to the Joint Chiefs, was nervous about the covert side of the plan. The operations could be risky. The plan was split into two parts. The Pentagon would handle the overt operations, such as making sure Iraqi soldiers knew a red cross meant a red crescent, and the covert operations would be left to the CIA, which had already put together a small psyops group. Langley had more cutouts and covers to hide covert operations. If exposed, not as much stink would be raised, the joint staff reasoned. It would just be another agency screwup.

But the CIA's psyops capability was pitifully weak compared to the 4th Group's. Unified command and control of the operation was essential if both a strategic and tactical campaign was to succeed. The dismemberment of the 4th Group plan had begun.

Normand spent the next couple of weeks wading through the defense bureaucracy and bouncing from agency to agency in Washington. Pentagon bureaucrats snarled the plan in mountains of red tape and regulations. The State Department organized an unwieldy public diplomacy group to mull over ways to influence international opinion on Iraq, but its work was ignored by higher-ups. No one at the White House seemed interested in forcing the government to agree on a broad strategic plan for waging psychological warfare against Saddam. Left on their own, the agencies squabbled among themselves.

Appalled by the narrow-mindedness, the turf wars, the bureaucratic gridlock, Normand flew back to Riyadh disgusted. To hell with Washington, he thought. He began implementing the parts of the psyops plan that the Central Command could undertake on its own without administration approval. A combined psyops team, made up of senior American, British, and Arab officers, began sketching out themes for leaflets.

Normand made several more trips back to Washington to win approval for a more comprehensive plan. But the bureaucracy would barely budge. About the most the CIA could manage was a clandestine radio station run by Iraqi exiles, which broadcast propaganda into the country. A ten-minute video the 4th Group had produced touting the allied military advantage and the dire consequences Iraq faced in occupying Kuwait rattled around the State Department for almost fifty days before officials there approved its distribution in the Middle East. By then, the film was out of date and had to be reedited before it could be sent to nineteen countries in the region and smuggled into Iraq.

Media events became unintended psychological operations. Hyped and sloppy press reporting conveyed the impression to Saddam, a CNN junkie, that more tanks and planes were pouring into Saudi Arabia during the early Desert Shield buildup than was really the case. In one instance, an embarrassing gaffe proved valuable. Air Force Chief of Staff Michael Dugan was fired from his job after he revealed to reporters Israeli cooperation in the crisis and bragged about his warplanes bombing Baghdad. American embassy officials later reported that the interview had a "sobering effect" on Iraqi officials.

It was easy to see why the agencies never had a coherent battle plan. The men at the top never did either. Bush and Secretary of State James Baker, who ran foreign policy consulting only a small circle of trusted aides, began a freelance psyops war on Saddam. But the message was mixed. One day, Bush would stand up in the White House press room and hint that the United States wanted to topple Saddam. The next day he would back off, fearing that the threat would keep Saddam's forces more firmly entrenched in Kuwait. One day, the reason for U.S. military intervention in the Persian Gulf was to restore democracy in Kuwait (where, of course, it had never existed before). The next day, the goal was to guard world oil supplies or preserve stability in the Middle East or, as Baker once propounded, to protect American jobs at home.

While Washington dithered, Saddam launched his own psywar campaign, which proved deceptively more effective than the American effort. American GIs laughed at broadcasts from Iraq, nicknamed "Baghdad Betty," which taunted that while they were stuck in the desert, Arab men and the cartoon character Bart Simpson were sleeping with their wives at home. But Arab males in the region wouldn't find it amusing, Normand and his staff in Riyadh knew. The broadcasts would demonstrate to Iraqi soldiers or other Arabs listening in that Saddam's government was not cowed by the Desert Shield buildup. The 4th Group's intelligence studies found that daily media themes formulated by Baghdad were quickly disseminated throughout the country and embassies worldwide so Iraqi officials spoke in unison. An elaborate, well-funded operation targeted Arab clans and religious sects in the region. The landing of planes bearing hostages finally released from Baghdad was staged so they occurred as Iraqi ambassadors in the Western capitals held news conferences in time for evening broadcasts. This was no backwoods operation, Normand realized. The Iraqis were pros.

By December, Normand had given up organizing a strategic psyops campaign against the Baghdad government. A plan to destabilize the regime or talk it out of Kuwait was overtaken by events. War was imminent. But Normand needed approval from Washington for most of the tactical psychological operations CENTCOM wanted to conduct in the region after the shooting started. Washington continued to drag its feet. Normand wasn't about to leave Riyadh until his part of the war plan was approved. Frustrated, he walked into Schwarzkopf's office with a draft of a top secret cable to be sent to the Pentagon, politely urging the service chiefs to reach a quick decision. Time was running out. The Pentagon had deliberated long enough.

Schwarzkopf read in silence.

"This is bullshit, they'll never react to this," he finally said grumpily and grabbed a pencil.

Schwarzkopf began scratching out Normand's tame words and inserting more pungent language. He, too, was fed up with Washington's dawdling. The delays in approving the psyops plan were "unconscionable," he now wrote. "Bungling bureaucrats" had sat on it for too long. It was time for the Defense Department to act or get out of the way.

The cable landed on the Pentagon like a tactical nuke. Within days the Joint Chiefs approved the entire plan, making only minor changes. One month before Desert Storm, the Central Command finally had a green light from

Washington to begin the psychological preparation of the battlefield.

Normand cleaned out his desk and headed for home.

There was no time to lose. Dunbar had been posted in Saudi Arabia since October so the change of command would go smoothly. Now, with an approved plan finally dragged out of the Pentagon, he had to move quickly to have radio equipment in place, leaflets printed, and Arabic-speaking loudspeaker teams assembled, all before the war started.

The work was classified top secret. When Dunbar had to obtain approval for specific psyops missions, he would seal the plans in a manila envelope and personally carry them to the general who must sign off. After the general had approved, Dunbar would reseal the papers in the envelope and carry them back to his safe. A psyops plan was worthless if it leaked to the enemy or the press.

Wading through Saudi decision making became a maddening experience for Dunbar. His Saudi counterpart on the coalition's psyops team was a Colonel Mohammed. Dunbar quickly found that Mohammed's okay for an operation was just the beginning of a long line of Saudi functionaries who were part of the approval process. But the endless meetings over leaflet themes turned out to be important. Dunbar's staff wanted to begin with an intimidating message for radio broadcasts and leaflet drops before the air war began. The Iraqi soldier should be confronted with the awesome military might assembled on the other side and the allies' determination to use it, he argued.

That was too harsh for the curtain-raiser, Mohammed complained. The other Arabs on the team agreed. Being provocative with Saddam might make him even angrier. "We don't want this to start the war," Mohammed worried.

The Americans gave in and agreed on an "Arab brotherhood" theme for the first leaflets. The message would be soft. Arabs should not fight Arabs. One design showed a simple color cartoon of an Iraqi and Saudi soldier walking off into a desert sunset hand in hand with the inscription on the back reading: "In peace we will always remain hand in hand."

Dunbar thought the theme a bit limp. At the Central Command headquarters, officers nicknamed it the "love and kisses leaflet." But the Americans would later discover from defector interviews that the brotherhood leaflets were among the most effective that were dropped. Shooting at fellow Arabs was troubling for an Iraqi soldier. Mohammed and the other Middle Eastern officers on the team knew better than any Americans what would sway their brethren across the border.

The American psyops officers learned other things from the Arabs. Senior officers at the Central Command complained that with all the expensive publishing equipment the 4th Group had available, it should be printing slick, well-designed leaflets. But the psyops team found that Iraqi soldiers would respond better to crudely drawn cartoons on cheap paper. The soldiers were more used to those type of pictures from the political cartoons they saw in newspapers or on billboards back home.

The psyops team agreed that leaflets with more intimidating themes would follow the first drops of Arab brotherhood paper. "Oh brother Arab, have you really thought about the power of the joint forces?" one leaflet asked with a drawing of Stealth planes and B-52s dropping bombs over the battlefield. Defector interviews revealed that front-line Iraqi soldiers were largely ill-equipped, poorly fed, and isolated on the Kuwaiti battlefield. Iraqi commanders gave them little information on why they were stuck in foxholes or what kind of force confronted them. Leaflets were designed to plant questions in their minds. One cartoon showed Saddam climbing on the back of a bedraggled soldier who complained in the drawing: "I obeyed your orders. I feel death is knocking on the door whenever we go on the offensive and I feel I am on my last breath."

Special themes were developed for different units. Leaflets for Scud missile operators asked why they were targeting innocent Arabs. Chemical warfare units were warned that they would be the first to die if they fired their weapons.

There were helpful suggestions from surprising quarters. Defense Secretary Dick Cheney and Powell had flown to Riyadh in December for a update on the Central Command's war plans. During Dunbar's psyops portion of the briefing, Cheney interrupted at one point and asked, "What's going to be printed on the leaflets?"

Before Dunbar had time to answer, Powell leaned over and said, "Oh, they'll say things like, 'Get away from your equipment. We're going to blow it up.'"

None of the leaflets said any such thing. But Dunbar didn't correct the chairman. Leaving the briefing room, he had to admit to himself that Powell had a good idea. Millions of leaflets were printed up with cartoons urging Iraqi soldiers to leave their tanks if they didn't want to be killed.

The leaflet drops began the first week in January. Air Force MC-130E Combat Talon planes, each crammed with one million leaflets, flew at 25,000 feet just south of the Kuwaiti border. Flimsy boxes filled with paper and attached to static lines were shoved out the back of the plane every thirty seconds, like an assembly line conveyor belt. The line broke the box apart and the sky was filled with tiny white sheets floating across the border and to the ground. Using computer models of wind patterns, 4th Group experts calculated that the paper would float up to 300 miles north into enemy territory.

To sharpen the message, special interview teams in Saudi Arabia then began surveying defectors who trickled across the border. One Iraqi sergeant pointed out that fellow soldiers inclined to surrender were so isolated and disoriented in their bunkers that they didn't know where the Saudi border was, nor how far they would have to walk to reach it. Radio scripts were rewritten. To direct them south, the broadcast would now say, "Walk three hours in the direction of Mecca," Islam's holiest city, in Saudi Arabia. Every Arab knew the direction of Mecca.

To broadcast radio messages into Kuwait and southern Iraq, a mobile green van that served as a radio studio was parked next to the Central Command's Riyadh headquarters. Land lines connected the van to the two secret transmitting stations 250 miles away. An EC-130 Volant Solo plane packed with electronic warfare equipment flew over the Gulf and Saudi Arabia to pick up the ground signal and retransmit it deeper into enemy territory.

On January 17, the first day of the air war, "Voice of the Gulf," as the program came to be called, began broadcasting eighteen hours a day on six frequencies, making it easy for any Iraqi soldier with a pocket radio to find it. Kuwaiti and Saudi announcers served as disc jockeys so the soldiers would not know that the broadcast was American-run. The show's format was carefully crafted so the psyops messages were slipped in between a heavy dose of straight news and music. Haranguing Iraqi soldiers with Baghdad Betty-like propaganda would do no good. They would just tune into the many other media outlets that flooded Middle East airwaves, such as CNN, the BBC, the Voice of America, or Radio Baghdad.

A typical day's broadcast began with music, then a news summary, which was simply an update on the Persian Gulf crisis taken directly from American or foreign wire services. A surrender hotline message would follow:

> Commanders, you have led your units courageously. You have served your country, your army, and your men well. You recognize by now that further resistance to the overwhelming air, land, and sea power of the coalition forces is folly. . . . If you recognize the futility of your position we offer the opportunity to surrender to your Arab brothers with dignity. You need only to tune your radio to 6.639 or 8.924 frequency and express your intention. A senior Arab officer will discuss with you the terms of an honorable and just withdrawal from the war. You and your unit can be out of this war within two hours.

The senior Arab officer sat aboard the Volant Solo plane ready to take any calls. Other bulletins instructed Iraqi soldiers on the mechanics of surrendering, such as waving a white flag or turning the barrel of a tank to the rear.

To wean enemy soldiers away from the competitors, the Voice of the Gulf began broadcasting details on CENTCOM operations, which weren't being released to the international media. Iraqi soldiers began flipping off the BBC and tuning in the Voice of the Gulf. "It was a quick way to increase our market share," Dunbar would later deadpan.

As the bombing campaign wore on, word soon began filtering back to the Central Command through intelligence channels that the radio and leaflet operations were having their intended effect. Bombing and psyops were crumbling the enemy's will to fight. A 4th Group liaison officer who had been given a chilly reception before, now received a standing ovation when he walked into the Air Force's operations center.

Several weeks into the air war, even Schwarzkopf began concocting psychological operations. Anxious to speed up defections or at least convince more Iraqi soldiers to abandon their equipment, Schwarzkopf summoned Dunbar to his office.

"Why don't we just tell them we're going to bomb them?" he asked the colonel.

"Can we?" Dunbar said, a bit startled. Bombing plans were usually closely guarded secrets. The Air Force did not want its bombers shot down by an enemy air defense system alerted in advance. But the allies controlled the skies and Iraq's antiaircraft batteries along the Kuwaiti front were all but silenced. The few operating would not be able to hit high-flying B-52s.

"Yeah, we can do that," Schwarzkopf said, becoming more enthusiastic about his own idea. "We can announce it one day and hit them the next. That would really heighten their anticipation, their sense of dread. They'd think about it for twenty-four hours in advance."

Schwarzkopf already knew the terrifying psychological impact of B-52 raids from his days in Vietnam. When the flying battlewagons delivered their bombs, the ground shook like an earthquake for miles around the impact sites. A fleet of bombers was put at Dunbar's disposal. The psywarriors had come a long way. Once shunned, now they were issuing bombing orders to B-52s.

Leaflets showing photos of B-52s dropping bombs were first dumped on an Iraqi division. The caption on one read:

> The 16th Division will be bombed tomorrow. Leave this location and save yourself.

The next morning at six o'clock sharp, the B-52s would fly over and drop their rain of steel. The following day, a second leaflet drop was made. It was written in red ink with a red border:

> We have already informed you of our promise to bomb the 16th Infantry Division. We kept our promise and bombed them yesterday.
> Beware.
> We will repeat this bombing tomorrow. Now the choice is yours. Either stay and face death or accept the invitation of the joint forces to protect your lives. This is your first and last warning! Tomorrow the 16th Infantry Division will be bombed! Flee this location now!

The Voice of the Gulf broadcast the same warning as the B-52s went from division to division. Iraqi soldiers now clambered out of their bunkers grabbing the latest leaflets to see if the planes would come the next day. An Iraqi general captured later told interrogators that his men kept their ears glued to the broadcasts. Surveys among Iraqi POWs showed that half listened to the Voice of the Gulf.

Shortly before midnight on February 6, Skip Davenport pushed forward the throttle of his MC-130E Combat Talon to accelerate for takeoff. Thank God they had a long runway at King Fahd Airport, he thought. The Air Force major would need it all to get enough speed to lift the load in the back of his Talon: a 15,000-pound BLU-82, the largest conventional bomb in the U.S. inventory.

The "Blue-82" or "Daisy Cutter" as it was also nicknamed, hadn't been dropped on an enemy since the Vietnam War, when the terrifying monster weapon had been used to clear dense jungles for aircraft landing zones. Tonight the bomb was to be used to clear minefields. Its other mission, just as important: psychological warfare.

It had taken all evening to load the single bomb into the aircraft's cargo hold. Behind Davenport's plane, Lieutenant Colonel Carl Henry piloted a second Combat Talon with another BLU-82 in its belly. The bombs would always be dropped in pairs. Davenport and Henry became known as the Blues Brothers.

Davenport didn't care what they called him. Finally, he was flying a true special ops mission in this war. That's all that mattered. The Combat Talons, part of the 8th Special Operations Squadron, were the long-range infiltration planes of the 1st Special Operation Wing. A souped-up C-130 Hercules transport, the plane had been equipped with a sophisticated navigation system and radar evasion equipment to fly troops and cargo on clandestine missions. So far, Davenport had been flying "trash hauler" missions in Saudi Arabia, ferrying equipment or standing by for search-and-rescue operations, which never materialized because so few pilots were shot down. But a BLU-82 operation was one of his plane's specialties. The Combat Talon was the only aircraft in the Air Force inventory that dropped the giant bomb, which was about the size of a Volkswagen Beetle.

Davenport was used to being in the thick of the fighting. He relished it. A silver-haired Arizonan, forty-five years old, Davenport had found flying Combat Talons a lot more interesting than being an airline pilot for the Military Airlift Command. He won his first Distinguished Flying Cross on combat missions in Vietnam. His second was awarded for piloting a crippled Talon off the Río Hato

Airport runway during the Panama invasion. He later flew
the plane that brought Noriega to the United States.

Shortly before the Desert Storm air war began, Davenport and his crew mates had been brainstorming ideas
for BLU-82 operations. If it could sweep jungles, the
weapon might also clear minefields. With over six tons of
explosives, the bomb could flatten everything within a
three-mile radius. If the mines weren't cleared, the BLU-
82 would still be a powerful psychological weapon if paired
with leaflet drops, the crew believed.

The Marines were eager to try it out. The leathernecks
would be among the first to have to cross the belts of
minefields, barbed wire, tank traps, and burning trenches
the Iraqi army had laid along the Kuwaiti border.

On January 28, Colonel George Gray, the 1st Wing's
commander, paid another visit to Schwarzkopf's office. A
former C-130 pilot himself, Gray knew the bomb's potential. Back at Hurlburt, he had drafted contingency plans to
use the BLU-82 for wiping out terrorist camps in Lebanon
if American strikes were ever ordered. But Gray hedged
his briefing.

"Sir, we've never tested this thing to see how it would
work opening up minefields," the colonel told Schwarzkopf. The Central Command's deputy commander, General Calvin Waller, sat beside Schwarzkopf along with several other staff officers.

The B-52's carpet bombing might be more effective as
a mine clearer, Gray continued. But the BLU-82 would be
a more powerful psyops weapon. "One thing is certain,"
Gray concluded. "Everybody within three miles of the drop
will be bleeding from every orifice of his body."

"Oh God," Waller said, a grin spreading across his
face. "How many do we have?"

Within a week, eighteen BLU-82s shipped from Hill
Air Force Base in Utah had arrived at King Fahd Airport.
Eleven would eventually be dropped on Iraqi positions.
Each bomb was covered with graffiti from every weapons
handler along the way who had scrawled a message. ("The

mother of all bombs for the mother of all wars." "This bomb's for you.")

An escort force of EF-111 Ravens and F-4G Wild Weasels surrounded the Blues Brothers as their Combat Talons climbed to an altitude of 16,000 feet. The planes would have to decelerate to about 140 knots to drop the two bombs. Moving that slow, they would be vulnerable to antiaircraft fire unless they cruised high up. The Ravens and Wild Weasels would attack SAM radars trying to lock on to the transports.

The two targets for the first night were a minefield and an enemy division headquarters in the southwest corner of Kuwait. As they neared the border, the Talons began flying a serpentine route to evade enemy radars. In addition to Davenport, the crew for this special flight consisted of two more pilots, three navigators, an electronic warfare operator, radio operator, two load masters to handle the weapon, and a gunner to arm it.

The BLU-82 was a big, dumb bomb. The trick was to slide the unguided weapon out the back of the Combat Talon at a precise point in the flight so it landed on target. Davenport's navigators had already carefully calculated the release point for the bomb based on the plane's position, speed, and altitude, plus the wind speed and direction, and the air density and temperature. The crew practiced dropping the bomb several times a year at a Utah test range and could hit a target within 200 feet or less.

The huge bomb sat on a drop pallet attached to rails with its nose pointed to the front of the plane. When the order to drop was given, a drogue parachute shot out the back of the bomb to help pull it out the rear ramp of the plane. The parachute then stabilized the bomb's descent and kept the nose down.

At the nose was a four-foot probe, which was the first part of the weapon to hit the ground. The probe rammed into a front detonator, which set off a charge and ensured that the explosion occurred above ground. That way the shock wave spread out from the impact site instead of into the ground.

Twenty minutes from the target, the plane's navigators began recalculating the release point variables to account for changes in wind speed and direction since the beginning of the flight. The load masters began the drop checklist, adjusting the pallet's rigging and the drogue chute. The gunner made sure the nose fuse arming lanyard was in its proper position for arming the bomb.

Ten minutes from the target, static lines for the parachute were double-checked. Safety pins were removed from the rails. The load masters donned their parachutes in case there was an accident and they were swept out the rear ramp.

Six minutes away, the gunner armed the fuses. The bomb was now "hot." Locks on the rails were removed.

Ten miles from the target, Davenport slowed the plane to 140 knots. A navigator recalibrated a radar to update the onboard navigational computers that determined the plane's precise position.

"One minute," the navigator announced. "Slow down now." The fuse safety clip for the detonator on the bomb's nose was removed.

Davenport kept the altitude steady as the navigator called off adjustments in the plane's direction.

Twenty seconds out, the drogue parachute was released.

"Drogue okay," a load master in the back announced over the intercom as the parachute unfolded in the wind. If the drogue had malfunctioned, the lever he gripped could have released it.

"Hot load," he continued.

"Ten seconds," the navigator announced. The parachute billowed as the wind caught it.

Davenport tightly gripped the steering column, which was called a yoke. The navigator announced the "distance to go" until the bomb was released.

"Stand by for countdown," the navigator continued.

He began to tick off the seconds. "Five, four, three, two, one. Hot!"

An electronic air drop system controlled by the plane's

navigation computer automatically released the bomb. Sparks flew from the rails as the pallet shot out the back with the BLU-82.

"Bombs away," a load master shouted as the BLU-82 flew briefly away from the plane's rear ramp, then began to sink.

The shifting load of a 15,000-pound bomb sliding out the back of the Talon created a seesaw effect in the aircraft that Davenport had to quickly control. As the pallet rushed to the rear of the plane, he shoved his yoke forward to compensate for the heavy load pushing the tail down and the nose up. Then as the bomb fell out the rear ramp, he yanked the yoke back to compensate for the plane's tail flipping up and its nose plunging down.

The steering maneuver worked. The plane held steady. Davenport took a deep breath.

Then he banked the Talon to the left for a clear view of the explosion from his side of the cockpit. On the green FLIR screen of his front console he saw a tiny white dot drifting to the ground.

The Air Force operations center 300 miles away in Riyadh fell silent. Staff officers who had been monitoring the Talon's frequencies stared mesmerized at SATCOM radios waiting for the announcement that the two bombs had impacted. Seven thousand miles away in the Special Operations Command headquarters at MacDill, senior officers did the same. This was the most powerful weapon to be dropped on the enemy.

The bomb detonated. A huge mushroom cloud rose up from the ground as if a nuclear device had been set off. In the clear cool night of the barren desert, the light from the fireball and the noise from the blast carried for hundreds of miles.

"Fucking awesome," a pilot on one of the escort planes said, breaking radio silence.

A British SAS commando team on a secret reconnaissance mission 110 miles away radioed back frantically to its headquarters: "Sir, the blokes have just nuked Kuwait!"

A GI sleeping under a Humvee fifty miles south of the

Kuwait border bolted up and banged his head on the bumper.

Colonel Jesse Johnson, Schwarzkopf's top special ops aide, cabled back to MacDill: "We're not too sure how you say 'Jesus Christ' in Iraqi."

Iraqi SAM radars along the Kuwaiti border lit up. Terrified operators thought the ground war was about to begin. American RC-135 planes on the Saudi side of the border quickly plotted all the radar positions so warplanes could knock them out when dawn broke.

In the morning, another Combat Talon flew south of the drop zone and dumped out leaflets. On one side of the paper was printed a drawing of the BLU-82. On the other side, the message read:

> You have just experienced the most powerful conventional bomb dropped in the war. It has more explosive power than twenty Scud missiles. You will be bombed again soon. Kuwait will be free from aggression. Flee south and you will be treated fairly. You cannot hide. Flee and live, or stay and die!

One contingent needed no more convincing. An Iraqi battalion commander and his staff raced across the border near the bomb site. Among the defectors: the commander's intelligence officer clutching maps of the minefields for their sector. The windfall helped CENTCOM officers pick out weak spots in the mine defenses.

When the ground war began, the effects of the constant bombing and psychological warfare quickly became evident. In postwar surveys the 4th Group conducted among Iraqi POWs, 98 percent of those interviewed said they had seen a leaflet and 70 percent said the pieces of paper influenced their decision to surrender or defect. Pentagon officials could not vouch for the statistical reliability of the surveys. No poll was taken of the Iraqis who stood and fought or escaped to the north. But it was clear the leaflets had their impact.

By the end of the 100-hour ground war, more than 80,000 Iraqi soldiers had surrendered. One soldier walked up to startled American GIs with 250 surrender leaflets sticking from his pockets. Thousands of ragged Iraqi infantrymen who couldn't wait to give up clogged roads and held up advancing American units. When allied trucks could hold no more prisoners, weapons were confiscated and Iraqi soldiers were told simply to walk south where they would eventually be collected at checkpoints. Schwarzkopf's ground forces had attacked an army on the verge of collapse.

BEHIND ENEMY LINES

Jim Kraus sat in a cramped room at the far end of the Bat Cave. In front of the Army colonel were several intelligence officers and staff aides, plus the three-man Green Beret team that was to brief him on one of the riskiest missions of the Desert Storm war. The Bat Cave was the nickname the 5th Special Forces Group had given the huge lower level of the mammoth air terminal still under construction at King Fahd International Airport. Much of the 5th Group, which Kraus commanded, had been garrisoned in the cavernous hall with its loading ramps large enough to drive in tractor trailers. Green Beret teams had piled sandbags to partition off sections of the hall for their quarters. Camouflage netting had been hung around cots to offer some privacy. Some teams had even constructed living room furniture from scrap boards found near construction shacks outside.

The room where Kraus now received his "briefback" had been designated an isolation area, in which Green Berets secluded themselves to prepare for clandestine missions. Jeffrey Sims, a stocky master sergeant from South Carolina, led the three-man team sitting before Kraus. The briefback was a ritual every Green Beret team performed before a mission, a time when its members assembled before the commanding officer to describe in minute detail how an operation would be conducted. The team also had to win the CO's approval.

Kraus was not the kind of Special Forces commander who rubber-stamped any mission, particularly not this one. He wanted to know every detail. The mood in the room was tense. Sims and his men had grim looks on their faces.

Kraus knew there was a chance they might not come back from this operation.

In a week, the Central Command would begin the ground war phase of Desert Storm. Two Army corps, the 18th Airborne from Fort Bragg and the 7th from Germany, would soon complete a secret 500-mile trek along the lonely Tapline Road to staging bases in the barren western deserts of Saudi Arabia. From there, the two corps—120,000 men strong with 12,000 tanks and armored personnel carriers—would dash across southwestern Iraq to envelop Saddam's army in Kuwait. A French light armored division plus a brigade from the 82nd Airborne Division would screen their flank to the far west. But the two corps also needed eyes watching for enemy movements coming from the north out of Baghdad. As the 18th and 7th turned east to encircle the Iraqis in the south they did not want to become trapped themselves by a northern counterattack. Sims was leading one of thirteen Green Beret teams that would be dropped inside Iraq ahead of H-hour to radio warnings if enemy reinforcements from the north tried to assault the Hail Mary flankers.

Satellite photos warning of such a counterattack would arrive too late. Poor weather that had kept much of Iraq covered in clouds lately might prevent reconnaissance planes from spotting movement. Army commanders wanted teams like Sims's and Balwanz's (see Prologue) to watch the north-south highways as allied tanks raced across the western Iraqi desert. They would radio back instantly if enemy reinforcements were mobilized to strike from the north.

The Green Beret teams would be helicoptered in at night. They would spend as long as five days peering out of underground hide sites at enemy convoys. Three teams of three to six men each would be placed north of the Euphrates to watch the roads. Ten teams would be positioned south of the river.

Sims and his men had been in isolation for almost twenty days preparing for the mission. Green Berets routinely went into seclusion before operations to preserve secrecy and to help them focus on the task at hand. In this case Sims and his men had also been kept in the dark about Balwanz's team and the other units conducting "strategic reconnaissance" deep inside Iraq. That way, if he were captured by the Iraqis—and almost surely tortured— he could not compromise other operations.

Kraus believed it was very likely that hide sites would be discovered and the Iraqis would capture some of his men. His stomach churned as Sims—ramrod straight and in a monotone voice—delivered his brief-back. The idea for the strategic reconnaissance had come from the Green Berets, who had lobbied the corps commanders and the Central Command to approve the operations. But now that they were on the verge of beginning, Kraus couldn't help but worry. He rubbed his face, which had become brown and weather-beaten from four months in the desert. His close-cropped hair was salt-and-pepper gray. He felt every bit his fifty-three years.

Jim Kraus kept a tight rein on his men in the 5th Group. He had spent more than thirty years in the Army, enlisting in 1956 and immediately joining the Green Berets, which was then in its infancy. He had been one of the first Special Forces advisers in Vietnam. He returned for two more tours and watched the war and the Green Berets corrupted by trashy recruits and incompetent officers. Discouraged, he drifted in and out of Special Forces; it was the only way to rise through the ranks of the conventional Army.

As head of the 5th Group, whose regional responsibility included the Middle East, Kraus was obsessive about training and discipline. By the very nature of their jobs, Green Berets were often plunked in politically delicate situations and given tremendous latitude. The nightmare years of Vietnam had taught him that Special Forces soldiers could not be left on too long a leash. Kraus spent as much as six hours a day away from his desk mingling among his commandos. He liked to think that he could walk into any unit and measure proficiency by the discipline and appearance of its soldiers.

Commando operations had ended up being a small part of the Special Forces mission in the Persian Gulf. Schwarzkopf too had kept a short leash, forbidding any Green Berets from sneaking into enemy territory before the air war started and then rejecting many operations they proposed after the bombing had begun.

Green Berets were allowed to join British SAS commandos in one operation to cut a fiber optic cable that stretched from Baghdad to southwest Iraq. The CIA warned that American tanks and trucks might become bogged down in sandy terrain as they conducted their Hail Mary maneuver across southern Iraq. Schwarzkopf, who was desperate for detailed intelligence on the region's weather and terrain, allowed six-man Green Beret teams to secretly helicopter into Iraq and scoop up soil samples for analysis in Riyadh. The teams also used camcorders and digitized still cameras to transmit photos back to headquarters. The soil samples showed the ground was firm enough and the pictures gave commanders a close-up view of their battlefields.

Otherwise, most of the Green Berets spent their time in Saudi Arabia working as military liaisons with the Arab units or training the remnants of the Kuwaiti Army. When the ground war started, Kraus wanted his men closely watching the Kuwaiti soldiers. He knew full well they would kill or torture Iraqi prisoners in revenge for occupation atrocities. The Green Berets would do their best to curb the abuses. They would not look the other way, as they had in Vietnam and Central America.

None of the Green Beret teams had objected to the strategic reconnaissance missions. But then again, none of them had been too excited about the operations. They would be hundreds of miles deep inside Iraq. If their hide sites were discovered by the enemy, the commandos might have to fend for themselves. Helicopter rescues would be difficult that far away. Kraus knew he could count on Sims to see the mission through no matter the dangers. Sims was one of his most senior sergeants. Solid as a rock. As team-oriented and confident as they came.

Jeffrey Sims was a true patriot. He was born in the tiny town of Winnsboro, South Carolina, just north of Columbia. His mother and father worked in cotton mills. His brother joined the Marines. As far back as Sims could remember, he wanted to be in the Army and become a Green Beret. At nineteen, he enlisted. It was 1975 and antimilitary sentiment after Vietnam ran strong throughout the country. He almost punched out his sister's boyfriend, who tried to talk him into going AWOL after he enlisted. In Sims's driveway was parked a Ford pickup truck. He would never drive anything but an American car.

Sims's A-team, Operational Detachment Alpha 523, had been surprisingly stable over the years. Sims, who was the team's senior sergeant, had been with ODA-523 since 1979. He and the other detachment veterans had long ago made a solemn pact. Never lie to a fellow team member. Do things right, not just the easy way. Bromides, but they lived by them.

The two other sergeants on the recon mission with Sims were Roy Tabron and Ron Torbett. A medic, Tabron was the first African-American Sims's A-team had had in a long time. Energetic, a hard worker, Tabron was an avid paratrooper. He lived for the airborne infantry. Torbett— or R.T., as Sims called him—was a newcomer, fresh out of the Q Course at Fort Bragg. He was full of enthusiasm like any rookie, and green like one. Within days he would embark on perhaps the most dangerous mission of his career as a Green Beret. Torbett crammed to learn quickly and pestered Sims with hundreds of questions.

Sims had tried to match compatible personalities for the mission. The men would be living in tiny holes together for almost a week, eating, sleeping, and defecating literally under one another's noses. Captain Christopher Conner, the young commander of ODA-523, would head up another three-man hide site just south of Sims's.

For weeks, Sims, Tabron, and Torbett practiced hide site designs in the desert south of King Fahd Airport. The holes were five-feet-by-three-feet wide and about chest-high deep. Techniques were mastered to conceal the fresh dirt dug from the ground. Until it dried, the dirt would be a darker color than the topsoil and would give away their position to passers-by. Some of the underground dirt was placed in sandbags to reinforce the walls. The rest was carefully mixed with the topsoil so the colors would blend. Special powders were then spread around the hole to throw dogs and other curious animals off the scent.

The three men experimented with different roofs. They decided on a prefabricated umbrella made of canvas and thin metal rods. The umbrella weighed more than other designs, but it could be unfolded and laid on top of the hole quickly. More importantly, with the sand covering, it better concealed the team in the ground.

Next they practiced constructing the site quickly. The mission called for them to be taken in by helicopter at night, walk for five hours to the recon point, and spend four more hours digging the hide site. That way, they would be hidden and ready to observe convoy traffic before the sun rose the next morning. The first time out, the entire operation—walking and digging—took them twelve hours. They practiced digging holes almost a dozen more times. The team eventually reduced the operation to under nine hours.

Each man would carry ten quarts of water, which weighed twenty pounds. They would drink two quarts a day. On the helicopter flight in, Sims's team would take a case of bottled water and gulp it down until their bladders about burst. The hydration would help them retain liquid during the grueling march to their final position. Green Beret doctors showed each man how he could cram into one plastic MRE sack no bigger than a lunch bag an all-protein diet that would sustain him for up to five days.

The three men practiced living together in the holes for twenty-four- and forty-eight-hour stretches. Some special reconnaissance teams urinated into condoms while in the holes. Sims's team used plastic bottles buried in the holes. Feces were placed in plastic bags with lime to keep odors from escaping that animals might detect.

Load distribution became a science. The three had to

share the weight equally and ensure that if one man's pack was lost the other two had enough equipment to complete the operation. Each man would be lightly armed with pistols, M-16 rifles, grenade launchers, and claymore mines. They were on a reconnaissance mission. They wanted to avoid enemy contact, so they packed light on ammunition. But not on radios. Four would be taken. All told, each man would have to carry 175 pounds.

The team pored over dozens of intelligence photos of their infiltration site. They would be flown 150 miles into Iraq to a point just west of Highway 8, which paralleled the Euphrates River southeast into Basra. Their hide site would be west of the road and less than five miles north of the small town of Qawam al Hamzah. Conner's hide site team would be just south of Qawam al Hamzah and also watching Highway 8. The Green Berets wanted two teams at each road. If one was compromised, the other would be a backup to continue the recon.

The team hunted for every scrap of information it could find on Qawam al Hamzah. How many people did it contain? Were there sheep, camels, and dogs in the area? Would there be high-tension power lines that might tangle up a helicopter landing? The unknown was population density. That close to Baghdad with small towns and villages all around the recon site, the area was bound to be heavily trafficked. But overhead satellite photos showed the land fallow and unattended for the winter.

Intelligence analysts guessed that most of Qawam al Hamzah's some 5,000 townsfolk had fled north because of the bombing. But there were precious few bomb damage photos taken of the area, which might prove that the village had been deserted. Kraus had wanted low-level reconnaissance planes to photograph all the infiltration sites just before the war started, but the Air Force had been busy with sorties for the two corps.

The colonel now probed for more details in Sims's briefback. What about the team's "go to hell plan." If everything went wrong at the hide site, what was their fallback for extraction? Sims explained the contingency plans. With the allies in complete control of the Iraqi skies, warplanes could be dispatched to protect them from the air. Rescue helicopters would likely be able to fly in at night under the cover of darkness to pick them up. If the team had to activate the escape-and-evasion plan, it would split up and meet later at a linkup point south of the Euphrates.

Kraus stood up and shook the hands of the three men. He knew they were as prepared as they would ever be. But Kraus still left the isolation room with a bad feeling. Sims and the other commandos would be largely on their own when they crossed the border. Kraus wished he was more sure about the enemy terrain into which his men were infiltrating. There would be little he could do to help them if something went terribly wrong. Getting them out was easier said than done.

It was after 8 P.M. on February 23 when the MH-60 Black Hawk helicopter bearing Sims's team finally landed about six miles west of Qawam al Hamzah and Highway 8. A second Black Hawk dropped Conner's team about fifteen miles south. The two groups would never see or communicate over the radio with each other during the entire mission. In eight hours the 18th and 7th Corps would cross the border.

The temperature had dropped below 40 degrees. The black winter night was crisp and clear with a light breeze and a full moon. Sims could have done without the light of the moon. He could have also done without all the dogs barking after the helicopter took off. Christ, it sounded like thousands of mutts yapping, he thought.

On top of that, the helicopter had landed thirty minutes late. The mission's start at Rafha, a staging base twenty-five miles south of the Iraqi border, had been delayed by higher-ups at headquarters. Sims had contingency plans in his head for a late arrival. He could have ordered the pilot to deposit the team a half mile closer to Highway 8 so the infiltration time on the ground would be less. But that might put the helicopter in more danger of being seen or heard by someone on the road. He chose the preselected spot. They would make up the time walking faster.

Only now he wished the pilot had been just 100 yards off the target. The helicopter had landed in a freshly plowed field, its furrows almost three feet deep. Boots sank into the loose dirt. The men practically had to climb over each furrow. With the 175-pound rucksacks on their backs, they cursed silently and trudged the 100 yards until, winded, they finally reached solid ground.

If any farmers had been awakened by the barking dogs, they didn't crawl out of their beds to investigate.

After hiking 500 more yards to the east, the team stopped and began digging a hole for the cache of radios and supplies they would hide. If they were compromised at their hide site near Highway 8 and had to abandon equipment to escape, they could always pick up the spare supplies at the cache.

The secret stash now buried and their loads made lighter, the team set out at a brisk pace for the highway. After five miles, they stopped again at a pasture of tall winter wheat. It would be a perfect rallying point if they were spotted at the hide site and had to flee in different directions and link up later. They committed the scene to memory.

Off in the distance Sims could see the power lines, which he knew from his maps paralleled Highway 8. "We're getting close, boys," he whispered to Tabron and Torbett. They picked up the pace.

About 1,000 yards from the road, the team stopped in a field laced with shallow irrigation ditches. From that distance, they would be able to identify vehicles traveling on the highway.

It was shortly after midnight. The team had made up the thirty minutes during the long march in. Torbett and Tabron took the first shift digging. Sims kept watch for intruders. A lone railroad stretched along the eastern side of the road. A fifty-car train rumbled down the track. Sims could not identify what was in the boxcars, but he unfolded the SATCOM radio and sent a message back to the 18th Airborne Corps anyway to alert them to the train.

The soil was firm as predicted. The hole was easier to shape than the ones they had shoveled in Saudi Arabia. The digging went quickly. As dawn broke, the three men were underground and hidden. Tabron took the first watch out the peephole.

But as soon as the sun shone, people came out. It was like a scene change in a play. Farmers and sheepherders began walking within hundreds of yards of the hide site. The intelligence boys had been far off in their trafficability assessments, Tabron grumbled. There was a damn traffic jam outside the peephole.

A sheepherder in flaming red pantaloons walked in front of the hide site, within a foot of the peephole. Tabron jumped back as the red pants strolled by. He felt like his heart was about to leap out of his chest.

Tabron motioned frantically to Sims.

Sims signaled him to remain calm.

Miraculously, the herder did not notice the hide site and walked on.

Sims had already radioed to the 18th Corps that his team was in place and observing the highway. They would report in every four hours on traffic along the road, using code words to describe the type of vehicles they saw. Their radio call sign was Husky Zero Two.

Another shepherd, this one with a dog, strolled dangerously near. For once, the team's intelligence estimates turned out to be correct. Unlike American canines, Iraqi dogs tended not to hunt. The ones that roamed on their own usually were shot. Domesticated animals stuck close to their masters and didn't stray when they picked up a scent.

As the dog walked near the hide site, Sims could see its head perk up and its nose begin sniffing, perhaps for something they had not sanitized. But the animal did not wander away from the shepherd to investigate.

The three commandos calmed one another down. It was still busy outside from what they could see looking through the peephole. But no one had yet spotted them. At 11 A.M., seven hours after the allied ground invasion had begun, the team radioed another message back to the 18th Corps. Highway 8 was still quiet.

And then it happened. Perhaps they had spotted the SATCOM radio antenna that the team had to protrude ever so slightly from the hide site so a signal could be sent back to the 18th Corps. Perhaps they caught a glimpse of canvas off which the sand had drifted. Or maybe it was just blind luck.

A little girl no more than seven years old and an elderly man who had been herding a half dozen sheep stood frozen, staring in the direction of the hide site.

"Hey Jeff, I believe they see us," Tabron leaned back from the peephole and whispered to Sims. Should they jump out of the hole and try to grab them?

Sims leaned over and squinted to take a peek out the peephole.

"No, no, just wait," he said. "They're not running up here so let's wait."

True, they were not running. But they were slowly making their way closer to the hole.

The old man tried to look inconspicuous, but Tabron could tell he suspected something was amiss. The old man turned his back on the hide site and spoke in a hushed voice to the little girl.

The little girl peeked around the old man in the direction of the hide site, then pointed.

For five minutes the two inched nearer until they stood within a hundred feet of the hole. Then the girl bolted toward the hide site. The old man, who appeared to be in his sixties, followed closely behind.

The little girl was dark-skinned with deep brown eyes. Her head was covered in a veil and she wore a red dress with a black cape.

Sims ordered Torbett out of the hole to grab the old man. Sims and Tabron followed quickly behind.

The little girl froze in terror.

The three Green Berets had drawn their 9-millimeter

pistols fitted with silencers. The old man and the girl could easily have been shot and dragged into the hole. The mission could continue.

But Tabron for one knew he could not live with himself if he had to shoot the pair. Neither could Torbett.

Sims believed it was a waste of lives. They were already compromised. Shooting the two civilians would serve no purpose.

Sims sat the old man down. Speaking Arabic he asked him where the Iraqi soldiers were.

The old man lied. He told Sims the soldiers were just a mile down the road. Perhaps he wanted to scare the Green Berets into surrendering. Sims knew from his intelligence reports that the army was further away.

Sims tried to calm the old man but it was no use. He started screaming at other sheepherders now wandering several hundred yards away. "Americans are here! Americans are here!"

Tabron jumped back into the hole and cranked up the SATCOM radio.

The old man and the little girl scrambled to their feet and ran toward Qawam al Hamzah. Sims let them go.

Tabron had raised the 18th Corps on the radio and now handed the microphone to Sims. "I've got them on the horn," he said almost out of breath.

Sims grabbed the mike. "Be advised that we've been compromised," he said in a surprisingly even voice considering his predicament.

What happened? 18th Corps wanted to know.

Sims recounted the run-in with the old man and the little girl.

Have shots been fired?

"Not at this time," Sims answered.

We'll get back to you, said the voice on the other end of the radio transmission.

The team quickly packed up the radio and grabbed the survival gear they would need for their escape and evasion. Some of the equipment would be left behind.

Crouched down, they ran southwest along an irrigation ditch. After about 500 yards, Sims halted the team. The three men lay against the shallow trench, their weapons pointed east, south, and north.

Sims collected his wits. Focus on what you're doing, he told himself. The team had contingency plans in case they were compromised. They could split up and meet at the rally point or the linkup site even further south across the Euphrates. Tabron and Torbett wanted to run. But where would they go to? The desert? They were all expert shots. Should they stay in the hole and fight until help arrived?

Sims decided to move the team 300 yards to the southwest, away from the road. Then he would again radio the special ops liaison officers at the 18th Corps to see what they had in mind.

After 300 yards, they stopped in an irrigation ditch about knee deep. Sims grabbed the radio's handset.

When would 18th Corps have jets overhead to protect them? he demanded, pacing up and down the narrow ditch. Tabron reached up and yanked him to the ground. They were already taking fire from the Qawam al Hamzah villagers who had hunting rifles. Sims was paying so much attention to the radio, he didn't realize the villagers were shooting at him.

"We need immediate exfiltration," Sims now said. They were practically surrounded by angry villagers.

"We're working on it," came the reply from the radio.

How long would it take for choppers to arrive?

The corps liaison officers back at headquarters were vague.

When would the jets arrive to cover the team from the air?

It would take some time.

That meant not in the next five minutes, Sims knew, which was when he needed the close air support. He shoved the SATCOM mike back in its receiver and turned to Tabron and Torbett, both of whom had frantic looks on their faces.

"We're going to have to sit in this ditch for a while," Sims said, continuing with their rules of engagement. "We have to start killing folks. If they've got guns or they're wearing a military uniform, you shoot them."

Sims sent Tabron to the left down the ditch. Torbett went to the right. Sims crawled forward. They formed a triangle to protect each flank.

Within a half hour, a bus pulled up along Highway 8 and disgorged about fifty Iraqi soldiers. The team didn't wait for them to deploy. All of them good shots at long range, the three began picking off bodies as they climbed off the bus.

The killing was methodical. No rifles were set on automatic. That would waste precious ammunition. Each Green Beret aimed. Soldiers were lined up in bore sights. Triggers pulled. The process repeated. Aim. Sight. Pull. Aim. Sight. Pull.

The remaining Iraqi soldiers scattered from the bus and crawled toward the Green Berets. Armed civilians began sneaking across the right and left flanks. Several village men stood on an old masonry wall surrounding a stone house nearby and waved their hands to direct the soldiers to Sims's position. The Green Berets picked off one of the men. The others quickly climbed down and crouched behind the wall.

But the precision firing could not protect them forever. Villagers and soldiers crept up along the irrigation ditches from the south. The team would gun down several and the squads would retreat. But not for good. A half hour later another bus screeched to a halt along the highway and emptied fifty more soldiers.

Finally, an hour and a half after they had been compromised, an F-16 Eagle roared overhead. Sims shot flare after flare into the sky until the Eagle spotted one and fixed the Green Berets' position. At Sims's direction, the plane dropped cluster bombs and thousand-pounders onto ditches just 300 yards from his position.

Sims screamed his fire direction commands into the radio. The F-16's call sign was Pointer Six. But Sims could barely hear the pilot's response over the earphone. He was now practically deaf from his M-16 firing next to his ear and the bombs exploding around him.

The F-16 bombing had stalled the enemy assault. At least two platoons' worth of Iraqi soldiers lay dead around the Green Berets. But the remaining soldiers continued firing periodically to keep the Americans pinned down.

It was past noon. The standoff could not last forever. Eventually the F-16 would run low on fuel and have to return to its base. Sims knew from his briefing back at King Fahd that the chances were slim that a helicopter would be able to rescue them in broad daylight. It was simply too dangerous. The team had now used up about a third of its ammunition. No matter how much they conserved, they would soon run out of bullets.

Sims assumed he would not walk on American soil ever again. He tried to make peace with his God and his family.

Before they ever set out on the operation, the three Green Berets had vowed never to be captured alive. Each kept a grenade clipped to his canvas webbing for one last act of defiance. They would never survive even if captured.

Sims would die on his terms, not the enemy's. He'd be choking an Iraqi throat and pulling the pin of the grenade on his last breath. They would not capture him and parade him before television cameras in Baghdad. His mother was too old. The pain she'd feel would kill her.

Sims could see his wife, Carolyn, and their two children in his mind now as if they were standing right there next to him. Thirteen-year-old Adam and seven-year-old Becky. He had pulled his truck out of the driveway of their house near Fort Campbell the previous September and the three of them had waved goodbye. That was the last time he had seen them and he would carry that picture in his mind for as long as he now lived. If he had to die, he was ready.

The SATCOM radio crackled. The special ops headquarters had decided to take a chance and launch a daylight rescue. A helicopter would try to reach the team in an hour and a half. Hold on.

* * *

Jim Crisafulli lay with his flight suit stripped to his waist underneath the MH-60 Black Hawk helicopter; he was wrestling with a landing light that had been broken on the flight the night before. Crisafulli had piloted the Black Hawk to infiltrate one of the Green Beret teams into Iraq. The helicopter was now parked on an airport tarmac at the Saudi border town of Rafha where Crisafulli thought it would likely remain on standby for the rest of the day. The noontime sun had warmed the desert so it felt like a hazy spring day. The temperature would again plunge to near freezing that night.

Staff Sergeant Bruce Willard, the aircraft's crew chief, chuckled to himself as he worked over Crisafulli in the cockpit. The pilots usually didn't get their hands dirty tinkering with the choppers. But Crisafulli was an energetic sort. A warrant officer, he was one of the 160th Aviation Regiment's top special ops pilots.

They called him "Monk," perhaps because he was so soft-spoken, but also because he was a short and wiry third-generation Sicilian. Crisafulli had nicknamed his copilot, Randy Stephens, "Beast Man." Stephens was a giant of a man with a round face and a warm smile.

Wires and parts dangled from the belly of the chopper as Crisafulli reached into its innards with a screwdriver and wrench to install the light fixture. The damn desert, he thought. It had taken its toll on the 160th's aircraft. The 135-degree heat of the summer could suck the power right out of the engines. The sand ingested by the turbines ate up their insides.

Crisafulli had flown to the Persian Gulf expecting to see something out of a Lawrence of Arabia movie with gently blowing sand and rising dunes. Nothing had prepared him for the hundreds of miles of absolute bleakness. Trails and landmarks on maps were often barely recognizable from the cockpit, making ground checkpoints almost impossible to establish for navigation. The only break from the desert monotony was an occasional herd of sheep or camels, or the ever present Toyota pickup trucks. The dull gray terrain could seem endlessly flat to a pilot, when suddenly a sand dune jutted up in front and he had to yank back the stick to avoid crashing.

Crisafulli loved Lady Godiva, the name the crew had given the $7 million helicopter. She didn't have all the fancy navigation aids the other Black Hawks in the special ops regiment sported. But she was powerful, like a stripped-down muscle car ready for a drag race. Every helicopter had its own personality. Some were mechanically temperamental. Others gulped fuel. Lady Godiva was extremely strong and reliable. When Crisafulli demanded high power that would overheat any other chopper in the baking desert, her engines ran cool.

The son of a NASA engineer, Crisafulli had grown up moving from town to town. He joined the Army in 1972 for a simple reason. His draft number was sixty-nine. He thought he'd stay in the Army several years, then go to college on the GI Bill. Instead he wound up as a pilot in helicopters. The Army was the only service that would allow him to fly without a degree. Most Army helicopter pilots were warrant officers, who had risen through the ranks as enlisted men. By 1983, Crisafulli was flying special operations helicopters.

The 160th Regiment began as Task Force 160, a top secret helicopter unit organized in the early 1980s after the Desert One debacle to transport Rangers, Green Berets, and Delta commandos on covert operations. The "Night Stalkers," as the Task Force's forty aviators were known, became famous for their daredevil flying in darkness. The unit's motto was "Death Waits in the Dark."

In the beginning though, the Task Force's pilots were doing most of the dying, killed in training accidents because they often were pushing helicopters beyond their mechanical limits. Flight procedures were tightened, which eventually reduced the accident rate. Today, the 160th Regiment has three battalions and more than 300 highly skilled pilots who fly special MH-60 Black Hawk and MH-47 Chinook transports, and AH-6 and MH-6 Little Bird attack ships for commando infiltrations and assaults.

Crisafulli was still on his back gazing up at a snarl of wires when Lieutenant Mike Miller, the team leader for two of the Black Hawks parked at Rafha, came sprinting up. Black Hawks assigned to rescue commandos, as Crisafulli's now was, always flew in pairs in case one of the choppers was shot down.

"Crank her up," Miller said out of breath. "We've got a mission."

"Oh shit," Crisafulli said, looking up at Willard. He was half dressed and the chopper was half disassembled.

Quickly, Crisafulli began cramming wires and parts back into their compartments and screwing on panels.

He crawled out from under the aircraft, leaped through the front side door and hopped into the pilot's seat. He had no idea where he was flying to. Willard tossed him his survival vest, which he shimmied into as he cranked up the engine and flipped switches for the helicopter's five radios.

Chris Durkin, the copilot for the other Black Hawk, came racing out of the headquarters shack to start up Miller's aircraft. Miller was back in the shack copying coordinates for the mission. Stephens, Crisafulli's copilot, stood by Miller scribbling down the numbers for his navigation computer. The pilots already had preplanned flight routes to all the Green Beret hide sites that would minimize—as much as they could—the helicopter's exposure to hostile fire from the ground. All Stephens and Miller now needed were coordinates and bare details on the Green Berets under siege and they would be ready to fly.

Stephens came loping up to the helicopter and bounded into the copilot's seat.

His words were clipped as he strapped himself in. "We've got a team. They're nailed down. I've got the coordinates."

"Punch it in, daddy, let's go!" Crisafulli shouted. He was more worried than he sounded. Daylight helicopter rescues were exceedingly dangerous that deep into enemy territory. Half of them usually failed and the chopper ended up having to be rescued itself. Those poor bastards out there must be in deep trouble for headquarters to approve a daytime pickup, Crisafulli thought.

Stephen's fingers danced over onboard computer and navigation panels. Crisafulli considered himself a fairly good stick man. He thought nobody could beat Stephens on the nav systems. Willard, who had more than a decade's experience in special operations helicopters, began checking out the left minigun he would man during the flight. On the right gun was Todd Diffendorfer, a tall and lanky private first class new to the regiment.

The four men had become a crew only two weeks earlier, but Crisafulli thought they mixed well. He and Willard were the crew's two cutups. Stephens was a skilled cockpit coordinator. Monk and Bruce would keep everyone laughing. The Beast Man would keep them on track. Dif, the new kid on the block, looked to Crisafulli like he was sixteen. But on training runs before the war, he proved to be a fast learner and adaptable.

As the rotor blades began to whirl, Gordie Hopple piled into the back of the aircraft. A Green Beret sergeant first class who specialized in search and rescues, Hopple would leap from the helicopter at the pickup point with his machine gun blazing and drag back to the aircraft anyone wounded.

With the radios yapping in the earpiece of his helmet and everyone shouting instructions at once for the preflight checklists, Crisafulli happened to glance over at Miller's helicopter parked near them on the tarmac.

It was on fire.

The helicopter's number one engine had burst into flames.

Stephens keyed his microphone and radioed Miller to warn him. The message never got through. But Miller's crew quickly saw the smoke billowing and scrambled out with fire extinguishers.

The blaze turned out not to be as serious as it looked. A burned-out starter in the engine. But it was enough to cripple the helicopter for that day.

Crisafulli slumped back in his seat. "Oh crud, they're

going to tank us," he said with a groan. No way would their headquarters allow a single chopper to fly in on a daylight extraction. If it were shot down, no one would be there to pull out the crew. Then two long-distance rescues would have to be mounted.

But just to be ready, Crisafulli and the crew went through the motions of preflight checks. They wheeled the Black Hawk over to a tanker truck to top off with fuel. But they expected it would be a wasted exercise.

They were wrong.

Within minutes, Captain Tim Childrey, the air base's operations officer, ran up to Crisafulli's cockpit.

"It's a go!" he shouted.

Crisafulli and Stephens exchanged a brief glance, but said nothing.

I guess we're alone on this one, Crisafulli thought to himself.

Rick Detrick, a Green Beret warrant officer who was the search-and-rescue specialist for Miller's aircraft, now ran to Lady Godiva and leaped into the back. Crisafulli would need every shooter he could muster. The helicopter took off.

The night before, his chopper had taken heavy ground fire when it crossed the border. This time, Crisafulli crossed twenty miles to the northwest.

It was shortly before 1 P.M. The haze had dissipated. The sky was now cooler and clear. Terrific, Crisafulli thought. Perfect visibility for an antiaircraft gunner on the ground.

As he crossed the border, Crisafulli dropped the helicopter to just eight feet off the desert, no higher than the ceiling of a living room. He gunned the turbo shaft engines to 135 knots. They wouldn't be able to outrun an antiaircraft gunner's vision, but maybe it would be fast enough so he couldn't lock on to the target.

But traveling that low and that fast left no room for mistakes. Recovery time from errors would now be milliseconds instead of seconds. The helicopter was flying at the edge of the performance envelope. Just an accidental twitch in the pilot's wrist could send the aircraft crashing into the ground.

The preplanned flight route had the Black Hawk heading northeast crossing over the tiny villages of As Salman and Irjal ash Shaykhiyan. The direct route would have been more northwesterly, but that would have taken the aircraft over a division of enemy soldiers garrisoned along the Euphrates, twenty miles south of the Green Beret position. Instead, Crisafulli planned to loop around to the right at the point where the Euphrates bent to the east at the town of As Samawah, then fly northwest to Sim's position near Qawam al Hamzah.

But the radio traffic Crisafulli monitored from the F-16 patrolling over the Green Berets now sounded ominous. The aerial attacks had kept the Iraqi soldiers at bay so far, but the F-16 pilot worried that the team could not be protected for long. The enemy was still closing in on Sims and his men. The Iraqis would soon be overrunning his position. Pointer Six radioed to Crisafulli: "Unless you're here in ten minutes there isn't going to be anybody left to pick up."

"We're not going to make it," Stephens said, turning to Crisafulli.

"Yes we are," Crisafulli said.

At Irjal ash Shaykhiyan, he banked the helicopter hard to the left. They now flew due north. They would take the shortcut to the team—over the Iraqi division garrisoned south of the Euphrates. Crisafulli accelerated to the last ounce of power Lady Godiva had: 140 knots. Now her engines were hot.

The crew could see the reflections of vehicle mirrors streaking by from the ground just below as they zoomed over enemy troops and trucks. By the time the dazed soldiers unslung their rifles to fire, the Black Hawk was far ahead. The pilots could just hear the sound of gunshots trailing them.

Twenty miles south of the Euphrates, a small dune rose up in front of the helicopter. In an instant, Crisafulli yanked back the cyclic stick in his right hand and cleared the dune by two feet. He shoved the cyclic forward so the Black Hawk would drop into the small depression behind the dune and his aircraft would be masked from enemy fire. But as he did a donkey stood motionless in front of the chopper. He snapped back the cyclic and the helicopter hopped over the braying animal.

"That was kind of close there, boss," Willard said over his intercom with a nervous laugh.

Within seconds, the Black Hawk skittered over the marshes and inlets surrounding the Euphrates. Cockpit windshield wipers were turned on as the spray from the muddy water of the river just below splattered the windows. Flocks of birds scattered as the helicopter roared past. Crisafulli zigzagged to avoid ingesting the terrified fowl in the aircraft's turbines.

The helicopter was within minutes of the pickup site. The crew could hear more gunfire from the outside. The F-16 had broken off its strafing, its pilot now radioing to the Black Hawk the enemy positions it could see on the ground.

As they raced up to the pickup point, Crisafulli and Stephens saw Iraqi soldiers running through the brush, darting from ditch to ditch and pointing their rifles up to fire at the Black Hawk. The crew had not yet spotted the Green Berets. The grid coordinates given to them back at Rafha on Sims's position indicated the team was on the east side of Highway 8.

Still traveling at about 130 knots, Crisafulli decided to scoot under the road's power lines, which stood about eighty feet above the ground.

"Yeah, do it, do it," Stephens said urging his pilot on. The higher in the air, the more vulnerable the helicopter was to ground fire.

But just as he approached the highway, Crisafulli saw a second set of power lines underneath that were about fifty feet high. The Black Hawk couldn't squeeze through.

"Randy, I've got to go over," Crisafulli said quickly.

"We got to go over, we got to go over," Stephens said.

They were repeating each other as they both talked their way through the harrowing maneuvers.

Crisafulli decelerated the chopper. He wanted to pop up as close to the top wires as he could to minimize the exposure to ground fire. Like a high jumper, he rolled the helicopter over the lines.

The crew spotted the Green Berets. Tabron had fired the team's last flare. Sims then unfolded a five-foot-long panel painted bright orange, which was used to mark landing zones for helicopters. He waved the panel frantically over the ditch. The Green Berets were on the other side of the highway.

Crisafulli repeated the maneuver, skipping over the power lines once more. The helicopter looked to Sims like it was dancing a ballet over the road.

Coming off the western side of the highway, the Black Hawk was still traveling at 120 knots. Crisafulli had to nail the landing next to the team the first time. There could be no second try. Every Iraqi rifle on the ground was now pointed toward his aircraft and firing.

Crisafulli quickly decelerated the helicopter. It streaked just south of Sims's position. Less than fifty yards to the left of where the Green Berets hunkered, Crisafulli shoved down the nose of the Black Hawk with the cyclic stick forward and kicked the floor pedals violently to turn the tail. Lady Godiva twisted to her right side, pirouetting on her nose to fly a tight circle around the team below.

In the next instant, Crisafulli leveled the aircraft and dropped it like a stone to the ground. It wasn't the prettiest of maneuvers. "Jesus, Jim!" Stephens shouted when the helicopter slammed onto the ground. His stomach was stuck in his throat.

But it had worked. The rotor blades whirled over the heads of the Green Berets in the ditch. The Black Hawk had landed between the three Americans and the Iraqi soldiers who were firing at them.

Hopple and Detrick jumped out the sides of the helicopter firing M-16s from their hips. The Iraqi soldiers began to converge on the helicopter. Some were as close as

thirty-five feet away. Willard sprayed the field with the mo-
tor-driven minigun mounted on the helicopter's left side. It
ripped out 4,000 rounds a minute. An Iraqi soldier charged
the plane. The minigun's rounds cut him in half at the
waist like a chain saw.

The noise from the two miniguns firing was deafening.
Every radio in the cockpit was screeching with staff officers
back at Rafha asking a million questions. Crisafulli and
Stephens screamed into the intercom to point out targets
to the gunners.

"Get them on the left!"

"There's some in front of us!"

Willard and Diffendorfer swung the miniguns back
and forth wildly to mow down what seemed like a swarm of
enemy soldiers closing in on the aircraft.

The helicopter was being raked with bullets.

"We're taking hits, we're taking hits!" Willard shouted
into the intercom. One bullet shot through a rear window
and ricocheted inside the cockpit, barely missing a grenade
rack and Diffendorfer's forehead. Two rounds struck the
blades' rotors. Another struck the chopper's self-sealing
fuel tank. Still another zipped past the rear of Crisafulli's
cockpit seat, missing his head by a foot, and out the window on Stephens's side.

The Black Hawk was now more than thirty seconds on
the ground. It seemed to Crisafulli like thirty minutes.
Time froze. Sims scrambled onto the helicopter dragging a
huge rucksack behind him. It took him no more than a
second. But he seemed to Crisafulli to be moving in slow
motion and with a wide smile on his face.

In times of intense combat, ridiculous things often
pass through soldiers' minds. As Sims clambered aboard,
the long antenna from a radio he carried in one hand
snapped off and fell to the ground. I wonder if he signed
for that piece of equipment, Crisafulli thought as he
twisted his head back to watch the boarding.

Two more Green Berets jumped into the aircraft. That
made a total of three rescued. Crisafulli thought six men
had been compromised at the hide site. The air crew didn't

know that Conner's three-man team had not been discovered.

The cabin was in chaos. The miniguns continued to fire. Smoke and dust from the whirling rotors engulfed the helicopter. Crisafulli didn't want to leave anyone behind.

"Where's the rest of them?" he shouted into the rear cabin.

"We're all up!" Sims shouted back. "Go, go!"

There were no more men to pick up. Bullets pinged off the sides of the helicopter. The aircraft's collective flight control was damaged on one side. Its heat signature suppression equipment was shot up.

They had everybody, the crew determined.

"*Go!*" Stephens screamed at the top of his lungs.

Wrenching the sticks, Crisafulli pivoted the helicopter again on its nose, swung the aircraft around so it was pointed south, and sped away ten feet off the ground. Several dozen Iraqi soldiers lay dead at the landing zone behind them.

This time, the helicopter banked to the southeast to avoid the enemy division along the Euphrates.

Sims, Torbett, and Tabron now knew they would live. They slapped one another on the back and laughed and shouted over the noise of the engines.

Sims could no longer hear a thing. He crawled to the front of the aircraft. If he could have kissed Crisafulli and Stephens then, he would have done it. As far as he was concerned, they were warriors sent from heaven. To pluck them out, 150 miles inside enemy territory.

"All right! All right!" Sims screamed, reaching over the cockpit seat and grabbing Crisafulli's shoulders. He patted it so hard, Crisafulli had to turn the controls over to Stephens. They were still only ten feet off the ground.

The radios, on full volume so they could be heard in the back of the plane, now crackled. The special ops headquarters wanted a status report. What about casualties?

Crisafulli turned around and shouted, "Is anybody hit?"

Sims, Torbett, and Tabron jumped up and began beating their chests like gorillas. They howled and laughed.

Crisafulli turned around and keyed the mike.

"No, we don't have any casualties," he said with a smile.

He banked the helicopter to the right and headed for the Saudi border.

As Colonel Kraus, the Green Beret commander, had worried from the beginning, the strategic reconnaissance operations had their problems, particularly the ones furthest north. The SATCOM radio with Conner's team would not transmit. When the team sneaked back to its cache to pick up the backup radio, it found Bedouins camped next to the hidden supplies. The Green Berets went into escape and evasion. They radioed back no intelligence on Highway 8.

Balwanz's eight-man team, which watched another highway north of the Euphrates, also was compromised and had to fight off enemy soldiers for seven hours before 160th helicopters could rescue them at night. Another nine-man team also operating north of the Euphrates was spotted by a Bedouin shepherd who stumbled across its hide site. Incredibly, one of the Green Berets on the mission, Sergeant First Class Gary Seideman, had the presence of mind to pull out a camera and photograph their desperate battle with Iraqi soldiers the next six hours until helicopters arrived. When Seideman returned home, his wife was furious with him for shooting pictures instead of his rifle.

Intelligence officers made other errors besides assuming that Iraqi farmers left their fields unattended in winter. Analysts told one Green Beret team that the large objects pictured in satellite photos of an Iraqi field were boulders. The helicopters taking in the Green Berets quickly aborted the mission when the pilots saw that the boulders were really Bedouin tents. It was one of two teams that had to abort its mission because the infiltration point turned out to be populated.

Miraculously, none of the Green Berets compromised

in recon operations was killed or wounded. Seven hide sites positioned south of the Euphrates were never spotted. For five days, the Special Forces soldiers in them radioed back reports as the 18th Corps and 7th Corps swept around from the west. Even the teams that were compromised managed to send some intelligence back to headquarters. The fact that no more than companies of Iraqi infantrymen were in the areas to try to capture them told the corps intelligence officers that no large reinforcements were prepared to counterattack. The roads on the northern flank were quiet. The Hail Mary play had taken the Iraqis by surprise. One hundred hours after the ground war had begun, Saddam's army in Kuwait and southern Iraq was almost surrounded.

Jeff Sims, who had already been awake for more than thirty-six hours, flew back to the Bat Cave at King Fahd. He would not sleep more than an hour a night for the next four days—not until Conner's three-man team was safely back. He had found in the past that a commando could survive on an hour or two of sleep a night for as long as a month. When the radio message finally arrived informing him that a helicopter bearing the team had crossed the border and had landed at Rafha, Sims went to his cot in the Bat Cave and collapsed. He woke up two days later.

DECEPTION AT MINA SAUD

The Persian Gulf waters off the coast of Kuwait were flat calm. Tom Deitz was grateful for that. The other times the Navy lieutenant and his SEALs had raced up the Kuwaiti coast in speedboats on reconnaissance missions the seas had been choppy. The boats had bounced from wave to wave, sometimes soaring as much as five feet into the air. The bone-jarring ride could break a man's knee. When the speedboats finally stopped along the Kuwaiti coast, some SEALs had to lean over the sides and retch. Others struggled in the rolling seas to unzip bulky thick wet suits and urinate because bladders had been bounced silly.

Tonight, however, the four naval special warfare speedboats, each powered by twin 1,000-horsepower Mer-Cruiser engines, glided serenely along the water, and Deitz for the first time had a chance to gaze around instead of hanging on for dear life. It seemed a creepy night to him. In the sky no more than several hundred feet above the sea hung black clouds created by the allied bombing and the oil fires Saddam's army had just started in Kuwait. A thin, bright slice of moon darted between the dark patches. In stark contrast, the Kuwaiti beaches to his left glowed bright white. Further inland Deitz could hear the thump of exploding bombs delivered by allied air strikes and see the silver streaks of anti-aircraft fire draw white lines in the sky.

It had been six in the evening on February 23 when Deitz and the fourteen other Navy SEALs had set off in the four speedboats from a staging base at Ras al Mishab, a Saudi coastal town about thirty miles south of the Kuwaiti border. From the border, the boats would motor another fifteen miles north and park off a beach at the Kuwaiti coastal city of Mina Saud.

As Deitz prepared to climb aboard his speedboat at Ras al Mishab, Commander Tim Holden, his immediate superior, had pulled him aside and whispered one of the most closely held secrets in the Central Command. The allied ground war to liberate Kuwait would begin in just ten hours, at 4 A.M. on February 24. Deitz and his fourteen SEALs must convince the Iraqi defenders at Mina Saud that 17,000 Marines were about to land. Their mission would be one of the major deception campaigns of the Desert Storm war. Deitz smiled and hopped aboard the speedboat.

The operation, he knew, would hardly be as strenuous as SEAL training. A Naval Academy graduate, Deitz applied for the SEALs in 1986. Soft-spoken, the twenty-nine-year-old lieutenant was hardly the commando type. He could count on one hand the number of times he'd ever fired a pistol before joining the SEALs. But the physical challenge intrigued him. Compact and muscular, Deitz had been recruited by the academy to wrestle and ended up playing intercollegiate lightweight football for students under 158 pounds. Nothing so far had matched the misery of BUDS training. His Hell Week had been in December, when the Pacific waters off Coronado were frigid. Barely a third of the students in his class had graduated.

Deitz grabbed the microphone for a secure radio in the speedboat. He transmitted back to the SEALs's main tactical operations center the code word that indicated the speedboats had safely crossed another checkpoint on their trip north.

He had no guarantee that he'd reach the next checkpoint. In this case the ride to work was as dangerous as the secret mission itself. The gulf was infested with mines. The speedboats had no mine detection equipment. It was no use posting sailors at the bows as lookouts. With the boats traveling at forty knots, running lights out, there would be no time to warn of an obstacle. At least death would be instantaneous, Deitz knew. The thin-shelled boats would be vaporized if they struck a mine.

Captain Ray Smith leaned over a navigation chart in the canvas tent that served as the SEALs's tactical operations center at Ras al Gar, a Saudi coastal outpost some seventy-five miles north of the Gulf port city of Dhahran. Plywood boards had been laid inside the tent for a floor. Tactical maps hung up along its walls. Stacked on field tables were radios of all descriptions, which communicated with Deitz and other SEAL team leaders spread out over Saudi Arabia. The code word Deitz had just radioed would be only one of a few he would transmit that night. Operational secrecy precluded lengthy conversations, even over secure radios. Nevertheless, that brief transmission was reassuring for the Navy captain.

The Naval Special Warfare Task Group Smith commanded in the Persian Gulf had been small—no more than 260 SEALs, small-boat operators, and support sailors—but incredibly busy. The night before Deitz's missions, SEALs had secretly inserted a team of CIA-trained Kuwaiti guerrillas onto a beach south of Kuwait City. SEAL scouts posted along the Kuwaiti border had been overrun when Iraqi soldiers launched an early incursion and briefly held the Saudi border town of Khafji. Other SEAL teams captured oil platforms and Qarah Island, the first piece of Kuwaiti real estate to be retaken in the war.

Smith, who was lean and trim and looked much younger than his forty-four years, had practically lived in the tactical operations center the past six months. His cot in another barracks had been no more than forty yards away. Never had he been so engrossed in a single event as this war. Everything else paled in comparison.

There was an unspoken pressure on Smith. Only a tiny fraction of the Navy's 2,500 SEALs were allowed in the Persian Gulf war. Smith, who had commanded Naval Special Warfare Group One back at Coronado, was responsible for SEAL operations in the Middle East. He had even been lucky and managed to slip part of his force aboard transport planes headed to Saudi Arabia in early August before Schwarzkopf bumped special operations units from the manifests to airlift in heavy combat divisions. Every SEAL back in the United States was desperate for a piece of this war. The SEALs had lost eight men in poorly planned combat operations during the Grenada and Panama invasions. Whatever Smith did in Desert Storm, it had to be successful. By tradition, casualties were not taken lightly in this small force. If any mission failed, he would be blamed, no matter the circumstances. The SEALs could afford no more debacles.

This was Smith's second tour in the Persian Gulf. In 1988 he had briefly headed a task force of SEALs clearing mines and fending off Iranian gunboats as Navy warships escorted Kuwaiti tankers. Schwarzkopf had now named him commander of the Kuwaiti Navy for this war, a dubious distinction since the Kuwaiti fleet that had escaped Iraqi occupation consisted of two patrol boats and a barge.

Deitz's deception operation was actually a by-product of another mission. By November, the Marines had begun intensive planning for what to them was the most important part of a likely ground war: an amphibious assault on the coast of Kuwait. Spy planes and satellites had photographed the Kuwaiti shoreline for a possible landing site. But the Marines would need SEALs swimming near the beach to gather finer details on the gradient and firmness of the sand, the coastal gun emplacements, bunkers, obstacles, enemy vehicle movements, and troop concentrations. Smith also proposed that the SEALs simulate a landing at one beach to divert the Iraqi defenders from the point where the Marines planned to land.

SEAL teams sailed north ten times to scout beaches along the Kuwaiti coast. Mines weren't the only danger during the trips up the gulf. Friendly fire gave Smith just as many sleepless nights. The northern gulf was bristling with allied warships that had been picking off any Iraqi boats that dared to set sail. Before each recon mission, Smith contacted every allied navy vessel with guns to warn them not to mistake his speedboats for the enemy. No-attack zones were established to protect the SEALs. For the Saudi Navy, Smith would phone the day before a mission, send a cable, then hand-deliver a message the day of the operation. He began to joke with his staff that it was more difficult to sail through friendly waters than into the jaws of his enemy.

Even all the cross-checks didn't prevent at least one friendly fire incident. A Kuwaiti patrol boat in Smith's own Navy shot at a SEAL boat with .50-caliber machine guns, mistaking it for an Iraqi vessel. Fortunately the Kuwaiti boat was too far away to do any damage with the fire.

On some recons, the SEALs remained in their black rubber rafts and scanned the Kuwaiti coast 200 yards away with night vision scopes. Other times, they left the rafts and swam to the shore, where they lay shivering in the shallow 54-degree water with nothing but their camouflaged faces poking out and just watched. They counted trucks moving along coastal roads and spotted antiship missile batteries that threatened American vessels. Iraqi defenders exercised poor light discipline. Doors to command posts were opened and the SEALs could catch glimpses of activity inside. Back in their rubber rafts, they would pull pocket tape recorders out of plastic bags to describe details along the shore.

Many beaches were quickly ruled out for amphibious landings. On one, beach houses were packed so closely together, the Marine brigades would not be able to squeeze through. At another, Iraqi defenders fired at a SEAL team as it approached in rafts. An enemy patrol boat almost spotted another SEAL team. Other beaches were too heavily defended with mines and obstacles.

The intelligence the SEALs sent back to the Marines quickly confirmed what the Central Command had already suspected. The Kuwaiti coastline was too heavily defended. An amphibious landing was not worth the casualties the Marines would suffer. Even the Navy balked at steaming its amphibious ships into the mine-strewn waters off the coast. There would be no amphibious landing, Schwarz-kopf decided.

The Marines protested the decision all the way up the military chain of command. Amphibious operations were their raison d'etre, the very capability that made the corps different from the Army. But not since Inchon in the Korean War had the Marines conducted a full-scale amphibious invasion. But Powell and Schwarzkopf held firm. The only Americans allowed near the Kuwaiti shoreline would be the fifteen Navy SEALs of Task Unit Mike.

Deitz and the other SEALs now scouted beaches for an amphibious feint. The Marines would join Saudi divisions on land in breaching the defenses in southeastern Kuwait and then driving north to Kuwait City. Deitz's mission now was to create a diversion with explosives and machine gun fire to convince Iraqi coastal defenders that the Marines were still launching their amphibious assault onto the beach. That way, the coastal defenders would keep their guns pointed to the gulf instead of turning them around to attack the Marine and Saudi divisions that would slip past their rear.

Deitz had to find a beach where an amphibious landing was plausible enough that the Iraqi defenders could be convinced the Marines were invading. Just such a beach existed at Mina Saud. SEAL scouts had spotted it during one of their recon missions. The crescent-shaped shoreline was clear of houses for about two miles. Roads exited off the beach that would make a drive inland feasible. There was only fifteen feet of sand between the shoreline and the grassy berms, but the beach was wide enough to handle an amphibious force. The Iraqis must have thought the same. Sandbagged bunkers had been built at the flanks. Barbed wire and obstacles had been laid along the shore.

Central Command officers purposefully fanned press speculation about an amphibious invasion. Navy officials leaked details about amphibious ship exercises in the northern gulf that normally would have been kept secret. Back at Ras al Mishab after his last recon mission before the ground war was to begin, Deitz wandered into a nearby Saudi store and picked up a copy of the international edition of *Newsweek*. The headline for a two-page story announced: "To the Shores of Kuwait." He read the article and chuckled. "In one sense," the piece began authoritatively, "an amphibious assault on Iraqi forces in Kuwait is already under way. It's just that the Iraqis don't know it. By now, U.S. Navy SEAL teams have staked out the beaches, gathering hundreds of details. . . . The U.S. Marine attack forces are rehearsed. . . . The landing point has been chosen."

This is fantastic, Deitz thought to himself. The Iraqis are already being deceived by the press.*

Seven miles off the coast at Mina Saud, the speedboat crews killed their engines. It was 7:30 P.M. Deitz's team was an hour ahead of schedule. The trip had taken half the time he had budgeted because the boats had been able to accelerate in the calm waters. That was fine by Deitz. It gave his men more time to arrange their gear and prepare for the infiltration.

Lashed to the speedboats were four Zodiac rubber rafts. Deitz would only use three. The fourth one was carried as a spare. Deitz had found the adage always to be true: whenever you didn't have spare equipment, something invariably broke down.

The SEALs took a stair-step approach to the mission. From the speedboats they would climb into the three rubber rafts and quietly motor in about six miles to a point 500 yards from the shoreline. There a team would jump out and swim to the shoreline with the explosives that would be detonated.

Everything had been planned and rehearsed down to the last minute. Deitz's team was to detonate 120 pounds of C-4 plastic explosives on the shoreline at exactly 1 A.M., in order to give the coastal defenders three hours to react before the ground invasion began at 4 A.M. From that 1 A.M. deadline, Deitz had worked backward in his planning:

---

*The article that made Deitz laugh was one to which I had contributed. My only excuse is that I wasn't the only journalist taken in by the ruse.

Starting at the end of the mission first, he calculated the minutes needed to swim from rubber rafts to the shoreline, where the timers for the explosives would be set.

Next, he figured out the minutes needed for the rubber rafts to motor from the speedboats to 500 yards off the shoreline, where the swimmers would be dropped off.

Then he computed the exact time the speedboats needed to be at the point seven miles off the coast of Mina Saud to launch the rubber rafts.

Nine of the fifteen SEALs would remain in the three rubber rafts. They were Deitz's best radio men, M-60 machine gunners, and engine repairmen. Deitz and the remaining five SEALs were the swimmers who would carry the explosives to the shore. In case the swimmers were spotted by the enemy or one of the raft's engines failed, Deitz wanted his top people bailing them out.

The six swimmers needed only dry suits, fins, and the explosives to carry out the mission. But they would each lug twenty-five pounds' worth of extra gear in case something went wrong. Three carried Heckler and Koch MP-5 machine guns to use if sentries patrolled the beach. The other three took M-16 rifles fitted with grenade launchers for enemy machine gun nests that might have to be taken out. Each had a pistol hooked to his waist belt, in case the main weapon jammed, and a knife strapped to his leg, in case he became tangled in underwater barbed wire.

If enemy soldiers fired at them, the swimmers had scuba bottles that gave them three minutes of air to escape underwater. Each had a red flashlight to signal if he became separated from the rest of the team during the swim, plus a backup strobe light and chemical light. If someone was wounded, the life vest each man wore could be quickly inflated so he could more easily be carried back to the raft. (One of the SEALs on the swim team was a hospital corpsman who would treat casualties.) Underneath their dry suits, the swimmers wore their camouflaged fatigues in case they became trapped at the shoreline and had to escape over land. In small, waterproof backpacks each stuffed a pair of jungle boots.

With their equipment loaded into the Zodiacs, the SEALs pushed away from the speedboats, the thirty-five-horsepower engines on their rafts puttering quietly.

Deitz gathered the rafts together when they had cleared the boats to let the other men in on the secret he had been told back at Ras al Mishab. "The fucking ground war starts at 0400 hours!" he said in a half whisper, half shout. "Let's go in and blow the shit out of the beach!"

The commandos whooped and hollered and let out a chorus of "hoo-yahs!" They knew they were too far from the shore for anyone to hear.

At 10 P.M., the three Zodiacs reached the 500-yard mark. Deitz unzipped a plastic bag and pulled out a night vision scope, which enabled him to see in the dark. For ten minutes he scanned the shore in front of him. Nothing was different from his last recon. Jet fighters and naval warships had bombarded the coast for several days before that night to simulate softening it up for an amphibious landing. The beach was now deserted.

The six swimmers, their hands and faces blackened with camouflage paint, slipped quietly into the water. Each carried a haversack packed with twenty pounds of C-4 explosives and two timers to detonate the charge. One timer served as a backup in case the first failed. The haversacks were equipped with air bags to make them buoyant.

The swimmers spread out in a straight line facing the shore. Ten yards separated each man. They pushed the haversacks in front of them as flotation devices and, kicking their fins, began swimming to the shore. Their eyes never left the coastline. Exploding bombs and oil well fires illuminated the area behind the berms and made the sand on the beach appear bright white. It was perfect illumination for the infiltration, Deitz knew. If sentries were posted on the berms they would see nothing past the sand. That was because of a back lighting effect that SEALs learned in their training. Enemy soldiers who build bonfires on the beach to watch for waterborne infiltrators end up being able to see only as far as the illumination provided by the flames. Beyond that everything appears pitch black.

It took no more than fifteen minutes before the swimmers were in six feet of water and could stand up. Using hand signals, Deitz motioned the men to spread out further. Fifty yards now separated each of them. They scanned the shore for another ten minutes. It was now eerily quiet.

With the haversacks bobbing in front of them, they drifted slowly to the shore, the gentle surf lapping over their heads. Deitz swam in the middle of the formation.

Lying on their stomachs, the SEALs stopped when they were in no more than two feet of water. They unslung their weapons and laid them on top of the haversacks, which now rested on the sandy bottom. Deitz checked his dive watch and signaled the team to wait. The timers had all been set back at Ras al Mishab to detonate the charges in two hours. All the SEALs had to do in the water was pull the pins so the haversacks would explode at exactly 1 A.M.

But the pins would not be pulled at exactly 11 P.M. Water temperature affected the clock mechanisms. Deitz had a table he could consult to calculate the minutes lost or gained. For the 53-degree water that night, the timer would detonate thirteen minutes late. At 10:47 P.M., Deitz began signaling his men to pull the pins.

The SEALs slithered back, leaving the heavy haversacks now sitting firmly in about a foot of water. Deitz knew that by 1 A.M. the tide would be out and the haversacks would be on dry sand. There would be no water around the bags to muffle the explosion, which would wake up everybody for miles around.

Back at the six-foot mark, the line of SEALs closed in again like choreographed dancers to ten-foot intervals and began swimming slowly out to sea.

A silent rendezvous with the Zodiacs could be tricky. In the darkness the SEALs could easily lose the black rafts. The swimmers were even more difficult to spot in the water. The two groups could easily drift past each other and spend all night trying to link up if they weren't careful.

Deitz knew it had taken the team fifteen minutes to

swim to the shoreline. After swimming back out for ten minutes, he stopped the formation. Treading water, he unhooked a pocket radio.

"Foxtrot Two, stand by for signal," he whispered into the radio. He next pulled out his red flashlight, pointed it out to sea and turned it on briefly. Anyone on the beach would not be able to see the light.

But the Zodiacs spotted it.

"Roger, got your signal. Leaving," came the response over Deitz's radio.

The swimmers waited. They didn't see the Zodiacs until they were finally within twenty feet. The rafts were now about 300 yards from the shoreline.

Two of the Zodiacs then separated so there was about 250 yards between them. The crews in each boat then strung out two large, orange channel buoys, each three feet in diameter. When the sun rose in the morning the Iraqi defenders would think that the buoys were markers for incoming amphibious ships.

Meanwhile, two of the four speedboats parked just over the horizon had crept in closer to about 300 yards off the shoreline and waited for Deitz's signal. When Deitz's Zodiacs reached the two speedboats at the seven-mile point, he radioed back to the other boats near the shore: "We're all safe. Go ahead and continue with the plan."

At 12:30 A.M., the fireworks began. The close-in patrol boats started raking the beach with gunfire from their .50-caliber machine guns and peppering it with 40-millimeter grenades from M-19 launchers. That would wake up the defenders in the bunkers. As the boats drifted, their crews also dumped five two-pound charges off the side, which were set to detonate every couple of minutes.

Five minutes later, the two speedboats raced back to their rendezvous point seven miles off the coast and the small charges began exploding.

For the first time, Deitz could relax. As the speedboat crew looked on somewhat baffled, the SEALs conducted an impromptu ceremony. One of the commandos nicknamed "Diamond" was led to the bow of the boat.

"Raise your right hand and repeat after me," Deitz ordered.

Diamond did as he was told.

"I do solemnly swear or affirm that I will support and defend the Constitution of the United States," Deitz said.

Diamond repeated the oath. He was up for reenlistment. By being sworn in during wartime, Diamond received a reenlistment bonus, tax-free.

At 1 A.M., the 120 pounds of C-4 on the beach began detonating. The explosions as each haversack went off were deafening. The low ceiling of clouds created an echo so the sound reverberated inland. The combination of heavy machine gun and grenade fire, small charges detonating in the shallow water, the huge C-4 explosions six in a row, then the sight of bright orange buoys marking a corridor to the beach could not help but leave the impression in the minds of the Iraqi defenders that Navy frogmen had just prepared Mina Saud for an amphibious invasion.

Deitz radioed back to the tactical operations center at Ras al Gar with the code word "Pamela." It meant that the feint had been completed. The crews shoved boat throttles forward and sped south.

Ten hours later, Deitz sat on a bunk in his barracks still feeling groggy. The SEALs had arrived back as Ras al Mishab at 2:30 A.M. and had finally finished stowing their gear and weapons by five. After a debriefing, they went into isolation, forbidden to tell even other SEALs about their mission. Deitz had tried to rest but sleep was impossible. The ground war had just begun and Ras al Mishab was a beehive of noise and activity. He'd just have to leave his body clock screwed up for another day.

It was shortly after ten in the morning. Deitz reached into a locker and pulled out a box of crackers and a bag of noodles, which he would boil in water. Crackers and noodles had become his break from a constant diet of those detestable MREs.

Later, he strolled down to the pier where the speedboats were moored and a command tent had been erected. A warrant officer monitoring the radios and teletype handed him a cable from Smith, who was still overseeing operations back at Ras al Gar.

"Tom: Please pass to your men an 'extremely well done' on last night's mission," the cable began. Smith's task force had just received an intelligence report from the Central Command's headquarters in Riyadh. Not only had the guns of the coastal defenders remained pointed toward the gulf, but "elements of two Iraqi divisions reacted" to the feint and moved east to Mina Saud.

"It worked!" Deitz said to himself. He rushed back to the barracks to tell his men.

THE SCUD HUNT

Something was not right. The start of the Desert Storm war had been picture perfect. But now the first piece of unsettling news arrived at the Air Force strike cell in Riyadh. It was the afternoon of January 17, little more than twelve hours since the beginning of the air campaign. Iraqi rocket batteries had launched two Scud missiles at Israel. Fortunately the missiles were off target. They plunged harmlessly into the Mediterranean Sea near Israel's coast.

But the errant rockets worried the targeters in the strike cell. There weren't supposed to be any Iraqi Scud missiles launched against Israel. Just hours before, F-15Es had sneaked across the border at the beginning of the war to destroy what the strike cell's targeters thought were all of the Scud sites with fixed launchers and their supply depots. Had the targeters underestimated Saddam's missile arsenal?

Shortly after 3 A.M. the next morning, jarring proof arrived. Seven Scuds slammed into Tel Aviv and Haifa, wrecking 1,587 apartments and injuring forty-seven civilians. Terrified Israelis grabbed masks and braced for a dreaded gas war. Some of the Scuds had detonated as if they were intended to disperse chemical agents. American spy satellites observed eleven trucks leaving the Samarra chemical weapons warehouse near Baghdad with suspected warheads for missiles. Saddam appeared to be fulfilling his promise to "scorch Israel."

It turned out that the Iraqi dictator never armed his missiles with chemical warheads. As a tactical weapon, the notoriously inaccurate Scuds were worthless on the battlefield. But that mattered little to Israelis who now streamed into air raid shelters with the whine of sirens. Schools closed. Merchants shuttered shops. As a terror weapon, the Scuds would be Saddam's version of the V-2s that Hitler rained on London during World War II.

The Central Command had guessed that Saddam could field no more than fifty mobile and fixed Scud launchers, which Air Force bombers had already targeted. The strike cell, which had not placed Scuds high on its targeting priority at the war's outset, would soon discover there were perhaps ten times that number. It would turn out to be one of the biggest intelligence failures of the conflict.

The air war was little more than a day old and Washington faced a crisis. The Bush administration had already sounded out its Arab partners on their likely response if Israel entered the war against Iraq. The Saudis did not expect the Jewish state to stand idly by if attacked, but warned that Arab forces would never allow themselves to be perceived as allies with Israel in any battle. Saudi Arabia would likely remain with the coalition, but Syria, Egypt, and the Persian Gulf emirates would bolt. To reach Iraqi targets, Israeli jets might fly over Jordanian air space against Amman's wishes, which would likely force Jordan to ally with Iraq. If Iraqi Scuds striking Israel were armed with chemical or biological warheads, Tel Aviv might well retaliate with nuclear arms.

The week before the air war began, Bush had telephoned Israeli Prime Minister Yitzhak Shamir pleading with him not to initiate a preemptive strike against Iraq. Shamir promised that Tel Aviv would not be the first to attack, but by no means would it forswear retaliation if Iraq carried out its threats to strike. A "Hammer Rick" secret phone line would also be installed between Defense Secretary Dick Cheney and Israeli Defense Minister Moshe Arens.

On the morning of January 18, the Hammer Rick line was busy with long conversations between Cheney and Arens. Bush telephoned Shamir later pleading for restraint. More than a dozen Israeli jets had sortied and headed north after the first Scuds landed. But the Israeli warplanes stopped short of the border. Two Patriot anti-missile batteries with thirty-two rockets were quickly loaded on Air Force cargo planes, which landed in Tel Aviv seventeen hours later. Bush promised that the allies would destroy the remaining western Scuds within several days.

The Israeli air force wanted to retaliate immediately. Shamir decided to sit tight for the moment. But his patience was short-lived. On January 19 four more Scuds landed near Tel Aviv. Schwarzkopf received an urgent message from Powell. Israel wanted to send 200 warplanes and Apache helicopters through Saudi airspace (instead of Jordanian airspace) for a massive counterstrike in western Iraq. King Fahd flatly refused overflight permission. Bush telephoned Shamir to argue that Israel could throw no more firepower against the Scuds than the allies were already employing.

Shamir was not persuaded. American spy satellites photographed Israeli mobile missiles armed with nuclear warheads being readied for firing against Iraq. Israel also test-fired a nuclear-capable space rocket into the Mediterranean "just so we'd get the message that they weren't fooling around," said a senior Pentagon official. Tel Aviv hoped Baghdad would receive the same message.

The Central Command headquarters was in an uproar. F-15E Eagle jets had been scrambled to bomb the sites where the first Scuds had been launched at Israel, only to find nothing when they arrived on target. Schwarzkopf fought off pressure from Washington to have Israeli air planners fly to Riyadh with suggested targets; the allies were hitting them anyway and the presence of Israelis in Riyadh would cause a mutiny among the Arab generals. Under intense pressure from Washington, CENTCOM and the Pentagon now moved in a very real way to stop the missile attacks. Almost one third of the some 2,000 air sorties flown each day were diverted to Scud hunting.

An elaborate tracking system was quickly cobbled together. U-2 and TR-1 spy planes began flying over western Iraq. The U.S. Space Command diverted a DSP early-warning satellite to overfly the region, which joined forces with newly fielded E-8A Joint Surveillance Targeting Attack Radar System (JSTARS) planes to spot Scud launches. Another communications satellite kept a channel open around the clock for Scud-hunting messages. Scud CAPs (close air patrols) were organized twenty-four hours a day. Air Force F-15Es fitted with LANTIRN targeting pods dropped cluster bombs at night while F-16 Falcons, A-10 Thunderbolts, and British Tornadoes attacked during the day.

Central Command targeters marked off two "Scud boxes" for the patrols—one in western Iraq around suspected launch points at Ar Rubtah, Al Qaim, and the H-2 pumping station, the other in eastern Iraq around Qal at Salih where Scuds were being launched at Saudi Arabia. (Baghdad fired its first two Scuds at Saudi Arabia on January 20; Patriot missiles intercepted them both. The Patriots would not always be so lucky. On February 25, a Scud eluded the antimissile defenses and landed on a barracks in Dhahran, killing twenty-eight Army reservists and injuring 100 others.)

When the DSP satellite detected the red-hot exhaust plume of a Scud being launched, it radioed a warning to the U.S. Space Command's Cheyenne Mountain Complex in Wyoming. Using a special hotline established for Scud hunts, Cheyenne Mountain flashed "Scud Warning" and the coordinates of the launch to the Tactical Air Command Center in Riyadh. The TACC then fired off a message to an AWACS plane loitering over western Saudi Arabia, which dispatched fighter bombers from the Scud CAP to strike the launch site. Meanwhile, Patriot battery search radars in Israel and Saudi Arabia acquired and tracked incoming Scuds, then launched surface-to-air missiles to home in on the Iraqi missiles.

But the system had its weaknesses. The Patriots turned out to be less accurate than the Army advertised; even the falling debris from a Scud intercept often did as much damage as a Scud landing intact. The allied warplanes were attacking targets after Scuds had been launched—often as not finding nothing to bomb. Schwarzkopf had been told by his intelligence agencies that it took an Iraqi rocket crew thirty minutes to pack up and move a mobile launcher after firing. Egyptian staff officers in Riyadh, who were experts in Soviet-supplied Scuds, which Cairo had once bought, soon let Schwarzkopf know that a rocket crew could evacuate within six minutes after firing.

The Central Command shortened the response time. But the mobile Scuds still proved elusive for the warplanes flying above at 10,000 feet or more. No larger than medium-sized trucks, the launchers remained on the move constantly. Iraqi engineers, the allies later discovered, had presurveyed launch points in western Iraq, to which rocket crews could drive, shoot, then scoot. Within ten minutes after firing, the mobile launchers could be five miles away from their original spots. Some crews hid launchers in culverts and aircraft hangars or under highway overpasses to let them cool so their infrared signatures would be reduced. Then the crews would drive to remote locations to await another launch the next night. Others fired missiles when patrol warplanes returned to their tankers to refuel. To complicate the hunt even more, the Iraqis had also deployed decoys.

On January 22, a Scud landed in the Tel Aviv suburb of Ramat Gan, injuring ninety-six and causing three people to die of heart attacks. The pressure on the Central Command and the Pentagon to destroy Scuds now became overwhelming. Every time Iraq launched them in the middle of the night, Schwarzkopf would traipse into the war room in his bathrobe demanding to know what his staff had done about the missiles. If Israel entered the war, not only would the allied air campaign be totally disrupted by Israeli jets roaming western Iraq; Schwarzkopf's Hail Mary sweep at the beginning of the ground campaign also would be imperiled. Attacking the launch sites after the fact was not enough. A way had to be found to destroy the missiles before they were fired.

A telephone call came into the National Military Command Center, a large sealed-off room on the second floor of the Pentagon. On the other end of the secure line were senior special operations officers with the Israeli defense ministry. They wanted to convene a conference call with their American counterparts to brainstorm ideas for special operations missions to hunt Scuds. Green Beret, SEAL, and Air Force special operations officers in the Joint Staff's Special Operations Division quickly grabbed telephones.

Nerves were on edge. Every time CNN broadcast that a Scud had been fired at Israel, the hotline phone connecting the White House situation room to the Pentagon command center jangled. How many Scuds were fired? a frantic aide on the other end would demand to know. How many Patriots were engaged against the target? Had any landed? Were any armed with chemical warheads? The command center would immediately telephone the U.S. embassy in Tel Aviv, where a special planning cell headed by a Joint Staff flag officer would phone the Patriot battery for the number of Scud kills.

The Israelis now on the line were far from satisfied with the Scud-hunting results. They now wanted to discuss ground operations that Israeli commandos could conduct in western Iraq to track and destroy missiles before they were fired. Israel already had special operations teams specifically trained to infiltrate that desert in order to blunt an invasion if Iraq ever decided to cross into Jordan to attack the Jewish state.

For three hours, the Israelis discussed with their American colleagues the tactics Tel Aviv's commandos might use. The conversation ended with a condition. The Israelis wanted to quickly insert their own teams into Iraq to hunt Scuds. But they would hold off if the Americans deployed their best commandos.

The message was received loud and clear at the Pentagon. Immediately, phone calls were placed to the Joint Special Operations Command near Fort Bragg.

Wayne Downing had already drawn up contingency plans for how Delta teams might track and destroy mobile Scuds. After the first Iraqi missiles began falling on Israel, he had flown back to Washington on his own and delivered a top secret Scud-hunting plan to Colin Powell's staff. General Carl Stiner, the head of the U.S. Special Operations Command, also had been on the phone directly to Powell, lobbying him to allow Downing's JSOC force to finally enter the war theater.

Powell summoned Downing and Stiner to his office on January 28. The week before, Iraq had fired thirteen Scuds at Israel. Patriots had intercepted most of the missiles, but some had slipped through, leaving another Israeli dead and sixty-five injured.

Up to this point, Schwarzkopf had stubbornly resisted allowing American commandos to cross the border to hunt for the missiles, clinging to the hope that warplanes could destroy them from the air. But now, even some of Schwarzkopf's own senior advisers privately complained that it was time for the CinC to set aside his paranoia over cross-border operations and allow Delta Force to deploy. Bad weather had hampered the air search for mobile launchers, and even when the skies were clear the pilots found it about as easy as looking for needles in haystacks. The hunters needed eyes on the ground.

If Powell had any doubts about sending in Delta, the afternoon edition of *The Washington Times* that lay on his desk on January 28 had erased them. Owned by the Reverend Sun Myung Moon's religious cult, *The Washington Times* had become a hollow log for Pentagon aides and right-wingers in the Reagan and Bush administrations who wanted to leak stories. On the front page that day ran a piece that quoted unnamed "military sources" complaining that America's secret warriors were frustrated because they were "not being used for political reasons . . . the elite Delta Force and SEAL Team Six have not been permitted to operate at all in the Kuwaiti theater." Meanwhile, British SAS commandos, the paper revealed, had been allowed to patrol in southern Iraq to "search for Iraq's mobile Scud missile."

Powell's staff was furious with the story, not just because the heretofore private complaints of special operators had been publicly aired, but also because *The Washington Times* had informed his staff of something that it did not know—that Schwarzkopf had secretly approved the SAS to cross the border.

Driving stripped-down Land Rover vehicles and motorcycles, the British commandos had entered Iraq on January 20. General Sir Peter de la Billiere, the British force chief and himself a twenty-year veteran of the SAS, had assiduously cultivated Schwarzkopf during the allied military buildup in the gulf. A week before the air war began, de la Billiere had finally persuaded Schwarzkopf that British special forces could be useful cutting communications lines, laying road ambushes, and creating diversions in Iraq's western desert.

British teams on cross-border missions sliced underground cables, blew up microwave relay towers and communications bunkers, and even captured an Iraqi artillery lieutenant with valuable battle maps. But when Scuds started falling on Israel, the SAS teams immediately began hunting mobile launchers.

They fought valiantly. Patrolling the desert day and night in their Land Rovers, the SAS teams called in air strikes on suspected Scud launch sites. Conditions were harsh and dangerous. Snow, sleet, and hail swept through the desert and plateaus. Fog and sandstorms at times made reconnaissance impossible. One team engaged in fierce combat with Iraqi soldiers for more than four hours before American jets drove away the enemy so the commandos could escape. Another SAS team on foot patrol was spotted by Iraqi soldiers and had to scatter; four of its eight commandos died of exposure or in firefights with the enemy.

But the SAS's Scud-hunting operation proved cumbersome. The British commandos had limited mobility, traveling mainly by desert vehicles or on foot. Their communications with rear headquarters was slow and erratic. Often it took almost an hour for an aircraft to arrive on a target that a team had spotted.

Downing's commando force—backed up by heavily

armed Army and Air Force special operations helicopters that flew undetected at night—could move about the desert quicker and bring more firepower to bear in short order. Coordinated with F-15Es and A-10s flying Scud CAPs, Downing was certain that air and ground teams could kill more mobile launchers.

Flipping charts in Powell's second-floor Pentagon office on the E Ring, Downing offered up three different-sized force packages that JSOC might deploy in Saudi Arabia. Powell selected the smallest package: one squadron of Delta Force commandos, a contingent of helicopters from the 160th Special Operations Aviation Regiment, plus Downing and part of his JSOC staff. (A week after arriving in Saudi Arabia, Downing would be allowed to bring over another Delta squadron plus a reinforced Ranger company and a small SEAL Team-6 element. His secret force would total about 400 men.)

With Stiner in tow, Powell walked up a flight of stairs to Cheney's office on the third floor to broach the JSOC plan. Cheney quickly returned with Powell to the chairman's office where Downing had set up his briefing charts. Downing repeated his presentation for the defense secretary.

"How soon can you leave?" Cheney asked after Downing had finished.

"I can go right now," Downing said.

"Okay, go right now," Cheney said in a rushed voice. Earlier that morning he had been on the Hammer Rick line with Arens. It had not been a pleasant call.

The last person with whom to clear the decision was Schwarzkopf. Powell lifted the receiver for the secure phone connecting him directly to the Riyadh headquarters. It was the middle of the night in Saudi Arabia.

"Norm, I'm sending Wayne and some of his boys to work on the Scuds," Powell told Schwarzkopf. He intended the statement to sound more as an order than a request. Powell had conveniently deferred to Schwarzkopf on Stiner's grand plan the previous fall. But now he would brook no argument from his theater CinC about deploying this smaller JSOC force. Neither would Cheney. Purists would later complain that the Pentagon had no business dispatching highly skilled Delta commandos on Scud-hunting missions that could just as easily have been accomplished by Army Rangers. Years of expensive counterterrorist training had been invested in each Delta operator. It was like having brain surgeons treat migraine headaches. But Powell and Cheney knew full well that the Israelis—already angry that the Pentagon had refused to allow them quick access to satellite intelligence on Iraq—would not keep their own commandos garrisoned unless Washington sent over its best team.

Downing and his commandos arrived in Saudi Arabia three days later, on January 31. There were now four special operations contingents in the war. General Richard Potter commanded a special operations unit in Turkey ready to rescue allied pilots shot down over northern Iraq. The British had their own special forces hunting Scuds and conducting commando raids. Colonel Jesse Johnson commanded what became known as the "White SOF," the some 7,000 Air Force, Army, and Navy special operations forces that served as liaisons with foreign units, rescued pilots in southern Iraq and Kuwait, launched reconnaissance missions, and attacked radars and bunkers. Downing commanded what was officially called the Joint Special Operations Task Force, the cover name for the "Black SOF," whose deployment in Saudi Arabia would never be publicly acknowledged.

While his Task Force set up shop at Ar Ar, the tiny border town on Tapline Road in northwest Saudi Arabia, Downing flew to Riyadh to present himself formally to Schwarzkopf.

He walked nervously into the general's office in the Central Command headquarters. The two men had had a run-in four years earlier when Schwarzkopf was the deputy chief of staff of the Army for operations, and Downing, then a young brigadier, headed up the Washington liaison office for the new Special Operations Command. The command had desperately wanted thirty new MH-47E special operations helicopters for the 160th Regiment, but Schwarzkopf had scratched the request from the budget. The commandos had talked Army Secretary Jack Marsh into restoring the helicopter money. Schwarzkopf was enraged, accusing Downing of going behind his back.

Did the Bear still hold a grudge? Downing didn't think so, but he saluted and decided to confront the sore spot diplomatically.

"Sir, I'm under your orders and your command," Downing said with a firm voice. "I work for you."

"You're goddamn right you are!" Schwarzkopf bellowed. Perhaps he hadn't forgotten the helicopter incident.

Schwarzkopf's face turned beet red. The veins in his neck bulged. It was as if his pent-up frustration with special operators and with Stiner's maneuvering to horn in on his war had burst.

"I don't want you calling Stiner or working behind my back," Schwarzkopf continued in a growl. "If I find out you went into Iraq with your soldiers against my orders, I'll relieve you on the spot!"

"Sir, you know me well enough to know that I wouldn't do that," Downing said soothingly.

"You sonofabitch!" Schwarzkopf shouted back. "You know why I'm telling you that!"

Downing took the dressing down in stride. Schwarzkopf just needed to get it off his chest. Downing would quickly win Schwarzkopf's confidence. He made sure every Scud-hunting operation was cleared by the general and his senior staff. The two men would later laugh about Schwarzkopf's outburst during that first meeting. But Downing never made an end run to Stiner.

Downing left Schwarzkopf's office and flew immediately to the half-deserted outpost of Al Jouf, southwest of Ar Ar, where the SAS was headquartered along with Air Force special operations helicopters and A-10 Thunderbolts on Scud patrols. The three units at Al Jouf had already begun to pool their resources into a "fusion cell." Air Force Pave

Low helicopters helped infiltrate SAS commandos, while A-10s bombed Scud sites the British teams spotted.

There was no time to lose. SAS commandos now helped Delta officers get up to speed on the enemy and terrain. The two outfits had worked together closely in the past. The SAS did not want Delta making the same mistakes that had gotten its men killed. Don't travel on foot, the Brits warned. Use helicopters and desert vehicles. It was like operating on the face of the moon. The barren Iraqi desert was bitterly cold and lifeless. How the Bedouins survived out there, the SAS commandos didn't know. They must eat rocks. But they were all armed and Iraqi patrols constantly scoured the countryside.

The American and British teams immediately divided up real estate. Each was assigned roads for ambushes, nicknamed "Scud alleys." Delta Force would patrol northwest of Highway 10 near the Syrian border. SAS would cover south of the highway to the Saudi border.

Delta teams made their first foray into western Iraq the night of February 6. By 4 A.M. the next morning, Downing telephoned Schwarzkopf with the good news.

"We got four Scuds!" Downing said excitedly. The general had ordered him to telephone every time Delta destroyed any missiles.

"Yeah, right," Schwarzkopf said groggily, then hung up and went back to sleep.

Downing didn't think Schwarzkopf was awake enough to realize what Delta had done. Later that morning, he hopped into a helicopter and flew to Riyadh with a videotape of the kills, which a hovering Black Hawk helicopter had taken at the site.

Downing marched into Schwarzkopf's office shortly before noon and shoved the tape into the general's VCR.

The video showed huge fiery explosions from the attack.

"Holy shit!" Schwarzkopf exclaimed. "That's a Scud."

"That's what I was telling you," Downing said proudly.

A Scud-hunting routine was set up. Air Force MH-53J Pave Lows or Army MH-47E Chinooks would helicopter teams and their specially equipped Land Rovers under cover of darkness. When a chopper landed in Iraq, the commandos would back out their four-wheel-drive vehicles, then drive off. The Delta teams would roam the desert at night and hide out during the day. Talking over secure radios to AWACS planes, Air Force combat control commandos who accompanied the teams on the ground would direct in the F-15Es or A-10s with cluster munitions and 1,000-pound bombs. Communications were kept short and simple. Each commando team's call sign began with "Charlie." When the warplanes roared overhead, Delta operators would shoot flares and relay coordinates from their GPS receivers to mark launch sites.

Downing organized strikes on other targets besides Scuds. Delta plus a platoon of Rangers attacked a telephone switching station and tower in the southwest corner of Iraq near Jordan, which cut off land line communications between Baghdad and Amman. Flying low to the ground, MH-60 Black Hawks from the 160th Regiment strafed enemy radar sites, convoys, and command posts. SAS commandos ambushed a Scud convoy on one road and attacked another Scud discovered under an overpass.

The work was exhausting and dangerous. Some Delta teams stayed in the field for as long as three weeks. Others stumbled into grazing Bedouins or battled Iraqi patrols and had to be evacuated by helicopters. Commandos were wounded in firefights.

On February 21, tragedy struck. Patrick Hurley, a Delta sergeant major and one of the original members of the force, had been scaling a cliff in western Iraq when he slipped and fell, injuring his back. Hurley's two teammates on the Scud-hunting mission, master sergeants Eloy Rodriguez and Otto Clark, radioed for an evacuation. The weather was miserable, but one MH-60 Black Hawk, piloted by Captain Charles Cooper and Chief Warrant Officer Michael Anderson, managed to reach Hurley's team.

The Black Hawk touched down. Quickly the chopper's two crew chiefs, sergeants Christopher Chapman and Mario Vega Velasquez, helped Clark and Rodriguez lift Hurley into the back.

The Black Hawk sped off, hugging the ground to avoid enemy radar detection.

The helicopter crossed the border safely into Saudi Arabia and headed south toward the air strip at Ar Ar. But a heavy fog had settled over the desert. The air strips at Ar Ar had few lights to guide in the chopper. The aircraft made two passes trying to land, unsuccessfully. It was about 3 A.M. and a pitch black night with fog, making it impossible for Cooper and Anderson to see much in front of them. On the third attempt, the Black Hawk plowed into the ground several miles short of the runway. There were no survivors.

Shortly after 7:30 A.M., Downing lay down on the cot in his tent at Ar Ar for the first time since the day before. He had been up all night waiting for word on the missing Black Hawk.

He was just about to fall asleep, when an aide tapped on his tent pole and walked in.

"We just found the aircraft," the aide said simply and quietly. "It crashed near the runway. They all died."

Downing sat up and swung his aching legs off the cot. He leaned over, his elbows propped on his knees and stared at the ground.

He had expected this kind of news. It had been a miracle that no more special operators had been killed in this war, considering the high-risk missions they had been assigned. Fourteen Air Force special operations airmen had died when an Iraqi surface-to-air missile shot down their AC-130H gunship, which had been loitering for too long in daylight protecting Marines at the northeast Saudi border town of Khafji. Another Green Beret had died accidentally testing weapons. Now seven of his men had been added to the list.

But the low casualty rate did not make these deaths any more bearable for Downing. Hurley had been an old and close friend. Just the other day, the young general and the seasoned sergeant had spent all night in the operations shack at Ar Ar talking and laughing about old times. They hadn't done that in ten years. A dull pain now throbbed in the pit of Downing's stomach. There would be no more bull sessions with Pat Hurley.

But the Scud hunters had no time to grieve. The next night a call came into the Air Force strike cell at Riyadh from the Pentagon. The CIA had passed along a disturbing tip from one of its assets in Baghdad. Saddam Hussein planned to barrage Israel with a last-gasp attack of twenty-six Scuds. Although satellite photos could not back up the human intelligence, the Riyadh strike cell had intercepts of Iraqi radio transmissions that seemed to indicate the informant might be telling the truth. The CIA asset had passed along warnings of other large Scud attacks that had proved to be remarkably accurate. The Central Command headquarters relayed a warning to the fusion cell at Al Jouf and Downing's task force at Ar Ar to be on the lookout.

What happened next occurred more by accident than design.

Four days later, on February 26, Lieutenant Colonel Seth G. Wilson cruised north in his A-10 to the Mudaysis airfield in southwestern Iraq. His wing man, First Lieutenant Stephen Otto, followed him in a second A-10. Nicknamed "the Warthog," the A-10 was a slow-moving, low-tech mud fighter with thick armor that fired uranium-tipped shells and Maverick antitank missiles. The Air Force had long since canceled further production of the aircraft and true fighter jocks disparaged the ungainly-looking plane. The Warthog was so slow ducks flew up its tail pipe, the joke went. But for the Delta and SAS commandos, the Warthog was a daytime workhorse that could loiter in the sky for hours attacking Scuds.

An Air Force reservist from New Orleans, Wilson piloted one of about a dozen A-10s parked at Al Jouf. He had never talked on the radio to the secret commando teams that roamed the desert below him. But he couldn't help but admire their work. Since this fusion cell had been patched together, he thought the intelligence he had been receiving on Scud sites had improved considerably. The ground teams also could give his Air Force briefers back at Al Jouf almost instant battle damage reports on the targets he had struck. The satellite photos alone had never provided him a clear picture of the sites. When he attacked one, it took days before the follow-up photos arrived that might tell him if he had scored a hit.

The missions on his dance card today seemed fairly cut-and-dried. He was first to cover the Mudaysis airfield with cluster bombs.

But bad weather covered Mudaysis instead. Wilson and Otto returned to their orbiting tanker to refuel, then proceeded to the secondary target the fusion cell had listed: a military depot just southwest of Al Haqlaniyah along the western leg of the Euphrates River. This time, the weather had cleared and the two planes dropped their cluster bombs.

Both planes had gas and munitions left over. Wilson and Otto banked left. The third target on their list from the fusion cell was the road and parallel rail line, that stretched from Al Haqlaniyah northwest to the town of Al Qaim near the Syrian border. Delta teams had patrolled around Al Qaim, where they suspected that Scuds were still being intermittently launched. Wilson's third mission for the day was to fly up the road and rail line looking for railroad cars or trucks bearing missiles.

What the two pilots eventually found made their eyes bulge. Just southeast of Al Qaim, at a runway marked only on their maps as "T-1," Wilson and Otto discovered a Scud park. They counted quickly. There might be as many as two dozen Scuds mounted on carriers that were scattered in a lonely field. Wilson had been lucky if he could find one or two Scuds a day. Now they'd hit the jackpot.

The two planes swooped down releasing their Maverick missiles. Three of the long black cylinders below burst into fiery explosions—a good sign that they were freshly fueled missiles being prepared for launch.

Low on fuel themselves, the two A-10s sped south for a second fill-up with their aerial tanker just across the border.

But as they eagerly headed back north, Wilson and Otto received a divert order from the fusion cell at Al Jouf. A Delta team had been compromised along a north–south highway running up from the town of Ar Rutbah near the Jordanian border. It had seemed that everywhere the team had traveled in southwestern Iraq it had attracted enemy soldiers. The task force at Ar Ar had nicknamed it the "shit magnet patrol." Now the team was in a fierce firefight with Iraqi forces. The A-10s were needed to bomb around the commandos so they could break off contact and be rescued at an evacuation site by helicopters.

Wilson and Otto dropped another load of cluster bombs. The Iraqi soldiers scattered. The Air Force combat controller on the ground with the Delta team—his call sign was Charlie-96—radioed to the two A-10s that the team had spotted what looked like a Scud park across a ridge. Wilson and Otto flew over the site to investigate. But Wilson could see that the cylinder-like objects the Delta team had spotted were really military supplies and ammunition stacked in bunkers to look like Scud missiles. The Iraqis were masters of these kinds of deceptions, the pilots knew. They didn't waste their bombs on the decoys. The two A-10s flew northeast, back to Al Qaim.

This time they dropped cluster bombs on five more suspected missiles before Iraqi SAMs drove them away. Wilson called in reinforcements. Seven Navy F/A-18 Hornets showed up along with more A-10s. The next morning, Wilson and Otto returned to Al Qaim and by their count bagged another four Scuds.

All told, the pilots were credited with twenty Scud kills at the Al Qaim site. Whether these missiles were part of the twenty-six Saddam reportedly planned for a final barrage against Israel, no one knew. The Air Force would later credit commandos on the ground with providing the A-10s the intelligence on the Al Qaim Scud park. But it was unclear whether any of the ground teams ever actually spotted that particular park. Later Wilson tried to determine who had supplied the intelligence that prompted the fusion cell to direct the A-10s up the road toward Al Qaim.

He never found the source. Most likely it was blind luck that they stumbled upon the Scuds. It happened in war, Wilson knew.

In any case, Baghdad never launched a mass attack. Desert Storm ended a day later.

During the first week in March, Schwarzkopf paid a secret visit to the commandos at Al Jouf and Ar Ar. At Ar Ar, the two squadrons of Delta operators plus the helicopter pilots from the 160th Regiment lined up in formation before the four-star general. During his famous "Hail Mary" press conference at the end of the war, Schwarzkopf had stunned his staff by publicly singling out special forces for praise. "It's very important that I not forget those folks," he said. This coming from a man who at first was content to leave half of the commandos back in the States. Now before the operators at Ar Ar, Schwarzkopf spoke like a convert.

"What you've done is never going to be made public and we can't make it public," he said solemnly. "You kept Israel out of the war."

Whether that was really the case remains a hotly debated topic within the Pentagon. The Joint Special Operations Command "conservatively" estimated that Delta Force directed in air strikes that destroyed eight mobile Scud missiles and damaged another four. Some Delta commandos claimed that when unconfirmed hits were factored in, the more accurate count was over forty.

But the CIA and Defense Intelligence Agency found that the Scud kill estimates were wildly inflated. Two years after the war, a comprehensive Air Force study of air power in Desert Storm concluded that there was "no hard evidence" of any mobile Scuds being destroyed. "A lot of flatbed trucks got blown up," said a senior intelligence official. Other experts say that even the count on fixed Scud sites destroyed may be an overestimate. United Nations inspectors touring Iraq after the war discovered that many of the Scuds the allies believed they had knocked out were either intact or had been destroyed by the Iraqis themselves later as part of the cease-fire conditions.

Battle damage assessment is more an art than science. Whether a target is deemed destroyed often depends on the analyst interpreting the satellite photo. Pilots excited after a sortie often pump up misses or slightly damaged targets into sure kills. On the other hand, pilots rightly complain that intelligence analysts ignore what the aviator has seen with his own eyes just because a satellite has not detected the hit.

In Desert Storm, the evidence of Scud kills often ended up being illusory. Many of the cylinders pilots thought were Scuds turned out to be gas tanks. Videotape of what the Air Force believed was a convoy of mobile Scud launchers being destroyed on a road from Jordan turned out to be oil trucks. Air Force intelligence officers suspect that the first four Scuds Downing thought his commandos had destroyed were actually decoys. The Joint Special Operations Command still insists that the missiles were real. The numbers will remain forever in dispute.

But though they may not have killed any missiles, it seems clear that the Scud hunters succeeded in keeping the Iraqis from firing many of them. Just the threat of the Scud hunt appeared to suppress the launches. During the first ten days of Desert Storm, Iraq averaged five Scud launches per day. During the last thirty-three days of the war, when the Scud CAPs were in full force and commando teams roamed the desert, the launches dropped to an average of one per day. On the run, Iraqi rocket crews had to fire missiles from unsurveyed points or during bad weather when allied air patrols were not overhead, both of which made the Scuds even less accurate. Quality control also became a problem. Crews slapped Scuds on flatbed trucks and propped them up for launch. In one case, a missile was fired with a warhead filled with concrete. The Scud hunters may not have destroyed Iraq's launch capability, but they had certainly intimidated it.

* * *

The Scuds had exacted a tragic toll. And that would never be in doubt. In the end, the missiles Saddam fired killed four Israelis, injured at least 289, and left some 4,000 homeless. One hundred and twenty-eight Americans lay dead or wounded from the attack on Dhahran.

In a remote corner of the military post at Fort Campbell, Kentucky, sits a monument erected by the 160th Special Operations Aviation Regiment. Wedged between two abandoned ammo bunkers, it is difficult to find—intentionally so. The memorial is meant for the 160th's own family, not visitors. A simple slab of black granite shaped in a square is flanked by two triangle-shaped slabs. On the smooth face of the monument's front is chiseled: "In Memory of Fallen Night Stalkers." Sitting on top of the center slab undisturbed are the silver wings a helicopter pilot wears on his uniform. The names of twenty-eight pilots had been inscribed on the monument before the 160th had deployed to the Persian Gulf—the regiment's men who had died since the unit was formed.

When the regiment returned after Desert Storm, four more names were added to the list: Charles Cooper, Mario Vega Velasquez, Michael Anderson, and Christopher Chapman.

A quiet service was held at the John F. Kennedy Memorial Chapel in the Special Forces compound at Fort Bragg. No announcements were made of the ceremony. Invitations went out by word of mouth. Inside, sat the members of Delta Force, their families, and former commandos who had retired from the unit.

On the altar of the church were placed three sets of jump boots, three green berets. The squadron commander called the roll.

"Here," each Delta soldier answered.

But there was silence after three names. Otto Clark, Eloy Rodriguez, and Patrick Hurley. A bugler sounded taps. In death, they would be remembered as they had fought, in secret.

Part III

THE
FUTURE

TOMORROW'S
WARRIORS

The commando crawls up to a nuclear research facility that the CIA believes is secretly producing an atomic bomb. His mission has been subliminally fed into his brain by tape recorders while he slept during the plane ride to the Third World country. Sensory enhancement pills enable him to see every detail of the facility in the dark and to hear the conversations of the scientists inside. From a wristwatch radio connected to a throat mike he can communicate with the Pentagon in Washington. To divert a sentry, the commando projects a three-dimensional hologram of himself at the main gate's guardhouse. A laser beam delivers a voice projection so the hologram speaks. The commando aims his shoulder-fired "Brilliant Pebbles" rocket launcher at the facility and fires. Another neat, clean operation in the twenty-first century.

So went the musings of Jim Van Buskirk, Jr., and Sal Raineri. They are futurists in the world of special operations. Neither has much in the way of technical training for the job. Van Buskirk graduated from the University of Illinois with a major in animal science. Raineri earned a business degree after retiring from the Green Berets. In a military-industrial complex that spends billions of dollars dreaming up fancy new weapons systems each year, theirs was little more than a mom-and-pop operation crammed into tiny offices on the sixth floor of the Army's Special Warfare Center at Fort Bragg. But Van Buskirk, Raineri, and the some two dozen other officers and civilians who worked in what the center called its Concepts and Studies Division were the dreamers who shaped the way commandos fight tomorrow's wars. They were paid to fantasize.

Van Buskirk headed up the fairly new division. Raineri

served as his chief idea man and nonconformist. Weapons labs and think tanks measure status by the size of their budgets. The Concepts and Studies Division was proud to be small.

They were an odd match. Van Buskirk was tall and muscular with sandy blond hair falling across his forehead. Inquisitive-looking eyes behind glasses made him seem more like a young computer whiz than a forty-three-year-old Green Beret lieutenant colonel. Before taking over the division, most of his time in Special Forces had been spent concentrating on Europe. He had never fired a weapon in anger. His passions were science-fiction books and military reform thinking that challenges the conventional wisdom of the Army. Maybe that was why he found crystal ball gazing so appealing. "I don't fight the wars other people do," he explained.

Raineri was a Vietnam-era Green Beret—two tours in the central highlands. Short, stocky, with a middle-aged bulge accumulated from more than a decade away from the service, he spoke with a clipped Bronx accent and stabbed his forefinger in the air to make his points. He became interested in combat development—military jargon for weapons research—while in Vietnam. Most of the equipment the Green Berets used was crap, he had found, unsuited to their kind of warfare. Raineri would change that one day, he vowed.

After retiring from Special Forces in 1981, he eventually returned to Fort Bragg as a civilian specialist developing new hardware for special ops units. He brought to the job a fertile imagination and combat experience on the ground. Propped on his desk, a sign now read: "There are three kinds of people. Those who make things happen, those who watch things happen, and those who wonder what happened."

The two men played off each other and argued like backyard inventors. Van Buskirk was a sponge for new ideas. Raineri was his intellectual loose cannon. They both vacuumed technology from unlikely sources. Computer journals have shown them how microprocessors, modems, and printers can be crammed into a businessman's brief-case. The hardware could just as easily fit in a Green Be-ret's rucksack. Hunting magazines offer the latest high-tech outdoor gear; it only has to be painted green for the military. Virtual reality technology, which NASA is devel-oping to simulate space flight for astronauts, can be used by Special Forces to rehearse missions. Surrounded by big-screen televisions, a commando may one day practice sur-gical procedures in a jungle or walk the streets of Baghdad to recon a target.

Just from watching his son play Nintendo, Van Bus-kirk could envision a more video-oriented commando of the future. Whereas Van Buskirk as a child played cowboys and Indians outside, his son is content to spend hours play-ing the same game in front of a television. His son's son will be even more comfortable with the visual displays of a video screen.

That trend has implications for military technology. "Today's armor commanders don't like being buttoned up in their tanks relying on vision blocks and monitors to track the enemy," Van Buskirk explained. "They want to pop their heads out of the turret to see the real thing." Like-wise, combat pilots have heads-up displays that flash sym-bols on their visors, yet they still can, and want to, see the outside world. But their children's children, inculcated by computers and video games, may eventually have motor skills and sensory perceptions completely at home with viewing the world totally through an electronic monitor.

For the twenty-first century commando, it may mean he will be perfectly happy to see things through a display screen—much like the Terminator character Arnold Schwarzenegger portrayed in the movies. His head would be encased in a multisensor helmet. Microwave, infrared, and radar detectors would display the environment on his goggles, plus enemy threats the naked eye could not see: mines, electronic surveillance, enemy soldiers in bunkers, terrorists hiding behind walls.

Today in a clearing operation, Delta antiterrorist com-mandos divide a room into sections for which each shooter is responsible. Making split-second decisions, a shooter decides if a target is friendly or hostile, fires accordingly, and depends on his fellow commandos to cover their sectors of the room. In the twenty-first century, machines would take over many of these tasks. Almost instantaneously, microcomputers with artificial intelligence would catalogue targets as friendly, neutral, or hostile on the commando's goggle display. The computers would select appropriate weapons for attack, then direct hands to shoot them in the order of the threat they pose.

Van Buskirk's fellow operators chuckle and shake their heads when he fantasizes. But this kind of creative thinking is overdue. Major Army training commands have long had combat development centers churning out studies and plans for the equipment and personnel conventional forces would need to fight tomorrow's wars. Only recently have special operations units begun seriously thinking about their future.

In the past, commandos were forced to accept the equipment the conventional soldiers used or receive nothing at all. Only grudgingly would the services buy hardware specifically designed for special operations. Navy SEALs have spent more than fifteen years trying to field underwater delivery vehicles that would land them on shore dry; their current 1960s-vintage submarine is open to the water. Army commandos have yet to receive long-range infiltration aircraft for their missions; production of the V-22 Osprey, a tilt-rotor Marine insertion plane that special operations forces would also use, has been delayed because of budget cuts. The special operations force is so small its equipment requests become lost among the big-ticket ships, tanks, and planes the Pentagon is preoccupied with buying. The entire special operations research budget costs no more than one B-2 bomber.

As a result, commandos have taken to unconventional tactics to buy hardware. During Desert Storm the SEALs headquarters in Coronado received an urgent request from one of its teams stationed with amphibious ships in the Persian Gulf: "Send fifty boogie boards." The SEALs needed the small surfboards for swimming long distances. A SEAL supply officer went to a local surf shop. The boogie boards were repainted black and loaded on a plane to Saudi Arabia within a week.

Today the Special Operations Command has its own Special Operations Research, Development, and Acquisition Center (called the SORDAC), a fledgling organization that is overseeing the R&D of new weapons and gadgets for Army, Navy, and Air Force commandos. About one third of the command's budget is now plowed into research and buying hardware. New equipment is already in the force. Green Berets in Desert Storm packed portable computers, whose data were transmitted on secure radios via satellites. The special ops headquarters in Saudi Arabia tapped into a new computer network called SOCRATES, which provides instant access to detailed intelligence and satellite photos. Navy SEALs cruised around Kuwait City in Fast Attack Vehicles, black dune buggies equipped with machine guns, antitank rockets, and GPS receivers. The $50,000 vehicles, which look like they came from a Mad Max movie, sent Iraqi soldiers scurrying when they barreled down the road.

On the drawing boards: Green Beret A-teams hope to fill tiny compact discs with data from medical textbooks. Medics can then call up the information instantly on portable computers in order to operate on the wounded in combat. Scientists are researching "acoustical hearing devices" that Special Forces soldiers would plug into their ears to amplify sound on clandestine reconnaissance missions. Unconventional warriors may one day talk into electronic "speech translators" that will simultaneously convert their English into the language of the country that they're in. Radios may operate off wafer-thin but powerful microbatteries that last for years; commandos now carry heavy batteries that must be recharged each week.

The SEALs are developing tiny computers for their closed-circuit oxygen tanks that would project a digital heads-up display on a diver's mask showing his dive time, the oxygen mix he's breathing, his coordinates underwater, plus warnings of enemy boats nearby. Submarine-quieting technology is now being borrowed to find ways to make frogmen and their underwater delivery vehicles less detectable by sonar and infrared sensors. Scientists are even studying barnacles to determine if the glue they secrete, which keeps them stuck to hulls, can be duplicated as an adhesive for limpet mines.

Special operations medicine is becoming a discipline of its own. Navy scientists are studying sports medicine, special diets, and electrically heated diver suits to help frogmen endure physically arduous missions in frigid waters. Just getting to work can be punishing for these commandos. A SEAL can go from a high-altitude parachute jump to being deep under icy water to a dry beach all in one day. Doctors are studying ways operators can steal more sleep during air infiltrations for missions. Delta commandos now take Halcion to nap on long flights. Physicians are investigating the physiology of moving in and out of time zones and arriving alert for combat.

Green Beret teams may spend up to six months in isolated Third World areas, far away from rear-echelon supplies or medical care. Scientists are researching medicines that won't spoil in humid tropical environments. Special operations doctors already compile secret studies of medical threats commandos can encounter in any part of the world. To cut down on the heavy loads medics must carry, researchers are investigating lightweight IV powders the operators can pack, then mix with water to produce instant intravenous solutions for wounded soldiers. To keep a commando alive in a jungle until he can be evacuated, special ops physicians are being trained in trauma and resuscitative medicine so they can perform "instant surgery" in austere conditions. They use battlefield medical equipment exempt from Food and Drug Administration review.

Yet for all the new gizmos being fielded, special operations is still at the tail end of technology. A cultural bias against high tech pervaded the force in the past. For decades, commandos were content with jungle boots, machetes between their teeth, and machine guns slung across their shoulders. Now scattered among the force are futurists like Van Buskirk and Raineri who have been prodding special operations into the next century and beyond. As far as they are concerned, the equipment being fielded now should be considered antiques. "If a contractor shows you something he's got and he tells you it's new, rest assured it's at least five years old," Raineri said. He and Van Buskirk preferred to fast-forward.

In the past, the soldier has always been the last thing the Army modernized. Now the commando is being thought of as a weapons system himself, much like a ship or a plane.

Van Buskirk and Raineri then worked backward. They began by asking what the commando needs for his type of combat.

This can be answered fairly simply. A special operator's supply line is carried on his back. He is usually isolated from higher headquarters and works under miserable and dangerous conditions. His numbers are small. Each man in any team is highly trained. Casualties cannot be suffered lightly. So to perform their mission, commandos must be stealthy, mobile, and protected. They also want to be warm, dry, fed, and watered—without the load needed to accomplish all this breaking their backs.

Start with what the commando wears. "The fatigue uniform for combat has basically been the same for the last sixty years," Van Buskirk said. Underwear, socks, pants, blouse, fatigue jacket. But now look at it, as the Concepts and Studies Division did, as a "battle dress system." Why does an undershirt simply have to be just the cotton cloth you pull over as the first layer of warmth in the morning? Why not make the shirt both breathe and be waterproof, plus have it treated with antimicrobial and antifungal chemicals so a commando can live in it dirty for weeks. That way, he doesn't have to bring so much spare clothing to the jungle, which adds weight to his rucksack.

Since the soldier dresses in layers anyway, why not have each layer offer him a degree of ballistic protection, so by the time he is completely dressed he is encapsulated

in a bulletproof vest. Each layer would also be chemical-
and fire-resistant.

To carry his supplies and ammunition, a commando
presently straps on an LBE (the acronym for load-bearing
equipment), to which he attaches his rucksack and clips an
assortment of other packs, weapons, and tools. He becomes a walking Christmas tree and just about as efficient
as one. He can't run fast with this load on his back. If he
needs a piece of equipment quickly he can't reach into his
rucksack to grab it. He can't roll over on the ground with it.
Before he can fight he has to strip down.

Why not have the uniform carry the load? Ammunition, supplies, and weapons could be distributed around
the battle dress system in easy-to-reach pockets, which in
turn would offer more ballistic protection for the commando. The load would be more evenly spread over the
body instead of just concentrated against the shoulders and
small of the back, as is the case with the rucksack. Van
Buskirk estimated that 90 percent of a commando's mission could be accomplished standing in this kind of suit
without having to strip off anything.

To cut down the bulk that must be worn in cold
weather, Van Buskirk and Raineri were tinkering with a
concept borrowed from the Energy Department, which
they called "reactive multi-layering." When treated with
chemicals, wood and paper can burn at different rates. If
chemicals can slow the burning process even more—say, to
100 degrees Fahrenheit for eight hours—then the commandos have found themselves a perfect heater. Activated by a
button, a layer of the battle dress system could slowly burn
to keep an operator warm in extremely cold environments.

The suits could also be made more stealthy. Camouflaged fatigue uniforms now are painted green and brown,
or tan and brown. But the scenery in which a commando
operates constantly changes; camouflaged colors that blend
in one setting are out of place in another. Scientists are
therefore studying chameleonic suits, which would have
chemical coatings or micromachines with flippers to
change colors with the scenery.

The stealth may one day be even more exotic. Biological disguises may be developed to change racial features so that, say, white commandos can blend in among Third World populations. Or the commando may not be seen at all. During World War II, scientists discovered that they could make planes fly almost invisibly in the daylight sky by lighting up the aircraft. By placing lights on the wings and fuselage the plane appeared as bright as the sky behind it. To antiaircraft gunners on the ground, it seemed to disappear. By the year 2030 light may be folded or bent around commandos so the enemy can't see them. Techniques would also be developed to reduce the infrared and magnetic signature of the operator and his equipment. Raineri called it "multi-spectral invisibility."

There will be medical advances the operators can use. Tissue regeneration research may mean that wounds one day can be quickly closed on the battlefield with biological bandages. Red blood cells may be freeze-dried in the future. When a commando is wounded, a medic will dip a packet of red blood cell powder into a solution as he would a tea bag and have instant blood for a transfusion. Body performance may be enhanced with a super vitamin pill commandos can take before a mission. (The blood doping and steroids that athletes have used is considered too controversial or risky.)

The most hazardous part of a mission can come after a commando parachutes out of a plane. With the hundred pounds or more that he carries on his back, he sometimes breaks bones or sprains ankles on impact. For an assault, regular airborne divisions dump thousands of men out of planes, usually over soft ground. They can afford to lose a hundred to leg or back injuries. But a commando can expect to land on parking lots, hard-surface runways, wherever the enemy does not expect it. One broken bone can have disastrous consequences. On a clandestine mission, each commando on a small team is critical to success.

The concepts division launched a program called LEAP, for Lower Extremity Assistance for Parachutists. Raineri prowled hospital wards and orthopedics clinics strapping on leg braces for ideas on body supports. The commando's brace would likely be made of lightweight carbon fibers that did not give off a radar signature when the parachutists drifted down from the sky. The brace would extend from the waist to the ankle, be rigid in order to support the bones during impact, but then become collapsible for quick disposal after the commando lands or if he strays off course and ends up in a lake.

Once a lower extremity brace has been developed, the next step is extending it over the chest, and powering it. Then the commando has what is called an "exoskeletal frame." Like RoboCop, he would wear it for superhuman strength to carry heavy loads or break down doors.

Today's machine guns and pistols may go the way of the crossbow in the future. Spinoffs of Star Wars space weapons research will produce laser pistols and particle beam rifles. "Nonlethal incapacitators," or stun guns, will be used to knock out guards on clandestine missions so they awake later not knowing that they've been attacked. Artificially intelligent robotic companions—like Luke Skywalker's R2D2—will do the dirty work of clearing mine paths and scouting enemy-infested areas.

Or the sidekick may be a plant. One of Raineri's pet projects was a "biogenetic sensor system." Special operations units already have electronic sensors they can place in the ground to detect enemy movement. Plants may eventually perform the same job. An enemy area would be laced with specially engineered fungi, which could sense objects and movement, then store the information in sugars. Satellites or reconnaissance planes would pass over periodically with a light signal that would enable them to read the fungi's intelligence on truck and troop traffic. The fungi may be particularly valuable in monitoring drug trafficking routes.

The mind will also be part of the weapons system. "There's got to be a better way of putting information into the computer between our ears," Van Buskirk believes. Hormone balances might be altered with "injectible learning" shots so the brain can absorb a foreign language or complex mission plans while the commando sleeps. Sensory enhancement devices might be implanted under the skin so the operator can see, smell, or hear objects far off. Radios might be replaced by "synthetic telepathy"—pulse generators attached to brains so commandos can read minds instead of talking to one another on missions.

No more than 20 percent of the research programs Van Buskirk and Raineri dreamt up were ever funded. Defense budgets have been shrinking. Also "the bureaucracy doesn't allow you to do things fast," Van Buskirk said with a touch of frustration. "It only supports big-ticket items because dollars are power in the Pentagon. Big dollars are big power."

Their ideas also are too far out in the future for many in the Pentagon. Resistance is breaking down in some quarters. But Raineri said that when he shows defense planners his briefing slides on the commandos of 2030, they still laugh or "tell me that we'll never get there. Or they'll say that's a great idea, but do we really need it? We did without it before." The same things soldiers said before they turned in their cavalry horses for tanks. "Reluctance to change," he sighed.

TOMORROW'S WARS

The Crisis Action Center is buried deep in the basement of the Special Operations Command Headquarters at MacDill Air Force Base. Access is tightly controlled. Officers gain entry by slipping their plastic identification cards through electronic scanners, then punching a secret code into cipher locks.

Inside, rows of computer terminals face a large electronic board that tracks special operations missions worldwide. Staff officers from the command's crisis action team are assigned to each terminal, which can transmit written messages to commando units and receive intelligence from the Pentagon and CIA. The terminals are also patched into the World Military Command and Control System that links all major headquarters. Beside each computer screen a red telephone provides secure satellite communications to the secret warriors. A special intelligence team operates from a nearby vault.

Flash reports come into a control booth, packed with SATCOM radios, video monitors, laser printers, and secure fax machines. The world is monitored twenty-four hours a day. A television is always tuned to CNN.

The "CAC," as the operators call it, could well be the crisis center for tomorrow's wars. In the post–Cold War world, with superpower confrontations replaced by a proliferation of mini-threats, small teams of special operators, instead of B-1 bombers and main battle tanks, may be the force of the future.

The Special Operations Command is preparing for action. Secret contingency plans have been drawn up for commando teams to infiltrate all the known Third World trouble spots if the White House orders an attack: Cuba in

Latin America; North Korea, Myanmar, and the Philippines in Asia; Iraq, Iran, Syria, and Lebanon in the Middle East; Libya, Liberia, and the Sudan in Africa. A country-by-country "global analysis" has been drafted to assess U.S. interests and the command's likely response if trouble flares. Computers spit out secret operational plans for infiltration routes, drop zones, intelligence contacts, assault points.

With old rivalries turned upside down, the command is considering missions that were unthinkable in decades past. Green Beret teams now have secret contingency plans, not to launch guerrilla raids to blunt a Warsaw Pact invasion, but rather to send advisers to train new armies in Eastern Europe and the republics of the old Soviet Union.

Whether that happens remains to be seen. As has been the case since World War II, special operations continues to be an alien discipline for the American military establishment. Nowhere was this more evident than in the Persian Gulf war. The missions the commandos conducted —the helicopter raids, the special reconnaissance forays deep inside Iraq, the Scud hunting, the daring rescues, the amphibious feint—all were exciting enough. The Green Berets also were allowed to use their special language and diplomatic skills as military liaisons among the coalition armies to keep their attacks coordinated with the Americans and no doubt reduce friendly fire casualties. But otherwise, special operations forces were relegated to support roles for Schwarzkopf's general purpose forces. They were tactical adjuncts to the battle. Their strategic value was never realized.

Will special operations in the future gain a measure of acceptance that it has sorely lacked in the past? Bureaucratically the force seems well protected. But the commandos still have a long way to go before their conventional brethren accept them into the fold. Few American generals and admirals are trained in special operations or have anything but a nodding acquaintance with its form of warfare. Until recently, commando units were excluded from major military exercises and war games. Special operations missions are still not included in many of the contingency plans of conventional commanders.

But the new world order—or disorder—may compel greater use of these forces. The danger of Soviet tanks barreling though central Europe has been replaced by nuclear proliferation, terrorism, regional insurgencies, and drugs. A civil war has raged in Yugoslavia. Turmoil is a given among the fifteen successor states to the Soviet empire. American troops have already intervened to quell the anarchy in Somalia. East-West competition will be replaced by North-South confrontations. Drug cartels in Colombia, Myanmar, and Southwest Asia operate on budgets larger than many governments. More than twenty nations may have nuclear arms in the twenty-first century. The number of terrorist attacks has decreased but the lethality of the attacks that do occur may increase, as the 1993 bombing of New York's World Trade Center demonstrated.

A group of government and private security experts recently convened by the National Strategy Information Center, a Washington think tank, coined a term for the new national security threat. They called it the "gray area phenomenon"—the influence "nongovernment forces" will have on regional and global affairs. The villains in this case are not dictators or belligerent nations, but rather drug traffickers, money launderers, counterfeiters, smugglers, bank embezzlers, terrorists. They are subnational groups or border crossers. They peddle arms, gold, black market food, "perhaps even body parts," according to a report the group issued.

Tomorrow's warriors will have to think small to survive. Future battlefields will be covered with tiny sensors to guide the fighting. The dinosaurs of the conventional age—the tanks, ships, and heavy bombers—will be replaced by mini-projectiles, precision-guided munitions, robots, and small remotely piloted vehicles in the air, on land, or at sea. Grinding battles for territory will be replaced by surgical strikes to blind sensors and destroy command and control centers.

In this type of environment, the Special Operations

Command envisions its highly skilled soldiers as the fighters of the future. JSOC's commandos have already begun secret training in counterproliferation warfare. If international inspections or diplomatic demarches failed to deter a rogue state from acquiring nuclear weapons, Delta commandos could be infiltrated to discretely destroy a facility or intercept a dangerous shipment—a special operations version of Star Wars, with a cheaper price tag. Contingency plans are also being drafted for strategic reconnaissance teams to sneak into countries if diplomats need clandestine inspectors for verifying arms control agreements.

"Peacetime engagement," which George Bush first articulated as a post–Cold War defense strategy, has now become a favorite buzzword in the special ops command. American military might would be aimed at counteracting local violence and promoting "nation building" around the world. The command expects to devote more manpower and attention to what has been nicknamed its "well digger" work: special operations teams teaching foreign armies counterinsurgency and counterdrug tactics, bringing health care and civil works projects to remote villages, organizing disaster relief. Special Forces soldiers have acted as interpreters for U.S. humanitarian operations in Mongolia. Civil affairs teams inoculated 58,000 persons in Cameroon against meningitis. Green Berets are even teaching counterpoaching techniques to African game wardens.

The world is entering the "fourth generation" of warfare, according to Bill Lind, a former defense aide to Senator Gary Hart and military reform advocate. The generations have evolved from the Revolutionary War era of smoothbore muskets and neat lines of attack, to the attrition warfare of fire and movement during the Civil War, to the nonlinear maneuver tactics the Germans employed during World War II. In fourth-generation warfare, the battlefield will "include the whole of the enemy's society," he speculates. Collapsing an enemy's social structure internally will be the goal, rather than just destroying him physically. Targets will be military and civilian. Psychological operations will be important. The distinctions between war and peace "will be blurred to the vanishing point." Regular armies will shrink. Combat will be conducted by small, highly skilled, and independent teams of special operations soldiers. They will be joined by border patrols, specially trained police, and antiriot troops.

The conventions of war will change. Political leaders will be increasingly targeted during battles. (In fact they already are; Washington tried but failed to assassinate Muammar Qaddafi during the 1986 bombing raid on Libya and Saddam Hussein during Desert Storm.) Low-intensity conflicts will employ weapons banned in today's combat, such as nerve gas. Military bases "will be replaced by hideouts and dumps," writes military historian Martin Van Creveld. Regular armies will degenerate, as they did in Lebanon, to police forces on one side and armed gangs on the other. Uniforms will be replaced by civilian clothes with insignias and armbands. Salutes and military chains of command will disappear. "It will be a war of listening devices and of car bombs," Van Creveld continues, "of men killing each other at close quarters, and of women using their purses to carry explosives and the drugs to pay for them. It will be protracted, bloody, and horrible."

It also may not come to pass. A word of caution is certainly in order. Many regional hot spots are cooling down because the Cold War has ended. And just because there may be instability in the future doesn't mean that commandos should be rushed into the breach. The hard fact of life: with the Cold War over many regional conflicts simply won't matter to the United States. Much of the Third World was important in the past because of its effect on the global balance of power between the superpowers. With the Soviets out of the race "there are likely to be numerous quarrels that ought to be irrelevant" to American interests, says Ted Galen Carpenter, director of foreign policy studies at the Cato Institute.

Today, only a handful of nations have a substantial military capability or a vital resource like oil. Most Third World nations are so poor or have such limited military potential that even if they did break into conflict it's unlikely to affect American security interests directly or indirectly. "Malawi just can't come up with a 200-division threat," says Joshua Epstein, a defense analyst with the Brookings Institution. "Neither can Libya."

One of the rationales for dispatching special operations forces is that they are ideal for situations where Americans have some interest in a foreign dispute, but not enough to compel a large military intervention. It begs the question: if the problem is of such marginal interest to begin with, why send American soldiers at all? "As soon as they tell me it is limited, it means they do not care whether you achieve a result or not," Joint Chiefs Chairman Colin Powell once said of politicians who commit American soldiers to ill-defined missions overseas. "As soon as they tell me 'surgical,' I head for the bunker."

History would suggest that Powell's instincts are correct. The West has had a miserable track record conquering Third World insurgencies. Many of Washington's attempts at nation building during the Cold War were suspect. Restoring democracy was just a convenient cover for American covert operations in Iran, Guatemala, and Chile, where legitimate leaders were toppled and replaced with repressive regimes. In the name of regional stability, the United States has backed a rogues' gallery of Third World despots: the Shah of Iran, Nicaragua's Anastasio Somoza Debayle, South Korea's Park Chung Hee, Ferdinand Marcos of the Philippines, and Manuel Noriega.

In the post–Cold War world, conflicts will erupt to redraw borders. Many ethnic groups and tribal clans, forced together into nations by colonial or Soviet masters, will want to break free. Yugoslavia's dismemberment is a perfect example. There is no reason for the United States to intervene as new nations are sorted out, unless it wants to prosecute war crimes committed in the turmoil.

For better or worse, an army also mirrors its country's values and traditions. No matter how much special operators preach otherwise, Americans simply have never been comfortable with low-intensity conflicts. The United States by tradition is shy about intervening militarily overseas, but extraordinarily violent when it does. "What we're really good at is D-days," says Seth Cropsy, a former deputy assistant secretary of defense for special operations. "The furthest imaginable warfare for us is small, stealthy actions with few numbers and large political or personal risks. It's just not us."

If the twenty-first century does usher in a fourth generation of warfare, special operations forces may not always be the best weapons. Drug trafficking is an example of a serious gray area threat, but one that will be defeated by education and treatment centers in the United States and economic aid to Andean nations, not by special operations forces. Bank regulators are the most effective combatants against money launderers. The targets of most anti-American attacks overseas are businesses, which would be better protected by private security consultants than commandos. In Latin America, "the best vaccine against insurgencies" is development aid for budding democracies, says American University expert William LeoGrande, not more Green Berets to strengthen militaries that have toppled civilian governments in the past.

Finally, how special operators are used in the future should not be a decision left solely to the operators. JSOC has become the best surgical strike force in the world. Air Force and Army air commandos are unflappable precision pilots. The Navy SEALs are some of the most physically fit and fearless fighters ever fielded. Green Berets add valuable language and diplomatic skills. But there are weaknesses in their strengths. So intensely focused are they on missions, they can become tunnel-visioned to larger strategy. So close do they become to the turmoil on the ground, "they are almost proud of the fact that broader political questions aren't their concern," says RAND Corporation analyst Benjamin Schwarz. So rigorous is their selection, so gruelingly thorough their training, they can be blinded by a can-do spirit.

Because of the nature of their work, they are the most politically sensitive force a country has. Their deployment cannot be left only in the hands of the military. They are

quiet professionals. But they should be under the firm political control of civilian leaders.

The American military has long shunned its commandos. They have never quite fit in with the spit and polish,
the drill and regimentation. They are trained to be unconventional in a service that prides itself on convention. They
are elites in an army that prefers egalitarianism. Yet they
are some of the most innovative soldiers in the arsenal.
They may be the best and brightest for the future. And
perhaps the most misunderstood in the past. They are the
warriors in the shadows.

SOURCE NOTES

PROLOGUE: THE SHARKMEN

The account of the special reconnaissance mission into Iraq comes from the author's interviews with Chief Warrant Officer Richard F. "Chad" Balwanz. Details of the mission were also drawn from the "5th Special Forces Group After Action Narrative," Feb. 30, 1991, ASOF-SFA-SB.

The brief histories of special operations and covert warfare are drawn from official histories published by the U.S. Special Operations Command Public Affairs Office; "U.S. Low-Intensity Conflicts, 1899–1990," by John M. Collins et al., Washington: Congressional Research Service, Sept. 10, 1990; *Instruments of Statecraft: U.S. Guerrilla Warfare, Counter-Insurgency, Counter-Terrorism, 1940–1990*, by Michael McClintock (New York: Pantheon, 1992); *Presidents' Secret Wars: CIA and Pentagon Covert Operations since World War II*, by John Prados (New York: William Morrow, 1986); and *Secret Armies: Inside the American, Soviet and European Special Forces*, by James Adams (New York: Atlantic Monthly Press, 1987).

Other reports and books consulted for the history of special operations included: "Special Operations and Low-Intensity Conflict Legislation," by Colonel William G. Boykin, U.S. Army War College, Carlisle Barrack, Pennsylvania; "U.S. and Soviet Special Operations," by John Collins, Washington: Congressional Research Service, Dec. 23, 1986; "Special Operations and Low-Intensity Conflict: U.S. Progress and Problems," by Jim Nichol, Congressional Research Service, May 18, 1990; "Special Operations Forces: Finishing the Job of Reconstruction," by David Silverstein (Washington: Heritage Foundation, May 3, 1991); *Secret Warriors: Inside the Covert Military Operations of the Reagan Era*, by Steven Emerson (New York: G. P. Putnam's Sons, 1988); *Best Laid Plans: The Inside Story of America's War Against Terrorism*, by David C. Martin and John Walcott (New York: Harper & Row, 1988);

Special Operations and National Purpose, by Ross S. Kelly (Lexington, Mass.: Lexington Books, 1989); and *Special Operations in U.S. Strategy*, edited by Frank R. Barnett et al. (Washington: National Defense University Press, 1984).

The cultural and sociological observations of special operations soldiers are drawn from the author's interviews with operators in all the services.

CHAPTER ONE: ROBIN SAGE

The narrative on the Green Beret Robin Sage exercise is based on interviews the author conducted during the twelve days he was bivouacked with the students of Operational Detachment Alpha 941 in February 1992. Extensive interviews were also conducted with instructors assigned to F Company, 1st Battalion, 1st Special Warfare Training Group: Sergeant First Class Dan Moran, Sergeant First Class Keith Phillips, Sergeant First Class Mark Goode, Captain David Wilk, and Major C. D. "Duke" Whittington. Further interviews were conducted with Special Forces training officers at the John F. Kennedy Special Warfare Center.

Training documents consulted included the 1st Battalion, 1st Special Warfare Training Group curriculum outline; "Special Forces Assessment and Selection Physical Training Handbook"; "Detachment Mission Planning Guide" (March 18, 1991); "Guerrilla Chief Field Training Techniques," ST-31-191, March 1981; "Ranger Handbook"; and "Pineland Area Study, Special Text," Special Forces School, U.S. Army JFK Special Warfare Center.

For the history of the Green Berets, the following books were consulted: *Inside the Green Berets: The Story of the U.S. Army Special Forces*, by Charles M. Simpson III (New York: Berkley, 1984); *U.S. Army Special Warfare: Its Origins*, by Alfred H. Paddock, Jr. (Washington: National Defense University Press, 1982); *The Second Oldest Profession; Spies and Spying in the Twentieth Century*, by Phillip Knightley (New York: Penguin, 1988); *The Army and Vietnam*, by Andrew F. Krepinevich, Jr. (Baltimore: Johns Hopkins University Press, 1986); *Secret Armies*, by James Adams; *A Bright Shining Lie: John Paul Vann and America in Vietnam*, by Neil Sheehan (New York: Random House, 1988); *A Murder in Wartime: The Untold Spy Story That Changed the Course of the Vietnam War*, by Jeff Stein (New York: St. Martin's, 1992); *American Military Policy in Small Wars: The Case of El Salvador*, by A. J. Bacevich et al. (Washington: Pergamon-Brassey's, 1988); *American Counterinsurgency Doctrine and El Salvador*, by Benjamin C. Schwarz (Santa Monica, Calif.: RAND Corporation, 1992); and *Inside Central America: Its People, Politics and History*, by Clifford Kraus (New York: Summit, 1991).

CHAPTER TWO: HELL WEEK

The account of Hell Week is based on the author's observation of the entire Hell Week for BUDS Class 183 at the Naval Special Warfare Center, Coronado, California. Interviews were conducted with the fifty-eight students of Class 183 during Hell Week. Extensive interviews were also conducted with Captain Tom Richards, commander of the Naval Special Warfare Center; SEAL lieutenants Michael Reilly, Jeff Cassidy, and Pete Oswald, who supervised Hell Week; lieutenants Bruce Thomas and Scott Flinn of the Naval Special Warfare Center medical staff; SEAL instructors Joe Valderrama, John Landry, Ron Cooper, Ken Taylor, Wally Graves, Mike Jaco, Mike McCarthy, Ivan Trent, Shane Ludwig, Kevin James, Jesse Gross, Kirk Dobstaff, and Jim Hillock. Three other SEAL trainers, who asked that their names not be used, also were interviewed extensively.

Documents consulted on BUDS training and Hell Week included: "BUD/S," *Full Mission Profile: The Professional Bulletin of Naval Special Warfare*, Spring 1991, vol. 1, no. 1, pp. 11–22; "A Guide to Naval Special Warfare," by the U.S. Navy Special Warfare Center; "Officer Guide to Naval Special Warfare: The Navy SEAL" Naval Special Warfare Center "Basic Underwater Demolition/Seal Training Course"; Naval Special Warfare Center "Hell Week History," 19 April 1990; and Class 183 Hell Week Briefing Document. Insights on Hell Week curriculum and medical issues were also drawn from *Brave Men—Dark Waters: The Untold Story of the Navy SEALs*, by Orr Kelly (Novato, Calif.: Presidio Press, 1992).

Background interviews by the author on BUDS training were also conducted with fourteen active duty or retired SEAL officers and enlisted men, who asked that their names not be used.

The history of the Navy SEALs was based on: *Brave Men*

—*Dark Waters*, by Orr Kelly; *SEALs In Action*, by Kevin Dockery (New York: Avon, 1991); *The Element of Surprise*: *Navy SEALs in Vietnam*, by Darryl Young (New York: Ivy, 1991); *SEALs*: *UDT/SEAL Operations in Vietnam*, by T. L. Bosiljevac (New York: Ivy, 1990); and U.S. Naval Special Warfare official histories of the Underwater Demolition Team and the SEAL Team.

CHAPTER THREE: THE COWBOYS

The first section of the chapter describing the Pave Low pilots and the Pave Low helicopter is drawn from the author's interviews with more than a dozen Pave Low pilots. Also consulted were 1st Special Operations Wing fact sheets on the Pave Low, and "Personality Correlates of Aircraft Commanders' Perceived Effectiveness," a research paper on Pave Low Pilots by David B. Porter and Shayne M. Hamel, U.S. Air Force Academy.

The history of Air Force special operations wings was drawn from: *First Air Commando Group*: *Any Place, Any Time, Any Where*, by R. D. Van Wagner (Montgomery, Ala.: Air Command and Staff College, 1986, Military History Series 86-1); "Heritage of the Quiet Professionals," Air Force Special Operations Command History Office, Hurlburt Field, Florida; Air Force Special Operations Command fact sheet on AFSOC; First Special Operations Wing fact sheets on the 1st SOW and Hurlburt Field.

The Pave Low history was drawn from author interviews conducted with Colonel Gary Weikel, former commander of the 20th Special Operations Squadron; Noel Koch; Ted Lunger; and six former or present members of the 20th SOS. Also consulted was "Pave Low III: That Others May Live," a monograph by Leo Anthony Gambone, History Office, Aeronautical Systems Division, Air Force Systems Command.

The narrative describing the training of a Pave Low pilot is drawn from the author's visit for one week to the 542nd Operations Group at Kirtland Air Force Base, New Mexico. Extensive interviews were conducted with twelve student pilots and engineers in the 551st Flight Training Squadron. Interviews also were conducted with Colonel Dick Jeffreys, commander of the 542nd OPG and Lieutenant Colonel Dale Cook. Trainers interviewed included: Captain Joe Becker,

Captain Ben Pulsifer, Captain Paco Burrell, Captain Scott Pugmire, Captain Jim Shaffer, Captain James Simon, Major George Selix, Staff Sergeant David Robinson, Staff Sergeant Jim Mecke, and Staff Sergeant Ron Wheeler.

Training documents consulted included: "542nd Operations Group Command Briefing"; "542nd CTW Aircrew Training Device Briefing"; Pave Low pilot training day schedule; "Flight Manual USAF Series MH-53J Helicopter," T.O. 1H-53(M)J-1, Feb. 13, 1990, with operational supplements; "MH-53J Unique Systems Pamphlet," November 1991, 542nd OG/DOTH53; "Pave Familiarization," 542nd CTW (22 AF), April 2, 1992; and "AFSOC Regulation 55-54: Helicopter Operations," Aug. 1, 1990, Department of the Air Force, Headquarters Air Force Special Operations Command.

CHAPTER FOUR: DELTA FORCE

Interviews were conducted by the author with eight former Delta Force operators and officers. Supplemental interviews were also conducted with four officers formerly with the Joint Special Operations Command and the 160th Special Operations Aviation Regiment. Delta training documents were also consulted.

For the history of Delta Force, the following books were consulted: *Delta Force*, by Colonel Charlie A. Beckwith (Ret.) and Donald Knox (New York: Harcourt Brace Jovanovich, 1983); *The Cult of Counterterrorism: The 'Weird World' of Spooks, Counterterrorists, Adventurers, and the Not-Quite Professionals*, by Neil C. Livingstone (Lexington, Mass.: Lexington Books, 1990); *Best Laid Plans*, by David Martin and John Walcott; and *Secret Armies*, by James Adams.

The account of the Delta Force missions before the Just Cause invasion comes from the author's interviews with seven officers from the U.S. Southern Command and U.S. Special Operations Command; plus *The Commanders*, by Bob Woodward (New York: Simon and Schuster, 1991).

The section on the rehearsals for the invasion of Panama is based on interviews with five officers from the U.S. Special Operations Command.

The account of the rescue of Kurt Muse comes from "Danger in the Air," by Neil C. Livingston, *The Washingtonian*, June 1990, pp. 92–94, 196–206; plus the author's interview with Muse and interviews with three officers in the U.S. Special Operations Command.

CHAPTER FIVE: THE ROAD TO WAR

Biographical information on General Stiner was developed from interviews with four senior Pentagon officials, three former officers with the 82nd Airborne Division, three senior U.S. Special Operations Command officers, and three congressional aides. Further biographical information came from the U.S. Special Operations Command official biography; public transcript of the Senate Armed Services Committee hearing May 23, 1990, on the nomination of Lieutenant General Carl Stiner to be commander of the U.S. Special Operations Command; *Operation Just Cause: The Invasion of Panama*, by Tom Donnelly et al (New York: Macmillan, Inc., 1991); *The Commanders*, by Bob Woodward; *Best Laid Plans*, by David Martin and John Walcott; "Inside the Invasion," by Douglas Waller et al., *Newsweek*, June 25, 1990, pp. 38–41; "U.S. Commander Decries Leak on Panama," by Patrick Tyler, *The Washington Post*, Feb. 27, 1990; and "Pentagon Corrects Panama Invasion 'Leaks' Report," by Patrick Tyler, *The Washington Post*, March 13, 1990, p. A23.

The rest of the narrative on the Special Operations Command and Central Command was developed through the author's interviews with eleven Pentagon officials, eleven U.S. Special Operations Command senior officers and operators, six U.S. Central Command senior officers, four State Department officials, four senior Administration officials, and four congressional aides.

Other material consulted included: U.S. Special Operations Command unclassified briefing documents on Desert Shield, Desert Storm, Elusive Concept, and Provide Comfort; "International Cooperation Counters Iraqi Terrorist Threats," Department of State, Bureau of Public Affairs Dispatch, vol. 2, no. 26; U.S. Army Special Operations Command biography of Major General Wayne Downing; U.S. Central Command Biography of Colonel Jesse Johnson; "The Road to War," by Tom Mathews and Douglas Waller et al., *Newsweek*, Jan. 28, 1991, pp. 54–65; "The Secret History of the War," by Tom Mathews and Douglas Waller et al., *Newsweek*, March 18, 1991, pp. 18–26; *The Outlaw State: Saddam Hussein's Quest for*

Power and the Gulf Crisis, by Elaine Sciolino (New York: John Wiley & Sons, 1991); *In the Eye of the Storm: The Life of General H. Norman Schwarzkopf*, by Roger Cohen and Claudio Gatti (New York: Farrar, Strauss and Giroux, 1991); *It Doesn't Take A Hero: General H. Norman Schwarzkopf, The Autobiography*, by H. Norman Schwarzkopf with Peter Petre (New York: Bantam, 1992); *Storm Command: A Personal Account of the Gulf War*, by General Sir Peter de la Billiere (London: HarperCollins, 1992); "Operation Desert Shield/Desert Storm," Hearings before the Committee on Armed Services, United States Senate, April–June 1991, S.Hrg. 102–326; and "Conduct of the Persian Gulf War: Final Report to Congress," U.S. Department of Defense, April 1992.

CHAPTER SIX: OPERATION EAGER ANVIL

The account of Operation Eager Anvil was drawn from the author's interviews with Major Bob Leonik, Lieutenant Colonel Richard Comer, Lieutenant Colonel Dick Cody, and Colonel George Gray. Interviews also were conducted with ten members of the U.S. Central Command air staff in Riyadh during Desert Storm, and two members of the Army's 160th Special Operations Aviation Regiment. Descriptions of the Iraqi air defense network and the Desert Shield air campaign were prepared with the assistance of Bill Arkin with Greenpeace.

Material consulted for this chapter included: Air Force Special Operations Command history of "Air Force Special Operations Command in Operation Desert Shield and Desert Storm"; 101st Airborne Division history of operations in Desert Shield and Desert Storm; "Reaching Globally, Reaching Powerfully: The United States Air Force in the Persian Gulf War," a report by the U.S. Air Force, September 1991; "Conduct of the Persian Gulf Conflict: An Interim Report to Congress," Department of Defense, July 1991; U.S. Army briefing charts on Operation Eager Anvil; U.S. Special Operations Command briefing charts on Desert Storm; U.S. Central Command situation reports; *Triumph without Victory: The Unreported History of the Persian Gulf War*, by the U.S. News and World Report Staff (New York: Times Books, 1992); *It Doesn't Take a Hero*, by General H. Norman Schwarzkopf; "Secret Warriors," by Douglas Waller, *Newsweek*; "The Road to War," by Tom Mathews and Douglas Waller et al., *Newsweek*; "The Secret History of the War," by Tom Mathews and Douglas Waller et al., *Newsweek*; "USAF MH-53J Pave Lows Led Army Apaches Knocking Out Iraqi Radars to Open Air War," by Benjamin F. Schemmer, *Armed Forces Journal*, July 1991, p. 34; "First Shots Fired in Anger," by SSgt. William H. McMichael, *Soldiers Magazine*, April 1991, pp. 21–24,; "Apache Attack," by Richard Mackenzie, *Air Force Magazine*, October 1991, pp. 54–60; McDonnell Douglas Fact Sheet on the AH-64 Apache Attack Helicopter; and 1st Special Operations Wing official biographies on Colonel Ben Orrell, Colonel George Gray, and Lieutenant Colonel Richard Comer.

CHAPTER SEVEN: PSYOPS

The sections on the 4th Psychological Operations Group missions during Just Cause and Desert Storm were written from the author's interviews with Colonel Tony Normand and Colonel Layton Dunbar. Also interviewed were three U.S. Special Operations Command officers, four Pentagon officials, and a senior White House official.

Also consulted were: "Leaflets of the Persian Gulf," by the 4th Psychological Operations Group; "Leaflet and Radio Operations of Desert Shield and Desert Storm," briefing book by the 4th Psychological Operations Group; *Political Warfare and Psychological Operations*, edited by Carnes Lord and Frank R. Barnett (Washington: National Defense University Press, 1989); "Psyops in the Gulf," a video by the 4th Psychological Operation Group; "Protocol to Freedom," a video by the 4th Psychological Operations Group on Operation Just Cause; and "Soviet Analysis of Operation Desert Storm and Operation Desert Shield," translated by the Defense Intelligence Agency, Oct. 28, 1991.

The account of the BLU-82 mission was drawn from author interviews with Major Skip Davenport, Colonel George Gray, two Central Command officers, and two members of the 5th Special Forces Group. Also consulted were: "Air Force Special Operations Command in Operations Desert Shield and Desert Storm," by the Air Force Special Operations Command History Office; *Airpower in the Persian Gulf*, by James P. Coyne (Arlington, Vir.: Air Force Association, 1992); CENTCOM situation reports; "BLU-82 Drop," Air Force video, July 9, 1992; 8th Special Operations Squadron history, Air Force Special Operations Command; and MC-130E Combat Talon, 1st Special Operations Wing fact sheet.

CHAPTER EIGHT: BEHIND ENEMY LINES

The accounts of Special Forces strategic reconnaissance missions in Iraq were drawn from the author's interviews with Colonel Jim Kraus, Lieutenant Colonel Jerry Thompson (commander of 1st Battalion of the 5th Special Forces Group), Master Sergeant Jeffrey Sims, Staff Sergeant Roy Tabron, Sergeant First Class Gary Seideman, Sergeant First Class Michael Flick, Captain Ed McHale, and Colonel Jesse Johnson. The account of the helicopter rescue came from interviews with Lieutenant Colonel Dell Dailey (commander of 3rd Battalion of the 160th Special Operations Aviation Regiment), Chief Warrant Officer Jim Crisafulli, and Chief Warrant Officer Rick Detrick.

Material consulted for this chapter included: U.S. Special Operations Command briefing charts on Desert Shield and Desert Storm; "The Gulf War: Operation Desert Storm/Desert Shield," *Military Review*, September 1991, vol. 71, no. 9; "Fifth Special Forces Group (Airborne) in Desert Shield and Desert Storm," Chapter 38, Special Forces Association, 1991; "Night Stalkers Don't Quit," by Greg Walker, *Soldier of Fortune*, March 1992, pp. 42–79; "Secret Warriors," by Douglas Waller, *Newsweek*; and "The 100-Hour War," *Army Times*, March 11, 1991, pp. 14–44.

CHAPTER NINE: DECEPTION AT MINA SAUD

The account of the beach reconnaissance missions along the Kuwaiti coast and the amphibious feint at Mina Saud were drawn principally from the author's interviews with Lieutenant Tom Deitz and Captain Ray Smith. Also interviewed were Hospital Corpsman Allen Schildgen of Task Unit Mike, four other SEALs from the Naval Special Warfare Task Group-Central, and three members of Naval Special Boat Squadron One. Other interviews were conducted with three Marine officers involved in the amphibious operations planning.

Also consulted were: "Desert Storm: Summary of Operations," by Naval Special Warfare Task Group-Central; medals

and awards citations for members of the Naval Special War-
fare Task Group-Central; *Brave Men—Dark Waters*, by Orr
Kelly; "Secret Warriors," by Douglas Waller, *Newsweek*; "The
Secret History of the War," by Tom Mathews and Douglas
Waller, *Newsweek*; and "To the Shores of Kuwait: The Marines
Expect Their Largest Amphibious Operation Since Inchon,"
by Tom Post with John Barry and Douglas Waller, *Newsweek*,
Feb. 11, 1991, pp. 28–29.

CHAPTER TEN: THE SCUD HUNT

The account of the air and ground operations to hunt Scuds in
Iraq was drawn from the author's interviews with seven members of U.S. Special Operations Command, eight senior officers from the U.S. Central Command, and three Pentagon
officials. Interviews on the number of Scud kills were conducted with Bill Arkin of Greenpeace, Mark Crispen Miller of
Johns Hopkins University, and a Pentagon analyst. The account of SAS operations in western Iraq was drawn from
Storm Command, by General Sir Peter de la Billiere, plus interviews with four Air Force and U.S. Special Operations
Command officers. The account of the A-10 Scud-hunting
mission on February 26–27 came from an interview with Lieutenant Colonel Seth G. Wilson.

Also consulted for this chapter were: "Conduct of the
Persian Gulf War: Final Report to Congress," April 1992, Department of Defense; "Gulf War Air Power Survey," April 19,
1993, U.S. Air Force Summary; "Reaching Globally, Reaching
Powerfully: The United States Air Force in the Gulf War,"
September 1991, Department of the Air Force; U.S. Special
Operations Command briefing paper on Desert Storm and
Desert Shield; U.S. Central Command situation report on the
air campaign for February 26–27; Air Force awards citation
and Air Force news release on the February 26–27 A-10 mission; "Roving Royal Commandos Fingered Scuds for F-15Es,"
by Tony Capaccio, *Defense Week*, May 28, 1991, p. 6; "U.S.
Bombs Pipeline to Stem Oil Flow; Preventive Strike Was
Ruled Out," by Bill Gertz, *The Washington Times*, Jan. 28,
1991, p. A1; "Operation Desert Shield/Desert Storm," hearings before the Senate Armed Services Committee, April–
June 1991; "Operation Desert Sham," by Mark Crispen Miller, *The New York Times*, June 24, 1992, p. A21; casualty re-

ports from the U.S. Special Operations Command; "Special Ops Teams Found 29 Scuds Ready to Barrage Israel 24 Hours before Cease-Fire," by Benjamin F. Schemmer, *Armed Forces Journal International*, July 1991, p. 36; transcript of U.S. Central Command press conference by Gen. H. Norman Schwarzkopf in Riyadh, February 27, 1991; transcript of Defense Department press conference by Pete Williams, assistant secretary of defense for public affairs, June 25, 1992; and "Secret Warriors," by Douglas Waller, *Newsweek*.

Books consulted included: *Military Lessons of the Gulf War*, by Bruce W. Watson et al. (London: Greenhill Books, 1991); *Storm over Iraq: Air Power and the Gulf War*, by Richard P. Hallion (Washington: Smithsonian Institution Press, 1992); *The Sampson Option: Israel's Nuclear Arsenal and American Foreign Policy*, by Seymour M. Hersh (New York: Random House, 1991); and *Triumph Without Victory*, by U.S. News and World Report.

CHAPTER ELEVEN: TOMORROW'S WARRIORS

The accounts of new technologies were drawn from the author's interviews with Lieutenant Colonel James Van Buskirk and Sal Raineri. Also interviewed were Major General David Baratto, then commander of the U.S. Army Special Warfare Center; Colonel William F. Hughes, command surgeon for the U.S. Special Operations Command; Colonel Doug Richardson, acting director of the Special Operations Research, Development and Acquisition Center; Colonel Paul Morgan, director of intelligence for the U.S. Special Operations Command; and J. Frank Wattenbarger, science adviser, Naval Special Warfare Command.

Also consulted were: U.S. Special Operations Command fact sheet on SORDAC; SORDAC briefing charts on future special operations weapons systems and medical research; Joint Special Operations Force medical acquisition decision package; Special Operations health service support briefing paper; Rockwell International fact sheet on the AC-130U gunship; U.S. Special Operations Command fact sheet on JASORS; "United States Special Operations Forces: Posture Statement," June 1992, Office of the Assistant Secretary of Defense for Special Operations and Low-Intensity Conflict; "Special Ops/Low-Intensity Conflict," *Armed Forces Journal*,

July 1992, pp. 14–17; and Chenwoth Racing Products, Inc. fact sheet on the Fast Attack/Light Strike Vehicle.

CHAPTER TWELVE: TOMORROW'S WARS

The description of the Crisis Action Center comes from the author's tour of that facility.

The account of the U.S. Special Operations Command's plans on future roles and missions comes from the author's interviews with General Carl Stiner; James R. Locher III, assistant secretary of defense for special operations and low-intensity conflict; retired General James Lindsey; Captain Bob Claytor, chief of the Joint Mission Analysis Team at the U.S. Special Operations Command; Chris Mellon, former aide to Senator William Cohen; Major General David Baratto; Dr. Elie Krakowski, former Defense Department aide on low-intensity conflict; and four senior Pentagon officials.

Documents consulted on the U.S. Special Operations Command's future roles and missions included: USSOCOM briefing paper on "Special Operations Forces Strategic Potential"; USSOCOM briefing paper on "Foreign Internal Defense: USSOCOM Perspective on Peacetime Engagement"; USSOCOM briefing paper on "Joint Mission Analysis"; "United States Special Operations Forces: A Strategic Perspective," USSOCOM, January 1992; "United States Special Operations Forces: Posture Statement," Department of Defense, June 1992; "U.S. Special Operations Forces: A Strategic Perspective," by Carl W. Stiner, *Parameters*, Summer 1992, pp. 2–13.; and "Providing Resources for Special Operations Forces: Completing the Transition," by James E. Giles III et al., Logistics Management Institute, Report No. SO901R1, March 1989.

Other documents and publications consulted on future defense spending reductions and future roles and missions for special operations included: "U.S. Military Force Reductions: Capabilities Versus Requirements," by John M. Collins, Congressional Research Service, 92-43S, Jan. 8, 1992; "New Directions for National Defense," by John M. Collins, Congressional Research Service, 90-323RCO, July 6, 1990; "National Military Strategy, the DoD Base Force, and U.S. Unified Command Plan: An Assessment," by John M. Collins, Congressional Research Service, 92-493S, June 11, 1992; "Structuring U.S. Forces after the Cold War: Costs and Effects of Increased Reliance on the Reserves," Congressional Budget Office, September 1992; "From Gettysburg to the Gulf and Beyond: Coping with Revolutionary Technological Change in Land Warfare," by Richard J. Dunn III, Institute for National Strategic Studies, no. 13, March 1992; "National Security in the 1990s: Defining a New Basis for U.S. Military Forces," by Representative Les Aspin, paper presented before the Atlantic Council of the United States, Jan. 6, 1992; "American Military Power: Future Needs, Future Choices," background paper, Office of Technology Assessment, U.S. Congress, OTA-BP-ISC-80, October 1991; "Melding Special Operations with Forces of the Future," speech by Admiral David E. Jeremiah, Dec. 9, 1991, *Defense Issues*, vol. 7, no. 7, Department of Defense; "Versatility Protects Special Operations Forces," speech by James R. Locher III, assistant secretary of defense for special operations and low-intensity conflict, Nov. 12, 1991, *Defense Issues*, vol. 6, no. 55, Department of Defense; "Must The U.S. Disengage?" by Jed C. Snyder, *National Review*, Nov. 16, 1992, pp. 29–33; and "Fighting Tomorrow's Wars," by Bruce B. Auster, *U.S. News and World Report*, Nov. 16, 1992, pp. 77–78.

The critique of the role of special operations forces in Desert Storm is drawn from author interviews with six senior Pentagon officials, three senior members of the U.S. Special Operations Command, Edward Luttwak, and William S. Lind.

The section on future threats and future warfare is drawn from interviews with: Alvin H. Bernstein, director of the National Defense University's Institute for National Strategic Studies; William S. Lind; John M. Collins; and a senior Pentagon official. Documents and publications consulted included: "Significant Incidents of Political Violence against Americans: 1991," U.S. Department of State, Bureau of Diplomatic Security; "American Intelligence and the New World," speech by CIA Director Robert M. Gates before the Dallas World Affairs Council, Nov. 10, 1992; "The Changing Face of War: Into the Fourth Generation," by William S. Lind et al., *Marine Corps Gazette*, October 1989, pp. 22–26; "Defending Western Culture," William S. Lind, *Foreign Policy*, Fall 1991, no. 84, pp. 40–50; *The Transformation of War*, by Martin Van Creveld (New York: The Free Press, 1991); *LIC 2010: Special Operations and Unconventional Warfare in the Next Century*, by Rod

Paschall (Washington: Brassey's, 1990); "Dangerous Links: Terrorism, Crime, Ethnic and Religious Conflict after the Cold War," a report on the gray area phenomenon from the National Strategy Information Center, Washington; "Balkan Battlegrounds: U.S. Military Alternatives," by John M. Collins, Congressional Research Service, 92-679S, Sept. 2, 1992; "Canada and the United States in the Year 2092," *New York Times*, Oct. 21, 1992, p. A23; and "Sneaking in the Scuds," by Douglas Waller, *Newsweek*, June 22, 1992, pp. 42–46.

The section critiquing the future threats and the role of special operations is drawn from interviews with Seth Cropsy, Joshua Epstein, John Steinbruner, Benjamin C. Schwarz, and three Pentagon officials.

Documents and publications consulted included: "The New World Disorder," by Ted Galen Carpenter, *Foreign Policy*, Fall 1991, no. 84, pp. 24–39; "Barking Up a Fallen Tree: The Death of Low-Intensity Conflict," by Seth Cropsy, *The National Interest*, Spring 1992, pp. 53–60; "Use of Force by the United States: Case Studies, 1950–1991," by Mark M. Lowenthal and Robert L. Goldich, Congressional Research Service, 92–757F, Oct. 14, 1992; "The Disorder of Peace," by Richard J. Barnet, *The New Yorker*, Jan. 20, 1992, pp. 62–74; "A New Concept of Cooperative Security," by Ashton B. Carter et al., paper by the Brookings Institution, Washington, D.C., 1992; "The Need to Know," the report of the Twentieth Century Fund Task Force on covert action and American democracy, the Twentieth Century Fund Press, New York, 1992; "Powell Delivers a Resounding No on Using Limited Force in Bosnia," by Michael R. Gordon, *New York Times*, Sept. 28, 1992, p. A1; "Rest Easy. It's Not 1914 Anymore," by Francis Fukuyama, *New York Times*, Feb. 9, 1992, p. A17; "Freedom Is the Best Revenge," by Bruce W. Nelan, *Time*, Dec. 16, 1991, pp. 24–29; "Civilian Mission Is Proposed for Post–Cold War Military," by Eric Schmitt, *New York Times*, June 24, 1992, p. A12; and "The Hemispheric Interests of the United States in the New World Order," paper presented by William M. LeoGrande to National Defense University Workshop on Refining U.S. Interests in Latin America, Nov. 20, 1991.

INDEX